ADVANCES IN PERSONAL RELATIONSHIPS

Volume 2 • 1991

ADVANCES IN PERSONAL RELATIONSHIPS

A Research Annual

Editors: WARREN H. JONES
Department of Psychology
University of Tennessee

DANIEL PERLMAN
School of Family and Nutritional Sciences
The University of British Columbia

Volume 2 • 1991

Jessica Kingsley Publishers
London

Copyright © 1991 Jessica Kingsley Publishers Ltd
118 Pentonville Road
London N1 9JN

All rights reserved. No part of this publication may be reproduced, stored on a retrieval system, or transmitted in any form or by any means, electronic, mechanical, photocopying, filming, recording or otherwise without prior permission in writing from the publisher.

ISBN: 1 85302 077 X

Printed in Great Britain by Southampton Book Company.

CONTENTS

LIST OF CONTRIBUTORS   vii

PREFACE   ix
    Warren H. Jones and Daniel Perlman

PART I: THE DEVELOPMENT OF RELATIONSHIPS

THE ROLE OF SOCIAL CONTEXT IN THE DYNAMICS OF
PERSONAL RELATIONSHIPS   1
    Malcolm R. Parks and Leona L. Eggert

INTERPERSONAL TRANSFORMATIONS IN INTIMATE
RELATIONSHIPS   35
    Victor M. H. Borden and George Levinger

TRUST AND THE APPRAISAL PROCESS IN CLOSE
RELATIONSHIPS   57
    John G. Holmes

PART II: SOCIAL SUPPORT

AN EXPERIMENTAL APPROACH TO STUDYING
SOCIAL INTERACTION AND COPING WITH STRESS
AMONG FRIENDS   107
    Barbara A. Winstead and Valerian J. Derlega

SOCIAL SKILLS AND INTERPERSONAL RELATIONSHIPS:
INFLUENCES ON SOCIAL SUPPORT AND SUPPORT
SEEKING   133
    Ronald E. Riggio and Judy Zimmerman

PART III: ATTRIBUTIONAL AND STRATEGIC ASPECTS OF RELATIONSHIPS

COGNITION IN MARRIAGE: A PROGRAM OF RESEARCH ON ATTRIBUTIONS 159
Frank D. Fincham and Thomas H. Bradbury

PLANNING AND PERFORMING INTERPERSONAL INTERACTION: A COGNITIVE-MOTIVATIONAL APPROACH 205
Daniel Bar-Tal, Yoram Bar-Tal, Nehemia Geva, and Kerry Yarkin-Levin

INTER-PERSONALISM: UNDERSTANDING PERSONS IN RELATIONSHIPS 233
Lynn Carol Miller and Stephen John Read

AUTHOR INDEX 269

SUBJECT INDEX 274

LIST OF CONTRIBUTORS

Dr Daniel Bar-Tal School of Education,
Tel-Aviv University, Israel

Dr Yoram Bar-Tal School of Medicine,
Tel-Aviv University, Israel

Dr Thomas N. Bradbury Psychology Department,
University of California,
Los Angeles, CA

Dr Victor M. H. Borden Office of Institutional Planning
and Research, George Mason
University, VA

Dr Valerian J. Derlega Psychology Department,
Old Dominion University, VA

Dr Leona L. Eggert Psychosocial Nursing,
University of Washington, WA

Dr Frank D. Fincham Psychology Department,
University of Illinois, IL

Dr Nehemia Geva JDC Israel, Department of
Research and Evaluation,
Jerusalem, Israel

Dr John G. Holmes Psychology Department,
University of Waterloo, Ontario,
Canada

Dr Warren H. Jones Psychology Department,
University of Tennessee, TN

Dr George Levinger Psychology Department,
University of Massachusetts, MA

Dr Lynn Carol Miller — Department of Communication Arts and Sciences, University of Southern California, Los Angeles, CA

Dr Malcolm R. Parks — Department of Speech Communication, University of Washington, WA

Dr Daniel Perlman — Family Science, University of British Columbia, Vancouver, Canada

Dr Stephen John Read — Psychology Department, University of Southern California, Los Angeles, CA

Dr Ronald E. Riggio — Psychology Department, California State University, Fullerton, CA

Dr Barbara A. Winstead — Psychology Department, Old Dominion University, Norfolk, VA

Dr Kerry Yarkin-Levin — WESTAT, Rockville, MD

Judy Zimmerman — Psychology Department, University of California, Riverside, CA

PREFACE

It is commonplace in the social sciences to observe the inherently and thoroughly social nature of human beings. We are gregarious, group living and culture-bearing creatures and most of what we do may be characterized as social action, that is, guided and influenced by interpersonal objectives and processes. Considerable recent research and theorizing has confirmed and extended the traditional view regarding the pervasiveness and centrality of interpersonal behavior in the human experience. However, it is becoming increasingly clear that close personal relationships are the cornerstone of interpersonal behavior and social contact and that such relationships are more than merely common in human experience, they are necessary for survival. Research indicating that the quality of one's intimate relationships predict the frequency, severity, and prognosis of both psychological and medical complaints and also possibly mediate the influence of environmental stressors on adjustment and well-being is a case in point. In addition, it would appear that relationships do more than influence important individual outcomes; they also provide the context in which individual lives unfold and the standard against which the quality of life is measured.

Whereas few contemporary social scientists would disagree with the above characterization regarding the role of personal relationships, it is also clear that many disagreements remain and that much work needs to be done in order to fully understand the nature and influence of relationships in our lives. For example, many conceptualizations of relationships continue to fall short of the genuinely dynamic nature of relationships as they are experienced. We know a good deal more about some types of relationships than others, and a good deal more also about certain aspects of relationships than others. For example, much has been written about the influence of parents on their children whereas the influence of children on their parents remains relatively obscure. Similarly, we know more about attraction and the initial stages of relationships than we know about the maintenance and the dissolution of relationships. Also, we know more about the positive aspects of relationships than we know about the limitations and hazards of close interpersonal bonds. Finally, much of the research in this area has been correlational leaving questions regarding the direction of causality unresolved.

In our view, therefore, the literature on relationships provides promising and empirically substantiated answers to a host of questions regarding the role of relationships in our lives, but also leaves unanswered many key questions and issues. In principle, the opportunity to complete the picture is at hand because of the considerable attention paid to these issues in recent years in psychology and related disciplines. Never before have so many researchers devoted their energies to both basic and applied problems regarding relationships. On the other hand, in our judgment, more and better research is not all that is needed. Stated simply, a fuller understanding of personal relationships also requires integration of the rapidly developing empirical literature. It is toward this end that the present series of volumes is devoted.

The purpose of this annual series is to encourage and contribute to the continued development, integration, and cross-fertilization of research and theory on personal relationships. In order to achieve these objectives this and subsequent volumes in the series will feature three types of manuscripts. First, some will present new or reformulated models and theories of relationships including both those which seek to explain one or more of the many facets of personal relationships more broadly conceived. In particular, emphasis will be given to conceptualizations which have received considerable empirical support or which directly and as unambiguously as possible translate into testable hypotheses. Obviously the purpose for doing so is to provide a forum for the continued development and evaluation of theories of personal relationships. Second, these volumes will present papers which summarize and integrate ongoing programs of research on important problems in personal relationships. The goal here is to encourage authors to 'step back' from the specifics and complexities of their individual studies to consider broader empirical and conceptual questions. At a minimum such questions might include: What has been learned from the research program? How have assumptions and research goals changed, if at all? What remains to be done? and Which concepts and/or methods are in need of revision or which need to be abandoned? Such papers, then, will highlight the most important and replicable features of these research programs while also suggesting directions for future empirical investigations. Third, subsequent volumes will contain comprehensive reviews of the literature on personal relationships. In some instances, authors who have been active and instrumental in the development of a research tradition will be invited to summarize the relevant published research in order to provide an insider's view of the important issues, problems, and lines of convergence. In some instances, other scholars will be invited to provide an 'outsider's perspective' of pertinent developments. In either case, the purpose of such papers is to bring the reader up-to-date on the literature in a manner typically unavailable even in review articles.

In essence this Series is designed to provide readers with broad statements on advances in the personal relationships area. Given the diversity among the potential readers, we seek contributors who can write in a clear fashion. We ask authors to remember that some readers will come from a different discipline than themselves and that other readers will have minimal statistical training. As an 'advances' series, our primary goal is to have chapters of high calibre that reflect recent or emerging developments. We make no pretense that the chapters of a given volume will fit snugly around a common theme or focal point. Nonetheless, in some volumes certain themes are likely to emerge, and from time to time, we will try to assemble a cluster of chapters on a specific topic. For example, in Volume 1, several of the chapters focused on love and emotions in close relationships.

The primary audience for the Series will be researchers and advanced students interested in relationships and related topics. In addition, it is anticipated scholars who do not consider this area their primary field will find useful and timely papers explicating the connections between personal relationships and other aspects of experience. Also, we would expect that mental health professionals and practitioners from various disciplines will find these volumes of relevance in that personal relationships play an important role in processes of adjustment, health, coping, and well-being. In addition, chapters in future volumes will focus on various applied issues such as therapeutic outcomes, disorders of relationships, and relationships in the workplace. Finally, although both editors for the series were trained in social psychology and although psychologists have made key contributions to the study of personal relationships, it is clear that the field should not and cannot be confined to a single disciplinary point of view. As a consequence, we intend to publish papers by the leading scholars in relevant fields such as sociology, family studies, and communication and we would expect researchers trained in those disciplines to find the volumes in the series of interest as well.

Volume 2 of the series contains a broad array of contemporary approaches to the study of personal relationships. At the same time, however, these chapters represent specific themes around which research on personal relationships has been focused in recent years. The first three chapters nicely illustrate the ways in which contemporary research on relationships differs from older approaches, by emphasizing issues of relationship development and the context in which such changes take place. For example, the essay by Malcolm Parks and Leona Eggert explicates the complex and interconnected social network in which the dynamics of personal relationships unfold and uses the concept of uncertainty reduction to explain how development of a specific relationship is closely connected to the relational partners' other relationships, in particular those with family and friends. The chapter by Victor Borden and George Levinger is, first of all, yet another in a long and distinguished series of contributions to the literature on relationships by George Levinger. In addition, this chapter addresses how two people with separate identities and life histories become a 'we' and the almost imperceptible transformations of accommodation and convergence which are at the heart of the development of close personal relationships. Alternatively, John Holmes addresses a related issue by emphasizing the dialectic between the rewards and joys of commitment and intimacy versus the fears and harsh realities often associated with these processes. Holmes focuses on the dynamics of trust as the prototypical dilemma in the approach/avoidance conflicts that typify the development of relationships. Each of these chapters, then, provides a unique perspective from which to understand the dynamics and the developmental nature of close personal relationships and thereby begin to redress older conceptualizations based on static models of interpersonal ties.

The second theme represented in this volume concerns the extension and refinement of a widely researched issue of relevance to personal relationships; specifically, the supportive relationships embedded in social networks. As noted earlier a large number of research studies have documented the effects of social support on health and well-being. What has been less clear has been the mechanisms which underlie such empirical relationships. Judy Zimmerman and Ron Riggio extend a recent trend of examining the extent to which supportive social relationships derive, in part, from individual differences by focusing on two important issues regarding the construct of social skills. First, they consider a conceptual framework for defining and assessing social skills. Second, they discuss the role of social skills in several relevant processes such as support seeking, perceptions of support and the nature of emotionally supportive interactions. By contrast, Barbara Winstead and Valerian Derlega add a much needed laboratory approach to the support literature which has relied largely on self-reported measures. In doing so, these authors not only illustrate how complex interpersonal processes such as social support may be studied under controlled laboratory conditions but also they have begun to 'unpack' the complex nature of support into specific questions which may be separately addressed such as when and why support fails and the situational and personal factors that shape the effects of social support? These chapters therefore serve to hone the connection between social support and well-being from a widely documented truism to a specifically articulated and differentiated set of empirical relationships.

The third theme represented in this volume concerns the cognitive and strategic aspects of interpersonal relationships. In the past, relationships were often portrayed as if participants were passive conduits of interpersonal information and influence. By contrast, these chapters make it clear that it not only matters what people think, but what they hope and strive for as well. For example, Daniel Bar-Tal, Yoram Bar-Tal, Nehemia Geva, and Kerry Yarkin-

Preface xiii

Levin explore the cognitive and motivational processes of interpersonal interactions and emergent personal relationships. Specifically, Bar-Tal et al. examine epistemic motivations for validity, structure, and specific content as well as automatic processes which help to explain an actor's interpersonal choices and biases. Lynn Miller and Stephen Read argue for assessing the individual differences in mediating structures that influence interpersonal behaviors and, in particular, self-disclosure. In addition, they explain the merits of a language for understanding the stable and changing patterns of interpersonal goals and plans and the mutual influence of such patterns in personal relationships. Finally, Volume 2 of the series concludes with a discussion of the role of cognitions in the marital relationship by Frank Fincham and Thomas Bradbury. Specifically, Fincham and Bradbury review an extensive program of research examining the association between attributions and marital satisfaction. In addition to documenting the specific accomplishments of their research, however, these authors also carefully outline the limitations of their work and the relevant literature in general -- a lack of research on the role of cognitive and affective processes as mediators of the connection between marital behavior and satisfaction -- and in so doing set the agenda for future research in the area. These chapters then not only meet the objectives of the series by integrating and summarizing available research on these topics, but they also provide both the direction and impetus for continued development along these lines by identifying missing elements in our understanding of these issues and, most importantly, by providing new conceptual tools for examining the strategic and cognitive factors of personal relationships.

We are quite pleased with these papers and believe that, individually and collectively, they demonstrate the breadth and vitality of recent work on personal relationships. In addition, each of these chapters raises important questions regarding the role and influence of relationships in human behavior and experience and each provides its own unique and heuristic mix of conceptual and empirical answers. Finally, each of these chapters, along with the essays contained in Volume 1 of the Series (Jones & Perlman, 1987) illustrate the type and quality of the papers intended for the subsequent volumes of the series and, we believe, make substantive contributions to the growing literature on personal relationships.

Warren H. Jones
Daniel Perlman
Series Editors

ACKNOWLEDGEMENT

The editors wish to thank Dolores Fischer for her assistance in preparing the author index.

REFERENCE

Jones, W. H., and Perlman, D. (Eds.). (1987). *Advances in personal relationships: A research annual* (Vol. 1). Greenwich, CT.: JAI Press.

PART I

THE DEVELOPMENT OF RELATIONSHIPS

THE ROLE OF SOCIAL CONTEXT IN THE DYNAMICS OF PERSONAL RELATIONSHIPS

Malcolm R. Parks and Leona L. Eggert

The study of personal relationships is peculiarly divorced from the study of the social contexts in which they are embedded. Instead, as we and others have noted, personal relationships are usually studied in terms of the individual characteristics of the participants (e.g., personality characteristics, physical attractiveness), the way these individual characteristics match up (e.g., attitude similarity), or the pattern of interaction or inter-dependence between the participants (e.g., Huston, Surra, Fitzgerald, & Cate, 1981; Milardo & Lewis, 1985; Parks, Stan, & Eggert, 1983; Ridley & Avery, 1979). Systematic and sustained concern with the social environment in which individuals and dyads are embedded is generally missing.

The central theme of this chapter is that the interior, dyadic dynamics of personal relationships are inextricably intertwined with the participants' surrounding social networks of family and friends. We believe that the environment created by these networks influences and is influenced by personal relationships every bit as much as by purely individual or dyadic factors. We begin by illustrating the depth and breadth of the historic bias against examining social contextual factors in personal relationships. From there we will go on to consider the role played by social contextual factors in the initiation, development, and dissolution of personal relationships. In some cases we will be integrating and summarizing published results of our research program (Eggert & Parks, 1987; Parks & Adelman, 1983; Parks et al., 1983), while in other cases we will be presenting previously unpublished results.

THE HISTORICAL BLINDNESS TO SOCIAL CONTEXT

The failure to consider environmental factors in personal relationships is deeply set in the social sciences. In spite of Lewin's (1951; p. 25) famous dictum that 'in principle it is everywhere accepted that behavior is a function of the person and the environment', researchers have historically focused on individual and dyadic factors rather than social environmental factors. In the 1940s, for instance, Bergler (1948) argued that divorce was the result of personality defects ranging from neurosis to psychosis. He believed that only psychoanalysis could help because divorce and remarriage merely transferred a problem individual from one relationship to another. In their review of marital adjustment measures Terman and Wallin (1949) suggested that some people simply had a higher 'marital aptitude' or ability to form successful marriages. Thus successful and unsuccessful personal relationships were viewed as the product of individual qualities.

Self-disclosure and interpersonal attraction, among the most widely researched variables of the last 20 years, are fundamentally individual level variables. Reviews of research on these variables (e.g., Berscheid & Walster, 1978; Chelune, 1979) testify to the vigor of research efforts, but are largely silent when it comes to specifying the larger social contextual influences on attraction and disclosure. Indeed this research has been criticized for failing to move from the individual level to even the dyadic or relational level (Berscheid, 1977), let alone to the still larger social contextual level. This 'conceptual blindness' (Ridley & Avery, 1979) has only been reinforced by a preference for simple laboratory studies that 'necessarily foreshorten and isolate interactions which, in real life, are not only extended but embedded in a context of other interactions' (Duck & Miell, 1986; p. 135). When attempts are made to bring the social context into the laboratory, the result is often so rarefied and sterile as to raise questions as to whether the context is really very social at all (e.g., Cramer, Weiss, Steigleder, & Balling, 1985).

Research on more general relationship types, such as friendship, has also been limited in its focus. Perlman and Fehr (1986), for example, observed that social psychologists have typically approached friendship in terms of interpersonal attraction. They identified four primary theoretic perspectives on attraction in friendship: (1) reinforcement theories (e.g., Clore & Byrne, 1974; Lott & Lott, 1974); (2) exchange and equity theories (e.g., Berscheid & Walster, 1978; Kelley & Thibaut, 1978; Rusbult, 1980); (3) cognitive consistency theories (e.g., Heider, 1958; Newcomb, 1961); and (4) developmental theories (e.g., Altman & Taylor, 1973; Levinger & Snoek, 1972). Yet all of these theories restrict their vision of the friendship process to the perceptions and behaviors within a focal dyad. None explicitly consider the influence of the surrounding social context on the developing relationship. To their credit, Perlman and Fehr (1986) noted this limitation, but the fact remains that even the best social psychological research on friendship has ignored the broader social contextual level of analysis. Consider, for instance, an otherwise excellent study of friendship formation by Hays (1985). Subjects selected two acquaintances for study at the beginning of their first quarter of college. Measures of friendship intensity, intimacy, companionship, consideration, perceived benefits and costs, affection, and desire for a future relationship were taken at three week intervals until the end of the university term and again three months later. While this study examined an unusually broad range of variables, the only contextual variable that appears to have been considered was the geographic proximity between the friends' residences.

Similar criticisms have been lodged against the research on romantic relationships and mate selection (e.g., Huston et al., 1981; Milardo & Lewis, 1985; Parks et al., 1983). In the main studies in this area have adopted a focus limited to individual and dyadic factors.

In short social scientists in general and social psychologists in particular have been blind to the role of social contextual factors in personal relationships (Ridley & Avery, 1979). This is not to suggest that our efforts to date have been wasted. Instead as Milardo (1986; p. 163) points out:

> There is little doubt that an understanding of the formation, ongoing character and eventual termination of personal relationships has been and will continue to be advanced by studies of individual and dyadic properties. Individuals and their relationships, however, are embedded within a social system, a system that profoundly influences people, their availability to one another, the choices they make with regard to one another, and the character of their relationships.

To appreciate just how completely the social system in which the participants are embedded is intertwined with their personal relationships, we now turn to a consideration of how communication networks are associated with the initiation, development, and dissolution of personal relationships.

COMMUNICATION NETWORKS AND THE INITIATION OF PERSONAL RELATIONSHIPS

The importance of relationship initiation processes has been forcefully underscored by Berscheid and Graziano (1979; p. 32):

> ...the *raison d'etre* of any social relationship, as well as the relationship's complexity of character at any stage of its growth or deterioration, cannot be fully understood unless one also understands the conditions under which it was initiated.

Previous Research on Relationship Initiation

In spite of its significance relatively little research has directly explored the relationship initiation process. Most studies of initial interaction and attraction are really studies of recently initiated relationships rather than of relationship initiation. That is, the experimenter usually begins by creating interaction between subjects or by supplying them with information about one another and then studies what happens next (Berscheid & Graziano, 1979; Snyder, Berscheid, & Glick, 1985). The determinants of initial attention and partner choice are thus already given by the design.

In an attempt to remedy this difficulty Snyder, Berscheid, and Glick (1985) conducted two studies of how the personality variable of self-monitoring might influence the type of partner information to which subjects paid the most attention. In Study I males who were either high or low in self-monitoring were given the task of selecting a date from a set of file folders containing personal attribute information and photographs of 50 females. While subjects did not differ in the number of file folders examined, low self-monitors spent more time inspecting the information on personal attributes than the photographs and they also reported that personal attributes were a more important factor in their final choices. High self-monitors displayed the reverse pattern. In Study II subjects were given just two file folders. One described a physically attractive person with undesirable attributes, while the other described a physically unattractive person with desirable personal attributes. When forced to choose, low self-monitors were more likely to select physically unattractive partners with desirable personalities, but high self-monitors were more likely to select physically attractive partners with undesirable personalities. Thus personality factors such as self-monitoring appear to play a role in determining how much attention a potential partner might receive and in determining the features of that person judged to be most salient in relationship initiation decisions.

However, as useful as it was, the general design of this study and the assumptions behind it must be seen as extremely narrow approaches to the study of relationship initiation. The design presents the subject with an array of potential partners who are floating in a social void. That is, they are not engaged in any activity, the source of information is not another person, and there is no information about the potential partner's relationship to anyone in the subject's social circle. The ecological validity of such a socially stripped design is open to question. More importantly, the assumption framing the study may not be the most useful one for studying relationship initiation. Berscheid and Graziano (1979; p. 36) defined the 'protypical problem for the study of relationship initiation' as predicting which of the several people in a potential initiator's perceptual field might receive his or her attention. We believe that a prior question, indeed the fundamental question about relationship initiation is: what brought those people into the potential initiator's perceptual field in the first place? Laboratory studies are inherently incapable of answering this question because they rip the individual out of his or her natural social context.

The traditional answer to the question of what brings individuals into initial contact is physical proximity, or geographic propinquity. We know, for instance, that people who live close to one another or whose daily routes bring them close to one another are more likely to meet and strike up friendships than those who live further apart (e.g., Caplow & Forman, 1950; Festinger, Schachter & Back, 1950; Menne & Sinnett, 1971). However, while the influence of physical proximity is undeniable, it does not provide a sufficient explanation for relationship initiation processes. For one thing, it does not explain why people do not initiate relationships with everyone in close physical proximity. Moreover, it does not account for factors that might cause an individual to reach beyond his or her daily routes to meet a specific individual.

In short recent and traditional approaches to the problem of relationship initiation are unsatisfying. While some theories acknowledge the importance of a prior 'field of eligibles' or a 'zero contact' period of relatedness, most theories of relationship development do not apply extensively until after a relationship has already begun (e.g., Altman & Taylor, 1973; Berger & Calabrese, 1975; Levinger & Snoek, 1972). Recent 'perceptual-cognitive' approaches (e.g., Berscheid & Graziano, 1979; Snyder et al., 1985) are informative, but do not come into play until after a potential partner is already in the subject's perceptual field. They do not explain how the potential partner got into the subject's perceptual field in the first place. Traditional research on physical proximity is also helpful, but unsatisfying because it explains so little about the forces that might create first meetings between individuals.

A Social Contextual View of Relationship Initiation

The prototypical problem for the study of relationship initiation from a social contextual perspective may be defined as: 'Given a potential initiator in a given social context structured by previous communication patterns, which individuals, if any, is the initiator most likely to meet?'

One of the chief impediments to understanding relationship initiation has been an uncritical acceptance of the belief that relationships in the United States and most other Western cultures are initiated in an 'open' rather than 'closed' contextual field. Closed-field settings are those in which interaction with a given person is forced or predetermined to a great extent, while open-field settings are those in which the individual has a great degree of choice in relationship initiation (Murstein, 1970).

While individuals obviously do have some choice as to their partners, relationship initiation is also contextually constrained in at least four ways. First, as we already noted, it is constrained by the dynamics of physical proximity. Moreover, it is constrained by the influence of social norms regarding appropriate and inappropriate relational partners (e.g., Kerckhoff, 1974; Lewis, 1975; Milardo & Lewis, 1985). These norms function to propel the individual toward some groups of potential partners and away from others. Third, relationship initiation is influenced by the relative positions of the initiator and the potential partner within a larger communication network. Finally, relationship initiation is influenced by the direct actions of third parties within the larger communication network containing both the initiator and the potential partner. We will focus on the last two of these factors because they have received the least attention and because they illustrate our social contextual approach most clearly.

We believe that the probability of any two given individuals meeting is partly a function of their relative positions within a larger communication network containing them both. More specifically, the greater their communication network proximity (as opposed to physical proximity) the greater the probability that they will meet. By network proximity we mean the number of links that separate them. For example, if A is communicatively linked to B, and B to C, and C to D; we would say that A was more proximal to C than to D because information from A would have to pass through fewer links to reach C than to reach D. Thus the social context of relationship initiation is actually a communication network in which people are positioned at varying communicative distances from one another. Our contention is that those who are separated by fewer links are more likely to meet that those who are separated by a greater number of links. Put in a different way, I am more likely to meet the friends of those who are already my friends than to meet the friends of those who are not already my friends.

The process of relationship initiation is also triggered by the direct actions of third parties within the communication network shared by the initiator and the potential partner. An obvious example is the formal role of matchmaker, but third parties also operate in less formalized, more casual ways. They partially 'close' an otherwise 'open' relational field by simply introducing people to one another. Sometimes these introductions are deliberate attempts to get two people together. Sometimes they occur for less strategic reasons. Whatever the motivations of the third party, we hypothesize that third party introductions play a major role in the process of relationship initiation.

Study I: Communication Networks and Relationship Initiation

If our social contextual view is correct, then we ought to be able to find evidence that future relational partners were connected indirectly through network proximity prior to their own actual meeting. One way of demonstrating this could be to show that they had already met members of each other's networks of close friends and family before their own initial meeting. In addition we ought to be able to show that relational partners were often brought together through introductions by other network members. An exploratory study was conducted to search for these two types of evidence.

Subjects. A total of 858 subjects (355 males, 503 females) participated in the study. The sample was composed of students from a large state university (61%) and from a suburban high school (39%). Subjects ranged in age from 14 to 36, but most (96%) were between 16 and 22 years of age. Most (77%) were Caucasian.

Procedures. Subjects were first assigned to report about one of their same-sex close friendships ($n = 478$) or an opposite-sex dating relationship ($n = 380$). Subjects were then instructed to obtain a list of their partner's 12 most significant network contacts: the names of the four family members or relatives to whom the partner felt the closest and the eight nonkin to whom the partner felt the closest. Once the partner's network membership was obtained, subjects were instructed to indicate which, if any, of the twelve people in the partner's network they had met *prior* to first meeting their friend or dating partner.

Subjects who reported about a dating relationship were asked several additional questions. They first were asked if another person had initially introduced them to their partner. If so, further questions sought to ascertain the sex of the third party, the relationship between the subject and the third party at the time and the relationship between the future partner and the third party at the time (i.e., close friend, friend, family/relative, acquaintance, co-worker).

Results. Nearly two thirds (66.3%) of the subjects had met at least one member of their partner's network of close friends, family, and other close associates prior to actually meeting the partner himself or herself. Most subjects (47.3%) had prior contact with one to three members of the partner's close network, although an appreciable proportion (13.2%) had met between four and six members and a few (5.8%) had met more than six members of the partner's 12 person list of significant others.

Further tests revealed that males and females were nearly identical in the degree of prior contact with their partner's networks, $t(856) = 0.10$, *ns*. Nor was there any overall difference in the amount of prior contact between high school students and university students, $F(1.49)$, *ns*. There was, however, a significant main effect for relationship type, $F(1,854) = 74.48, p < .0001$. Those in dating relationships ($M = 2.68$) had prior contact with nearly twice as many people in their partner's network as did those in same-sex friendships ($M = 1.40$). This trend was even more pronounced among those in the university sample as indicated by a significant two-way interaction between relationship type and cohort, $F(1,854) = 5.23, p < .025$. University students tended to have much more prior contact in their dating relationships than in their friendships (M's = 2.74 vs. 1.19), while the difference in prior contact was smaller for high school students (M's = 2.54 vs. 1.68).

Almost half of the subjects (43.6%) could remember having been introduced to their dating partner by a third party. The proportions of people being introduced by third parties were almost identical in the university sample (44.2%) and the high school sample (42.7%). Data on the sex of the third party were available only for the university sample and they showed that introductions were somewhat more likely to be performed by women than by men (54% vs. 46%). Data on the relationships between the third party and the two potential partners were available for both samples. Third parties were more likely to come from the ranks of less close relationships (e.g., friends, acquaintances, co-workers) than from the ranks of close friends and family members. More notable, however, is the pattern of these relationships. The most common pattern was for introductions to be performed by a person who was close to one potential partner, but not to the other. The least common pattern was for the third party to be close to both potential partners.

Summary. Current theories of relationship development and previous research on relationship initiation do not adequately explain why some people meet and why other, perhaps equally viable, pairs never get an opportunity to meet. By default, most social psychologists appear to treat first meetings as if they took place randomly in an arena of almost complete free choice.

The social contextual model begins by conceptualizing the potential initiator and the potential partner as members of a communication network. Before they meet they may be indirectly connected through one or more third parties. Their communicative distance from one another may be calculated as the number of people one would have to go through to reach the other. As this distance decreases, the probability of the two parties actually meeting increases. The results of Study I, though not a full test, suggest that future relational partners usually have at least some contact with each other's network of close friends and family prior to actually meeting each other for the first time. Thus the larger communication network that defines the social context 'passes' potential friends and romantic partners in each other's direction and thereby increases the chances of an initial encounter. This seems to be particularly true for premarital romantic relationships. That is, our subjects appeared not to 'reach' quite as far beyond their existing networks for new romantic partners as for new friends.

The social contextual forces that produce initial encounters between prospective relational partners often go beyond this relatively passive ability of a network to pass people in each other's direction. Network members often intervene by introducing potential partners to one another. The results of Study I indicated that premarital romantic partners had been introduced to one another in nearly half of the almost 400 cases examined. Although our data were limited, it appeared that women were somewhat more likely than men to perform introductions. A more detailed social and personality profile of the types of people who are most likely to perform introductions awaits future research. In general our results demonstrated that introductions served a 'bridging function'. The person doing the introduction reaches out to connect someone he or she does not know well with someone he or she does know well.

One of the most important strengths of the social contextual model is that it theoretically unites the process of the relationship initiation with the later process of relationship development. As we noted, existing theories of relationship development are not explicitly concerned with the factors that bring prospective partners into each other's perceptual field. The social contextual model, on the other hand, not only identifies factors that create first meetings, but also suggests that these same factors are actively involved in the development of the partners' relationship.

COMMUNICATION NETWORKS AND THE DEVELOPMENT OF PERSONAL RELATIONSHIPS

Personal relationships do not develop in a social vacuum. Nor is the social context merely a stage upon which the developmental dance is played out. Instead the communication networks that form the participants' social context are actively involved in the process of relationship development. Fortunately this point is increasingly acknowledged by those studying personal relationships (e.g., Huston & Levinger, 1978; Huston et al., 1981; La Gaipa, 1981; Levinger, 1974; 1980; Lewis, 1975; Milardo, 1986; Milardo & Lewis, 1985; Ridley & Avery, 1979). In spite of all the discussion, however, only a few studies have actually examined the interplay between communication network factors and relationship development.

In this section we will overview previous theoretic notions about the interplay of networks and dyads. Next we will extend the social contextual model to identify specific linkages between network factors and developmental factors within dyads. Finally we will summarize the results of three studies (Eggert & Parks, 1987; Parks et al., 1983) in support of our theoretic perspective. We will begin, however, by considering the process of dyadic withdrawal, a process that is often thought to limit the influence of the social context on developing romantic relationships.

Dyadic Withdrawal or Dyadic Realignment?

Theorists have long drawn on the image of dyadic partners withdrawing from society into the private world of their developing relationship (e.g., Freud, 1961;

Goode, 1960; Krain, 1977; Lewis, 1972; Slater, 1963). Withdrawal from other relationships is merely the consequence of allocating greater time to the partner for some theorists, while for others the act of withdrawal helps define and stabilize the developing dyad itself (e.g., Johnson & Leslie, 1982; Krain, 1977; Lewis, 1972). It was only recently, however, that researchers sought to put this image to an empirical test. One strand of support was provided by Huston and his colleagues (Huston et al., 1981) who found that courting couples tended to increase the proportion of their leisure and recreational activities with the partner, while the proportion with outsiders decreased as their relationship developed. This finding was extended by Surra (1985) who found that couples who recalled shifting more of their affectional, instrumental, and leisure activities from the network to the partner also recalled moving toward engagement and marriage more rapidly.

A more extensive test of the dyadic withdrawal hypothesis came in a study by Johnson and Leslie (1982). They compared individuals at different points in the courtship process: occasionally dating, regularly dating, dating exclusively, engaged, or married. Johnson and Leslie found that subjects who were married or engaged had somewhat fewer friends, placed a bit less importance on the opinions of their friends and kin, and disclosed somewhat less to their friends and kin than subjects who were in the earlier stages of courtship. These results appeared to reveal a modest, but significant, dyadic withdrawal effect in the sectors of the network containing the subject's friends and relatives. Yet because only these network sectors were examined, the study could not determine whether dyadic withdrawal was a limited or general phenomenon. It may be that withdrawal occurs only for some sectors of the individual's relational network or even that withdrawal in some sectors is offset by expansions in some other sectors, say for example, increasing contact with the partner's friends and relatives (Parks et al., 1983).

A study by Milardo, Johnson, and Huston (1983) addressed some of these concerns by using a structured diary method in which subjects recorded all interactions of 10 minutes or more for two 10 day periods that were approximately three month apart. There were three primary measures of dyadic withdrawal: average duration of interaction, the frequency of interactions with a given person, and the overall number of people with whom the subject interacted. These variables were examined across five sectors of the subject's personal network: close friends, kin, intermediate friends, acquaintances, and total network. In addition two types of analysis were conducted. One was a cross-sectional analysis comparing individuals who were casually dating, regularly dating, exclusively dating, pre-engaged, or engaged. The other was a longitudinal analysis of differences over three months. All together, this combination of variables, network sectors, methods yielded 30 tests of the dyadic withdrawal hypothesis. Unfortunately, support for the dyadic withdrawal hypothesis was found in only about 10 of these tests. Only one of the tests involving network size and only one of the longitudinal tests provided evidence of withdrawal. When withdrawal did occur, it took place more in the peripheral sectors (intermediate friend and acquaintance) than in the central sectors (close friends and kin) of the individual's network. As their romantic relationship developed, individuals maintained contact with about the same number of people, but tended to interact with them somewhat less.

The studies conducted to date support only a limited version of the dyadic withdrawal hypothesis. It appears to be selective rather than general and its effects appear to be smaller rather than larger. One reason for this may be that dyadic withdrawal is only one of the changes accompanying the development of a romantic relationship. We believe that it is just part of the larger process of dyadic realignment that occurs as both network members and romantic partners alter their relationships with one another. Withdrawal is not an escape from the network, but rather part of the shaping of a new network and social context. This shaping probably involves some selective withdrawal, but it also involves greater contact with the partner's network and the expansion of network sectors that the romantic partners share (e.g., Eggert & Parks, 1987; Lewis, 1975; Milardo. 1982; 1986; Parks & Adelman, 1983; Parks et al., 1983; Surra, 1988).

Previous Theoretic Links Between Networks and Dyads

If social withdrawal is simply part of the larger interplay between the developing relationship and its networks, then we must look for additional ways in which the developing dyad and the surrounding networks influence each other. Some of these influences appear to be relatively diffuse. For example, behavior within the developing relationship should be influenced by the roles and values communicated over time by network members (e.g., Kerckhoff, 1974; Lewis, 1975; Milardo & Lewis, 1985). Another diffuse effect might be the sort of generalized social conditioning that occurs when group members are gathered together in a context that provides rewards (Lott & Lott, 1961). If a romantic couple and several network members all attend an extremely good concert together, for example, we might expect them all to become somewhat more attracted to one another.

A more encompassing approach to the link between dyadic development and network activity comes from research on transitivity by structural sociologists (e.g., Davis, 1970; Hallinan, 1974; Holland & Leinhardt, 1972; 1977). Transitivity is often treated by structural sociologists as one of a series of lower order principles upon which larger, higher order social structures are built (e.g., Berkowitz, 1982; Blau, 1977). Simply put, the principle of transitivity predicts that: 'if A likes B and B likes C, A will like or will come to like C'. Expressed another way, transitivity predicts that there is a greater chance that two people will become friends if they share a mutual friend already than if they do not (Hammer, 1980; Hammer & Schaffer, 1975; Salzinger, 1982). Thus we would expect that greater involvement with the partner and greater involvement with the partner's network would reciprocally promote each other. The partners and their networks should therefore become more intertwined and densely interconnected as their relationships develop (e.g., Salzinger, 1982).

The concept of structural interdependence has also been used to link the developing relationship to its surrounding networks (e.g., Milardo, 1982, 1986; Surra, 1988). Structural interdependence is based on social psychological theories of social exchange and interdependence (e.g., Kelley, 1979; Kelley & Thibaut, 1978). These theories view relationship development in terms of increasing mutual influence and interdependence between the partners. Milardo (1983, p. 11) simply applies the image of growing dyadic interdependence to the structural level in order to explain why romantic partner's networks become more overlapping as their dyadic relationship develops:

> As pairs become interdependent in their personal lives, they will become interdependent in their social lives as well and the emergence of overlapping networks is largely the result of increasing interdependencies...Mutually involved pairs develop a jointly held orientation toward themselves, a jointly held orientation toward the social environment and a jointly held network of relations that reflect the pairs' interdependence with one another and their interdependence with the social environment.

Increases in the partners' social environmental or structural interdependence, in turn, are characterized by increases in the mutuality or overlap, density, clustering, and interconnectedness of their communication networks (Milardo, 1986). In one excellent study, for example, Milardo (1982) showed that couples in the later stages of courtship had roughly twice as many mutual contacts in their communication networks as couples in the earlier stages of courtship. Over a three month period couples whose relationship developed also reported a greater number of mutual contacts, while couples whose relationship deteriorated reported a reduced number of mutual contacts.

Lewis' (1972; 1973; 1975) social reaction theory of mate selection focuses even more specifically on how interactions with network members can support the development of romantic dyads. According to this theory, romantic relationships develop as network members reinforce the couple's joint identity by directly expressing approval, by using symbolic labels that emphasize the participants' togetherness, by treating them as a couple socially, and by negatively reinforcing behavior which network members view as threatening to the relationship. These support processes have been linked both empirically and theoretically to several different indicators of courtship development (e.g., Lewis, 1973; Milardo & Lewis, 1985).

A Social Contextual View of Relationship Development

Each partner in a developing personal relationship is simultaneously a member of other dyadic and group relationships. Each individual and each relationship is thus embedded in a larger communication network that in its broadest sense actualizes the social context. Previous theory and research demonstrate that the developmental path of the partners' relationship covaries with their interactions within the larger network. They do not provide, however, an entirely adequate explanation for the linkages between dyadic development and network involvement. Explanatory concepts like transitivity and structural interdependence offer useful global summaries, but they do not clearly identify the more specific interactive processes in which they are manifested or which produce them. And while support from network members (e.g., Lewis, 1975) is surely one of the more specific interactive processes behind transitivity and structural interdependence, it is not the only one.

We believe that the role played by the social context in the development of personal relationships is best understood by considering a series of specific, but interrelated, processes arising in the interaction of partners and network members. These include: (1) the satisfaction of social expectations, (2) cognitive balance, (3) support or reinforcement, (4) information exchange, (5) the creation of opportunities for joint interaction, and (6) barrier forces.

Satisfying social expectations. Some of the expectations partners have about each other's behavior are undoubtedly relationship specific. Others may be linked to broader values and social norms (e.g., Kerckhoff, 1974; Lewis, 1973; Milardo & Lewis, 1985). One general expectation is that relational partners will be introduced to each other's friends and family. Failing to meet the partner's friends and relatives may create uncertainty regarding the partner's feelings or about the individual's own desirability. Conversely, meeting the significant members of the partner's network helps satisfy a basic social expectation, reduces uncertainty, and thereby promotes further relational development (Parks & Adelman, 1983).

Creating cognitive balance. Traditional balance theories predict that as the individual's attraction to his or her partner increases, the strain toward cognitive balance should result in greater attraction to the partner's friends and family (see Cartright & Harary, 1956; Davis, 1970; Heider, 1946; Newcomb, 1961). And one may be more attracted to a partner with attractive friends and family. On the other hand, cognitive imbalances should occur when the individual and the partner's network dislike each other or when members of the individual's own network dislike the partner. Such imbalances should create conflicting feelings about the partner, uncertainty regarding the relationship, and perhaps even reductions in attraction to the partner.

Providing support. Expressions of support or opposition have been the most consistently identified interactive process linking relationship development and network involvement in previous research. Partners and network members have long been known to try to influence each other's perceptions of the developing relationship (e.g., Bates, 1942; Leslie, Johnson, & Huston, 1986; Sussman, 1953). We have already noted how network members reinforce the developing relationship by expressing direct support, by treating the partners as a couple socially, and by using social labels that recognize the partners as a unit (Lewis, 1972, 1973, 1975; Ryder, Kafka & Olson, 1971; Waller & Hill, 1951). As their relationship develops the partners may make greater efforts to elicit support from network members (Leslie et al., 1986; Parks et al., 1983). By the same token, network members may become more supportive if it looks like the partners' relationship is going to develop and endure (Driscoll, Davis, & Lipetz, 1972; Leslie et al., 1986). Finally, the overall support in the network may increase as partners selectively withdraw from members who are thought to oppose the relationship (Johnson & Milardo, 1984).

A number of studies have reported positive associations between support from friends and family and relationship developments. Lewis (1973), for example, examined 316 premarital romantic couples over a 10 week period. Couples who had received the greatest support from friends and family at the beginning of the study also tended to have higher scores on measures of commitment, attraction, and courtship progression 10 weeks later. Positive associations between indicators of dyadic development and the level of support from network members have also been reported in other studies on premarital romantic relationships (e.g., Krain, 1977; Leslie et al., 1986). Research has also shown that marital adjustment is positively associated with support from network members, especially parents (Burgess & Cottrell, 1939; Burr, 1973; Locke, 1951).

Exchanging information. The information exchanged between individuals and members of their own and their partner's networks also allows the partners to reduce uncertainty about one another by enhancing their ability to predict, explain, and compare each other's behavior (Parks & Adelman, 1983). Communication with network members provides information about the partner's past behavior and personality. Network members can serve as sounding boards for the individual's own perceptions of the partner and as sources of explanation for the partner's behavior. They may tell one partner things the other partner has said about the first. More generally, the information exchanged among network members and the partners can help reduce uncertainty by providing a rich field for social comparison. Titus (1980), for example, reported that interactions with friends helped spouses to assess their own abilities, validate their relational and self images, and establish a frame of reference for evaluating their marital relationship.

Creating joint interactions. As personal relationships develop the participants usually endeavor to spend more time together. Additional time can be gained by withdrawal from other relationships or using time previously spent alone. In addition participants may create joint interactions between themselves and network members as a way to spend more time together (Anderson, 1979). Network members may create joint interactions as a way to cope with the couple's withdrawal, to express support, or to gain information. However created, joint interactions tie the developing dyad to its surrounding networks and create social arenas in which both greater dyadic development and greater convergence of the partners' networks occur.

Imposing barriers. Commitment to a personal relationship stems not only from its attractive features, but also from the constraints imposed in interactions among network members (Johnson, 1982; Levinger, 1979). Access to alternative partners is reduced as the partners become more involved with each other's networks. Once involved in the partner's network, the individual may find that network members provide resources that would be lost if the relationship were to dissolve. Indeed greater access to these resources may make the partner more attractive in the individual's eyes (Eggert & Parks, 1987; Parks & Adelman, 1983; Parks et al., 1983).

Two themes run through these more specific interactive processes that link relationship development and network involvement. One theme is *uncertainty reduction*. Uncertainty is reduced as partners become better able to predict and explain each other's behavior to themselves and become more attributionally confident (Berger, 1979; Berger & Bradac, 1982; Berger & Calabrese, 1975). Interaction with network members reduces uncertainty for all parties by satisfying expectations, creating cognitive balances, providing support, and by exchanging other uncertainty reducing information (Parks & Adelman, 1983). When uncertainty is reduced, the relationships between the partners and between the partners and members of each other's networks should exhibit greater amounts of interaction, disclosure, attraction, and intimacy. A second theme is *network structuring*. Beyond their potential for uncertainty reduction, interactions with network members promote and sustain relationship development by providing material assistance, creating opportunities for joint interactions, and by imposing barrier forces. Moreover, as the mutual or overlapping network becomes larger, partners and network members become better able to coordinate their interaction with one another (Milardo, 1986).

Study II: Communication Networks and Romantic Relationship Development in a Young Adult Sample

The theoretic processes discussed in the previous paragraphs imply that the development of dyadic relationships should covary with network factors. Some of these factors may already be at work when the relationship is initiated, or even before, as we noted in Study I. The goal of the next study (Parks et al., 1983) was to explore additional linkages between the later development of romantic dyads and patterns of interaction with network members. Specifically, we hypothesized that the level of relationship development should be positively associated with the level of perceived support for the relationship from members of one's own network, the level of perceived support from members of the romantic partner's network, the number of people met in the partner's network, the amount of communication with members of the partner's network, and the individual's attraction to members of the partner's network.

Subjects. Undergraduate university students (94 males, 99 females) who were currently involved in heterosexual premarital relationships were contacted through classes and campus advertisements. The typical subject was 19 years old. Subjects reported on relationships varying widely in duration (less than two weeks to 72 months), but the typical relationship had a duration of approximately 11 months.

Procedures. Subjects began by listing the names of the four family members or relatives and the eight friends or nonkin to whom they felt the closest. A similar list was then submitted from the subject's romantic partner. These lists were combined to create a 24-person network containing the 12 people to whom the subject felt the closest and the 12 people to whom the partner felt the closest. Subjects then completed measures of support from, communication with, and attraction to each network member as well as a series of measures of romantic involvement.

Previous studies in this area have often relied on single-item measures of relationship development. Many, for example, merely categorize relationships according to comparatively crude courtship labels such as 'regularly dating' or 'engaged' (e.g., Johnson & Leslie, 1982, Johnson & Milardo, 1984; Leslie et al., 1986; Milardo, 1982; Milardo et al., 1983). Our approach was to gain a more sensitive assessment of relationship development by examining six measures: (1) Rubin's (1970) love scale; (2) Wheeless' (1976) interpersonal solidarity scale, (3) the number of days (0-14) in the last two weeks in which the subject and partner had communicated face-to-face, (4) the percentage of free time (0-100%) spent with the partner in the last two weeks, (5) the subject's estimate of the probability (0-100%) that the relationship would last three more months, and (6) the subject's estimate of the probability (0-100%) that the relationship would lead to marriage.

We also examined a greater range of network factors than previous studies. First, the level of support from the subject's own network was measured with a six-item scale developed by Lewis (1973). In addition subjects were asked to judge the amount of support perceived from and expressed by each member of their own network. Scores on these scales were summed and averaged to yield two more indicators: support from own family and kin and support from friends and other nonkin. Second, the level of support from the partner's network was measured in terms of the amount of support perceived from and expressed by each member of the partner's network whom the subject had met. Separate measures of support from the partners' family and kin and support from the partner's friends and other nonkin were obtained. Third, the subject's range of contact with members of the partner's network was measured with two indicators: the number of family and relatives in the partner's network whom the subject had met and the number of friends and nonkin in the partner's network whom the subject had met. Fourth, two indicators were used to assess the amount of communication with members of the partner's network: a global item regarding how often the subject generally talked with network members and a specific item asking how often the subject had communicated with network members in the last two weeks. Finally, two indicators were used to assess the subject's degree of attraction toward known members of the partner's network. Responses to each item were averaged across known network members.

General results. These procedures yielded scores on a total of 17 indicators grouped into six general factors: a relational development factor and five network factors. The general analysis was conceptualized as a confirmatory factor analysis in which the indicators were grouped according to factors and in which the hypothesized links between relationship development and network involvement were estimated as correlations among factors using Joreskog and Sorbom's LISREL (1978) program. Because each factor was assessed with multiple indicators, this program allowed us to incorporate a measurement model and thereby to correct the correlations between factors for attenuation. Preliminary analyses showed that the indicators loaded significantly on their assigned factors and that correlations among indicators did not differ significantly as a function of the subject's sex, religious affiliation, and intensity of religious belief (See Parks et al., 1983).

In spite of the complexity of the analysis, the primary findings can be expressed simply as the correlations between the relational development factor and the five network factors. All correlations were significant ($p < .05$). The largest correlations were between dyadic relationship development and perceived support from one's own network ($r = .82$), perceived support from the partner's network ($r = .68$), and the number of people known in the partner's network ($r = .68$). Smaller, but significant, correlations were found between dyadic relationship development and attraction to members of the partner's network ($r = .39$) and between dyadic relationship development and the amount of interaction with members of the partner's network ($r = .27$). Thus, as we hypothesized, the level of romantic involvement between the partners was positively associated with the amount of support received from one's own network, the amount of support from the partner's network, the degree of contact and communication with members of the partner's network, and the level of attraction to members of the partner's network.

Romeo and Juliet revisited. A strikingly different approach to the relationship between romantic involvement and network support was taken in an oft-cited study by Driscoll and his colleagues (1972). They argued that opposition from network members set up a 'Romeo and Juliet Effect' in which the reactance and goal-frustration resulting from parental opposition actually created greater romantic involvement. Because this view runs nearly opposite to our own, we undertook a more extensive examination.

Our results suggested that overall relationship between romantic development and network support was positive and linear, rather than negative as Driscoll and his colleagues had hypothesized. We found no evidence of the Romeo and Juliet effect in those network sectors involving the subject's own family and relatives, the subject's own friends, and the partner's friends. Limited evidence of the effect was found in the network sector involving the partner's family and relatives, but only then with some levels of some indicators. Similar results were obtained for those who had been dating both shorter and longer periods of time. Other studies have also failed to replicate the Romeo and Juliet effect (e.g., Krain, 1977; Leslie, 1982/1983; Lewis, 1973). In short it appears that support from network members is positively associated with romantic involvement, while in most cases opposition is negatively associated with romantic involvement.

Study III: Communication Networks and Romantic Relationship Development in an Adolescent Sample

The next study (Eggert & Parks, 1987) extended the previous study in two ways. First, we expanded the scope of our research program by sampling the romantic relationships of high school age adolescents. Nearly all previous studies have been limited to samples of college age young adults. Second, we got an even more sensitive assessment of dyadic development by including additional indicators of romantic involvement.

Subjects. Subjects (46 males, 88 females) were drawn from 16 different classrooms in two different high schools in a predominantly middle-class, white community. The typical subject was about 17 years old. Subjects reported on relationships which ranged in duration from less than two weeks to 72 months, but which averaged about six months in duration.

Procedures. This study employed basically the same procedures as Study II. A 24-person network was constructed from lists of the 12 kin and nonkin to whom the subject felt the closest and from lists of the 12 kin and nonkin to whom the dating partner felt the closest. Subjects then responded to items concerning the amount of communication with, attraction to, and support from members of the network as well as to items assessing the level of development in the romantic relationship itself.

Relationship development was conceptualized in terms of three distinct, yet interrelated, dimensions: sociability, intimacy, and commitment. The sociability or interaction dimension was measured with two indicators: the proportion of free time the subject spent with the partner and the number of days out of the last two weeks in which the subject and partner had communicated. The intimacy dimension was assessed with six multiple-item scales: Rubin's (1970) scales for love and liking, Wheeless' (1976) general interpersonal solidarity scale, a perceived similarity scale, a measure of relational uncertainty (Parks,

1978), and a measure of communication satisfaction (Hecht, 1978). Finally, the commitment dimension of relationship development was assessed with two indicators: the subject's estimate of the probability that the dating relationship would continue for three more months and his or her estimate of the probability that it would result in marriage.

Communication network involvement was conceptualized in terms of four dimensions or factors: support for the relationship from the subject's own network, support from the partner's network, attraction to members of the partner's network, and the range of contact or communication in the partner's network. As in Study II, multiple indicators were used to measure each dimension. Subjects were asked to judge the amount of support perceived from or expressed by each member of their own network and each known member of the partner's network. Individual items were summed and averaged to yield estimates of support from each of four different network sectors: own family and relatives, own friends, partner's family and relatives, and partner's friends. Subjects also responded to two items indicating how much they liked or how close they felt to each known member of the partner's network. Answers were summed and averaged to yield separate measures of attraction to the partner's family and relatives and to the partner's friends and other nonkin. Finally, subjects reported whether or not they had actually met each member of the partner's network. These yielded separate measures of the range of contact with the partner's family and relatives and with the partner's friends and other nonkin.

Results. The analysis of these data followed the same general plan as the analysis of the data from the previous study. We used LISREL to test a confirmatory factor model linking indicators to factors and linking the relational development and network involvement factors (see Eggert & Parks, 1987).

Table 1: Study III: Correlations among romantic development and network involvement factors

Factor:	1	2	3	4	5	6	7	8
Interaction time with partner:	1.00							
Perceived similarity with partner:	.07	1.00						
Intimacy with partner:	.22	.80*	1.00					
Commitment to romantic relationship:	.43*	.58*	.46*	1.00				
Support from own network:	.32*	.42*	.35*	.23*	1.00			
Support from partner's network:	.36*	.62*	.55*	.43*	.80*	1.00		
Range of contact in partner's network:	.32*	-.08	.14	.15	.39*	.09*	1.00	
Attraction to partner's network:	.14	.69*	.68*	.56*	.62*	.53*	.44*	1.00

* Significant correlation - i.e. at least twice its standard error. Estimates drawn from Phi matrix in confirmatory factor analysis using LISREL V.

Our initial analysis suggested that the data better fit a four dimensional model of relationship development. Indicators were thus ordered according to four developmental factors: interaction time, perceived similarity, intimacy, and commitment. The correlations among these factors are reported in Table 1. Although the amount of time the subject spent interacting with the romantic partner was not significantly related to either perceived similarity or intimacy, all the remaining correlations among these four developmental factors were positive and significant.

The four network involvement factors were also highly interrelated, as noted in Table 1. Support from the subject's own network, support from the partner's network, and attraction to members of the partner's network were all positively and significantly associated. While the number of people the subject had met in the partner's network was not related to the level of support perceived from those who had been met, subjects who had met more members of the partner's network did tend to like the partner's network more and perceive their own network as more supportive of the romantic relationship.

Our greatest interest, of course, was in the linkages between the four relationship development factors and four network involvement factors. As predicted these two sets were highly related to one another (Table 1). People who perceived that their own and their partner's networks were more supportive also interacted more, perceived their partners to be more similar, felt more intimate with their partners, and experienced greater commitment to the romantic relationship. Moreover, as the subjects met more people in their partners' networks, they also interacted more with their partners. And the more subjects liked members of their partners' networks, the more intimate with and committed to their partners they became. While there were exceptions, the general pattern emerging from these findings bears witness to the strong association between the internal, developmental dynamics of romantic relationships and the communication networks surrounding those relationships.

Study IV: Communication Networks and Same-Sex Friendship Development in an Adolescent Sample

In the next study (Eggert & Parks, 1987) we extended our social contextual approach to relationship development by applying it to same-sex close friendships. Previous research in this area has been almost completely limited to studies of heterosexual romantic relationships. Yet the interactive processes theoretically linking relationship development and network involvement are not limited to romantic relationships.

Subjects. Subjects (69 males, 135 females) were drawn from the same high schools used in the previous study. The typical subject was 16 years old. Subjects were asked to report on a same-sex friendship. The duration of these friendships varied from less than two weeks to over 10 years, but averaged about 13 months.

Procedures. The procedures and measures employed in this study mirrored those of the previous study. Once again we obtained lists of both the subject's and the partner's four closest family and kin relationships and eight closest nonkin relationships. The lists were then combined to create a 24-person network composed of the subject's 12 closest significant others and the partner's 12 closest significant others.

Friendship development and communication network involvement were assessed with the same indicators used in Study III. An item asking subjects to estimate the probability of marriage was changed to an estimate of the probability of remaining 'friends forever', but otherwise the measures remained the same. Friendship development indicators were grouped into four factors on the basis of our initial confirmatory factor analysis: interaction time with the close friend, perceived similarity, intimacy, and commitment. Communication network involvement indicators were also grouped according to the same four dimensions used in the previous study: support for the relationship from the subject's own network, support from the partner's network, attraction to members of the partner's network, and the range of contact or communication in the partner's network.

Results. The analysis followed the same general procedures used in the previous study. A confirmatory factor analysis was first used to load indicators on the four developmental and four network factors and then used to calculate corrected correlations among the eight factors (Eggert & Parks, 1987).

Table 2: Study IV: Correlations among friendship development and network involvement factors

Factor:	1	2	3	4	5	6	7	8
Interaction time with partner:	1.00							
Perceived similarity with partner:	.28*	1.00						
Intimacy with partner:	.27*	.67*	1.00					
Commitment to friendship:	.16	.40*	.47*	1.00				
Support from own network:	.28*	.46*	.54*	.44*	1.00			
Support from partner's network:	.26*	.46*	.40*	.44*	.81*	1.00		
Range of contact in partner's network:	.30*	.30*	.01	.33*	.14	.19	1.00	
Attraction to partner's network:	.13	.40*	.35*	.80*	.50*	.33*	.23	1.00

* Significant correlation - i.e. at least twice its standard error. Estimates drawn from Phi matrix in confirmatory factor analysis using LISREL V.

As Table 2 illustrates, the four developmental factors were significantly correlated with each other. How much the subject interacted with the close friend, how similar the subject believed the two of them to be, how intimate the subject felt the friendship was, and how committed the subject was to the friendship all covaried positively. The lone exception to this pattern was the finding that commitment to the relationship was unrelated to how much the two friends interacted with each other.

Three of the four network involvement factors were significantly correlated with each other. Support from the subject's own network, support from the partner's network, and attraction to the partner's network were all positively associated with each other (Table 2). The subject's range of contact, however, was not significantly correlated with the other three network factors. That is, how many people in the partner's network the subject had actually met did not covary with perceptions of support and attraction for those whom the subject had met.

Again, our greatest interest was in the pattern of association between the four developmental factors and the four network involvement factors (Table 2). All but two of these correlations proved to be significant. Friends who perceived greater support from their own and their partners' networks also interacted more, felt more similar, experienced greater intimacy, and were more committed to maintaining their friendship. Although meeting more people in the partner's network was not associated with intimacy, those who had met a greater number of their partner's friends and family tended to interact more with each other, perceive greater similarity, and be more committed to the relationship. Finally, while those who saw their partner's friends and family as more attractive did not necessarily interact with their partner more, they did report greater similarity, intimacy, and commitment. In short, the general pattern of association between measures of friendship and measures of network involvement was positive and significant.

Summary of Studies II, III, IV

We argued at the outset of this section that the communication networks of dyadic partners were deeply involved in the developmental course of their relationship. This contention was strongly supported by the results of all three studies described above, although there were also differences between the studies which we have discussed elsewhere (Eggert, 1984/1985; Eggert & Parks, 1987). Other studies using different measurement strategies have also supported this general contention (e.g., Krain. 1977; Lewis, 1973; Milardo, 1982). Together these studies suggest that the development of dyadic relationships, whether measured with global indicators like courtship progression or with more specific indicators, is positively associated with the level of support perceived from the partners' networks of friends and family, the amount and range of communication partners have with each other's networks, the extent to which partners are attracted to members of each other's networks, and the extent to which the partners' networks merge or overlap. The studies presented here also testify to the generality of social contextual factors by showing that they apply to the development of both premarital romantic relationships and same-sex close friendships in at least two different age groups. In the next section we will further extend the social contextual model by exploring the role of communication networks in the dissolution of dyadic relationships.

COMMUNICATION NETWORKS AND THE DISSOLUTION OF PERSONAL RELATIONSHIPS

A Social Contextual View of Relationship Dissolution

Personal relationships deteriorate as the bonds that once held the partners together are eroded. While a few of these bonds may be purely individual or dyadic in character, more are probably social contextual in nature or at least deeply influenced by social contextual forces. These forces are involved in relationship deterioration in much the same way they are involved in relationship development. We have noted that relationships develop when communication with network members helps the partners reduce uncertainty about one another and when the emerging network structure creates joint interactions and imposes barriers to alternative relationships. Conversely, relationships should deteriorate when communication with network members increases rather than reduces partners' uncertainty about one another. By the same token, when communication with network members fails to create joint interactions or to impose barriers to alternative relationships, and when cognitive imbalances are created and social expectations remain unsatisfied, dyadic relationships should be more likely to deteriorate (Parks & Adelman, 1983).

These theoretic considerations imply that personal relationships should be more likely to dissolve when interactions with network members fail to provide support for the participants' relationship. Lewis (1973), for example, found that dating couples who felt that parents and friends were unsupportive of their relationship were significantly more likely to have broken up over a 10 week period than couples who perceived higher levels of support. Similarly, Johnson and Milardo (1984) reported that dating partners who thought that network members believed they spent too much time with each other were more likely to have broken up or experienced some sort of decline in their dating relationship when follow-up data were collected a year later.

The literature on divorce provides further evidence of the role of network support and opposition. Thornes and Collard's (1979) comparison of divorced and married individuals in England, for instance, revealed that family opposition to the marriage was over three times more common in the group that ultimately divorced. Opposition also continued after the marriage more often in the group that divorced than in the group that remained married. Moreover, individuals who are considering divorce usually seek emotional support for their decision from network members (Mitchell, 1981). This often leads to alliances between the dissatisfied spouse and network members which function to shut out the other spouse and to further distance the spouses from each other. Jacobson (1983) speculated that these alliances might have occurred in nearly half of the marriages ending in divorce.

Relationship deterioration is influenced not only by the content of the communication passing through network linkages, but also by the structure of the network itself. Personal relationships should be more likely to dissolve when they are embedded in networks which are only loosely knit and when the partners maintain largely separate networks (e.g., Milardo, 1982/1986; Miller & Parks, 1982; Salzinger, 1982).

Empirical support for this proposition can be found in the literature on a variety of personal relationships. Salzinger (1982), for example, found that over a three month period only 58% of the college aged men in densely interconnected friendship clusters lost or gained friends, while 90% of the men in loosely interconnected friendship clusters lost or gained friends. In a study of dating relationships Milardo (1982) found that the percentage of daily network contacts which the partners shared dropped significantly as their romantic relationship deteriorated over a three month period. Thus the dyadic bonds of a personal relationship and the social fabric of its surrounding network tend to unravel together. Such changes may originate either from the focal couple or from network members. Miller (1970), for instance, observed that divorce often becomes contagious as the divorces of some network members destabilize the marriages of other network members. More generally, cross-cultural comparisons have suggested that divorce is more common in cultures where spouses keep relatively separate networks than in cultures where spouses develop a more shared network (e.g., Ackerman, 1963; Zelditch, 1964).

Study V: Predicting Breakups in Romantic Relationships

If the deterioration of personal relationships covaries with the content and structure of network linkages, than it should be possible to use network factors to predict which personal relationships will last and which will dissolve over a given period of time. Doing just this was one of the goals of our next study (Parks & Adelman, 1983). We combined measures of the amount of communication to members of the partner's network and amount of support perceived from members of the partners' networks with dyadically oriented measures of the amount of communication with the romantic partner, uncertainty regarding the partner, and the degree of perceived similarity of the partner in order to predict breakups in premarital romantic relationships.

Subjects. The sample (n = 172) consisted of equal numbers of males and females who were involved in premarital heterosexual romantic relationships, but who were not cohabiting. The typical subject was 19 years old. He or she had known the romantic partner for approximately 18 months and had been dating the partner for just over 11 months.

Procedures. As in our previous studies, subjects began by obtaining a roster of the partner's significant others which included the four family members and relatives to whom the partner felt the closest and the eight friends or nonkin to whom the subject felt the closest. The first measure of communication with the partner's network was simply the proportion of the partner's significant others that the subject had met face-to-face. The second measure of communication with the partner's network was based on separate items asking subjects to report how often they generally communicated with each known contact in the partner's network and how often they had communicated with each known contact in the last two weeks. Responses to these items were summed across the partner's network and averaged to yield a proportion. The final measure was constructed by averaging the two more general proportions to create a scale ranging from 0 to 100. Higher scores implied that the subject had met more members of the partner's network and communicated with them more often.

Perceived support from the partners' networks was assessed with a six-item scale developed by Lewis (1973). Responses were summed to yield a total.

Three additional measures were constructed to assess the romantic relationship itself. These were a measure of uncertainty regarding the partner (Parks, 1978), a measure of perceived similarity to the partner, and a measure of the amount of communication with the partner. The latter measure was created from an item asking the subject to report the number of days in the last two weeks in which the partners had communicated face-to-face and an item asking the subject to report the percentage of his or her free time in the last two weeks that had been spent with the partner.

Subjects were contacted for a short telephone interview three months after these initial measures were taken. During the telephone interview subjects were asked if they were still 'going out' with the romantic partner named at Time 1. Approximately 30% of the relationships had terminated by Time 2.

Results. Our preliminary analysis revealed that relationships which had terminated at Time 2 differed on each of the Time 1 measures from those that had stayed together. Those that had broken up at Time 2 had significantly less (all p's < .0001) communication with the partner's network, received less support from the partners' networks, less communication with the partner, greater uncertainty regarding the partner, and less perceived similarity to the partner at Time 1.

The Time 1 measures were next used to form a discriminant function that predicted the status of romantic relationships at Time 2. The overall discriminant function was significant (Rc = .73, p < .0001) and all of the individual discrimination coefficients for the Time 1 predictors were significant (all p's < .001). Finally we examined how accurately the discriminant function could classify relationships according to whether they had terminated or stayed together. These results showed that the network and dyadic variables combined to correctly classify the status of relationships three months later with nearly 90% accuracy.

Another way to appreciate the significance of these findings is to compare them to the findings of another study which also attempted to predict breakups in romantic relationships over time. While we used a relatively small set of network and dyadically oriented predictors, Berg and McQuinn (1986) used much larger sets of predictors, but their predictors were all limited to the dyadic level. One set of predictors was composed of general relationship measures of satisfaction, love, conflict, ambivalence, and a variety of maintenance behaviors. Another set of predictors was composed of a series of social exchange measures including the amount of aid given to the subject by the partner, the amount of self-disclosure, perceptions of the comparison level, the comparison level for alternative, and equity. Separate discriminant functions were computed for each set and for males and females in an effort to predict whether or not the romantic relationship had terminated at Time 2, four months later. In spite of the greater number of Time 1 predictors, none of Berg and McQuinn's analyses were able to classify cases more accurately than ours and, in general, their predictor sets were slightly to substantially less correlated with the later status of the romantic relationships. Some of these differences might be attributed to the larger sample in our study. Nonetheless, it does appear that including direct measures of the structure and content of romantic partners' communication networks adds a certain amount of predictive power that is not obtained from examining much larger sets of dyadically oriented measures. And, as we demonstrated in the previous section, the dyadically oriented measures themselves are probably influenced by network factors.

SUMMARY AND DISCUSSION

No relationship is an island. Instead the participants in any one relationship are simultaneously participants in other relationships and in turn these relationships combine to form still larger social patterns that ultimately create a social context, without which no one individual or relationship can be fully understood. This social context is not an empty stage upon which isolated individuals play out their lives, but rather a vibrant representation that both defines and is defined by the interactions making it up. Its only reality stems from the communication patterns of its participants over time.

Our goal in this chapter has been to show that what happens in any one personal relationship is intimately and necessarily connected to what happens in the participants' other relationships, especially those with family and friends. Other reviewers (e.g., Milardo, 1983, 1986; Milardo & Lewis, 1985, Lewis, 1975; Surra, 1988) have pursued the same goal, though they, like us, have tended to highlight the contribution of their own particular research. Taken together, however, these reviews reach compatible, generally consistent, conclusions testifying to the interplay of personal relationships and social contexts.

Previous explanations of the link between the developmental path of a given personal relationship and interactions in its surrounding communication networks have often relied on larger images of social transitivity and structural interdependence. We believe that these theoretic images are most fruitfully portrayed in terms of the more specific interactive process in which they are manifested or which create them. As the participants in a personal relationship interact with each other and with the other members of their communication networks a series of theoretic processes come into play. These in turn serve to create interdependencies between the dyadic relationship and its surrounding networks.

We have chosen to group the specific theoretic processes linking dyads and networks into the broader categories of uncertainty reduction and network structuring. Uncertainty reduction refers to the ways in which interactions with networks function to enhance the dyadic participants' abilities to predict and explain each other's behavior, to enhance their attributional confidence, and thus to increase their actual and perceived control over the course of their relationship. This occurs as interactions with network members allow the relational partners to satisfy their expectations, to achieve a sense of cognitive balance, to increase their understanding of one another, and to obtain social support for their relationship. Beyond this, interactions with network members can structure the participants' dyadic relationship by initially bringing prospective partners together, by creating additional opportunities for them to interact with each other, and by reducing their access to and the desirability of alternative partners.

The origin of these processes can not be neatly assigned to either the personal relationship or to the networks. The processes that ultimately link a given dyad to its participants' networks emanate from the actions of both participants and network members. Changes in the level of social support for a given relationship, for instance, can result either because the participants decide to seek more support from network members or because network members decide to provide more support. It is probably misleading to argue that changes in the structure of a given relationship are caused solely by changes in network activity, or to argue that changes in network activity are caused solely by changes in the structure of a given relationship. Instead, changes in a given personal relationship and in its surrounding networks drive each other in a reciprocal fashion.

The five studies from our research program as well as the studies of other investigators that we have summarized in this chapter demonstrate clearly the associations between communication networks and the initiation, development, and deterioration of personal relationships. In Study I we found that by the time most prospective partners met for the first time they had already developed relationships with members of each other's existing networks. Moreover, we found that first meetings between prospective partners were often created through introductions by network members. Whether these introductions were initiated at the request of one of the future partners or through the unilateral actions of network members is still unknown, but in either case, networks were involved in the initiation of many relationships. Thus the friendships and romantic relationships we examined were not born in a social void but rather in a social context that already indirectly linked the partners to each other.

The results of Studies II, III, and IV extended our theoretic perspective to the later development of romantic relationships and same-sex friendships. These studies replicated and expanded upon the results of earlier studies (e.g., Krain, 1977; Lewis, 1973) by showing that the level of social support friends and romantic partners perceive from network members for their relationship is strongly and positively associated with several different measures of personal relationship development. We also found that the partner's attraction to members of each other's networks was positively associated with the development of their personal relationship. Moreover, we found that partners tended to have more and more contact and communication with members of each others' networks as their dyadic relationship developed. These findings fit nicely with the results of a study by Milardo (1982) who found that romantic partners tended to develop more shared or overlapping networks as the relationship developed. Our studies expanded upon previous studies in three ways. First, we were able to show that relationship development and network involvement were positively associated not only in premarital romantic relationships among college students, but also in the same-sex friendships and dating relationships of a younger age group. Second, we were able to show that relationship development was positively associated with a broader range of network factors, including support from one's network and from the partner's network, attraction to network members, and the range of contact and communication with members of the partner's network. Finally, we were able to show that these network factors were positively associated with a broader range of developmental factors, including the partners' intimacy and attachment to one another, their perceived similarity, their satisfaction, their perceived understanding, their commitment to one another, and their amount of interaction with one another.

The role of social context in the lifecycle of personal relationships was extended the final step in Study V where we examined the deterioration of romantic relationships. We found that romantic relationships were more likely to deteriorate over a three month period when the participants perceived that members of their own and their partner's network had lower levels of support for their relationship. Compatible findings have emerged from other studies of premarital romantic relationships and marriages (e.g., Jacobson, 1983; Johnson & Milardo, 1984; Lewis, 1973; Thornes & Collard, 1979). In addition we found that romantic relationships were more likely to deteriorate over time when the participants lacked extensive communication and contact with each other's networks. Other researchers have also linked the deterioration of romantic relationships and marriages to the separation of the partner's networks (e.g., Ackerman, 1963; Milardo, 1982; Zelditch, 1964). Moreover, when these network factors were combined with basic dyadic variables, we found that it was possible to create a discriminant function which not only predicted which relationships would deteriorate over time with nearly 90% accuracy, but which also lead to more accurate predictions than studies which ignored network factors.

While we think that the combination of studies reviewed here provides overwhelming evidence of the role of social context across the entire lifecycle of personal relationships, research in this area is obviously only beginning. Many methodological and substantive concerns still remain. On the methodological side, much of the research, including our own, can be fairly criticized for its over reliance on inferences from cross-sectional data. And even those studies with a longitudinal component (e.g., Johnson & Milardo, 1984; Lewis, 1973; Milardo, 1982; Parks & Adelman, 1983; Salzinger, 1982) lack sufficiently rigorous designs to yield clear data on the relative weight and causal priority of dyadic and network factors. In addition many of the studies to date have been limited by comparatively crude single-item measures of relational development and network involvement. The limited measurement strategies and essentially bivariate focus of many of these studies probably reduce the ability to identify true relationships among variables and to detect change over time. Moreover, few if any of the major studies to date go beyond perceptions of the dyadic participants themselves to directly assess the perceptions of other network members. This makes it difficult to sort out how much of the linkage between dyadic development and network involvement is due merely to the dyadic participants' potential response biases (see Parks et al., 1983).

Many exciting questions remain on the substantive side. We know little about how networks are involved in the initiation of personal relationships in their natural context. While the results of Study I are suggestive, research has yet to explore the degree of prior linkage between the potential partners' networks or the role of informal matchmaking in any detail. The relationship of selective dyadic withdrawal to the larger process of dyadic realignment is largely unexplored. Studies which more clearly identify why withdrawal occurs in some relationships and not in others are badly needed as are studies that more closely examine how people manage interference, opposition, and disliking in on-going social networks. Finally, studies that extend the social contextual view to an even wider range of age groups and relationships are needed to test the generality of the linkages we and others have observed.

Over 35 years ago Kurt Lewin (1951) reminded social scientists that the observation of social behavior was of little value if it failed to specify the context in which the behavior occurred. Nowhere should Lewin's reminder echo more loudly than in the contemporary study of personal relationships. While some researchers (e.g., Kelley, 1986) see the study of personal relationships as a means of linking an understanding of the individual with an understanding of larger, societal processes, this potential is not likely to be realized until both the individual and his or her relationships are set within their broader social context (Parks, 1982).

REFERENCES

Ackerman, K. (1963). Affiliations: Structural determinants of differential divorce rates. *American Journal of Sociology*, 69, 13-20.

Altman, I., & Taylor, D. A. (1973). *Social penetration: The development of interpersonal relationships*. New York: Holt, Rinehart & Winston.

Anderson, B. (1979). Cognitive balance theory and social network analysis: Remarks on some fundamental theoretical matters. In P. W. Holland & S. Leinhardt (Eds.), *Perspectives on social network research* (pp. 453-469). New York: Academic Press.

Bates, A. (1942). Parental roles in courtship. *Social Forces*, 43, 483-486

Berg, J. H., & McQuinn, R. D. (1986). Attraction and exchange in continuing and noncontinuing dating relationships. *Journal of Personality and Social Psychology*, 50, 942-952.

Berger, C. R. (1979). Beyond initial interaction: Uncertainty, understanding, and the development of interpersonal relationships. In H. Giles & R. St. Clair (Eds.), *Language and social psychology* (pp. 122-144). Oxford: Basil Blackwell.

Berger, C. R., & Bradac, J. J. (1982). *Language and social knowledge*. London: Edward Arnold.

Berger, C. R., & Calabrese, R. J. (1975). Some explorations in initial interaction and beyond: Toward a developmental theory of interpersonal communication. *Human Communication Research*, 1, 99-112.

Bergler, E. (1948). *Divorce won't help*. New York: Harper.

Berkowitz, S. (1982). *An introduction to structural analysis*. Toronto: Butterworth.

Berscheid, E. (1977). Interpersonal attraction. In B. B. Wolman & R. R. Pomeroy (Eds.), *International encyclopedia of neurology, psychiatry, psychoanalysis, and psychology* (Vol. 2, pp. 201-204). New York: Van Nostrand Reinhold.

Berscheid, E., & Graziano, W. (1979). The initiation of social relationships and interpersonal attraction. In R. L. Burgess & T. L. Huston (Eds.), *Social exchange in developing relationships* (pp. 31-60). New York: Academic Press.

Berscheid, E., & Walster, E. H. (1978). *Interpersonal attraction* (2nd ed.). Reading, Mass.: Addison-Wesley.

Blau, P. (1977). *Inequality and heterogeneity: A primitive theory of social structure*. New York: Free Press.

Burgess, E. W., & Cottrell, L. S. (1939). *Predicting success or failure in marriage*. New York: Prentice-Hall.

Burr, W. (1973). *Theory construction and the sociology of the family*. New York: Wiley.

Caplow, T., & Forman, R. (1950). Neighborhood interaction in a homogeneous community. *American Sociological Review*, 15, 357-366.

Cartwright, D., & Harary, F. (1956). Structural balance: A generalization of Heider's theory. *Psychological Review*, 63, 277-293.

Chelune, G. J. (1979). *Self-disclosure.* San Francisco: Jossey-Bass.

Clore, G. L., & Byrne, D. (1974). A reinforcement-affect model of attraction. In T. L. Huston (Ed.), *Foundations of interpersonal attraction* (pp. 143-170). New York: Academic Press.

Cramer, R. E., Weiss, R. F., Steigleder, M. K., & Balling, S. S. (1985). Attraction in context: Acquisition and blocking of person-directed action. *Journal of Personality and Social Psychology*, 49, 1221-1230.

Davis, J. (1970). Clustering and hierarchy in interpersonal relations. *American Sociological Review*, 35, 843-851.

Driscoll, R., Davis, K. E., & Lipetz, M. E. (1972). Parental interference and romantic love: The Romeo and Juliet effect. *Journal of Personality and Social Psychology*, 24, 1-10.

Duck, S., & Miell, D. (1986). Charting the development of personal relationships. In R. Gilmour & S. Duck (Eds.), *The emerging field of personal relationships* (pp. 133-143). Hillsdale, NJ: Lawrence Erlbaum Associates.

Eggert, L. L. (1985). *Adolescents' personal relationships and communication network involvement* (Doctoral dissertation, University of Washington, 1984). Dissertation Abstracts International, 45, 1238A.

Eggert, L. L., & Parks, M. R. (1987). Communication network involvement in adolescents' friendships and romantic relationships. In M. L. McLaughlin (Ed.), *Communication yearbook 10* (pp. 283-322). Beverly Hills, Ca.: Sage Publications.

Festinger, L., Schachter, S., & Back, K. W. (1950). *Social pressure in informal groups: A study of human factors in housing.* New York: Harper.

Freud, S. (1961). *Civilization and its discontents.* New York: W. W. Norton.

Goode, W. J. (1960). A theory of role strain. *American Sociological Review*, 25, 483-496.

Hallinan, M. (1974). *The structure of positive sentiment.* New York: Elsevier.

Hammer, M. (1980). Predictability of social connections over time. *Social Networks*, 2, 165-180.

Hammer, M. & Schaffer, A. (1975). Interconnectedness and the duration of connections in small networks. *American Ethnologist*, 2, 297-308.

Hays, R. B. (1985). A longitudinal study of friendship development. *Journal of Personality and Social Psychology*, 48, 909-924.

Hecht, M. L. (1978). The conceptualization and measurement of interpersonal communication satisfaction. *Human Communication Research*, 4, 253-264.

Heider, F. (1946). Attitude and cognitive organization. *Journal of Psychology*, 21, 107-112.

Heider, F. (1958). *The psychology of interpersonal relations.* New York: Wiley.

Holland, P., & Leinhardt, S. (1972). Some evidence on the transitivity of positive interpersonal sentiment. *American Journal of Sociology*, 77, 1205-1209.

Holland, P., & Leinhardt, S. (1977). Transitivity in structural models of small groups. In L. Leinhardt (Ed.), *Social networks: A developing paradigm* (pp. 49-66). New York: Academic Press.

Huston, T. L., & Levinger, G. (1978). Interpersonal attraction and relationships. *Annual Review of Psychology*, 29, 115-156.

Huston, T. L., Surra, C. A., Fitzgerald, N. M., & Cate, R. M. (1981). From courtship to marriage: Mate selection as an interpersonal process. In S. Duck & R. Gilmour (Eds.), *Personal relationships 2: Developing personal relationships* (pp. 53-88). London: Academic Press.

Jacobson, G. F. (1983). *The multiple crises of marital separation and divorce.* New York: Grune & Stratton.

Johnson, M. P. (1982). Social and cognitive features of the dissolution of commitment to relationships. In S. Duck (Ed.), *Personal relationships 4: Dissolving personal relationships* (pp. 51-73). London: Academic Press.

Johnson, M. P., & Leslie, L. (1982). Couple involvement and network structure: A test of the dyadic withdrawal hypothesis. *Social Psychology Quarterly,* 45, 34-43.

Johnson, M. P., & Milardo, R. M. (1984). Network interference in pair relationships: A social psychological recasting of Slater's theory of social regression. *Journal of Marriage and the Family,* 46, 893-899.

Joreskog, K., & Sorbom, D. (1978). *Lisrel IV: Analysis of linear structural relationships by the method of maximum likelihood.* Chicago: International Educational Resources.

Kelley, H. H. (1979). *Personal relationships: Their structure and processes.* New York: Wiley.

Kelley, H. H. (1986). Personal relationships: Their nature and significance. In R. Gilmour & S. Duck (Eds.), *The emerging field of personal relationships* (pp. 3-19). Hillsdale, NJ: Lawrence Erlbaum Associates, 1986.

Kelley, H. H., & Thibaut, J. W. (1978). *Interpersonal relations: A theory of interdependence.* New York: Wiley.

Kerckhoff, A. C. (1974). The social context of interpersonal attraction. In T. L. Huston (Ed.), *Foundations of interpersonal attraction* (pp. 61-78). New York: Academic Press.

Krain, M. (1977). A definition of dyadic boundaries and an empirical study of boundary establishment in courtship. *International Journal of Sociology of the Family,* 7, 107-123.

La Gaipa, J. J. (1981). A systems approach to personal relationships. In S. Duck & R. Gilmour (Eds.), *Personal relationships I: Studying personal relationships* (pp. 67-90). London: Academic Press.

Leslie, L. A. (1983). Parental influences and premarital relationship development (Doctoral dissertation, Pennsylvania State University, 1982). *Dissertation Abstracts International,* 43, 277A.

Leslie, L. A., Johnson, M. P., & Huston, T. L. (1986). Parental reactions to dating relationships: Do they make a difference? *Journal of Marriage and the Family,* 48, 57-66.

Levinger, G. (1974). A three-level approach to attraction: Toward an understanding of pair relatedness. In T. L. Huston (Ed.), *Foundations of interpersonal attraction* (pp. 99-120). New York: Academic Press.

Levinger, G. (1979). A social exchange view of the dissolution of pair relationships. In R. L. Burgess & T. L. Huston (Eds.), *Social exchange in developing relationships* (pp. 169-193). New York: Academic Press.

Levinger, G. (1980). Toward the analysis of close relationships. *Journal of Experimental Social Psychology,* 16, 510-544.

Levinger, G., & Snoek, J. D. (1972). *Attraction in relationship: A new look at interpersonal attraction.* Morristown, NJ: General Learning Press.

Lewin, K. (1951). *Field theory in social science.* New York: Harper & Brothers.

Lewis, R. A. (1972). A developmental framework for the analysis of premarital dyadic formation. *Family Process,* 11, 17-48.

Lewis, R. A. (1973). Social reaction and the formation of dyads: An interactionist approach to mate selection. *Sociometry,* 36, 409-418.

Lewis, R. A. (1975). Social influences on marital choice. In S. Dragastin & G. H. Elder, Jr. (Eds.), *Adolescence in the life cycle* (pp. 211-226). New York: John Wiley & Sons.

Locke, H. J. (1951). *Predicting adjustment in marriage.* New York: Holt.

Lott, A. J., & Lott. B. E. (1961). Group cohesiveness, communication level, and conformity. *Journal of Abnormal and Social Psychology*, 62, 408-412.

Lott, A. J., & Lott, B. E. (1974). The role of reward in the formulation of positive interpersonal attitudes. In T. L. Huston (Ed.), *Foundations of interpersonal attraction* (pp. 171-189). New York: Academic Press.

Menne, J. M. C., & Sinnett, R. E. (1971). Proximity and social interaction in residence halls. *Journal of College Student Personnel*, 12, 26-31.

Milardo, R. M. (1982). Friendship networks in developing relationships: Converging and diverging social environments. *Social Psychology Quarterly*, 45, 162-172.

Milardo, R. M. (1983). Social networks and pair relationships: A review of substantive and measurement issues. *Sociology and Social Research*, 68, 1-18.

Milardo, R. M. (1986). Personal choice and social constraint in close relationships: Applications of network analysis. In V. J. Derlega & B. A. Winstead (Eds.), *Friendship and social interaction* (pp. 146-166). New York: Springer-Verlag.

Milardo. R. M., Johnson, M. P., & Huston, T. L. (1983). Developing close relationships: Changing patterns of interaction between pair members and social networks. *Journal of Personality and Social Psychology*, 44, 964-976.

Milardo, R. M., & Lewis, R. A. (1985). Social networks, families, and mate selection: A transactional analysis. In L. L'Abate (Ed.), *Handbook of family psychology and therapy* (Vol. 1, pp. 258-283). Homewood, Ill.: Dorsey Press.

Miller, A. A. (1970). Reactions of friends to divorce. In P. Bohannan (Ed.), *Divorce and after* (pp. 56-77). Garden City, N. Y.: Doubleday.

Miller, G. R., & Parks, M. R. (1982). Communication in dissolving relationships. In S. Duck (Ed.), *Personal relationships 4: Dissolving personal relationships* (pp. 127-154). London: Academic Press.

Mitchell, A. K. (1981). *Someone to turn to: Experiences of help before divorce.* Aberdeen: Aberdeen University Press.

Murstein, B. I. (1970). Stimulus-value-role: A theory of marital choice. *Journal of Marriage and the Family*, 32, 465-481.

Newcomb, T. M. (1961). *The acquaintance process.* New York: Holt, Rinehart & Winston.

Parks, M. R. (1978). *Communication correlates of perceived friendship development.* Paper presented at the annual convention of the Speech Communication Association. Minneapolis, Minnesota.

Parks, M. R. (1982). Ideology in interpersonal communication: Off the couch and into the world. In M. Burgoon (Ed.), *Communication yearbook* 5 (pp. 79-107). New Brunswick, NJ: Transaction Books.

Parks, M. R., & Adelman, M. B. (1983). Communication networks and the development of romantic relationships: An expansion of uncertainty reduction theory. *Human Communication Research*, 10, 55-79.

Parks, M. R., Stan, C. M., & Eggert, L. L. (1983). Romantic involvement and social network involvement. *Social Psychology Quarterly*, 46, 116-131.

Perlman, D., & Fehr, B. (1986). Theories of friendship: The analysis of interpersonal attraction. In V. J. Derlega & B. A. Winstead (Eds.), *Friendship and social interaction* (pp. 9-40). New York: Springer-Verlag.

Ridley, C. A., & Avery, A. W. (1979). Social network influence on the dyadic relationship. In R. L. Burgess & T. L. Huston (Eds.), *Social exchange in developing relationships* (pp. 223-246). New York: Academic Press.

Rubin, Z (1970). Measurement of romantic love. *Journal of Personality and Social Psychology*, 16, 265-273.

Rusbult, C. E. (1980). Commitment and satisfaction in romantic associations: A test of the investment model. *Journal of Experimental Social Psychology*, 16, 172-180.

Ryder, R. G., Kafka, J. S., & Olson, D. H. (1971). Separating and joining influences in courtship and early marriage. *American Journal of Orthopsychiatry*, 41, 450-464.

Salzinger, L. L. (1982). The ties that bind: The effects of clustering on dyadic relationships. *Social Networks*, 4, 117-145.

Slater, P. (1963). On social regression. *American Sociological Review*, 28, 339-364.

Snyder, M., Berscheid, E., & Glick, P. (1985). Focusing on the exterior and the interior: Two investigations of the initiation of personal relationships. *Journal of Personality and Social Psychology*, 48, 1427-1439.

Surra, C. A. (1985). Courtship types: Variations in interdependence between partners and social networks. *Journal of Personality and Social Psychology*, 49, 357-375.

Surra, C. A. (1988). The influence of the interactive network on developing relationships. In R. M. Milardo (Ed.), *Families and social networks* (pp 48-82). Beverly Hills: Sage Publications.

Sussman, M. (1953). Parental participation in mate selection and its effects upon family continuity. *Social Forces*, 32, 76-81.

Terman, L. M., & Wallin, P. (1949). The validity of marriage prediction and marital adjustment tests. *American Sociological Review*, 14, 497-504.

Thornes, B., & Collard, J. (1979). *Who divorces?* London: Routledge & Kegan Paul.

Titus, S. L. (1980). A function of friendship: Social comparisons as a frame of reference for marriage. *Human Relations*, 33, 409-431.

Waller, W., & Hill, R. (1951). *The family: A dynamic interpretation*. Hinsdale, Ill.: Dryden Press.

Wheeless, L. (1976). Self-disclosure and interpersonal solidarity: Measurement, validation, and relationships. *Human Communication Research*, 3, 47-61.

Zelditch, M. (1964). Family, marriage and kinship. In R. E. L. Faris (Ed.), *Handbook of modern sociology* (pp. 680-733). Chicago: Rand McNally.

INTERPERSONAL TRANSFORMATIONS IN INTIMATE RELATIONSHIPS

Victor M. H. Borden and George Levinger

Two individuals in a long-term intimate relationship are often identified as a couple. This term is more than merely a label. It reflects a transformation from self-oriented to jointly-oriented criteria for formulating goals and evaluating experiences - a transformation from an 'I'- to a 'we'-orientation. The importance of mutuality in social relationships has been long recognized in analyses of interpersonal conduct by thinkers both outside and inside the social sciences. It is central to the conception of the Golden Rule, 'Do unto others as you would have them do unto you,' in Martin Buber's (1923/1958) advocacy of an 'I-Thou' as contrasted to an 'I-It' stance toward other human beings, and in the definition of love as a state in which the happiness of another person is essential to your own.

Social scientists have also written about the contrast between 'I' and 'we' orientations in their analysis of 'secondary' versus 'primary' groups (Cooley,

1909), of competitive versus cooperative relations (Deutsch, 1949), and of short-term 'surface contact' versus long-term 'mutuality' (Levinger & Snoek, 1972). Huesmann and Levinger (1976) showed how such a transformation from self-seeking toward altruism could be modeled theoretically in computer simulations of relationship development. Subsequently, Kelley and Thibaut (1978; Kelley, 1979) incorporated the concept of 'motivational transformation' into their general theory of social interdependence.

This chapter concerns the interpersonal transformations by which individuals in close relationships develop a sense of unity or partnership - and, conversely, by which partners' feelings of unity may decrease. Whereas previous writings (e.g., Kelley, 1968, 1979) have emphasized processes of mutual accommodation, we here propose the existence of a broad continuum from transient, situation-oriented 'accommodation' at one extreme, to interpersonal 'convergence' at the other extreme. The gradations of adaptation are subtle, but our model emphasizes two major processes: 'motivational' transformations (Kelley, 1979) and 'dispositional' transformations. After reviewing Kelley's conception of motivational transformation, we develop the companion concept of dispositional transformation and indicate how these two processes work together.

THE CASE OF SUSAN AND TOM DARBER

The development of Susan and Tom Darber's relationship (see Levinger, 1983) provides numerous illustrations of we-oriented changes during this couple's courtship and early marriage. Later, as the relationship deteriorates and moves toward breakup, it illustrates contrasting instances of the lack of mutual accommodation and the growing divergence between Susan's and Tom's desires or goals.

> When they met one another, Susan and Tom were both American students spending a year abroad at the Sorbonne in Paris. Although it took special circumstances for them to take an interest in each other, after they did so Susan and Tom soon fell in love. Yet they encountered various interferences with their relationship. For one thing, Susan and Tom lived an hour apart. For another, they had rather different recreational tastes: Susan loved skiing in the mountains; Tom, an architecture student who did not ski, preferred visiting painters and sculptors in the city.
>
> How did they resolve such difficulties? First, since Tom's apartment was less cramped than Susan's little room, Susan took the bold step of moving in with him. This gave them much more time together.
>
> Second, Susan soon began teaching Tom how to ski, and he found ways of introducing her to his artist friends. By the end of that spring, Tom had become an excellent first-year skier, and Susan was truly appreciating paintings and sculpture, something she had never before been very interested in.

How do we interpret these changes in Susan and Tom's relationship? The first change - that of Susan's place of residence - was primarily her *accommodation* to their current situation. They both were bothered by the length of their commuting trips. Although Susan preferred her old neighborhood, she felt that moving in with Tom would improve their relationship. She did not especially like Tom's apartment, but she really enjoyed being together with him.

Other changes reflected a long-term *convergence* in values and preferences, although they began as an accommodation to the other person's desires. Until Tom knew how to ski well, he kept telling Susan that he was doing this 'stupid thing' just to please her. Similarly, Susan at first went on Tom's jaunts along the Left Bank just to be with him, and not because she herself cared much about art. In both instances, though, each partner started to enjoy these activities for their own sake. Tom soon began yodeling joyfully as he skied down the snowy slopes, and Susan began going out by herself to talk to sculptors whose work she had come to prize.

More than mere accommodation to the other's preferences, this second type of change represents a significant long-term change in one's own preferences in the direction of those of the partner. Such change becomes internalized, or *independent* of the other's continued influence.

Now consider the Darbers' relationship after they had been married for about 19 years. We first summarize earlier happenings in their marriage and then the pair's later marital difficulties.

After they returned to the US and were married, Susan finished her last year in college while Tom started architecture school. Six months after Susan had completed college their first child was born, and then two more children arrived during the following four years. Meanwhile, Tom was on his way to a successful, sometimes brilliant career with a major architectural firm.

Although Tom's architectural work was highly original and although Susan's own interests and friendships were uncommon, their marital relationship became fairly conventional. That is, Tom worked extremely hard at his office - often late into the night and on weekends - and he often came home too tired to do more than fall into bed. He did love playing with the kids when he had the time, and the family did occasionally take good vacation trips together, but Tom and Susan rarely devoted time to talking about their marriage or their future.

When their youngest child was 8, Susan decided to go to evening law school. Five years later she had a law degree. She postponed accepting a good job offer because Tom asked her to stay home a while longer, but during this period she began to realize that the two of them had drifted apart. No longer was she thrilled by Tom's presence. Instead, Susan now began to feel a certain resentment and competitiveness toward him. Tom, however, remained oblivious to Susan's feelings; his behavior only tended to aggravate what had gradually become a shaky marriage. For example, he failed to listen to Susan's stories about the volunteer legal work she was doing and he remained almost totally absorbed by his own career.

A year and a half later, after Susan had received another good job offer, she told Tom she wanted to separate from him. Tom was stunned and tried to find ways of repairing the marriage, but his efforts were too little and too late. After 22 years of marriage, Susan Darber obtained a divorce.

These later changes in the Darbers' relationship indicate instances of their inability to accommodate to each other behaviorally, and also of a growing divergence in their needs, values, and goals. By the time Tom became aware of Susan's dissatisfaction and tried to reverse the decline, the two of them had drifted too far apart to enable them to reconnect adequately.

PROCESSES OF INTERPERSONAL TRANSFORMATION

The excerpts from the Darber case illustrate how intimate partners may change as they develop their relationship. Such changes, both minor and major, have been examined extensively in the literature on close relationships (e.g., Kelley et. al., 1983). This chapter, though, is concerned with the underlying processes by which such changes occur.

Two persons in a relationship can deal with their differences or conflicts in many ways. Figure 1 identifies three broad categories on a continuum of mutual adaptation: (1) situation-oriented tactical accommodation, (2) relationship-oriented systematic accommodation, and (3) relationship-transcendent interpersonal convergence.

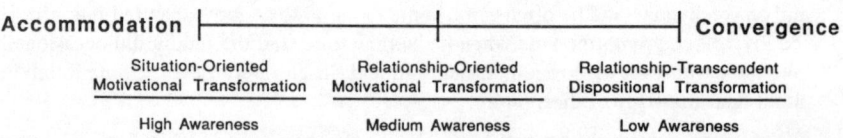

Figure 1. A Continuum of Mutual Adaptation

These three categories parallel in a sense Kelman's (1958) basic processes of social influence: compliance, identification, and internalization. Tactical accommodations cope with an immediate situation; they are a form of overt compliance that is highly dependent on the influencer's presence (Kelman, 1958; French & Raven, 1959). At the most superficial extreme, they occur without any pair relationship at all, as when two strangers meet each other in a corridor and one or both swerve to the right to avoid bumping into the other.

Systematic accommodations reflect how one's preferences are influenced by identification with a close partner. Here we put aside or alter our own preferences so as to adapt to those of the partner. Such adaptations are based mainly on one's caring for the other and the relationship. If the relationship should sour, however, the impetus for adapting would disappear. Like Kelman's identification, therefore, systematic accommodation depends on the continued existence of an interpersonal relationship.

Interpersonal convergence reflects long-term changes in our own attitudes, interests, or preferences. These changes reflect the 'internalization' of our earlier situationally-altered preferences. That is, our personal likes and dislikes have actually changed in the direction of those of the partner; although these changes derived from the relationship they have now become independent of it. For instance, Tom Darber eventually became genuinely fond of skiing and went skiing by himself, although initially he went only to please Susan.

Kelley and Thibaut (1978) described a process of motivational transformation that characterizes the left side of the present adaptation continuum. Subsequently, Kelley (1979) described how motivational transformations become systematized in close relationships. He thus moved more toward the middle of our present continuum.

INTERPERSONAL ACCOMMODATION: THE TRANSFORMATION OF MOTIVATION

Accommodation means adapting one's own interests to those of another. It is based on mutual interdependence; only if one's actions affect or are affected by another person does one need to account for the other's interests. Kelley and Thibaut (1978) employed pair *outcome matrices* to represent the interdependence between two interactants' outcomes; they conceptualized discrepancies between two interacting persons according to a characteristic of the matrix which they labeled *outcome correspondence*. They described a process called the *transformation of motivation*, wherein interacting individuals adjust their outcome matrices to increase outcome correspondence and thereby accommodate to the other.

Kelley (1979) subsequently focused on transformations between intimate partners: intimate pair members consistently try to reduce discrepancies among their interests. He developed the concept of *interpersonal disposition* to characterize the systemic motivational transformations typical of close relationships.

Outcome Matrices

An outcome matrix represents the potential outcomes of interacting individuals according to all possible combinations of actions. For example, the 2 x 2 outcome matrix in Figure 2 shows the potential satisfactions and dissatisfactions of a husband and wife who are faced with the task of cleaning their apartment. The wife would be most satisfied if both she and her husband cleaned the apartment together (+5); she would still be satisfied, but less so, if either she or her husband cleaned the apartment alone (+3); and she would be dissatisfied if neither cleaned the apartment (-5). Thus the wife feels it is important to get the cleaning done, but would be most satisfied if she and her husband share this activity.

The husband, on the other hand, would be most satisfied if his wife cleaned the apartment by herself (+8) and least satisfied if he had to clean it by himself (-6); his desire not to take part in cleaning exceeds his desire to have a clean apartment. If this situation dictates the pair's actions, it is most likely that the

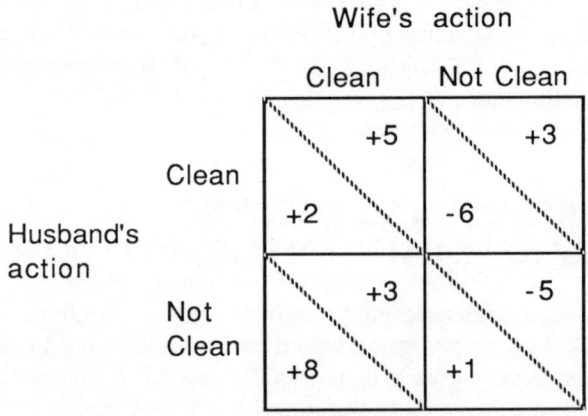

Figure 2. A 2 x 2 Outcome Matrix

wife will clean alone but, as explained later, neither spouse's preferences are necessarily fixed.

Outcome Correspondence

Kelley and Thibaut's term 'outcome correspondence' refers to the degree of congruence between a pair's interests as indicated in their outcome matrices. In the outcome matrix for apartment cleaning (Figure 2), the husband would rather not participate in cleaning the apartment, but the wife would like him to participate. This reflects an incongruency between the husband's and wife's preferences.

Kelley and Thibaut describe a measure of outcome correspondence - the 'index of correspondence' (IC) - that is similar to a product-moment correlation between the partner's outcomes. IC ranges from *-1*, indicating completely *noncorrespondent* outcomes, to *+1*, indicating completely *correspondent* outcomes. For the apartment cleaning matrix in Figure 2, IC = 0.04, indicating that the husband's and wife's outcomes are neither correspondent nor noncorrespondent, but somewhere in between.

Incidentally, note that outcome correspondence is sometimes based on preference *similarity* (e.g., enjoying the same recreation) and sometimes on preference *complementarity* (e.g., taking different but compatible roles in performing a household task). Similarity is useful in primarily the socio-emotional aspects of a relationship; in order to enjoy leisure and companionship, it helps if partners have the same likes and dislikes. Such similarity is often unnecessary, though, in the realm of task achievement; wherever tasks permit a division of work, it may be beneficial for each partner to play a different role. Empirical research on marriage has confirmed that partners in satisfying marriages show a far greater similarity in their socio-emotional than in their task-oriented behavior, whereas task specialization is more common than mutuality (Levinger, 1964).

The Transformation of Motivation

Kelley and Thibaut conceptualize the transformation of motivation by distinguishing between 'given' and 'effective' dyadic outcome matrices. The *given* matrix summarizes each person's outcomes from all the pair's possible actions, *without taking into account* the effect of those actions on the partner's outcomes. In game research, the given matrix is the set of payoffs specified for each person by the experimenter. In ordinary life, the given matrix is 'a set of outcomes provided to the person by external reward and incentive systems' (Kelley, 1979, p. 69).

In contrast, the *effective* matrix summarizes the outcomes the pair members perceive and will obtain from their actual behavior in this situation. These 'effective' outcomes are determined not only by self-interest, but also by one's interest in the partner's outcomes. When aware of an event's consequences for other people, 'a person can and does evaluate the event ... in relation to those consequences. This constitutes a transformation of the person's motivation' (Kelley, 1979, pp. 68-69). In other words, in the effective matrix one's own 'given' outcomes are transformed by one's concern for the partner's welfare.

Figure 3 shows one way in which the married partners in the apartment cleaning situation can transform their motivations. Figure 3a, the given matrix, is a reproduction of Figure 2. Here, we consider these outcomes to be each partner's ratings of satisfaction for the four behavioral possibilities as determined by their respective *self-interests*. The near-zero value for IC in the given matrix indicates that the pair's outcomes are neither very correspondent nor particularly noncorrespondent. As noted earlier, if this situation were to persist, the wife would clean the apartment alone.

Figure 3b, however, shows this couple's *effective* matrix. It shows how their individual feelings toward cleaning are affected by each partner's concern for the other. Upon further reflection, the husband realizes that he can make his wife

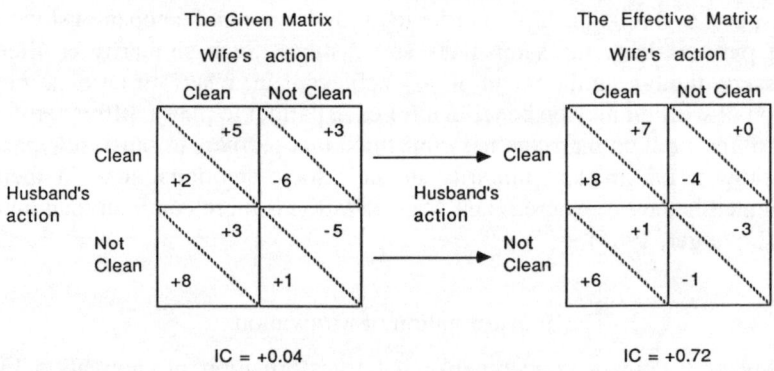

Figure 3. An Outcome Matrix Showing A Motivational Transformation

happy by cleaning the apartment. Furthermore, he remembers the surprisingly good time he and his wife had the last time they both participated in a similarly mundane task. At the same time, the wife reevaluates the situation, and she shifts her primary concern from getting the apartment clean to doing something with her husband. *Effectively*, then, this couple is more likely to clean together than to have the wife clean alone. Furthermore, the IC for the transformed matrix (+.72) indicates that the partners' effective outcomes are far more correspondent than their given ones.

More generally, motivational transformations are ways in which persons reconceptualize a given situation. A transformed set of outcomes no longer reflects only each individual's private preferences, but the context of the entire relationship (Kelley & Thibaut, 1978, p. 139). Most conducive to intimate interaction is maximizing either the pair's or the partner's joint outcomes, rather than one's own outcomes (McClintock, 1972).

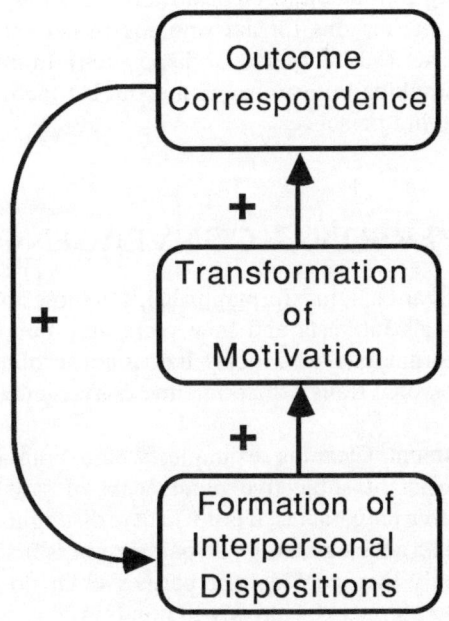

Figure 4. Formation of Interpersonal Dispositions as a Feedback Process

Interpersonal Dispositions

Kelley (1979) has noted that, as two partners become increasingly close, they tend to accommodate to each other's outcome preferences in predictable ways. That is, their inclination to modify their personal preferences in the direction of the partner's preferences becomes increasingly stable and dependable. Kelley calls this the formation of 'interpersonal dispositions.'

Figure 4 displays Kelley's idea as a circular feedback loop. As a pair experiences rewards from its high outcome correspondence, its members form interpersonal dispositions to maintain this correspondence. Thus, whenever the partners encounter situations with seemingly discrepant, noncorrespondent outcomes, they become inclined to transform their self-oriented motives into pair-oriented ones. This restores outcome correspondence, which in turn serves to further reinforce the pair-oriented dispositions.

Imagine, for example, a man who likes to smoke, building a relationship with a woman who intensely dislikes smoking (their 'given' preferences). In the pair's earliest encounters, he may forego smoking in her presence so as not to dissuade her from seeing him again (a tactical transformation). As their relationship builds further, his reasons for not smoking in her presence become based on his caring for her (an interpersonal disposition). In other words, the man would still enjoy smoking but care enough about her feelings to sacrifice his own interest when in her presence.

INTERPERSONAL CONVERGENCE

Kelley's concept of motivational transformation helps to show how two partners may adapt to each other's interests and how pairs may build closeness by developing stable transformational tendencies. It does not account, however, for another form of interpersonal transformation - the convergence of individual preferences over time.

Consider the Apartment Cleaning example, where both the given and effective outcomes consist of subjective judgements of satisfaction. When considering such subjective judgements, it is difficult to distinguish 'given' from 'effective' outcomes. In an actual situation, do pair members first consider their own self-interest and only then consider the partner's? Or do they approach situations with the partner's interests already in mind? And at what point may a partner's interest become identical to one's own?

Such questions lead us beyond Kelley and Thibaut's notion of accommodative transformations to the recognition of long-term changes within one or both partners. That is, accommodative adaptation can occur in even the most casual or cursory encounters, but in lasting relationships there are likely to be long-term changes in the individual members' underlying preferences.

The Transformation of Disposition

Members of long-established relationships are sometimes found to have more correspondent preferences than are members of shorter relationships (e.g., Borden, 1983). That finding is explainable by two contrasting, but not necessarily exclusive, possibilities. One possibility is that partners with *initially* correspondent preferences are more likely to build long-term relationships than are partners with initially noncorrespondent preferences. For example, tidy people would be likely to build partnerships with other tidy people, untidy ones with other untidy individuals; smokers would be attracted to smokers, nonsmokers to nonsmokers. Some research findings support such a homogeneous-selection principle (e.g., Kelly, 1955; Kerckhoff, 1974) but other findings indicate its limitations (Levinger & Rands, 1985).

A second possibility is that two partners' private preferences become increasingly correspondent over the course of their relationship. For example, the smoker we referred to above may stop smoking not only in his partner's presence - the motivational transformation displayed earlier in the relationship - but he may stop smoking altogether, under any and all circumstances. He now actually dislikes the very smell of cigarette smoke. This form of change is here be labeled a 'dispositional' transformation, a change in the person's underlying preference or attitude. Although initially instigated by his pair membership, it has become totally internalized and independent of the relationship. Dispositional transformations, then, are changes in the individual partner rather than in the relationship. The more such dispositional changes occur, the less necessary will be motivational changes.

INTERPERSONAL TRANSFORMATIONS: A TWO-PROCESS MODEL

The concepts introduced above can now be linked more systematically. Figure 5 conveys their interplay. At the top, it refers to interactive situations between two individuals. In even a brief encounter, two interacting individuals must accommodate to each other; this means adjusting their initial preferences or working out some sort of behavioral compromise to take account of discrepancies. For example, Paul, who usually prefers to sit in the sun, adjusts his preference in order to introduce himself to Olivia, who is sitting in the shade. This form of accommodation is a tactical transformation of Paul's motives, i.e., a motivational transformation induced by his current situation.

As two individuals establish a more lasting relationship, they encounter situations that require new forms of accommodation. Over time, the pair members' transformational tendencies become more predictable; they develop interpersonal dispositions that dictate the types of transformations each partner

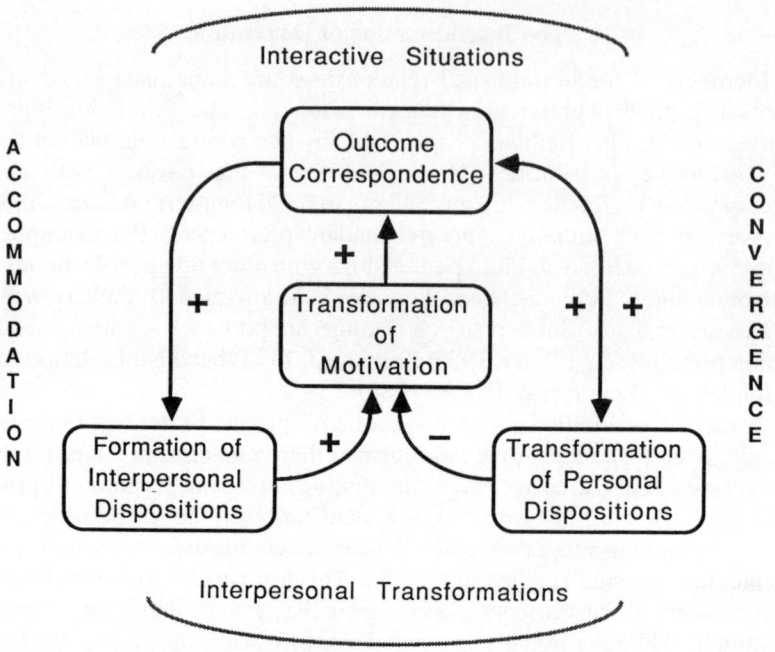

Figure 5. Interpersonal Transformations: A Two-Process Model

may expect of the other. For example, if Paul and Olivia were to grow closer, they might develop a pattern wherein they sit in the sun for a certain amount of time, to satisfy Paul, and then move to the shade, to satisfy Olivia. These kinds of transformations are examples of a 'max joint' motive pattern (McClintock, 1972); both partners strive to maximize the joint outcomes of the pair.

Such pair-oriented transformations have several implications: First, they give evidence to both self and partner that one cares sufficiently for the relationship to forego self-centered preferences. Second, if such interpersonal concern is found rewarding in one set of circumstances, then one may adapt to the partner's interests in other types of situations. The left part of Figure 5 shows the accommodation processes of Figure 4 - i.e., the positive feedback loop between building we-oriented 'interpersonal dispositions' and making further positive motivational transformations.

Accommodation can now be related to the supplementary process of interpersonal convergence. Not only do pair members accommodate to each other's given interests but, over time, their given interests may become increasingly correspondent. Such long-term changes are here labeled the 'transformation of personal disposition.'

Transformations of disposition consist of long-term changes in a person's attitudes, outcome preferences, or behavioral styles. In line with Figure 5, we first emphasize those changes that lead to a convergence in previously discrepant pair interests. Returning to our example, Paul may find that spending too much time in the sun reduces the total time that the two of them can remain outdoors; thus he comes to enjoy the longer time they spend outside in the shade. Eventually, Paul actually prefers the shade even when he is not with Olivia. When this happens, his attitude toward the advantage of shade over sun has converged with hers.

The greater such dispositional convergence, the less will be the discrepancies that previously necessitated the partners' motivational transformations. Therefore Figure 5 shows a negative feedback loop among motivational transformation, outcome correspondence, and dispositional transformation.

THE LIMITS OF ACCOMMODATION AND CONVERGENCE: UNION VERSUS INDIVIDUATION

If the accommodation and convergence processes described in Figure 5 occurred in a closed system, we could imagine a gradual but predictable movement toward total convergence between Person and Other. The more rewarding that P and O found their transformed outcomes, the more likely they would be to shift their given preferences toward the transformed ones. Eventually, in such a closed system, the two partners' preferences would coincide in all realms.

Interpersonal relationships, of course, are not closed systems. Factors influencing the functioning of intimate relationships can be categorized into three general sets of 'causal conditions': the two partners' physical and social environment, P's and O's individual personalities, and the P-O relationship system itself (Kelley et al., 1983).

The Physical and Social Environment

One reason that people's functioning changes over time pertains to alterations in their environment. Beginning with the initial difference between their parental families, two partners' social and physical environments will always differ in significant ways. From these differences there emanate discrepant pressures or demands, many of which require accommodations to third parties outside the relationship.

Consider, for example, the members of a young married couple who both strongly desire a child. After the baby's arrival, each spouse must respond to the infant's demands; some of those demands, and the partners' responses, will interfere with the spouses' previous dyadic accommodations. Furthermore, the birth of a child leads to other significant changes in each spouse's environment.

Living arrangements are likely to change at least minimally, and often drastically, as when the family moves to a larger apartment or buys a house. Job situations are likely to change; one or both spouses may take time off or change jobs in response to the new responsibilities. Various other aspects of the couple's life are also likely to change.

The Darbers. During the course of their marriage, the Darbers experienced many different changes in their physical and social environment, each of them requiring some form of adaptation. After Susan graduated from lawschool, however, she discovered a wholly new set of pressures from her social environment; they strengthened her sense as an individual but weakened her connection to Tom. For example, when classmates or friends urged Susan to take an attractive law position she at first replied: 'But how will that affect my marriage?' However, she found that these friends put far more value on her developing professional skills than on her family obligations. And, since Tom took little interest in furthering Susan's new identity, she interacted more and more with people who supported it at the cost of worsening her marital situation.

P's and O's Personalities

The maintenance of an intimate relationship depends in part on each member's well-developed and stable dispositions; this seems to run counter to the notion of convergence. However, the considerable differences that exist even between two highly compatible individuals allow for the occurrence of significant convergence without approaching total unity.

Even if partners were to mesh their needs totally, as might occur at times in highly intimate relationships, it could only be temporary. Even in relationships where one partner dominates the other totally, it is impossible to suppress the other's personal needs entirely. And although some close relationships do lead to suppression - sometimes without either partner's full awareness - the submerged needs are likely to reappear eventually, requiring new accommodations or adjustments. In other words, the individual partners' biological and psychological needs exert demands that prevent the total unity of outcome preferences suggested by the transformation model of Figure 5.

The Darbers. Initially, when Tom and Susan Darber were married, they felt so attuned to each other that they assumed their needs would always continue to mesh satisfactorily. For a considerable length of time this assumption remained valid. But, as Susan moved from being a young wife and mother to becoming a woman in her mid-thirties with growing children, her personal needs did change.

When Susan met Tom she was a college student studying for a year in France; she had an advanced education and experience traveling abroad. Raising young children and maintaining a family home was enough of a challenge and provided enough rewards to keep her satisfied. However, as the children became more independent and household maintenance more manageable, Susan required new challenges. Attending law school allowed Susan to rekindle her intellectual and social interests, which she had willingly put aside early in marriage.

After law school, however, when Susan started to look for a job, she began to realize how much her personal interests had changed and how much she looked forward to playing a new role in her later life. Only then did she begin to realize that her personal goals had been diverging from those of her husband, who still regarded her as mainly a helpmate. And only after this realization did it become increasingly difficult for Susan to accommodate in other ways to Tom's desires: suddenly, it became irritating to change her schedule to suit his, to think of special recipes for dinner, or to ask him about his day at work when he came home in the evening.

Susan Darber's experiences suggests an important hypothesis: Whereas people are generally aware of their motivational accommodations or their failures to accommodate, dispositional convergence or divergence occurs with much less awareness. This makes it hard to document dispositional changes, except over long periods of time and sometimes only after there has been a dramatic reversal in interpersonal involvement.

The P-O Relationship

There is a noteworthy balance between the processes of accommodation and convergence. Accommodation to a partner requires the existence of a significant difference between self and partner. Convergence, on the other hand, reduces such differences between self and partner. But the more that two people converge in their preferences - or the more that their likes and dislikes become identical - the less opportunity they have to accommodate so as to demonstrate their willingness to sacrifice for the partner. In other words, both processes are vital for close relationships; but, if either is taken too its extreme it can become dysfunctional.

Overaccommodation and overconvergence. In even the closest relationship, extremely accommodating behavior by one's partner may become dysfunctional. For one thing, it can make us less inclined to go out of our way to please the other; if our partner were totally compliant at all times, it would eliminate our thoughts of 'quid pro quo' and thus lower our expressions of concern or even ordinary politeness. This is indicated in the finding that many marriage partners are less polite to each other than to strangers (see Levinger, 1983). Furthermore, accommodation can become so routine that we no longer acknowledge our partner's continual supportiveness, although his or her withholding support would probably elicit hurt or anger (e.g., Rook & Pietromonaco, 1987).

Another extreme form of accommodation is where two partners, whenever they have a disagreement, always try to compromise so as to reach 'middle ground.' That too can have its problems. In every relationship, there are times where we should express our individuality, or permit our partner to do so. Halfway compromises often satisfy neither individual. Furthermore, unless both partners can express their true preferences, they will be unable to search creatively for 'integrative' solutions (Pruitt, 1981) that reflect both individuals' basic interests.

Convergence through dispositional transformation reduces the likelihood of overaccommodation. But how desirable are extreme degrees of convergence? On the one hand, such convergence seems highly desirable. Highly correspondent preferences limit the potential for conflict, and presumably couples wish to avoid conflict. On the other hand, an extreme degree of pair convergence can also have disadvantages. If two partners were to agree about *everything*, they would no longer have opportunities to show that they care more for the other's wishes than for their own. Difference not only provides variety and stimulation, but it also gives each partner the chance to demonstrate concern for the other through making observable adaptations. The existence of differences permits us to make motivational transformations, and such transformations show evidence of our caring.

Taking the partner for granted. In other words, either overaccommodation or overconvergence can lead partners to take the other's feelings for granted. If our own interests were always accommodated to by our partner, we would lose sight of our partner's own interests. Eventually we would no longer be pleased by the other's compliance, even though we could be strongly displeased by its absence.

Overconvergence leads to somewhat different problems. If our partner's interests were to become identical to our own, they would no longer have to be considered; we would then think only of our own interests, in the belief that the other is similarly disposed. It would be a mistake, however, to generalize from one or a few such areas of identity to all others; such a supposition could eventually lead to frictions for which the partners are unprepared.

The Darbers. To illustrate the dangers of partners taking each other for granted, let us return once more to the marriage of Susan and Tom Darber. These dangers seem especially clear in regard to Tom's perceptions, but Susan's beliefs and actions indicated that she too tended to see her spouse as a fixed entity.

Tom Darber, when he was interviewed after the marital breakup, said that he had not realized the extent of Susan's disaffection. He had accepted her sacrifices gratefully but without question. *Yes*, he had thanked Susan profusely for postponing her own career move so as to help advance his career; but *no*, he had not in turn tried to find ways of putting aside his own job concerns to help advance her professional interests. *No*, he had not made any great effort to support Susan's attempts to retool from her housewife-mother role to a career she would find gratifying after their children had grown up. In other words, Tom had come to assume that Susan would continue to accommodate to him without his having to reciprocate. He also assumed that her personal goals would always remain identical to his own and he was unaware that they had been changing significantly.

Susan also had difficulties in this area. She had felt somewhat guilty about her changing interests and had worried about how to discuss them with Tom. Having insufficient previous basis for talking with him about serious interpersonal issues, she postponed such discussion and it became harder and harder to confront the issue honestly. Thus Susan did not make it easy for Tom to notice the growing differences between them. Between Tom's lack of attention to her new interests and Susan's hesitation to broach the subject, her divergence became irreconcilable.

Asymmetry. One critical problem in the Darber's marriage was its inequality. Neither spouse realized this until it was too late to remedy because, on the surface, Tom and Susan adhered to an egalitarian ethos. For example, each would consult the other about what they ought to do on a weekend evening, what they should have for dinner, or how they should decide on most major purchases. At this level, they showed mutual respect and concern for the other's wishes. At a deeper level, however, they showed a remarkable lack of reciprocity; Susan accommodated far more to Tom's needs than he did to hers, but she failed to see this until she reexamined their relationship 18 years into the marriage.

Such asymmetry is common in close relationships: Younger, weaker, or subordinate partners are likely to change more toward older, stronger, or dominant partners than vice versa. Interdependence is rarely equal, and the more dependent partner is usually more influenceable than the less dependent one.

But such inequalities are not necessarily permanent. For example, parents can become more dependent on their children later in life; employees can become more influential than their employers; students can become smarter than their teachers. The same kind of reversal can occur between spouses. Although some recent evidence suggests that wives' personal characteristics are likely to converge more toward those of their husbands than are the husbands toward their wives' characteristics (Gruber-Baldini & Schaie, 1986), there surely are many exceptions. In the case of the Darbers, for example, their earlier asymmetry was followed by Susan's strivings for a professional identity; and still later, when her needs for greater equality were not adequately responded to by Tom, she began to drift away from him emotionally. In other words, asymmetric accommodations or convergences are likely to be unstable in an unstable normative environment.

THE SOCIAL PSYCHOLOGICAL COMPONENTS OF ACTIVITIES: TASK VERSUS SOCIO-EMOTIONAL ASPECTS

The limiting factors described above make total convergence improbable. It is unlikely that any intimate pair ever ceases to have *some* conflicting interests, even if their conflicts rarely come to the surface. To further complicate matters, partners often evaluate events or activities according to more than one outcome component. For example, a meal can be evaluated not only according to its tastiness, but also according to how pleasurable it was to cook or to clean up after it. And, the correspondence of two partners' outcomes for an event or activity can be considered separately for each outcome component. Kelley and Thibaut (1978) refer to these as the social-psychological components of interdependence.

We here discuss two primary components of activities - the task and the socio-emotional components - that have important implications for pair coordination and accommodation. Generally, partners' satisfaction from doing a job together depends on both how well the job is performed (the task component) and how enjoyable it is to work on it together (the affective component). Activities differ according to which of these two factors is given more weight, and partners differ according how much they weigh each factor for any given activity.

Consider, for example, a couple's house cleaning. Its success is probably measured by how well the house is cleaned, but it also depends on how well the two partners get along while doing the cleaning. Although the success of house cleaning is likely to depend mainly on its task outcome, for many other activities - e.g., going out for dinner or to a concert - the socio-emotional tone of the performance is more important than its externally judged goodness.

The task component of pair activities often requires specialization and the coordination of the partners' differing contributions (Levinger, 1964). The social component, in contrast, implies mutuality and doing things together. An example of the first would be one spouse shopping at the hardware store while the other picks up the groceries; an instance of the second is both partners doing all their shopping together so that they can spend more time together.

The task versus socio-emotional distinction is important for understanding interpersonal accommodation and convergence. If two spouses care primarily about maintaining their home efficiently (i.e., a task outcome), then accommodation to the other entails a willingness to do jobs that *complement* those the partner is most able or willing to perform. If, on the other hand, they are primarily interested in spending time together (i.e., a socio-emotional outcome), then accommodation entails a willingness to do *similar* jobs.

What happens, however, when an activity combines these two components in fairly equal proportions? Or, what if partners differ according to whether they see an activity as primarily a task or a social activity? Accommodation and convergence require more than a simple meshing of preferences; they also require a meshing of evaluative criteria.

DIVERGENT TRANSFORMATIONS

Our main emphasis has been on convergent transformations and facilitating accommodations - that is, on positive changes whereby two individuals become closer or where two separate 'I's' move toward defining themselves as one joint 'we.' Divergent transformations or interfering actions have so far received far less attention. Nonetheless, it seems obvious that many close relationships show signs of decline or deterioration after having built considerable interdependence.

One can look for causes of divergent transformations in the same causal conditions discussed above - the partners' environment, their personalities, and their pair interaction - or in some combinations among these factors (Kelley et. al., 1983). In the case of the Darbers, all three factors seemed to have some effect.

Both Susan's and Tom's environmental demands helped to further the breakdown of their relationship. Susan's law career brought her into contact with new expectations and new friends that conflicted with her former self-identity as primarily a wife and mother. At the same time, Tom's all male architectural environment failed to prepare him for adjusting to such changing circumstances; his firm's work pressures involved him so totally in his professional work that he was largely oblivious to his wife's new needs.

Looking back, one can also note certain personality characteristics that contributed to the split. Susan was unable to confront her husband when she felt angry or disappointed with him. Having earlier adapted herself almost totally to Tom's expectations of an ideal wife, she could not talk with him about her new feelings of unfairness. Meanwhile, Tom's personal rigidity and emotional unexpressiveness - which had caused no problems previously, when their marriage adhered to his expectations - now interfered with his ability to work things out from his side.

The Darbers' marriage was the third causal component in furthering divergence. As mentioned earlier, it had evolved into a highly asymmetric relationship, which conformed to the cultural norms of the 1950s and 1960s. When Susan did begin to focus on the unfairness of the arrangement, she and Tom lacked both the basic mutuality and the practiced problem solving skill wherewith to work out a joint resolution.

In other words, once the relationship had begun to deteriorate, environmental factors - including supportive friends and changing cultural norms, the spouses' personal characteristics, including both timidity and rigidity, and their relational history - combined to hasten the marital decline. In this way, Susan's earlier convergent transformations were succeeded by gradual divergences. This process was associated with physical and psychological strains that she failed fully to understand - such as frequent headaches and back aches, as well as a growing irritation at Tom's behavior. After a while, ostensibly because of her back aches, Susan began sleeping separately in another room. And, as this separation proceeded, she found herself less and less able to talk to Tom about anything emotionally meaningful. The psychological counterpart of the physical separation was the breaking of her emotional connections with her husband, as well as the building of a new sense of herself as an independent individual.

CONCLUSION

Transformations of motivation and of disposition are important concepts for understanding the development of close relationships. They help to explain how two separate individuals become a pair unit, how two 'I's' become a 'we.' But, transformations are often so gradual and so diffuse that the persons are unaware of the precise changes; if later asked about how or when the changes occurred, respondents often cannot point to any specific markers or events. For one thing, their accommodations become so routine as to be second nature. For another, people are accustomed to changing their preferences as they mature and cannot easily identify the particular influences.

Intimate relationships are crucial contexts for personal and interpersonal growth. And, accommodation and convergence are processes by which such growth occurs. It should be asked, however, how transformational processes either parallel or differ from other forms of social influence or attitude change?

As we discussed earlier, each of these processes involves familiar forms of social influence. Tactical transformations of outcome preferences - or situation-oriented transformations (see Figure 1) - parallel the 'compliance' found in experimental studies of social conformity, in which one adapts to another's wishes temporarily but with little long-term significance (Kelman, 1958). Relationship-oriented transformations are similar to Kelman's process of 'identification'; such transformations are recurrent, but depend on thinking about the partner and are eroded by the partner's absence. Finally, dispositional transformations parallel Kelman's notion of 'internalization'; they transcend the relationship and are independent of the other's presence or absence.

One might also want to consider the mechanisms whereby transformations occur. Mechanisms of change include various forms of social learning, including conditioning and modeling processes, as well as other processes of attitude formation and change - e.g., dissonance or self-perception. In other words, the psychological processes of outcome transformation are akin to other forms of personal change.

The interpersonal transformations considered in this chapter require a *dyadic* context and the existence of a long-term relationship. Although they pertain to changes in individuals, these changes derive their meaning only from the relationships in which the individuals are embedded. For instance, we would not look for transformational processes in purely superficial contacts; conversely, if someone's outcome preferences are markedly altered by a particular encounter or new relationship, then that encounter or relationship would appear to be rather significant.

ACKNOWLEDGMENTS

We are indebted to Icek Ajzen, James Averill, John G. Holmes, L. Anne Peplau, and Robert Sternberg for their helpful comments on a previous version of this chapter.

REFERENCES

Borden, V. M. H. (1983). *Interpersonal transformations in married and cohabiting couples.* Unpublished master's thesis, University of Massachusetts at Amherst.

Buber, M. (1958). *I and thou.* New York: Scribner (Originally published in 1923).

Cooley, C. H. (1909). *Social organization.* New York: Scribner.

Deutsch, M. (1949). A theory of cooperation and competition. *Human Relations.* 2, 129-152.

French, J. P., Jr., & Raven, B. (1959). The bases of social power. In D. Cartwright (Ed.), *Studies in social power* (pp. 150-167). Ann Arbor, MI: Institute for Social Research.

Gruber-Baldini, A. L., & Schaie, K. W. (1986). Longitudinal-sequential studies of marital assortativity. Paper presented at the meeting of the Gerontological Society of America, Chicago, IL.

Huesmann, L. R., & Levinger, G. (1976). Incremental exchange theory: A formal model for progression in dyadic social interaction. In L. Berkowitz (Ed.), *Advances in experimental psychology* (Vol. 9, pp. 191-229). New York: Academic Press.

Kelley, H. H. (1968). Interpersonal accommodation. *American Psychologist*, 23, 399-410.

Kelley, H. H. (1979). *Personal relationships: Their structures and processes.* Hillsdale, NJ: Erlbaum.

Kelley, H. H., Berscheid, E., Christensen, A., Harvey, J. H., Huston, T. L., Levinger, G., McClintock, E., Peplau, L. A., & Peterson, D. R. (1983). *Close relationships.* San Francisco: Freeman

Kelley, H. H., & Thibaut, J. W. (1978). *Interpersonal relations: A theory of interdependence.* New York: Wiley-Interscience.

Kelly, E. L. (1955). Consistency of adult personality. *American Psychologist*, 10, 659-681.

Kelman, H. C. (1958). Compliance, identification and internalization: Three processes of attitude change. *Journal of Conflict Resolution*, 2, 51-60.

Kerckhoff, A. C. (1974). The social context of attraction. In T. L. Huston (Ed.), *Foundations of interpersonal attraction* (pp. 61-78). New York: Academic Press.

Levinger, G. (1964). Task and social behavior in marriage. *Sociometry*, 27, 433-448.

Levinger, G. (1983). Development and change. In H. H. Kelley et al., *Close relationships* (pp. 315-359). San Francisco: Freeman.

Levinger, G., & Rands, M. (1985). Compatibility in marriage and other close relationships. In W. Ickes (Ed.), *Compatible and incompatible relationships* (pp. 309-332). New York: Springer-Verlag.

Levinger, G., & Snoek, J. D., (1972). *Attraction in relationships: A new look at interpersonal attraction*. Morristown, NJ: General Learning Press.

McClintock, C. G. (1972). Social motivation - a set of propositions. *Behavioral Science*, 17, 438-454.

Pruitt, D. G. (1981). *Negotiation behavior*. New York: Academic Press.

Rook, K., & Pietromonaco, P. (1987). Close relationships: Ties that heal or ties that bind? In W. H. Jones & D. Perlman (Eds.), *Advances in personal relationships: A research annual* (Vol. 1, pp. 1-35). Greenwich, CT: JAI Press.

TRUST AND THE APPRAISAL PROCESS IN CLOSE RELATIONSHIPS

John G. Holmes

As a close relationship develops, the tension between two opposing forces is likely to become more acute. On the one hand, a desire for increased closeness is fed by people's positive feelings and the mutual benefits anticipated from moving further into the relationship. On the other hand, increased closeness raises the spectre of giving more to the relationship and becoming more dependent on the partner's reciprocated benefits. The risks of being wrong, of being exploited or abandoned go with the territory. This dialectic between people's hopes and fears may be temporarily resolved, only to appear again at some later juncture in the relationship where events conspire to remind people of the risks of intimacy.

This prototypical dilemma has several critical ingredients that serve to highlight the issue of trust. An approach/avoidance conflict is apparent, where people can readily imagine a range of alternative scenarios which vary in their consequences. The extent of the internal conflict hinges on people's subjective forecasts of the likelihood of positive as compared to painful consequences. A sense of trust, a confident set of expectations about a partner, transforms the situation and psychologically diminishes the perception of risk. In contrast, if uncertainty about a partner prevails and thoughts of negative outcomes come all too easily to mind, people are likely to seek avenues of safety and avoid choices that increase their dependence and vulnerability.

In this depiction of events, the term trust is used to refer to people's expectations about what a partner is likely to provide in a relationship. To understand trust then, we must understand the ways in which people evaluate a partner in order to reduce uncertainty about what the future holds. In the first part of this chapter I will set the stage by describing the major themes that have emerged from the extensive literature on people's chronic tendencies to trust or distrust others. I will then consider the issue of how trust is formed in particular relationships. The emphasis will be on the types of information about a partner that have most impact on people's sense of security at various stages in the growth of intimacy. Different sets of concerns about a partner emerge during the development of a relationship and the meaning of trust is colored by experiences that are central at that window in time. In later sections of the chapter we will reverse our perspective and examine how *existing* states of trust influence perceptions, and at times, trap people in a circular type of logic.

GENERALIZED TRUST

A large part of the research literature on trust deals with people's general expectations about the social motives of others, rather than their particular expectations about a partner in a close relationship. People's chronic tendencies to trust or distrust others are assumed to result in a readiness to evaluate particular partners as trustworthy if their behavior warrants such a conclusion, or to exercise excessive caution in doing so (Erikson, 1963; Sroufe, 1983).

In the Beginning

The notion of *basic trust* has a central place in a number of theories that focus on the first stages of psychosocial development, when the infant-caregiver relationship is characterized by extreme dependency. In earlier models, an affective bond metaphor was used to describe the intensity of attachment to caregivers. It was assumed that children form mental models of significant others that reflect the qualities of their seminal experiences, a reformulation of the psychoanalytic concept of 'the good object'. The adult capacity to rely trustingly on others in situations of dependency was expected to echo these more archaic forms (Bowlby, 1973; Erikson, 1963).

A number of more specific hypotheses have emerged from recent work in this domain. First, there appears to be some agreement about what constitutes quality in infant-caregiver interactions, at least at more abstract levels. Various theorists have suggested that the critical ingredient is the attachment figure's *responsiveness* to the needs of the infant. This includes a mother consistently and appropriately satisfying the basic needs of the infant as they occur, rather than on the basis of her own schedule or mood (Ainsworth, 1979; Erikson, 1963; Sroufe, 1983). Stern (1985) argued that sensitivity to the *affect* of the infant is also a necessary basis for responsiveness. He suggested that children are capable of sensing the degree to which the mother mirrors and is attuned to their emotional state at an age as early as six months.

Second, various theorists have concluded that the consequence of a mother who is available, sensitive and responsive is a state of secure attachment in the infant. The confidence that this breeds facilitates both exploratory and affiliative tendencies, with the mother as a 'secure base'. The child will be less prone to intense or chronic anxiety, will adapt better to distressing circumstances such as separation and will find comfort in contact with the caregiver on reunion (Ainsworth, 1979; Sroufe, 1983).

The third but more controversial theme, is that general confidence in the responsiveness of attachment figures is built up slowly during the years of immaturity through adolescence, and that 'whatever expectations are developed during those years tend to persist relatively unchanged' (Bowlby, 1973). A number of recent studies on adult relationships have been based on this premise. Hazan and Shaver (1987) classified *adult* orientations to relationships on the basis of Ainsworth's descriptions of three major styles of attachment in infants - secure, avoidant and anxious/ambivalent. People's categorizations of their own styles related both to memories of the nature of their relationships with parents and their experiences of romantic love. Of particular note, secure individuals described themselves as having more trust, less fear of closeness and fewer emotional extremes. Anxious/ambivalent individuals reported the strongest desire for reciprocation of feelings, for union or merger with their partners and more jealousy.

Other studies have focused on Erikson's (1963) stage theory, which stresses the successive hurdles that must be bridged for a person to achieve the potential for mature intimacy. In simplified form, both an adequate sense of trust and autonomy are seen as developmental accomplishments that permit adolescents to form a positive identity and move successfully through the 'intimacy crisis' in the young adult years. For instance, Gold and Yanof (1985) have shown that the degree of intimacy in the friendships of women in the senior years of high school related to their perceptions of their mothers on the dimensions of emotional warmth and granting autonomy. Similarly, in a series of studies Orlofsky and his associates have pursued Erikson's theme that a strong sense of ego identity is linked to the capacity for mature intimacy. Based on the object-relations theory notion of separation-individuation (Mahler, 1963) they delineated two groups of people, merger and low-intimacy status. These groups were characterized by unresolved dependency issues, that is, the inability to feel secure as separate individuals (Levitz-Jones & Orlofsky, 1985).

The findings of their studies with college women seem much in accord with those of Hazan and Shaver (1987) and an attachment-theory perspective. Like anxious/ambivalent individuals, merger women exhibited needfulness, ambivalence and enmeshment in their relationships. Their symbiotic union appeared to serve as a means of dealing with trust through fusion with another. Like avoidant individuals, the low-intimacy women dealt with issues of dependency very differently. Their relationships were pseudointimate, marked by fears of closeness and a need to maintain clear boundaries and distance. Both groups demonstrated more defensiveness, depression and self-esteem loss in the face of potential separation when compared to a high-intimacy status group of women. Their anxiety supposedly reflected their uncertainty that an attachment figure could be trusted to be available when needed.

Two themes. Claims of continuity in interpersonal tendencies across the developmental time span and across situations remain controversial (Hazan & Shaver, 1987). The studies I've chosen as examples used retrospective reports of earlier experiences or concurrent measures of adult attachment styles, and of course do not offer tests of such claims. However, in each case the studies furthered our understanding of adult close relationships by considering the psychological *dynamics* postulated by developmental models. At least two important themes emerge from this theoretical perspective.

The first is that genotypically similar concerns about trust and dependency may give rise to very different displays. We saw that some people coped with issues about trust by 'loving too much', by needing to merge with their partner, whereas others dealt with the risks of intimacy by remaining distant and superficially self-reliant. In both cases, latent anxieties about being exploited or abandoned were apparent.

In this vein, the naive depiction of a trusting relationship in the popular literature is that it can be recognized by the extent of attachment displayed by the partners and by the degree to which they depend on each other. In fact, trusting individuals may often appear to be *less* attached than those identified as anxious/ambivalent (mergers), at least in terms of the manifest intensity of affiliative behaviors. They are also likely to be *more* autonomous in their relationships, though not to the extent displayed in the defensive self-sufficiency of avoidant individuals. Thus evidence about tendencies toward affiliation or independence (autonomy) in a relationship is not a straightforward reflection on trust, though it is often interpreted that way.

The second theme is that the consequence of perceived responsiveness by caregivers in situations of dependency is a state of 'felt security' (Sroufe, 1983). Confident, benign expectations about attachment figures stretch the threshold for perceiving threats, cushion their impact and hasten recovery after an experience of distress. In contrast, anxious/ambivalent infants are more easily dislodged from their fragile sense of security and may experience affect in reaction to events that might appear to be only minimally stressful. Though the details of analysis might differ in the adult case, this model offers some useful insights into the possible impact of different states of trust.

Generalized Trust in Adults

Several authors have constructed personality scales to assess current states of general trust in adults, without directly considering the imprint of developmental conflicts. Wrightsman (1972) focused on the extent to which people's philosophy of human nature reflects a belief that others are basically honest as opposed to immoral and irresponsible. Rotter (1967) defined interpersonal trust as a generalized expectancy that other persons can be relied on to live up to their verbal promises. Neither scale has proven to be particularly useful in predicting behavior in close relationship contexts (Larzelere & Huston, 1980). These results could be interpreted as evidence that the trust construct is only viable with reference to specific target persons, not as a chronic tendency (Johnson-George & Swap, 1982). The research reviewed earlier on the related concept of chronic attachment styles suggests such a conclusion really is not warranted. Instead, the problem may be that the two scales focused rather exclusively on the notion of honesty in communications, an issue that represents only one rather limited aspect of trust in close relationships.

It is interesting to note that when Rotter's trust scale was used along with his locus of control measure, the combination was quite successful in predicting constructive behavior in the marital communication and problem solving domains (see Doherty & Ryder, 1979). The locus of control construct reflects people's beliefs that events in their lives are contingent on their efforts and are under their personal control (internals), as compared to being determined by outside forces (externals). Internal locus of control has consistently been found to correlate positively with Rotter's trust scale (Sabatelli, Buck, & Dreyer, 1983). Together the two measures may depict more effectively the qualities of a trusting orientation in close relationships.

The reasoning behind this hypothesis is that locus of control is linked to risk-taking in interpersonal disclosure, which in turn promotes a sense of shared security. Miller, Lefcourt, Holmes, Ware and Saleh (1986) found that internals tended to directly engage issues by stating their feelings to their partners. In general, individuals who were assertive in expressing their needs achieved better quality solutions in marital problem-solving and experienced more satisfaction with the outcomes than those who avoided the issues. This pattern is consistent with the earlier theme that trusting individuals expect others to be responsive to them: they should have a stronger sense of efficacy and fewer anxieties about engaging issues by stating their needs in relationships. According to the Miller et al. results, this process should only serve to foster mutual satisfaction and reinforce their confidence in the strength of their relationship.

In summary, the locus of control construct helps to capture nuances in the meaning of trust. Trusting individuals typically have a sense of personal control predicated on the assumption that attachment figures will respond to their efforts if they make their needs clear. In contrast, a pervasive sense of distrust is usually associated with a 'defensive external' orientation (Sabatelli et al., 1983). In this passive (aggressive) stance people tend to blame others for their interpersonal failures, thereby strengthening their basic attitude of suspicion. At other times distrust in others is countered more directly. People resort to direct forms of influence to control interaction and ensure their needs are met.

Basically, power provides some security in the absence of trust, and Holmes (1987) has found that the two variables show a strong negative correlation in close relationships. This is a very different translation of control, one that serves to reduce dependence on others. The sense of control described for trusting individuals was achieved by their taking the risk of *increasing* dependence, with the expectation that the closer the ties they forged, the more responsive partners would be to their efforts.

Trust as Risk-taking Behavior

In social psychology the concept of trust has a rich history, but one that is very different from that in the developmental and personality traditions. The emphasis has been on predicting trusting *behavior* in situations involving risk, usually in simulated social dilemmas or conflict scenarios in the laboratory. The analysis of risk has usually involved a subjective expected utility model that focuses on the perceived likelihood of different outcomes. For instance, Deutsch (1973) defined trust as 'confidence that one will find what is desired from another, rather than what is feared'.

Most studies in this research tradition examined how *situational* factors influenced people's assessments of others' behavioral intentions. Distrust in intentions was strongest in situations where the pattern of outcomes was perceived as tempting them to exploit vulnerability on the part of subjects (Webb & Worchel, 1986) and where subjects had little effective counterpower over the opponents' welfare (Pruitt, 1965; Solomon, 1960). Thus, this research focused on behavioral expectations about others that may have had no relation to trust in their *personal motives*. To put it another way, the more others are compelled to cooperate by the exigencies of the situation, the less reason to attribute the behavior to their benevolent intentions (Holmes, 1981; Strickland, 1958). We learn least about people's trustworthiness under the very circumstances that foster our making supposed 'trusting' choices.

The irony then, is that in order to develop trust in a person one must first take the *risk* of trusting in situations where uncertainty remains, where there are indeed temptations for the other to exploit one's vulnerability without implied threats of counter control. Thus scenarios involving personal risk are most diagnostic of partners' motives because 'good reasons' then exist for them to act in their own interests rather than recognizing ours (Holmes, 1981; Kelley & Thibaut, 1978).

A second important theme in this discussion of strategic choice in social dilemma research relates to the common practice of focusing on the interaction of two strangers. This ambiguous situation is like a Rorscharch that pulls for the expression of people's assumptions about what others are really like, whether they can be trusted or not. In this vein, Kelley and Stahelski (1970) argued that the expectations people hold about typical others are indeed a reflection of generalized beliefs that emerge from their social experience, but that actors may play an unwitting part in maintaining such beliefs. In a series of studies, they discovered that people who intended to act competitively invariably expected others to behave the same way. Their opponents, including those with cooperative intentions, were forced to assimilate to the actors' competitive style to defend themselves. The basic distrust exhibited by competitors may be in part projection, but they also helped create a social reality that only served to confirm their beliefs about others. In contrast, cooperators did not have fixed expectations and tailored their actions to the others' cooperative or competitive style.

The Impact of Generalized Trust on Specific Relationships

Most researchers assume that generalized tendencies toward trust contribute to the development of trust in specific relationships, though the link has not been directly established. The Kelley and Stahelski (1970) results introduce a note of caution in terms of assuming any simple rule of correspondence, however.

Cooperators indeed showed a 'readiness to trust' by taking risks and encouraging reciprocation, but ultimately their actions were contingent on their partners' behavior. Competitors went further than simply displaying a readiness to distrust: their initial expectations were relatively hardened and their behavioral style ensured that their perceptions of others would remain frozen. Miller and Holmes (1975) also found that competitors, as compared to cooperators, tended to view a situation which featured a potential for being exploited as 'just like real life'. One could speculate about the extent to which competitors are primed to interpret a wide variety of situations as raising issues of trust.

These findings suggest the possibility of an *asymmetry* in the capacity of trusting and distrusting individuals to adjust effectively to the special features of situations and partners. A tendency to be trusting might best be regarded as a preferred adaptation, a readiness to attribute good intentions if experiences in a relationship seem to warrant such conclusions (Erikson, 1963). In contrast, a tendency to be distrusting might be viewed as a more imperialistic interpersonal ideology, one that introduces substantial distortion into the social learning process. If it is associated with a fixed set of negative expectations and a risk-avoidant style, it may be very difficult for partners to provide evidence that would be construed as diagnostic of their good intentions.

THE DEVELOPMENT OF TRUST IN CLOSE RELATIONSHIPS

This extensive literature on the genetics and impact of chronic tendencies to trust does much to clarify the dynamics of the construct and to characterize the ways in which it will be displayed. Considerably less attention has been paid by researchers to the *process* by which trust develops within the boundaries of a particular close relationship. The realization of a state of trust is expected to be heavily contingent on the unique set of experiences encountered with a partner. These experiences will be shaped by the particular attributes of the other person and by the properties of social interaction that characterize the development of relationships. Thus the eventual form that trust takes will reflect people's ways of handling the psychological dilemmas that mark each phase of development.

The early, evaluative and accommodation stages that will be described in portraying the development of relationships roughly correspond to the phases depicted by Braiker and Kelley (1979) and Levinger (1979). The goal is to relate the evaluation of trust to the particular psychological issues that people typically confront at different points as relationships grow. I will suggest that the meaning and functions of trust depend on the issues most salient at the time and the type of appraisal process triggered by those current concerns. The use of stages in the presentation is intended to highlight these critical *processes*, rather than to argue for a particular stage model *per se*.

The Early Stages of Romantic Love

For most people, the early stages of romantic involvement are a blur of experience, made opaque by a rush of rather unreflective positive feeling toward a partner. The initial focus is very much on the rewarding qualities that make the relationship seem worthwhile (Eidelson, 1980; Rusbult, 1983). Some authors contend that people achieve an intuitive grasp of what a partner can provide very early, and that these impressions successfully predict continuity in most relationships four to six months later (Berg & Clark, 1985). It may be the case that we know quite early that someone seems 'right' for us. The decision to move further into the relationship may initially be made in an implicit, unself-conscious manner, governed by the pull of mutual attraction.

The emotional highs and intense absorption of passionate love have fascinated both the layperson and scientist (e.g., Brehm, 1985). However this picture may mask the undercurrents of anxiety that are often experienced. At some point, people are apt to become more explicitly aware that their hopes have begun to ride on the growth of intimacy and that rejection would prove to be very painful. As this awareness surfaces, people often deal with concerns in a simple way: they deny that trust is an issue - 'Of course my partner loves me'.

At this stage trust is often little more than a fragile expression of hope. The projection of people's intense feelings, bolstered by displays of affection from partners, creates a sense of optimism that belies a lack of hard evidence. The working assumption is made that the other's feelings of love are similar to their own. Larzelere and Huston (1980) reported that trust tends to be high and strongly related to love for couples at the exclusively dating stage. Similarly, Sternberg (1986) described Fatuous Love and Hendrick and Hendrick (1986) described Eros as passion accompanied by a mutual sense of commitment and common destiny, without a core of sustained intimacy to supported such longings. Dion and Dion (1976) reported that love and a sense of trust went hand in hand even during the more volatile infatuation period experienced by low self-esteem individuals. Thus it appears that for some, the cocoon of romantic love need not be seriously penetrated by occasional concerns about whether one's feelings are fully reciprocated. In fact, Blau (1964) even suggested that these anxieties are the very fuel of passionate love!

The Evaluative Stage

At some point, sterner realities must be faced. Our partner's imperfections start to intrude on our images, where previously we had filled in the gaps with the imagined attributes of an idealized other. A subtle shift in perspective occurs that influences people's orientation toward their partners. Their agenda or current concern (Klinger, 1977) becomes more explicitly evaluative. They need to consolidate their feelings and establish the worth of the other in their lives in a way that does not simply deny the negative elements. Essentially, the motivation increases to reduce uncertainty about the ultimate designs of the partner, to develop a sense of trust that acknowledges realities and concerns that had been largely suppressed.

The emergence of this evaluative perspective is keyed to a more explicit understanding of the *prospective nature* of experience in close relationships. People discover that for the relationship to grow they must be willing to give more, and increasingly sacrifice personal interests to accommodate the needs of the partner. Of course, efforts to maximize joint outcomes may be done in a spirit of caring and will often show quite immediate dividends. But it is the promise of increasing rewards in the future, the anticipation of the benefits of deeper levels of intimacy, that ultimately controls decisions to give more and increase the level of involvement (Kelley & Thibaut, 1978; Huesmann & Levinger, 1976).

The nuances of this social contract may remain obscure to most people, whereas the emotional impact of the pact may be quite salient: the risk is that the more you care, the more you have to lose. This conclusion is usually hard to escape. People's emotional investment is underlined by both their own accommodations and their increasing dependence on the partner's reciprocated benefits. As the risks and the sense of vulnerability grow, people become concerned with the issue of whether the other's feelings and qualities make their investment a secure one.

Thus the central theme is that people's decisions to move further into the relationship become increasingly tied to their subjective forecasts of what the future holds. This prospective analysis involves not only people's sense of what the partner is capable of providing, but also their confidence that the other can be depended on to reciprocate their affection and to actualize the potential of the relationship (Holmes, 1981; Kelley & Thibaut, 1978). The first issue focuses more on the intensity of attachment and love, whereas the second concerns matters of trust. Taken together, these value and likelihood components remind us of the expected utility model discussed earlier.

The self-regulation of emotions. In the early romantic stages love appeared to be the basis for trust, however inarticulate or unfounded the latter may have been. In this evaluative stage love and trust are more likely to promote each other in a circular fashion. The idea is that current feelings of trust in a partner's affections serve to *regulate* the pace and level of one's involvement in a relationship (Holmes, 1981). Whereas the romantic period might indeed be described by a sense of falling in love, the development of conjugal love (Driscoll, Davis, & Lipetz, 1972) is likely to be more controlled, governed by cues that one's affections are being reciprocated and that one is not alone out on a limb.

Several lines of research are consistent with this view that reciprocal love enhances a sense of trust. Perceptions of unequal involvement are probably the best single predictor of the dissolution of dating relationships (Brehm, 1985; Hill, Rubin & Peplau, 1976; Walster, Walster & Traupmann, 1978). In a similar vein, Berscheid and Fei (1977) reported that people who were insecure about their partners' feelings toward them said they were not sure they were in love, even though they admitted being dependent on the other person. In contrast, expressions of love and feelings of security went hand in hand. It appears that trust in a partner enables people to diminish psychologically the risk of moving further into the relationship, allowing emotions to crystallize in a way that lets people more fully acknowledge feelings of being 'in love'.

These various issues that mark the evaluative phase could be described as reflecting concerns with the pragmatics of self-regulation (Kelley, 1983). They stand in contrast to the unreflective absorption, the sense of being carried away that is characteristic of the early, romantic stages. Kelley's use of the term pragmatic is perhaps misleading if the reader is left with the impression that people's focus turns largely to an accounting of the concrete benefits partners are capable of providing. A prospective analysis certainly contains such elements, but his point, and mine, is that the process of attachment becomes more controlled out of concerns about the reciprocity of caring, the mutuality of love. The point at which this type of self-regulation emerges is by no means clear, and I suspect the onset has as many variations as occur in the interpersonal tendencies that contribute to the 'colors' of love (Hendrick & Hendrick, 1986). For instance, there is some evidence that relationships are experienced as less mysterious and volatile and more continuous for people who had a secure attachment history (Hazan & Shaver, 1987) and who are characterized by internal locus of control (Dion & Dion, 1973).

The process of uncertainty reduction. In the evaluative stage, the development of trust could be described in terms of a process of uncertainty reduction. Rempel, Holmes and Zanna (1985) have proposed a typology for characterizing the various forms of information that people use for this purpose. The first and most basic type of information that people seek relates to their need for *predictability* in the face of ambiguity. It deals with people's efforts to consolidate their expectations about a partner's *behavior*, with the goal of more accurately forecasting the pattern of rewards and costs experienced in everyday social exchange.

The perceived stability of patterns of behavior in close relationships has been largely ignored in the literature, in spite of the fact that variability is a critical component of prediction (Holmes, 1981; Kelley, 1983). Theorists in the social reinforcement tradition have focused heavily on analysis at this behavioral level, but they have typically considered the cumulative bank account of rewards and costs as the criterion for evaluating how satisfying a relationship is likely to be (e.g., Gottman, 1979). However the anticipated benefits from developing a relationship would have a very different flavor in cases where variability is high compared to the balance of rewards and costs experienced. Volatile, inconsistent behavior by a partner would inhibit a sense of confidence and control, and would cause anxiety and attributional ambiguity as expectations are violated.

Patterns of consistent behavior contain some important messages about conditions that foster them. A stable, rewarding orientation by a partner at the dating stage implies a commitment to shared norms and a convergence of interests (Kelley & Thibaut, 1978). Most critically, an accurate understanding of a partner's patterns of behavior early in a relationship serves as an informational source for *attributions* about his or her personal dispositions (Kelley & Thibaut, 1978). In fact, it is not at all clear that we retain much in the way of detail in our memories of interpersonal experiences (Wyer & Srull, 1986). In close relationships our memories of past events may be colored to fit contemporaneous images of partners (McFarland & Ross, 1987). Thus the type of accounting alluded to by behavioral theorists may lose its articulation rather early, and predictability may be largely an emergent general impression of a partner's behavioral consistency in domains important to the relationship.

As time passes a partner's behavioral profile is essentially transformed: the focus shifts to the reasons for the observed patterns. Thus for purposes of cognitive economy we come to place our trust in the attributes of a person, not specific actions. To this end, theorists have considered one component of trust to be a set of trait inferences about a partner that seem to resemble a *dependability* prototype (Rempel et al., 1985). A partner would be seen as trustworthy if he or she is the type of person who can be counted on to be honest, reliable, cooperative and essentially benevolent (Johnson-George & Swap, 1982; Larzelere & Huston, 1980; Rempel et al., 1985). People's confidence in such trait inferences will reflect their experiences in a limited set of situations involving personal risk and vulnerability, where trust is a salient concern. Partners' benevolent responses will be seen as most genuine and diagnostic of dependability when salient temptations exist for them to exploit their advantage in such encounters, as I suggested earlier.

An important aspect of trust is simply not captured by the predictability and dependability perspectives. One can imagine a rather exemplary partner who is consistently rewarding and is virtuous in character, but who still fails to instill any sense of security about the relationship. This is because neither of these components of trust addresses the issue of whether the partner's display of positive qualities is *uniquely* tied to feelings of attachment for the particular person. If anything, the currency value of these two attributes makes the partner more desirable to others, which could potentially heighten feelings of insecurity! However trust can be defined in a different way, one that perhaps raises the ultimate question: Will my partner love and care for me, in particular, and be responsive to my needs in the future?

The reciprocal attachment process. This third perspective centers on the perceived strength and quality of *attachment* on the part of a partner. It was suggested earlier that people tend to calibrate the level of their own emotional involvement to such perceptions, and that a rough balance in perceived attachment at each level of development is essential for trust. If this is the case, then the growth of trust is a conjunctive responsibility (Kelley & Thibaut, 1978), requiring that each person provide reassurance to the other about their feelings at each step in the evolution of the relationship. The outlines of a conjunctive model depicting the growth of mutual trust were first presented by Osgood (1962) as a proposal for a 'graduated reciprocation in tension reduction (GRIT)' in the domain of international relations. He suggested that unilateral initiatives are most likely to be successful if they involve a cost or sacrifice and are accompanied by a clear statement of intentions. Each overture offers reassurance to the other party and invites a confirming countermove. Trust grows in an upward spiral, anchored by the delicate balance in the reciprocation process.

Kelley and Thibaut (1978) contended that a similar logic can be applied in the realm of close relationships. The formation of trust was depicted as an exchange of actions or messages that gradually reduces uncertainty and increases mutual assurance that the relationship will endure. The process is keyed to attributions about risk taking: confidence in a partner increases when the other's behavior involves some sacrifice of self-interests or acceptance of risk (Pruitt, 1965; Swinth, 1967). Acceptance of risk by a partner implies that he or she must go further than simply validating or confirming the person's expressions of attachment by responding in kind. Rather, the partner must at times take the more vulnerable position of being further out on a limb. This behavior involves finding a response meaningfully greater than what is immediately justified by the person's prior behavior.

The normal flow of this escalation process can be endangered if partners 'come on too strong'. The risk is that people will become reactive to what might be seen as excessive expectations now thrown on their shoulders, or a level of dependency that has outstripped their own involvement. Of course the balance could also be upset if partners were seen as dragging their feet, unless the hesitation is interpreted as indicating personal insecurities that essentially equalize the risks accepted by both parties (Kelley & Thibaut, 1978). For instance, women may find themselves in the role of the pace setter in disclosing feelings, but rationalize it by concluding that men incur extra costs because they find it hard to communicate emotions.

The escalation of mutual attachment and dependency as I have described it is very much a dyadic process that involves the metamorphosis of trust from individual beliefs about a partner to a concept perhaps better depicted in relationship terms. This is not to deny that some part of a shared sense of security might conceal latent asymmetries or at least differing perceptions: the potent combination of wishful thinking by one person and self-presentation by the other almost assures a degree of noise in the system. However, the trust that does evolve is in important ways an attribute of the relationship itself, one that emerges as a product of joint endeavors. As we shall see later, the focus of the participants themselves becomes more truly interpersonal, centering on the couple as a unit with an identity growing out of the unique fabric of their interactions.

Judging responsiveness. To understand the dynamics of this process model, it is important to consider the critical issue of *how* people judge their partners' attachment to them. Kelley (1979) suggested that people code a partner's behavior for signs that the other is acting in a way that is responsive to their needs and preferences, rather than solely in terms of self-interest. It is this shift in agenda, this *transformation* of motivation in the context of the relationship (see also Borden & Levinger, 1990, Chapter 2), that serves as the basis for people's attributions about a partner's 'interpersonal dispositions'. The problem is, our partners have much to gain from convincing us that they are attuned to our interests and willing to put them before their own. To add to the ambiguity of the task, people must also distinguish partners' more chronic altruistic dispositions, their dependability, from interpersonal attitudes that are uniquely tied to their specific relationship. To illustrate these ideas, it is useful to discuss several interaction contexts that may serve as arenas or testing grounds for evaluating people's intentions.

Theorists have long assumed that *self-disclosure* is both a barometer of trust and a platform for its development (Altman & Taylor, 1973). Indeed, trust is associated with the depths of intimate self-disclosure across the life-span of relationships, though the correlation is strongest for married couples (Larzelere & Huston, 1980). In that regard, Hendrick (1981) found that intimate disclosure was an important ingredient for marital satisfaction and that both revealing one's feelings and being a confidant for one's partner's disclosures contributed to this effect.

Altman and Taylor (1973) argued that the development of trust is linked to reciprocity in self-disclosure in the early stages of relationships. Reciprocal communication demonstrates a shared interest in furthering the relationship and offers reassurance about each person's good intentions. Evidence of reciprocity at increasing *depth* of disclosure would be consistent with a model of escalating attachment, where progress is keyed to mutual risk-taking. This is especially true where people are revealing information that could be evaluated negatively, leaving them vulnerable to exploitation or rejection. This perspective focuses on the role of self-disclosure in signalling and pacing depth of involvement. Reciprocity provides a sense of security by ensuring equality in the bearing of risks and in involvement in the relationship.

Another view is that our partners' reactions to personal disclosures afford opportunities to judge their responsiveness to our concerns and to develop the sense of 'a special connection' when they affirm our social reality. When this goal is primary, we would not expect to see any urgency to reciprocate in kind. Expressions of understanding and support by the recipient of a self-disclosure may better convey a sense of caring (Berg & Clark, 1985). However, this type of response presumes a degree of mutual security in the relationship, as it does not balance the emotional vulnerability of both partners. In this regard, Altman and Taylor suggested that the need to maintain the safety net of immediate reciprocity will diminish as the foundations of trust are strengthened. There is then less concern about momentary imbalances in the bearing of risk. This logic leads one to predict that evidence of direct reciprocity in disclosure will be weaker in more established relationships. Several studies offer support for this conclusion (Derlega, Wilson & Chaikin, 1976; Morton, 1978).

Patterns of *social exchange* provide another important testing ground for evaluating the extent of a partner's attachment. The process is predicted to reflect themes similar to those in the domain of self-disclosure, based on the reciprocal attachment model being proposed. Partners' behavior will be coded for evidence of their willingness to moderate self-interest and respond to our needs and preferences. The perceived *costs* involved in their being responsive and accommodating will be evaluated as diagnostic of attachment, in much the same way as risks were in the disclosure process (Holmes, 1981; Kelley, 1979). From the present perspective, signs of *increasing* responsiveness and giving by partners have critical symbolic value. This behavior can more easily be interpreted as evidence of growing emotional investment in *the relationship itself*, rather than as reflecting partners' dispositional qualities such as dependability.

Trust in a partner depends not only on these attributions about his or her level of involvement, but also on perceptions that the other's attachment is comparable to one's own. As in the case of self-disclosure, there will be pressures toward *reciprocity* in exchange caused by a need to maintain the security of equal involvement. This does not necessarily imply expectations of behavioral reciprocity in particular interactions. However, it does suggest that people will be concerned with the balance of investments because of the message it contains about the state of their relationship. An important implication of this idea is that constraints are put on the degree to which people will feel comfortable responding to a partner's needs as they occur. The degree of responsiveness shown will be tailored to current levels of perceived involvement and limited by concerns about reciprocal attachment. In other words, the state of trust that has developed is likely to govern people's flexibility around rules of reciprocity.

A number of other authors have also argued that partners are more concerned with the balance of exchange in earlier phases of relationships (e.g., Brehm, 1985; Walster et al., 1978). Several recent studies illustrate the point. In research on dating couples, Lloyd, Cate and Henton (1982) found that a general sense of equity or fair exchange was more strongly related to satisfaction at earlier rather than later stages in relationships. Schmidt, Kelley and Fujino (1987) examined the outcome patterns preferred by dating couples across a wide range of decision situations. They found a variety of exchange rules reflected in their analysis of couples' preferences. People in shorter-term relationships tended to show concerns with equality, expressed through efforts to minimize the differences between their respective costs or benefits. In contrast, people in serious, longer-term relationships showed an increased preference for maximizing the joint welfare of the pair, even though it might involve a temporary imbalance in outcomes. These studies seem to indicate that people have concerns about fair exchange earlier in relationships that later recede in importance.

Clark and her colleagues have presented an apparently contrasting view on whether reciprocity is important in the beginning stages of relationships. For example, Clark and Mills (1979) argued that rules of economic exchange, including reciprocity, are seen as inappropriate very early on, even at the point where people decide to pursue a friendship. They suggest instead that in 'communal relationships' people benefit one another in direct response to their needs, with no expectation of receiving comparable benefits in return. Berg and

Clark (1985) make the intriguing argument that norms for close relationships are fundamentally different, and that people show an abrupt transition to them rather than shifting by a matter of degree. They reported a number of studies showing that individuals exhibited relatively selfless behavior when they were entertaining hopes of forming a relationship with someone, and reacted positively to a communal orientation in their prospective partner.

A recent study by Lydon, Jamieson and Holmes (1985) explored this theme further by focusing on people's concerns behind the rules they adopted. Individuals were asked to describe how they behaved in a set of different situations, and how they felt about their actions. People who were asked to describe their interactions with an established friend (a unit relationship) indicated little adherence to rules of reciprocity and seemed comfortable doing so. People describing interactions with someone they liked and with whom they were developing a relationship (pre-unit) expressed an equal willingness to ignore short-term reciprocity. However, they also indicated considerably more anxiety about following that path. They expected that a balance of exchange would be restored in a shorter period of time than those in unit relationships. Both conditions were in contrast to a control group describing interactions with a casual acquaintance, where reciprocity was clearly expected.

These results and those of Clark and her colleagues clearly show that people understand the social scripts that *should* differentiate close encounters from others. A shared understanding of the norm means that the display of such altruistic scripts carries messages about people's intentions. The communal script becomes a *language* for communicating interest in the other, for defining the nature of the relationship, and for conveying evidence of 'good character' and positive feelings. In attributional terms, the expressive value of one's contributions would be undermined if one's motivation for being responsive were seen as part of an explicit process of quid pro quo (Clark & Mills, 1979; Holmes, 1981).

In summary, conformity to the communal script may be prevalent in *particular encounters* very early on in relationships because such behavior is an important means for expressing a caring attitude. I suspect that a pact of selfless absorption can be more easily maintained in the early romantic period discussed previously, where trust appears to be surprisingly high. However as couples move into the evaluative phase, the issue of equal attachment becomes increasingly significant. When it does, concerns for balanced exchange and reciprocity over the shorter term are likely to be evident. People may still avoid underlining rules of reciprocity in particular interactions. Rather, the accounting process will be tighter until sufficient trust has developed to loosen the reins and extend the time frame within which fairness will eventually be served.

As mutual attachment grows, the psychological foundations are laid for taking the risk of departing from the strategically secure orientation of monitoring investments and minimizing momentary imbalances. People become increasingly able to set security concerns aside and respond more directly to a partner's needs, with an eye to maximizing the joint welfare of the unit. This reflects the fact that a critical aspect of the motivation for reciprocity was to ensure a balance in attachment, not simply to negotiate a fair deal in economic terms. Thus as the symbolic value of the behavior recedes, the pattern loses its impetus. Of course, the shift also reflects a genuine desire to take the partner into account as love grows, less encumbered by the restraints of self-regulation.

The heart of the matter. Holmes (1981) suggested that even evidence of a partner's positive attitudes toward the relationship is not simply taken at face value over the course of time. Behavior is coded not only for its responsiveness, but also for the *reasons* that ultimately lie behind demonstrations of considerateness and altercentric concern. Rempel, Holmes and Zanna (1985) distinguished three types of motivation that might be perceived as responsible. First, a partner might be responsive now in order to secure anticipated benefits of an extrinsic kind, tangible resources facilitated by the relationship, such as money, status and so on. Second, the anticipated benefits may depend on a partner's perceptions of how rewarding the person is, his or her value or worth in an intimate relationship. The qualities that a partner values might have common currency, such as appearance, intellect and social competence, or be targeted more directly, like support, praise and companionship. The common thread is that a partner may make present sacrifices to maintain the relationship, precisely *because* it is expected to be rewarding. Their behavior is in this broad sense, *instrumental*.

Rempel et al. distinguished these two orientations from responsiveness that is seen as *intrinsically* motivated. Various theorists have stressed the notion that the pleasure derived from gratifying the needs of an intimate partner may become an end unto itself, through a process of empathic identification (e.g., Blau, 1964; Levinger, 1979). The desire to be responsive to the partner is seemingly without reason, in a way that suggests the motive becomes functionally autonomous from its roots. Loving is its own reward.

Earlier it was suggested that the spiral of attachment is a dyadic process that produces a strong sense of shared attitudes, of mutuality. A sense of 'we-ness' develops out of the dyadic process and people come to talk of 'our love' rather than 'my love' (Kelley, 1983). This experience of union, where the boundaries of one's own interests and the partner's become blurred, captures the meaning of intrinsic attachment. In this state, it is increasingly difficult to do a rational accounting to justify our actions, and we cease to count the reasons for our feelings.

The conviction that a partner is intrinsically motivated to care for us and to be responsive to our needs is hypothesized to be the cornerstone of trust. The concept may seem ephemeral, but in one sense it is the strongest evidence of attachment precisely because it goes *beyond* reasons (Brickman, 1987). Value is placed on the relationship itself by partners over and above their evaluations of our desirable features (their instrumental motives), whose currency we may fear, is not written in stone for all time. In a less logical way, intrinsic attachment is appropriate to our cultural understanding about what 'true love' really is: it seems inimical to people's thinking to conceive of their partners' love as rooted largely in what they provide for them. The very spectre of an instrumental arrangement seems to discount the worth of a partner's love (Rempel et al., 1985; Seligman, Fazio & Zanna, 1980).

The impact of intrinsic motivation may be related as much to the *experience* of unconditional acceptance within relationships as to any such attributional analyses (Baldwin & Holmes, 1987). People's sense of felt security may be a more direct result of a responsive partner who is attuned to their affect and mirrors their sense of worth. This process resembles the more archaic one proposed by developmental theorists as the basis for secure attachment in infants. Such feelings of trust are rooted in a subtle, dynamic process in the dyad, and people may have little apprehension of these ties.

Rempel, Holmes and Zanna (1985) attempted to test some of these notions by constructing scales to measure the three types of motives and feelings of trust. They found that trust was strongly related to beliefs that a partner was intrinsically motivated to be in the relationship ($r = .52$), but not to beliefs that the other was motivated by instrumental ($r = .17$) or extrinsic ($r = -.03$) concerns. Perceptions of an intrinsic orientation in self and other were tightly linked ($r = .77$), as one would expect if the attachment process indeed promotes a sense of mutuality and shared feelings. It is important to note that unlike trust, love and satisfaction were both significantly associated with perceptions of instrumental motives in a partner ($r = .52$), and this pattern was particularly strong for women. It seems that being valued by a partner for what one has to offer, for one's qualities, is self-affirming and bolsters reciprocal good feeling (e.g., Sternberg & Barnes, 1985). However, in spite of this positive glow and the sense of control implied by the partner's dependency on one's resources, perceptions of being needed in this way seemed to do little to strengthen trust.

These results go beyond the idea that people code a partner's behavior in terms of its responsiveness to their needs. In relation to trust, the responsiveness must be seen as coming from the heart and symbolizing a lack of conditionality, a caring that is somehow above concerns about reciprocity. After all, to give to the relationship is not to give anything away if people have come to see themselves as a natural cognitive unit (Lerner, Miller & Holmes, 1976). This perspective portrays trust as having almost a Gestalt-like quality, a sense that a relationship somehow transcends each individual, is greater than its parts. Such perceptions emerge from the fabric of shared experience in the attachment process, through the subtle transformations in the nature of social exchange and self-disclosure that have been described.

The Accommodation Stage

Most people would have some trouble recognizing this rather idealized depiction of events in their relationships. The path to a secure, loving relationship is typically not a smooth one. A number of authors have suggested that the developmental course of relationships tends to culminate in a period of crisis. Eidelson (1980) found a marked drop in satisfaction across couples as relationships became defined as serious. This occurred at a point where people became more aware of the restrictive costs of modifying behavioral preferences to suit the partner's needs, evoking concerns about the demands of intimacy that often conflicted with chronic tendencies toward independence and affiliation. Braiker and Kelley (1979) and Driscoll, Davis and Lipetz (1972) also reported an increase in interpersonal conflict, negativity and personal ambivalence as people became aware of their growing dependency on each other. The incidence of conflict was orthogonal to feelings of love and apparently was not a harbinger of the demise of the relationship (as even the confused participants themselves might have concluded).

Kelley (1983) has argued that as *interdependence* increases, objective incompatibilities are more likely to surface not only at the behavioral level, but at the level of personal styles and attitudes. People start to confront issues of commitment, whether the partner is the kind of person they wish 'to spend a lifetime with'. Concerns about independence may provoke feelings of ambivalence and any apparent asymmetry in involvement that results may lead to open conflict.

Some people may avoid these rather turbulent experiences, but most will come to recognize that their relationship is different from the fantasy they once envisioned. This accommodation process need not diminish the relationship even if it promotes open conflict. It is the final testing ground for trust, an opportunity to learn about a partner's reactions when interests seem opposed. In earlier stages it is often difficult to find optimal scenarios that are diagnostic of interpersonal motives because the preferences of intimates so often appear to correspond. These perceptions of similarity are sometimes projections fueled by attraction, but are more often a reflection of a biased sample of interaction situations. People manage their self-presentations, choose situations to enjoy together and avoid others that might highlight their differences. In this stage, the pressure of deeper levels of interdependence often exposes conflicts that previously could not have been anticipated.

Not only do events become more diagnostic, but emotions are magnified as couples shape their terms of endearment - the stakes are very high and the issues are often deeply rooted and tied to self-esteem. But as Braiker and Kelley (1979) put it, this period offers a platform for 'growth through conflict'. When vulnerabilities are running high, empathy and responsiveness by a partner are all the more meaningful and draw the couple together. Compromises and personal accommodations are attributed to the strength of attachment and in the same breath, bolster it. As the pair navigates this terrain by forging innovative arrangements tailored to their styles and needs, they are likely to develop a sense of the uniqueness of their relationship, that they have created something special.

This process does not merely involve an exchange of concessions between two fixed entities. It consists of mutual influence by two individuals who often discover that the experience of intimacy is self-defining, as well as affirming of some aspects of identity but not others. New preferences may evolve in the context of the relationship and some of the convergence between partners may constitute permanent changes in dispositions rather than simply adaptations to the other person (Borden & Levinger, 1990, Chapter 2). Sociologists in the interactionist tradition have gone so far as to argue that partners collude to construct a shared social reality, a 'little world that crystallizes through the conversational process with little apprehension by its authors' (Berger & Kellner, 1972).

There are several important themes in this analysis that I want to underline. First, the accommodation stage is a platform for confronting the issue of conflict over the conflict process itself, or meta-conflict (Braiker & Kelley, 1979). To the extent that a couple learns that they can deal effectively with issues, and with cooperative efforts feel closer, they will experience the security that derives from a sense of control over the fate of the relationship (Miller et al., 1986). In contrast, if issues are avoided and go underground because of a clash of styles for resolving conflicts, confidence is liable to be eroded and areas of vulnerability will linger.

Second, intimate partners increasingly tend to evaluate interactions on a dual basis, partly in terms of the concrete outcomes experienced but also in terms of the attitudes, the interpersonal tendencies revealed by the behavior (Kelley, 1983). An action may be valued more for the thoughtfulness and caring it expresses than for its substance. This process is likely to be marked during this stage, where people may value diagnostic information about the state of their relationship far more than particular rewards. Kelley argued that the affect evoked by a partner's behavior may then be derivative, linked to the perceived causes of the concrete event. For instance, a fight about doing the dishes may be fueled by interpreting the situation as a negotiation around power and sex roles in the relationship.

Situations diagnostic of trust. Certain types of situations highlight issues about trust. The features of these situations are structured so that partners' behaviors are likely to be construed as diagnostic of their attitudes. The prototypical situation focuses attention on whether a partner will accommodate his or her interests in a way that is responsive to the joint concerns of the pair. Several examples are depicted in matrix form in Figure 1.

In the first example, a modified Martyr scenario, individuals have a safe choice (A) that does not leave them dependent on a partner's actions and that assures a degree of equality in the outcomes. If instead people were to risk

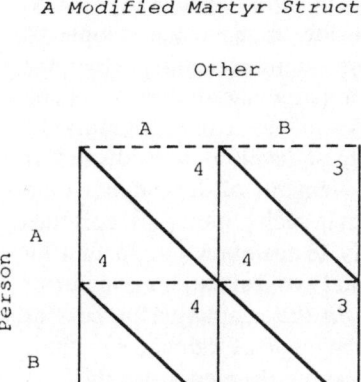 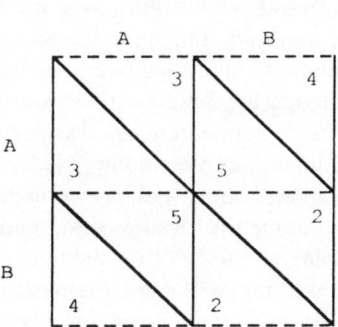

Figure 1. Situational structures that highlight issues of trust. (The number in the lower left of each cell reflects one's own outcome, the number in the upper right reflects one's partner's outcome.)

choosing option B which is more attuned to their needs, they become vulnerable to the other's desire to choose behavior A. Partners might do so to serve their self-interests, to minimize differences in outcomes, or to maximize their relative gain. Nevertheless, the risk might be accepted in the hope that the other would show concern for their needs and the joint welfare of the pair. The second example is a modified Hero scenario. If both persons act in their own short-term interest without taking the other into account, the pair will receive only moderate, but equal rewards (3,3). However, if either person steps forward and takes the initiative of selecting B, then both gain and the joint welfare of the couple is served. The cost involves receiving less than the other, even though the person's foresight and flexibility were responsible for the benefits.

In both of these examples, the message conveyed by a partner's willingness to sacrifice some form of self-interest and the derivative good feeling evoked by attributions of caring may be given far more weight than the substantive rewards represented in the situation. In the Martyr case, the outcome of 6 might have a transformed, symbolic value that was far greater to the person. Also, the perception would be strengthened that the partner had reacted to the (6,3) configuration as if it were perhaps (6,5), reflecting an understanding of the partner's personal satisfaction in being able to respond to the person's needs: Your happiness is ultimately mine.

This representation captures events only at a fixed point in time and fails to adequately portray the temporal and sequential aspects of trust central to a prospective model. Kelley (1984) used the term *transition control* to describe the tendency for outcomes in a particular episode to shape the sample of situations people choose to enter over time. From the present perspective, the positive affect resulting from successful risk-taking motivates individuals to be less cautious and exercise less control in moving into a broader range of encounters involving potential vulnerability. As trust develops, it results in less vigilance for features of situations that contain elements of dependency on a partner's good intentions. However, if experiences in such prototypical episodes fail to reduce uncertainty, individuals are likely to maintain a tight rein on transition control and have a readiness to detect and avoid situations that mirror their concerns. Kelley described such failures in the adaptation process as causing a 'lifestyle' for the relationship, where the range of intimate situations that partners will risk is narrowed and certain areas are deemed 'off limits'.

Faith and the need for closure. When all is said and done, a sense of conviction or psychological closure about a partner's attachment is seldom fully warranted by the evidence that is available. This is because trust is prospective in nature, and there will be times when the future does not mirror the past. People and circumstances change and feelings do not always remain constant as relationships confront the strains of new and unforeseen forces. Also, the evaluation of a partner typically leaves a residue of ambivalence, particularly during the accommodation stage. Imperfections mar the once shimmering surface of the relationship and subtle strains are experienced in domains where incompatibility in interpersonal styles remains unresolved. Inserted into this equation is the ultimate point of comparison: Do I live up to my partner's ideals for the right mate?

Rempel, Holmes and Zanna (1985) speculated that at some point most people need to act as if a sense of security were justified, and set their doubts aside. To do so requires a 'leap of faith', in the face of evidence that can never be conclusive. Thus trust becomes a necessary construction, an emotionally-charged sense of closure. It permits an illusion of control, an intimate life free from continual uncertainty, where one can plan ahead without anxiety - a more permanent peace. As Jones and Gerard (1967, p.181) put it, a sense of conviction allows us to avoid being 'forced to listen to the babble of competing inner voices'.

Although faith is built on the firm foundations developed during the reciprocal attachment process, it is still an aspect of trust that is in part a personal rather than an interpersonal construction. It is an internal construction in service of imposing some order on an unruly set of feelings, and it is likely to reflect properties that are an outcome of the integrative process itself. Holmes and Rempel (1986) predicted that the attitude structure of trusting individuals will show a high degree of affective-cognitive consistency, particularly among symbolic attitudes about a partner's attachment. Beliefs and affect about the other's responsiveness, affection and intrinsic motivation, for instance, are expected to show a coherent pattern, simple in form and high in redundancy among its elements. In contrast, the organization of the structure would be looser and less consistent at levels less central to its function (e.g., Wyer & Srull, 1986). For example, beliefs about a partner's dependability and predictability were described as less critical to the goal of felt security than beliefs about attachment. These and other attributes viewed by people as less relevant to trust would show less evidence of integration in the hierarchical structure.

On the other hand, the process of defining the relevance of particular characteristics may in itself be a consequence of efforts at synthesis and the resolution of ambivalence (Holmes & Rempel, 1986). A woman in one of our studies treated a husband's reluctance to share his feelings with her as having little relevance to her sense of trust: 'He's a rather closed type of man, but that's not so important. He shows he cares in other ways'. Thus she essentially disavowed or encapsulated that aspect of him, limiting its implications and relegating it to a lower rung in the hierarchical structure. Another woman seemed to turn a lack of expressiveness in her partner into a virtue: 'He's a strong, silent man, that's why I can depend on him'. In this case, a subtle shift in meaning enabled her to maintain her convictions.

I suspect that negative elements and experiences like these are often integrated into the attitude structures of people with a strong sense of trust, and that this is an active and continuing process. Consistent with this view, Chaiken and Yates (1985) demonstrated that individuals with attitudes showing strong affective-cognitive consistency on an issue reacted to challenges to their beliefs by assimilating discrepant information. They did this by generating refutational thoughts that enhanced their attitudes, discrediting the information or minimizing its importance. In the present context, people have recourse to a wide variety of such attributional mechanisms to shield themselves against any adverse implications for the relationship itself.

Thus the hypothesis is that trust involves coming to terms with the negative aspects of a partner, accepting or perhaps tolerating issues by buffering them in the broader context of positive elements. In an 'economy of surplus', to use Levinger's (1979) phrase, one can be generous. In large part then, the consequence of a successful formulation process is a relatively integrated structure, one that avoids the separation of cognition or affect into positive and negative compartments in domains critical to trust. The strength or fragility of the solution depends of course on the degree to which people are removing the sting of their lingering doubts by suppressing them or denying their importance, rather than by consolidating them into a unified representation with all that is positive.

Brickman (1987) has argued cogently that an important consequence of forming a synthesis is that it then becomes harder for people to think of its constituent parts in isolation. His point is that the integration of elements often serves the purpose of masking ambivalence, which then leaves people open to sudden swings in emotion if the construction becomes unravelled. It is an important point, but the occurrence of such 'catastrophes' hinges on the degree to which people have had to stretch the fabric of their perceptions and feelings to achieve a sense of closure. If the integration was firmly anchored by experiences in the mutual attachment process and was woven without disavowal of major issues connected to trust, then I would expect it to be relatively impervious to challenges to its integrity.

For many people a sense of faith in their partner may be an elusive goal. Their interpersonal history with a partner or their personal issues about trusting may make it difficult to forge a more permanent peace between their reasons to trust and their reasons to doubt. Some individuals may develop a close approximation, but be unable to dispel their residual fears or to surmount them by leaning on their hopes. Pockets of ambivalence may leave people feeling uncertain, caught in an approach/avoidance conflict in terms of allowing themselves to take the risk of truly depending on their partners, with no questions asked.

Alternatively, individuals may not achieve even this level of integration, where at least the positive and negative aspects of their feelings in important domains are in contact with each other. Instead, the hurts and fears may be relatively compartmentalized, isolated from areas of positive affect. If there is only a weak integration of component attitudes in the associational network involving trust, situations might prime a negative category without also priming the broader range of positive feelings about a partner's attachment that could moderate a person's overall reactions. Thus people would be susceptible to a 'splitting' of their attitudes, to polar swings in emotion of the sort described earlier in the reactions of anxious/ambivalent or merger individuals. This notion is similar in some ways to the psychoanalytic idea of ambivalence/amplification, where one side of people's feelings is suppressed while the other is enhanced.

Trust and love. Driscoll et al. (1972) and Dion and Dion (1976) reported that love and trust were associated more strongly in married than in dating couples, and suggested the change was due to a shift from romantic to conjugal love. Conjugal love supposedly reflects people's more temperate, integrated view of a partner, and it would be expected to develop hand in hand with the faith component of trust. However, Larzelere and Huston (1980) noted that during the period when couples were cementing their commitment, when they were engaged, cohabiting or newlywed, the correlation between love and trust dropped dramatically. They speculated that this relates to the turbulence experienced during the later parts of the accommodation stage, as couples come to realize that their attributions must now take into account a dramatically lengthened period of time.

This explanation is not fully satisfactory, because their own data indicated that trust itself remained high during the accommodation phase. From my perspective, people's appraisals of a partner indeed become truly prospective in nature as the issue of commitment surfaces. As this occurs, factors relevant to trust but independent of love enter the picture as I suggested earlier. For instance, people must adapt to potential incompatibility in their interpersonal styles, including their ways of handling conflict. Braiker and Kelley (1979) reported that conflict and feelings of ambivalence were both unrelated to feelings of love during this period. But successful accommodation would be expected to have a constructive impact on trust; however uncomfortable the adjustments may be, they provide the arena for building confidence in a partner's responsiveness and the couple's ability to communicate and surmount problems together. The Larzelere and Huston data thus lead me to speculate that there are periods when love and trust grow independently and that the consolidation of attitudes is a process that extends through into marriage, eventually restoring the link between love and trust.

THE IMPACT OF TRUST IN ESTABLISHED RELATIONSHIPS

Trust is not a static concept, an edifice that once erected simply continues to provide a warm place to house a relationship. One might get that impression however, given the dearth of research focusing on the impact of different levels of trust on experiences in established relationships. Studies have dealt almost exclusively with the development of feelings of security rather than the consequences. In this section I hope to take a step in the direction of remedying this imbalance by considering the dynamics of trust, its influence on the process of interpersonal evaluation in marriages.

Earlier I presented the notion that in the appraisal process, behavior is coded both at the concrete level and at the level of its symbolic value (Kelley, 1983). But what are the psychological origins of the meaning that gets attached to a partner's actions? The hypothesis guiding my thinking is that the symbolic value of specific behaviors is often generated in a top-down fashion, by the general feelings of trust that exist in the relationship. People's central attitudes about their partners' motives are thus expected to color their interpretations of events. This idea is best explained by portraying the interpretative styles displayed by people at various levels of trust.

The Appraisal Process of High Trust Individuals

The interpretative process of trusting individuals is shaped by their sense of confidence in the partner's attachment to the relationship. This implies that the core of the other's motives is not at issue, is not a current concern. Thus there is little reason to monitor behavior for diagnostic signs of caring. A trusting relationship can probably be recognized by the absence of an active appraisal process in the normal course of events (Holmes, 1981). Second, trust serves to dampen or buffer the impact of particular behaviors because they are likely to be given little weight or meaning in the broader scheme of things. Against the elaborate backdrop of people's firmly anchored expectations, single events add little that does not seem redundant.

A wide range of positive behaviors by a partner is liable to be assimilated to these benevolent expectations, and credited as further examples of the other's good intentions. I might add that there is a potential cost to this process if the coding becomes relatively automatic and little depth of elaboration takes place. Acts of caring may be taken for granted and lose their emotional punch (Berscheid, 1983). In contrast, negative behaviors are typically relegated to lower levels of concern by limiting their implications for deeper relationship issues. This charitable orientation rests on the premise that trusting individuals do not treat a partner's central motives as an open question. Behavioral transgressions can therefore be more easily endured because they have already been discounted in advance, in attributional terms. For example, an argument over household chores may cause very real frustration at the behavioral level. However, the sting is largely removed because the conflict is not interpreted as a sign that the other doesn't really care.

Even recurring negative aspects of a partner's behavior are often integrated into the attitude structure in a way that shields people from any adverse implications for their core attitudes. In the housework example, the wife may indeed see the husband as lazy or pampered by his rather traditional mother. She thus reverts to dispositional or normative attributions at lower, less threatening levels in the trust structure. Any anger coupled to even these conclusions could be further drained by refutational thoughts of the 'yes, but' kind: 'He's lazy about cooking, but he's really considerate about helping with the children'. His transgressions only serve to remind her of his virtues! These various mechanisms play a self-fulfilling role in maintaining people's confidence.

Despite these tendencies, events may sometimes conspire to more seriously challenge or threaten their beliefs. When this happens, a more active appraisal process will be triggered. The outcome of this process is liable to be largely overdetermined, unless the partner's actions truly merit suspicion. This is because the hypothesis being tested is framed at the abstract level - does my partner really care? The evidence is at a specific, behavioral level and the translation of it into diagnostic form is subject to considerable poetic licence. Like a centripetal force, the weight of the past will be brought to bear on the present and a confirmatory bias is most likely to result.

Trust not only influences people's reactions in specific encounters, but it also shapes the *psychological perspective* adopted in the overall evaluation process (Holmes, 1981). Trusting individuals tend to assess the flow of events in a relationship over a more extended period of time. Their broad time perspective has the effect of stabilizing perceptions. Conclusions are moderated by aggregating the balance of rewards and costs over the longer term because this accounting practice itself has a levelling effect on impressions of momentary disturbances, smoothing out the ups and downs of everyday experience. Larger samples of behavior provide more stable inferences and give the appearance of less volatility in behavior. This is not to suggest that trusting individuals consciously calibrate a current ledger. Rather, their sense of security tends to free them from concerns with monitoring contributions, permitting a looser, less deliberate accounting based on feelings of general satisfaction.

The Appraisal Process of Individuals Uncertain about Trusting

Individuals with more moderate levels of trust, who feel uncertain or ambivalent about a partner's motives, present a rather different picture. If they are motivated to reduce this uncertainty and attain closure, their concerns will lead them to test actively the hypothesis that the partner cares for them and is responsive to their needs. Thus these individuals are expected to be relatively vigilant and to monitor behavior for any diagnostic signs. There are competing influences on the appraisal process, however.

On the one hand, their emotional investment in the relationship leads them to be hopeful, primed to detect clear positive evidence of caring and to have the hypothesis confirmed. On the other hand, their hopes are constrained by feelings of vulnerability, by the risk of drawing positive conclusions that aren't justified, and being hurt, perhaps once again. These concerns are likely to result in hardened criteria for accepting positive behavior as truly diagnostic of corresponding motives of caring in the partner. This conservative inference process of requiring relatively unequivocal behavioral evidence is rather like setting a high alpha level in statistical terms. I suspect that individuals who have lingering anxieties related to experiences of rejection in their present or previous relationships would be most hesitant and risk avoidant in drawing positive conclusions.

At first blush this may seem like a confusing if not contradictory portrait. But it is one that captures the approach/avoidance conflict that these individuals are caught in. The emotional tone of their relationships is expected to reflect this latent conflict, resulting in an unstable dialectic between polarities of feeling as they focus on one side of their attitudes or the other. This tendency will be most pronounced in people who show little evidence of having consolidated their hopes and fears, as I suggested earlier. On the one extreme, uncertain individuals will be reactive to positive behaviors. They are both ready to detect positive signs and to code them for their relevance to larger issues. Thus their positive affect often derives from the process of attaching meaning to the behavior, seeing it as a sign of caring. To compound matters, the more limited, short-term perspective evoked by their uncertainty may also serve to amplify their feelings. A positive experience can more easily take center stage, without being absorbed into the broader context of expected events as just one more credit in an already healthy bank account.

However, these same three tendencies add to the emotional impact of negative experiences as well. Compared to trusting individuals, uncertain individuals are likely to be more vigilant and primed to interpret a wide range of acts in a negative way. The hurt will be greater because of their willingness to consider the implications of a partner's negative behavior for deeper issues about caring. Their refutational structure is less capable of placing limits on the generalization process, of containing the damage at lower levels of concern. Finally, the more narrow frame of reference of these individuals intensifies the impact of negative behavior, by allowing it to loom larger in the figure to ground context. Their limited perspective essentially promotes overdrawn inferences, because restricted but vivid samples of behavior will tend to bias their perceptions.

People's vulnerability to such tendencies will depend on the relative strength and integration of their positive and negative expectations, and the depth of their concerns about avoiding rejection. As positive expectations consolidate and the balance shifts, negative construals should drop out more rapidly, undercut by the stabilizing influence of hopefulness about their prospects. However, I suspect that the avoidance gradient often becomes steeper as uncertain individuals approach a state of reaching a positive conclusion. The spectre of things going well reminds people of the costs of their being wrong, and to remove their final doubts they may show remnants of their former defensive styles of attribution.

The Appraisal Process of Low Trust Couples

Compared to couples at other levels of trust, low trust couples may already have experienced some of the heavy emotional costs of taking risks in their relationships and feeling disappointed or even betrayed. A lack of trust in established relationships usually implies that a crisis of confidence has occurred. The decline may sometimes be dramatic, but more often it involves an accumulation of violated expectations about their partners' responsiveness and caring that exceeds the thresholds of tolerance. As confidence erodes, people develop a sense of defensive pessimism to protect themselves against further risk and being hurt, once again.

In some ways, their attitudes are a mirror image of those of high trust individuals. They are likely to have a relatively closed mind and to react as if they have concluded that the partner is not truly concerned about them or the relationship. Positive behavior by the other will be viewed with suspicion. Low trust couples may retain some residual hopes, but they understand all too well the risks of drawing positive conclusions about their partners' motives that later prove to be unwarranted. Their fears of being let down again make them vigilant for signs of negative attitudes. Conversely, negative behavior by the partner is likely to prime these fears and be interpreted as further evidence that their pessimism and caution are justified.

A RESEARCH STRATEGY

These various ideas about the impact of trust in established relationships are complex and obviously very difficult to test in any direct fashion. In order to get some leverage on the issues, a research strategy is needed that provides data on both people's affective reactions to particular behaviors by their partners and their perceptions and attributions of what had taken place during an interaction episode. To accomplish these goals, Holmes and Rempel (1986) designed a novel set of procedures for measuring the impact of levels of trust on people's reactions to their partners' behavior during a problem-solving session in a laboratory setting.

The problem with simply observing couples with different levels of trust in this way is that the design is essentially correlational in nature, as are almost all studies in the marital interaction literature. This descriptive approach has provided some impressive insights, but there are inherent limitations in using it to narrow the range of causal interpretations. Thus it seemed worth taking the risk of trying to identify experimental conditions that might put differences in trust into sharper relief by making certain feelings about partners very salient.

I have argued that the foundations of trust involve people's experiences of their partners' responsiveness in situations of uncertainty, usually involving conflict or risk. Our research strategy was to remind people in a vivid way of either the darker or the brighter side of these types of experiences before their discussion of a serious issue in their relationship. Our goal was to selectively focus on only one side of the beliefs they harbor, to evoke a set of feelings associated with an acute sense of either trust or distrust. Thus we hoped to clarify the dynamics of trust by facilitating the accessibility of different aspects of their chronic beliefs with these two types of relationship memories. I might add that the recapitulation of relationship memories and their ability to intrude on the present is an issue worthy of consideration in its own right.

The Methodology

Eighty couples who had been living together for at least two years were asked to take part in a study on marital problem solving. After an introduction to the research, participants completed a Trust Scale (Rempel et al., 1985) and a Problem Inventory designed to flag the area of stress or disagreement that caused the most difficulty in their relationship. The experimenters selected the issue for discussion while the partners engaged in a five-minute warm-up exercise to accustom them to the idea of being videotaped. After we specified the topic, we asked each person to complete a short questionnaire comprised of semantic differential items probing expectations about the partner's behavior and motives, in the context of the forthcoming problem-solving session. A fifteen-minute discussion of the identified issue then ensued.

After a short break, we seated each person at a table facing a TV monitor. A button-box with four keys was placed on each table and interfaced with a microcomputer in an adjacent room. The color videotape of the couple's discussion was then played, and we asked each person to rate any of the partner's behaviors 'that had some impact on you, resulting in either positive or negative feelings.' Thus people were requested to segment or punctuate the interaction in the units that had most meaning to them. Their *affective ratings* could range from very negative, to moderately negative, to moderately positive or very positive. This on-line procedure for measuring people's immediate evaluative expressions provided us with a valuable time line of responses to specific behaviors. People's spontaneous reactions to events could later be compared to their retrospective, overall appraisals of the interaction.

Following the replay procedure, participants completed the same set of semantic differential scales that had been administered prior to the interaction. In this case, we asked them for their perceptions of the partner's actual behavior during the interaction, and then their inferences about the other's motives for acting that way. I will discuss the nature of these questions when the results are presented.

The experimental conditions. The experimental manipulation was administered to each participant in the privacy of a separate room, just before the start of the couple's discussion. In the *Positive Recall* condition we tried to prime a vivid memory of a stressful incident where a partner showed evidence of being responsive to the person's needs. Each person was asked to 'Think back to a time when you faced a conflict or disagreement between you that for the most part was successfully resolved. We are interested in getting you to remember a problem which seemed difficult, but your partner responded positively to your concerns and came through as you had hoped.'

Participants were given a minute to recall a specific incident of this type. They were reminded to think of an example where the partner made an effort to be considerate and was responsive to their feelings. We then asked them to describe the incident and to recall the particular things the partner did that left them feeling good about the experience. The whole procedure took only about five minutes and was recorded on audio tape.

The instructions for the *Negative Recall* task were almost identical to those in the Positive Recall condition, except of course, for certain key phrases. In this case, we asked individuals to think of an example where the partner did not respond positively to their needs, where they were left feeling that they had not really dealt with the problem. They were also asked about the particular things the partner did that left them feeling disappointed with the experience.

For purposes of comparison, a *Control* group was included in the design. Participants in this condition were simply given several minutes to consider the issues before the discussion took place. Eighty couples were recruited for the study from a wide variety of sources. The large sample was very heterogeneous in composition, across such factors as social class, education and age.

The Pattern of Results

As a first step, couples were classified as high, medium or low trust on the basis of their total Trust Scale scores. The conservative criterion of total couple scores was used because partners' responses were likely to be dependent on what occurred in the dyad and because the present conception of trust focuses on the emotional tone in the relationship itself. Whatever the case, the results are substantially the same if the categorization is done on the basis of individual scores. The middle tertile of couples was thought to approximate pairs I have been describing as uncertain, with residual ambivalence about trusting. The low-trust label for the bottom tertile is probably justified: Locke-Wallace marital adjustment scores for these couples were typically in the range considered to be clinically distressed.

Expectations. Couples at each level of trust had very different expectations as they entered their discussion period. People had been asked to rate themselves and their partners on a series of scales reflecting both the behavior they anticipated in the interaction and the motives they felt would represent the attitudes behind such actions. In both cases, seven-item composite scores were created by averaging scales that loaded cleanly on an evaluative cluster in a factor analysis. For example, *behavior* was described on seven-point scales as pleasant/unpleasant, helpful/hurtful, positive/negative and agreeable/angry. Attributions about *motives* were made on scales indicating causes such as a positive/negative attitude, compassion/hostility, a considerate/self-centered attitude and tolerance/intolerance.

Table 1. Expectations about Motives as a Function of Trust and Target

Trust Level	Self	Partner	Partner-Self
High	5.14	5.36	+.22
Medium	4.67	4.70	+.03
Low	4.31	4.09	−.22

Expectations for behavior and motives showed the same pattern. The results for motives are displayed in Table 1 and support the notion that dyadic trust is associated with importing very different assumptions into interactions. People viewed both their own and their partners' motives as more suspect as trust decreased. Also, self versus partner attributions interacted significantly with level of trust. Low trust individuals seemed defensively pessimistic and judged their partners' attitudes even more harshly than their own. The correlation between self and partner attributions in this group was -.26. This means that people who credited themselves with good intentions were especially likely to blame their partners for the anticipated poor outcome. In contrast, high trust individuals were generous in their assumptions, expecting their partners' motives to be even more positive than their own. This sense of optimism about the mutuality of good intentions seemed to be bolstered by some amount of projection on their part. The correlation between own intentions and perceptions of the partner's intentions in this group was +.76, whereas the correlation with the partner's actual intentions was not significant. In any case, high trust couples appeared to enter the discussion ready to give each other every benefit of the doubt.

Affective responses to partners' behavior. With such divergent expectations, it is perhaps not surprising that people's reactions to the partner's behavior during the interaction might be colored by their level of trust. The average affect ratings made during the on-line replay procedure are depicted in Table 2. The ratings were scaled from 1 to 4, with 4 representing a very positive rating. The neutral point was 2.5.

Table 2. Spontaneous Affective Responses to the Partner's Behavior

Measure		Level of Trust		
	Source	*Low*	*Medium*	*High*
Mean Affect Rating	Couples	2.40	2.41	2.64
	Judges	2.43	2.52	2.62
Percent Negative Affect	Couples	54.9	54.4	43.3
	Judges	53.2	42.6	37.5

The couples' ratings clearly discriminate between high and low trust groups, but the medium couples closely resemble the low trust ones in terms of their emotional reactions to events. These findings contrast with ratings made by independent judges focusing on the same behaviors. This yoking procedure was accomplished by having the computer signal the trained observers to make ratings at the same points in time as the spouses. The yoked judges clearly saw the medium trust couples as acting more positively than the low trust pairs. This pattern is even more apparent when we examine the total proportion of responses across the two negative categories. In this case, the medium trust group is closest to the high trust one in the eyes of the observers, but obviously not from the perspective of the couples.

Table 3: Trust and the extreme affect categories

Percentage of total responses	Level of trust		
	Low	Medium	High
Very negative	16.82	16.79	7.20
Very positive	12.50	15.47	18.96
Difference score	-4.32	-1.30	+11.76

In Table 3 the results for the two extreme response categories are depicted. High trust pairs, as expected, were largely characterized by the small amount of *very negative affect* they experienced, even when dealing with a problem they identified as very difficult for them. In contrast, the medium trust pairs reported dramatically more strong negative affect, as much as the low trust couples. However, they did acknowledge some more positive feelings than the lows, with the cumulative effect that they reported the largest total percent of extreme affect ratings of any group.

I want to highlight the fact that for couples, it was only in the use of the two extreme affect categories that the differences among levels of trust became apparent. This finding is important because the triggers for this strong affect appear to have resided in the private agendas of particular couples. The independent judges were quite unable to track the couples' extreme reactions, in spite of a robust degree of agreement on the other two categories.

In summary, the judges' ratings suggest that couples across each of the three levels of trust did in fact behave differently during the discussions. In contrast to these findings, medium trust couples reacted to their partners with as strong negative affect as the low trust couples. I would speculate that medium trust couples are particularly sensitive to the symbolic content of behavior, as suggested earlier. High trust pairs were marked by their tendency to dampen such negative reactions, whereas lows were unique in their inability to experience very positive feelings toward their partners.

Evaluations of the partner's behavior and motives. Before we examine couples' overall evaluations after the interaction, it is important to consider the manipulation check results across experimental conditions. The recall sessions were recorded on audio tape and coded by judges blind to the experimental induction. The incidents recounted by individuals in the Negative Recall condition were rated as very significantly more negative and more upsetting than those in the Positive Recall condition. The example chosen was also coded as a more serious concern, representing a recurring theme from the deeper past. Clearly people seem to have memories like elephants for past hurts. There was much evidence of spontaneous attributions, with subjects in the Negative Recall condition assigning more blame to both partners' attitudes and dispositions. There were no effects of level of trust on these measures or on ease of recall ratings.

These results indicate that the recall procedure was successful in eliciting different types of relationship memories. We will now explore how these memories affected the perceptions of people with different levels of trust. The dependent measure is the change score from pretest expectations to posttest appraisals of partners. The scales for expectations were described previously. In the case of the post-discussion appraisals, the measures reflect people's perceptions of their partners' behavior during the interaction, and attributions about their partners' motives for acting the way they did. The overall effect is a very significant interaction involving trust level and condition, modified by behavior versus motive ratings.

The results for evaluations by *low trust couples* are presented in Figure 2. Looking at the graph, it is obvious that perceptions of behavior were not affected by the manipulations. The pessimistic behavioral expectations of low trust individuals appear to firmly anchor their evaluations. These couples had little reason to be selectively vigilant for new answers to an old, and probably sore

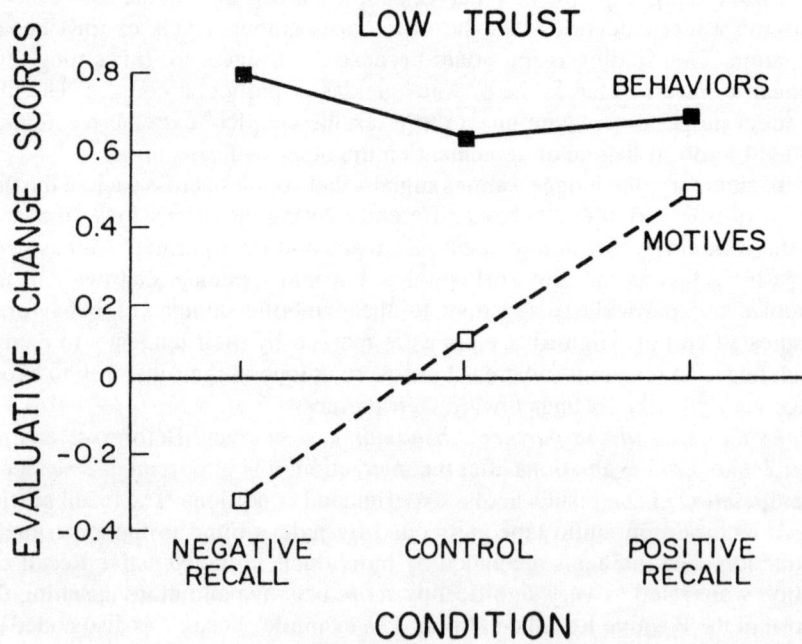

Figure 2. The impact of recall conditions on low trust couples' evaluations of their partners' behavior and motives.

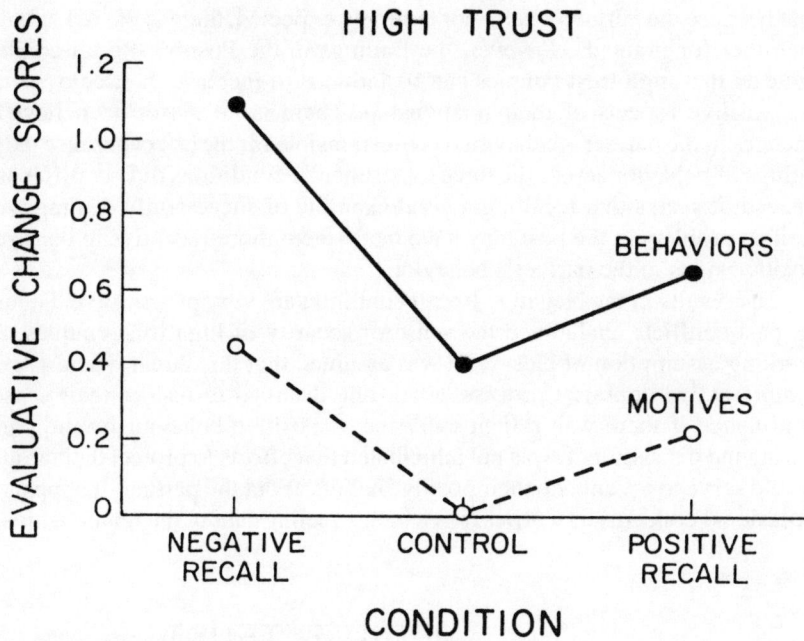

Figure 3. The impact of recall conditions on high trust couples' evaluations of their partners' behavior and motives.

question. Their appraisals of motives, however, were strongly influenced by remembering their past, in a way that seems unconstrained by their descriptions of behavior.

In the Negative Recall condition, it was expected that the focused recall would prime a wider constellation of unhappy memories in low trust people, relating to a more intense history of disappointments and feelings of rejection. The results indicate that their past can easily cloud the present, cogently reminding them of the risks involved in depending on the partner's good intentions. The findings in the Positive Recall condition were quite unexpected. Even low trust couples seem to retain some vestige of hope, and remembering their strengths seems to have given them the courage to be generous in their attributions for their partner's behavior.

The next graph shows the results for *high trust couples* (Figure 3). The close correspondence between the behavior and motive ratings suggests that impressions of behavior were taken at face value in terms of granting credit to the partner. Second, their change scores in the Control condition were the lowest of all groups, indicating that events unfolded very much as they expected. High trust individuals had little reason to either accentuate or elaborate positive behavior that only confirmed their convictions. This pattern of results warns us that because the partner's behavior is simply expected, there is the risk of taking the other for granted. However, the findings in the Positive Recall condition indicate that high trust couples can be induced to increase their enjoyment of the positive aspects of their relationship. There is no reason to believe that changes in the partner's behavior were responsible for the effect because judges' ratings of behavior across the three experimental conditions did not differ at all. Instead, it seems that recalling a vivid example of successfully dealing with a serious problem in the past may have made them more receptive to construing positive signs in the partner's behavior.

The results in the Negative Recall condition are very provocative. Focusing on past conflicts challenged the sense of security of high trust couples, their working assumption of closure. It was assumed that this threat would provoke a more active appraisal process, albeit one destined to restore their sense of confidence if there was salient evidence of positive behavior by the partner during the discussion. It was not anticipated that efforts to protect their attitudes would serve to accentuate their positive beliefs about the partner. It appears that occasional concerns or worries may vitalize feelings about the relationships and

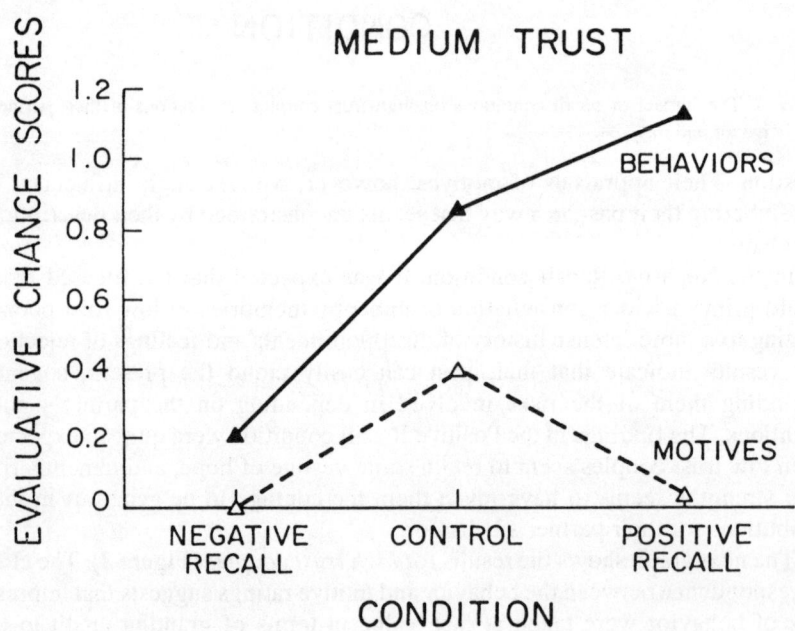

Figure 4. The impact of recall conditions on medium trust couples' evaluations of their partners' behavior and motives.

somehow throw them into sharper relief. One could speculate that negative experiences have the power to resurrect a fuller spectrum of feelings for trusting couples in a way that positive ones do not. Thus the impact of a deeper elaboration of their convictions about trust is to polarize their attitudes, as long as the challenge can be absorbed by their refutational framework (Chaiken & Yates, 1985).

The results for the medium trust, *uncertain couples* are perhaps the most fascinating (Figure 4). In the Negative Recall condition, a readiness to attend to and interpret behaviors in a negative way was expected when feelings of vulnerability were made salient, when anxieties about trusting were primed. Compared to similar couples in the Control condition, these individuals in fact seemed more sensitive to portraying the negative side of the partner's behavior. They also tended to construe the other's motives in an equally dark way, perhaps adding a surfeit of meaning where it was not warranted. Unlike couples in the high trust group, there was no evidence of the negative memory being buffered by the positive side of their attitudes.

Finally, uncertain couples in the Positive Recall condition showed a pattern of results that is encouraging for the present theoretical perspective. They showed evidence of being very ready to perceive their partners as behaving positively, in line with the hopes we had primed. On the other hand, they also showed rather extreme hesitation in drawing conclusions about the other's good intentions. Their evaluations of motives actually decreased significantly compared to the Control condition. It is as if when things appear to be going too well, ambivalent individuals pull back and harden their criteria for reaching positive conclusions. The spectre of feeling close to a partner seems to be inextricably linked to an associated set of anxieties about the risk of not truly having one's hopes realized. Indeed, avoidance motives seem to become salient as uncertain couples approach the point of making positive attributions.

If the results for the different groups are examined together, it becomes clear that the Negative Recall condition acted like a stressor in polarizing people's reactions, exposing their attitude structures in a way that clearly discriminated the three levels of trust. When people's scores on our Trust Scale were simply correlated with their overall evaluations of their partners' motives in this condition, the coefficient was .65, accounting for 42% of the variance. It appears that trust is truly diagnostic of people's appraisals when unhappy memories from the past intrude on the present and underline the risks of depending on their partners. The contrasting correlation in the Control condition was .34, accounting for less than 12% of the variance.

The final topic to consider is the relation between people's overall evaluations and their affective responses to particular behaviors on the part of their partners. What type of process links the sequence of discrete emotional reactions to the general impressions that people reported? The average affect rating correlated .37 with changes in evaluations of the partner's behavior from pre-discussion expectations. However, only negative ratings on the button box were predictive of people's appraisals. The influence of strongly negative reactions was the most pronounced, in spite of the low frequency of such extreme ratings. In the Control condition, the correlation was a rather startling -.56. The correlations in both Recall conditions were significantly lower. Thus it appears that thoughts about the past in the Recall conditions activated attitude structures related to trust that interfered with the process linking feelings and general impressions.

SUMMARY AND IMPLICATIONS

The Impact of a Breakdown in Trust

The portrayal of low trust individuals painted by the results is a rather depressing one. They entered the interaction with a sense of dread and pessimism, expecting little of themselves and even less of their partners. The outcome seemed preordained and the judges' ratings suggest their behavior in fact lived down to their expectations. In their affect ratings they seemed to experience strong emotions largely when they felt hurt, seldom when they felt happy. When the recall manipulation reminded them of the unhappy side of their past, low trust couples were particularly inclined to distrust their partners' motives. Thoughts about such relationship concerns may be close to the surface and have an intrusive quality in their every day lives, leaving people vulnerable to interpreting events in line with their fears.

To our surprise, positive memories induced low trust couples to be more generous in their attributions, but there was no evidence of any behavioral change that might support any hopes for a sense of closeness. Holmes and Rempel (1989) argued that any remaining hopes are often undercut by the self-fulfilling nature of a lack of trust. As people's fears grow, they are tempted to take out various forms of security insurance to protect themselves against the rising tide of risk. They essentially move to decrease interdependence in the relationship (Levinger, 1979) by forging an implicit social contract that puts their fate less in the hands of the partner (Holmes, 1981). Rules evolve to protect people's interests in contentious areas and more vulnerable domains are simply deemed off limits and avoided. The exchange process becomes less flexible and more measured as the issue of the partner's willingness to be responsive increases in salience. The theme is that more effort is expended at controlling situations to ensure that one's needs are met, reducing dependency on the partner.

These tendencies indicate that people are withdrawing psychologically from the relationship. As an aversion to taking risks grows, problems in the relationship are dealt with more superficially in an arm's-length, avoidant way. Rempel

(1987) studied the spontaneous attributional statements made by couples during their discussions. He found that low trust couples actually avoided focusing on contentious current issues and instead provided explanations for specific, less stable events from the past. This lack of commitment to confronting ongoing issues in the relationship removes the opportunity to restore trust by showing concern and caring. As people pull back, diminished evidence of concern by one person is likely to be reciprocated by the other, creating a reality that mirrors their fears.

Distortions in the Process of Ambivalence Reduction

Uncertain individuals showed evidence of the ambivalent, volatile reactions that were anticipated. Their perceptions of the partner's behavior were controlled in an almost linear fashion by our experimental manipulation of the different sides of their feelings. Their susceptibility to such influence is consistent with the view that their attitudes are not affectively consolidated. Positive and negative aspects of their approach/avoidance conflict can be primed more or less independently because their views are relatively compartmentalized. These results are also consistent with the idea that uncertain individuals engage in an active appraisal process that involves a readiness to attend to both positive and negative signs of caring in their partners' behavior.

This tendency to be more reactive to the perceived tone of the partner's behavior was also evident in their negative affective responses during the video replay procedure. However, in this case the pattern of results for positive affect ratings did not conform to what was predicted. Uncertain couples made fewer strongly positive responses than high trust couples, though more than low trust pairs. One explanation for these results is that the discussion of a very serious relationship problem, for the most part, tended to underline the concerns and doubts of individuals who were ambivalent. Alternatively, the context may have provided fewer opportunities for feeling very good about the partner's behavior than would occur in their every day lives.

Their reactivity to perceived negative behavior by the partner was very apparent, however. These couples often responded with anger in their ratings of behavior, expressing extremely negative feelings as frequently as the low trust pairs. The independent judges were not able to discern the triggers for these reactions, and actually rated the partner's negative behavior as more closely resembling that of high trust individuals. The implications of these findings are important because people's overall evaluations were tied to the experience of negative but not positive affect in reaction to their partners' behavior (e.g., Levenson & Gottman, 1985). In summary, uncertain couples seemed vulnerable to interpreting behavior in a negative way and to reacting strongly to it. These tendencies were predicted from the assumption that they bring a limited perspective to the appraisal process and consider the implications of particular events for deeper issues about caring. They seem unable to apply the cumulative weight of past experience and their hopes for the future in a balanced way that would drain the significance from a moment in time.

Couples who are ambivalent also seemed trapped in their uncertainty by a critical asymmetry in the types of conclusions they were willing to draw about their partners' motives. In the Positive Recall condition, they evaluated the partner's behavior very positively, but were extremely hesitant to grant any credit for it. In contrast, they were all too ready to blame the partner's motives for the negative behavior they perceived in the Negative Recall condition. Rempel (1987) found a similar theme when he focused on attributions that were actually communicated by uncertain couples during their discussions. Their dialogues contained more very negative and fewer very positive attributional statements than did those of either high or low trust couples. In addition, they made more global and fewer specific attributions for very negative events than did other couples.

It may be the case that for uncertain couples, the threshold differs for drawing positive and negative inferences. A risk-aversive strategy seems to predominate, as though people were framing the hypothesis being tested as, 'Will my partner demonstrate that he or she cannot really be counted on to respond to my needs'. Reeder and Brewer (1979) suggested that inferences about moral dispositions such as honesty might follow such an asymmetrical pattern, where negative instances are treated as more diagnostic. Of course, that would not explain the tendency for uncertain individuals to draw back in the Positive Recall condition. In that case it was as if the hopes that were raised sharpened the criteria for the attributional process. Perhaps conservative rules of inference are primed in which the partner's positive behavior is tagged to specific situational features and attributions are held in abeyance until future behavior consolidates the generalization. Such people may consider themselves to be 'situationally skeptical' rather than distrusting.

The origins of ambivalence. A state of uncertainty has been assumed to portray the thread of experience common to couples categorized as having moderate levels of trust. It is important to recognize that the causes of uncertainty may vary considerably among such couples and influence the prognosis for their relationships. The fabric of some relationships may simply not merit a sense of conviction. In other cases the personal dynamics of one or both partners may constrain feelings of trust, as Hazan and Shaver (1987) suggested in their analysis of people with anxious/ambivalent attachment styles.

Another group may suffer from a malaise brought on by forces of time and habituation that dampen the emotions that once cemented a sense of mutual dependency and connectedness. Trust appears to be at its lowest for those married from 6 to 20 years (Larzelere & Huston, 1980). Berscheid (1983) speculated that people in this group may find that emotional intensity fades in their relationships as the mutual facilitation of goals becomes relatively automatic and expected. She argued that people may be dependent on each other in important ways that go unrecognized unless events expose the emotional ties concealed by the adaptation process. One can only hope that a crisis of confidence acts largely to provoke a better understanding of the foundations of attachment that remain intact. Trust draws its sustenance from the challenges of intimacy and to restore a sense of vitality, couples must find the strength to risk confronting their concerns.

The Moderating Effects of Trusting Attitudes

The results of the present study confirm that high trust couples indeed expect positive outcomes in their relationships and interpret events in ways that maintain their optimistic expectations. They resisted attaching significance to negative behavior by the partner and seldom reacted very angrily. It was suggested that the impact of negative events is buffered by placing them in the broader, stable context of their positive convictions. This anchoring of perceptions was most apparent in the Control condition, where the evaluations of high trust couples departed least of all from their initial expectations.

The results from Rempel's (1987) study on attributions made during interactions suggest that the charitable perspective of high trust individuals is directly communicated to their partners. They made more spontaneous attributions for positive events than people at lower levels of trust and their inferences were more stable and global. Trusting people also made fewer very negative attributions, but they did not naively ignore negative events. Instead they made more moderately negative attributions than would be expected by chance. These findings reinforce the theme that high trust couples are distinguished by their capacity to place some limits on the negative implications that events could have for their relationships.

The dynamics of trusting individuals were put in stark relief in the Negative Recall condition of the present experiment. When their sense of confidence was challenged, they seemed to respond by more actively considering the wider issue of the partner's general motives. The integrated nature of their attitudes about trust allowed them to reach back into their store of positive feelings, and prevented them from falling prey to the momentary impact of a salient negative aspect of their experience. This appraisal process served not only to restore the status quo, but to actually vitalize their positive feelings. In this case, the rich only get richer.

Alternative Explanations

The complex research design of the Holmes and Rempel (1986) study provided a rich store of findings, but it did so at the expense of precision in ruling out competing notions. A number of alternative explanations do not seem very plausible, however. The Recall manipulation was carefully designed to permit a content analysis of the memories people reported. High trust individuals did not remember negative incidents that were judged to be somehow less serious or vivid, and there was no evidence that it was more difficult for them to recover an example of feeling let down. We chose to have them recall a single incident to avoid a problem whereby a protracted search for negative experiences would only serve to make salient the positive balance in their interpersonal histories. Actually, such an effect would be both interesting and plausible under those circumstances. In this case it is not consistent with either the ease of recall measures or the pattern of findings across conditions. Several other important properties of personal memories are similarly relevant, but again do not seem to provide a portrait that fits the results very well. For instance, Strack, Schwarz and Gschneidinger (1985) demonstrated that recalling an unhappy time from the past may result in a contextual contrast effect if people are relatively happy now (like high trust participants), accentuating their positive judgments of the present. However, they noted that such effects occurred only when the memory was pallid and abstract; assimilation effects resulted when the memory aroused stronger affect, a result that is in fact inconsistent with the high trust, Negative Recall finding (and others).

Another concern relates to the discriminant validity issue. Is it the level of trust that is important or other factors such as marital adjustment, self-disclosure, or satisfaction that might be associated with trust? The Locke-Wallace scale of marital adjustment did not show significant interaction effects with the experimental conditions in the present study, despite the fact that it is an umbrella measure that asks about satisfaction, conflicts, commitment and so on. The breadth of most adjustment or intimacy scales is often a liability, because one cannot discern the particular aspects that are having an effect and a theoretical focus is harder to achieve. Trust is a more focused construct that is specifically concerned with people's perceptions of their partners' motives. It permits more precise theoretical statements of an a priori nature, that in this case proved useful. A note of caution is certainly warranted, however, and the possibility remains open that other factors were responsible for the pattern of results.

The point is not to argue that the results can only be explained by the notions developed in the chapter. Other perspectives are no doubt possible, and the design was not intended to be sufficiently fine-tuned to serve the purpose of examining competing explanations. On the other hand, the study appears to have been successful in demonstrating some aspects of the dynamics of trust in established relationships and the results are at least generally consistent with the postulates that were developed.

CONCLUSIONS

Most earlier formulations on trust focused on people's state of confidence in a partner at different stages in relationships and on the connections between trust and other qualities of intimacy such as love and self-disclosure. In the present chapter, I have tried to expand our perspective on trust. I have considered the process by which it develops and the consequences of different states of trust on the fabric of experience in relationships and the nature of interpersonal appraisals. The etiology and dynamics of trust in close relationships are not only important in their own right, but reflect on features of the state of trust at a particular point in time.

A central theme in the chapter is that the foundations of trust change as relationships develop. In the early stages, feelings of love hold center stage and trust is not a salient issue unless signs of unequal attachment intrude. As relationships progress and people come to recognize the risks of increasing dependency, concerns about their prospects come into focus. Partners' behavior is increasingly coded for evidence of the quality of their feelings and people's own level of involvement becomes regulated by their perceptions that their love is being reciprocated. A window of reciprocity at the behavioral level offers some security in the face of risk, but the central function of reciprocity is to convey reassurance about the mutuality of feelings.

The process of reducing uncertainty about the partner's attitudes is facilitated by the demands of accommodation as interdependence grows. Couples face situations that are increasingly diagnostic of each person's motives, as differences in preferences and styles are gradually exposed. A partner's attachment is inferred from behavior that seems responsive to the needs of the person and the welfare of the unit. Trust is strengthened most by perceptions that considerate behavior has become an end unto itself, that it is intrinsically motivated. If these adjustments are successfully confronted, people develop a shared sense of security that the relationship will endure and feelings of efficacy in controlling its future course.

Few people negotiate this terrain without discovering negative aspects of a partner. Despite this, high trust individuals achieve a sense of closure by integrating such elements into the broader context of a coherent set of positive attitudes. Their optimistic expectations are maintained by interpreting the partner's behavior in ways that confirm their attitudes. Negative experiences are tolerated by relegating them to lower levels of concern. In contrast, other people have difficulty resolving feelings of ambivalence by setting their doubts aside. Instead they monitor the partner's behavior for diagnostic signs that might dispel their uncertainty or provide substance to their fears.

The relationship histories of uncertain couples may merit their sense of caution, or personal issues about trust and dependency may inhibit a sense of security that is perhaps justified. In either case, the nature of the appraisal process triggered by their concerns may, in itself, structure their experiences in predictable ways. The impact of the partner's behavior is likely to be magnified by their willingness to consider its implications for deeper relationship issues and by their inability to interpret it within the broader perspective of their relationship attitudes. To complicate the issue, the results from several studies reported in the chapter suggest that the hypothesis-testing strategy of uncertain individuals tends to be risk-aversive. Their rules for venturing positive inferences about the partner's motives seemed very conservative. They also showed a marked tendency to focus on negative behavior and a readiness to interpret it in line with their concerns that the partner will ultimately fall short of their expectations. In an ironic way uncertain people become directed toward the very fears they hope to surmount.

This chapter departs from other portrayals of trust in its strong emphasis on how feelings of trust in a partner influence people's emotions and perceptions in their relationships. In both developing and established relationships, a need to attain and consolidate a sense of emotional security was postulated to have a significant impact on the appraisal process. Much of the research relevant to this theme for established couples focused on people dealing with serious issues in their relationships. It remains to be seen whether similar conclusions would be warranted if people's reactions to events in their daily lives were examined. If it is the case that risk-aversive rules of inference indeed capture the psychological experiences of couples struggling with issues of trust, further research in controlled settings may then enable us to articulate these dynamics with considerably more precision. The problem represents a challenge not only for scientists, but for the many couples who feel trapped in a continuing cycle of uncertainty.

ACKNOWLEDGMENT

Preparation of this manuscript was facilitated by a Grant from the Social Sciences and Humanities Research Council.

REFERENCES

Ainsworth, M. D. S. (1979). Infant-mother attachment. *American Psychologist*, 34, 932-937.

Altman, I., & Taylor, D. A. (1973). *Social penetration: The development of interpersonal relationships*. New York: Holt, Rinehart & Winston.

Baldwin, M. P., & Holmes, J. G. (1987). Salient private audiences and awareness of the self. *Journal of Personality and Social Psychology*, 52, 1087-1098.

Berg, J. H., & Clark, M. S. (1985). Differences in social exchange between intimate and other relationships: Gradually evolving or quickly apparent? In W. Ickes (Ed.), *Compatible and incompatible relationships* (pp. 101-128). New York: Springer-Verlag.

Berger, P., & Kellner, H. (1972). Marriage and the construction of reality: An exercise in the microsociology of knowledge. *Recent Sociology*, 2, 50-71.

Berscheid, E. (1983). Emotion. In H. H. Kelley, E. Berscheid, A. Christensen, J. H. Harvey, T. L. Huston, G. Levinger, E. McClintock, L. A. Peplau & D. R. Peterson (Eds.), *Close relationships* (pp. 110-168). New York: Freeman.

Berscheid, E., & Fei, J. (1977). Romantic love: Sexual jealousy. In G. Clanton & L. G. Smith (Eds.), *Jealousy* (pp. 101-109). Englewood Cliffs, NJ: Prentice Hall.

Blau, P. M. (1964). *Exchange and power in social life*. New York: Wiley.

Borden, V. M. H., & Levinger, G. (1990). Interpersonal transformations in intimate behavior. In W. H. Jones & D. Perlman (Eds.), *Advances in personal relationships: A research annual* (Vol. 2, pp. 35-56). London: Jessica Kingsley Publishers.

Bowlby, J. (1973). *Attachment and loss: Vol. 2. Separation: Anxiety and anger*. New York: Basic Books.

Braiker, H. G., & Kelley, H. H. (1979). Conflict in the development of close relationships. In R. L. Burgess & T. L. Huston (Eds.), *Social exchange in developing relationships* (pp. 135-168). New York: Academic Press.

Brehm, S. S. (1985). *Intimate relationships*. New York: Random House.

Brickman, P. (1987). *Commitment, conflict, and caring*. Englewood Cliffs, NJ: Prentice-Hall.

Chaiken, S., & Yates, S. (1985). Affective-cognitive consistency and thought-induced polarization. *Journal of Personality and Social Psychology*, 49, 1470-1481.

Clark, M. S. & Mills, J. (1979). Interpersonal attraction in exchange and communal relationships. *Journal of Personality and Social Psychology*, 37, 12-24.

Derlega, V. J., Wilson, M., & Chaikin, A. L. (1976). Friendship and disclosure reciprocity. *Journal of Personality and Social Psychology*, 34, 578-587.

Deutsch, M. (1973). *The resolution of conflict: Constructive and destructive processes*. New Haven, CN: Yale University Press.

Dion, K. L., & Dion, K. K. (1973). Correlates of romantic love. *Journal of Consulting and Clinical Psychology*, 41, 51-56.

Dion, K. L., & Dion, K. K. (1976). Love, liking and trust in heterosexual relationships. *Personality and Social Psychology Bulletin*, 2, 187-190.

Doherty, W. J., & Ryder, R. G. (1979). Locus of control, interpersonal trust, and assertive behavior among newlyweds. *Journal of Personality and Social Psychology*, 37, 2212-2220.

Driscoll, R., Davis, K. E., & Lipitz, M. E. (1972). Parental interference and romantic love: The Romeo & Juliet effect. *Journal of Personality and Social Psychology*, 24, 1-10.

Eidelson, R. J. (1980). Interpersonal satisfaction and level of involvement: A curvilinear relationship. *Journal of Personality and Social Psychology*, 39, 460-470.

Erikson, E. H. (1963). *Childhood and society*. New York: Norton.

Gold, M., & Yanof, D. S. (1985). Mothers, daughters, and girlfriends. *Journal of Personality and Social Psychology*, 49, 654-659.

Gottman, J. M. (1979). *Marital interaction*. New York: Academic Press.

Hazan, C., & Shaver, P. (1987). Romantic love conceptualized as an attachment process. *Journal of Personality and Social Psychology*, 52, 511-524.

Hendrick, C., & Hendrick, S. (1986). A theory and method of love. *Journal of Personality and Social Psychology*, 50, 392-402.

Hendrick, S. S. (1981). Self-disclosure and marital satisfaction. *Journal of Personality and Social Psychology*, 40, 1150-1159.

Hill, C. T., Rubin, Z., & Peplau, L. A. (1976). Breakups before marriage: The end of 103 affairs. *Journal of Social Issues*, 32 (1), 147-168.

Holmes, J. G. (1981). The exchange process in close relationships: Microbehavior and macromotives. In M. J. Lerner & S. C. Lerner (Eds.), *The justice motive in social behavior* (pp. 261-284). New York: Plenum.

Holmes, J. G. Unpublished data, 1987.

Holmes, J. G., & Rempel, J. K. (1986, August). *Trust and conflict in close relationships*. Invited address at the meeting of the American Psychological Association, Washington, DC.

Holmes, J. G., & Rempel, J. K. (1989). Trust in close relationships. In C. Hendrick (Ed.), *Review of Personality and social psychology: Close relationships* (Vol. 10, pp. 187-220). Beverly Hills, California: Sage Publications.

Huesmann, L. R., & Levinger, G. (1976). Incremental exchange theory: A formal model for progression in dyadic social interaction. In L. Berkowitz & E. Walster (Eds.), *Advances in experimental social psychology* (Vol. 9, pp. 151-193). New York: Academic Press.

Johnson-George, C., & Swap, W. (1982). Measurement of specific interpersonal trust: Construction and validation of a scale to assess trust in a specific order. *Journal of Personality and Social Psychology*, 43, 1306-1317.

Jones, E. E., & Gerard, H. B. (1967). *Foundations of social psychology*. New York: Wiley.

Kelley, H. H. & Stahelski, A. J. (1970). The social interaction basis of cooperators' and competitors' beliefs about others. *Journal of Personality and Social Psychology*, 16, 66-91.

Kelley, H. H. (1979). *Personal relationships: Their structures and process*. Hillsdale, NJ: Erlbaum.

Kelley, H. H. (1983). Love and commitment. In H. H. Kelley, E. Berscheid, A. Christensen, J. H. Harvey, T. L. Huston, G. Levinger, E. McClintock, L. A. Peplau & D. R. Peterson (Eds.), *Close relationships* (pp. 265-314). New York: Freeman.

Kelley, H. H. (1984). Affect in interpersonal relations. In P. Shaver (Ed.), *Review of personality and social psychology* (Vol. 5, pp. 89-115). Beverly Hills, CA: Sage.

Kelley, H. H., & Thibaut, J. W. (1978). *Interpersonal relations: A theory of interdependence*. New York: Wiley.

Klinger, E. (1977). *Meaning and void: Inner experience and the incentives in people's lives*. Minneapolis: University of Minnesota Press.

Larzelere, R. E., & Huston, T. L. (1980). The dyadic Trust Scale: Toward understanding interpersonal trust in close relationships. *Journal of Marriage and the Family*, 42, 595-604.

Lerner, M. J., Miller, D. T., & Holmes, J. G. (1976). Deserving vs. justice: A contemporary dilemma. In L. Berkowitz & E. Walster (Eds.), *Advances in Experimental Social Psychology* (Vol. 9, pp. 134-162). New York: Academic Press.

Levenson, R. W., & Gottman, J. M. (1985). Physiological and affective predictors of change in relationship satisfaction. *Journal of Personality and Social Psychology*, 49, 85-94.

Levinger, G. (1979). A social exchange view of the dissolution of pair relationships. In R. L. Burgess & T. L. Huston (Eds.), *Social exchange in developing relationships* (pp. 169-193). New York: Academic Press.

Levitz-Jones, E. M., & Orlofsky, J. L. (1985). Separation-individuation and intimacy capacity in college women. *Journal of Personality and Social Psychology*, 49, 156-169.

Lloyd, S., Cate, R., & Henton, J. (1982). Equity and rewards as predictors of satisfaction in casual and intimate relationships. *Journal of Psychology*, 110, 43-48.

Lydon, J. E., Jamieson, D. W., & Holmes, J. G. (1985). *From acquaintanceship to friendship: The affective and behavioral metamorphosis of social exchange.* Paper presented at the meeting of the Canadian Psychological Association, Halifax, Nova Scotia.

Mahler, M. S. (1963). Thoughts about development and individuation. *Psychoanalytic study of the child*, 18, 307-324.

McFarland, C., & Ross, M. (1987). The relation between current impressions and memories of self and dating partners. *Personality and Social Psychology Bulletin*, 13, 228-238.

Miller, D. T., & Holmes, J. G. (1975). The role of situational restrictiveness on self-fulfilling prophecies: A theoretical and empirical extension of Kelley and Stahelski's triangle hypothesis. *Journal of Personality and Social Psychology*, 31, 661-673.

Miller, P. C., Lefcourt, H. M., Holmes, J. G., Ware, E. E., & Saleh, W. (1986). Marital locus of control and marital problem solving. *Journal of Personality and Social Psychology*, 51, 161-169.

Morton, T. U. (1978). Intimacy and reciprocity of exchange: A comparison of spouses and strangers. *Journal of Personality and Social Psychology*, 36, 72-81.

Osgood, C. E. (1962). *An alternative to war or surrender*. Urbana: University of Illinois Press.

Pruitt, D. G. (1965). Definition of the situation as a determinant of international action. In H. C. Kelman (Ed.), *International behavior* (pp. 393-432). New York: Holt, Rinehart and Winston.

Reeder, G. D., & Brewer, M. B. (1979). A schematic model of dispositional attribution in interpersonal perception. *Psychological Review*, 86, 61-79.

Rempel, J. K. (1987). *Trust and attributions in close relationships*. Unpublished doctoral dissertation, University of Waterloo, Ontario.

Rempel, J. K., Holmes, J. G., & Zanna, M. P. (1985). Trust in close relationships. *Journal of Personality and Social Psychology*, 49, 95-112.

Rotter, J. B. (1967). A new scale for the measurement of interpersonal trust. *Journal of Personality*, 35, 651-655.

Rusbult, C. E. (1983). A longitudinal test of the investment model: The development (and deterioration) of satisfaction and commitment in heterosexual involvement. *Journal of Personality and Social Psychology*, 45, 101-117.

Sabatelli, R. M., Buck, R., & Dreyer, A. (1983). Locus of control, interpersonal trust, and nonverbal communication accuracy. *Journal of Personality and Social Psychology*, 44, 399-409.

Schmidt, G. W., Kelley, H. H., & Fujino, D. C. (1987). *Some new insights into interpersonal motives.* Paper presented at the 67th annual convention of the Western Psychological Association Long Beach, California.

Seligman, C., Fazio, R. H., & Zanna, M. P. (1980). Effects of salience of extrinsic rewards on liking and loving. *Journal of Personality and Social Psychology*, 38, 453-460.

Solomon, L. (1960). The influence of some types of power relationships and game strategies upon the development of interpersonal trust. *Journal of Abnormal and Social Psychology*, 61, 223-230.

Sroufe, L. A. (1983). Infant-caregiver attachment and patterns of adaptation in preschool: The roots of maladaptation and competence. In M. Perlmutter (Ed.), *Minnesota symposium on child psychology* (Vol. 16, pp. 41-83). Hillsdale, NJ: Erlbaum.

Stern, D. (1985). *The interpersonal world of the infant: A view from psychoanalysis and developmental psychology.* New York: Basic Books.

Sternberg, R. J. (1986). A triangular theory of love. *Psychological Review,* 93, 119-135.

Sternberg, R. J., & Barnes, M. (1985). Real and ideal others in romantic relationships: Is four a crowd? *Journal of Personality and Social Psychology,* 49, 1589-1596.

Strack, F., Schwarz, N., & Gschneidinger, E. (1985). Happiness and reminiscing: The role of time perspective, affect, and mode of thinking. *Journal of Personality and Social Psychology,* 49, 1460-1469.

Strickland, L. H. (1958). Surveillance and trust. *Journal of Personality,* 28, 200-215.

Swinth, R. L. (1967). The establishment of the trust relationship. *Journal of Conflict Resolution,* 11, 335-344.

Walster, E., Walster, G. W., & Traupmann, J. (1978). Equity and premarital sex. *Journal of Personality and Social Psychology,* 36, 82-92.

Webb, W. M., & Worchel, P. (1986). Trust and distrust. In S. Worchel & W. G. Austin (Eds.), *Psychology of intergroup relations* (pp. 213-228). Chicago: Nelson-Hall.

Wrightsman, L. S. (1972). *Social psychology in the seventies.* Monterey, CA: Brooks/Cole.

Wyer, R. S., & Srull, T. (1986). The role of chronic and temporary goals in social information processing. In R. M. Sorrentino & E. Tory Higgins (Eds.), *Handbook of motivation and cognition* (pp. 503-549). New York: Guilford Press.

PART II

SOCIAL SUPPORT

AN EXPERIMENTAL APPROACH TO STUDYING SOCIAL INTERACTION AND COPING WITH STRESS AMONG FRIENDS

Barbara A. Winstead and Valerian J. Derlega

Consider the following examples:

> Roy Campsen is an instructor at a community college. This morning he woke up with a toothache. He called his dentist for an appointment. The tooth has been giving him trouble for several months and Roy's dentist has suggested that this morning might be a good time to extract the tooth. After speaking with the dentist, Roy telephones a friend and colleague at work, Lou McIntire, to ask him to teach his classes today. Lou agrees to help. Lou also mentions as they both talk that he dislikes going to dentists and would feel upset if he were in Roy's position. Roy, who already is feeling bad about his own plight, winces and agrees that getting the tooth pulled will be unpleasant.

> Jane Howard is a mechanical engineer who works for the Navy in Washington, DC. She is flying with a friend and colleague, Deborah, to a conference in a rural community on the eastern shore of Virginia. Jane is nervous about flying on small aircraft and this

plane holds only eighteen passengers. As the plane is getting ready for take-off, Jane and Deborah are talking about the presentation which they will be making at the conference. The discussion distracts Jane from thinking about flying aboard the small plane and she doesn't feel as upset as she expected.

These anecdotes focus on how social interactions between friends (and in these two examples, also between colleagues) influence how individuals cope with a potentially stressful situation. Talking with a friend about negative feelings associated with going to a dentist made Roy Campsen feel worse about having a tooth pulled. On the other hand, talking with a friend about a topic unrelated to flying in a small airplane helped Jane temporarily forget about flying.

We suggest that knowing the types of interaction that occur between friends (and possibly between other providers of social support, such as family members, spouses, and neighbors) can help in understanding when social support aids or detracts from coping with a stressful situation. In the first section, we review how previous studies of social support, using surveys and interviews, have focused on perceived social support rather than on the social behaviors that enact (or implement) social support. Despite the enormous knowledge gained from this research (cf. Brownell & Shumaker, 1984; Cohen & Syme, 1985; Fleming & Baum, 1986; Heller, 1986; Sarason & Sarason, 1985; Shumaker & Brownell, 1985), we still need studies to explicate the mechanisms and ingredients involved in providing social support (Wortman & Conway, 1985).

In the second section, we describe two experiments which examine, in a laboratory setting, the therapeutic value of same-sex friendships in coping with stress. The goal of our research is to investigate experimentally how persons who are in close relationships (such as same-sex friends) are successful in assisting one another in coping with a stressful event. The goal of this chapter is to suggest the value of a laboratory-oriented, experimental approach to studying how friends help one another to cope with stress.

CORRELATIONAL STUDIES OF PERCEIVED SOCIAL SUPPORT

Considerable research indicates that social support reduces the negative psychological impact of stressful life events (Cohen & Wills, 1985). For instance, Lowenthal and Haven (1968), in a study of adaptation among older adults, found that the presence of a confidant served as a 'buffer' against various life crises, including the risk of becoming depressed in the face of losing a spouse or of retirement. Fleming, Baum, Gisriel, and Gatchel (1982) report that residents living near the Three Mile Island nuclear power station during the 1979 accident who had social support (e.g., 'having a close friend to talk to about things,' 'having someone to turn to for support when unhappy or under stress') had fewer psychological and behavioral (but not physiological) symptoms of stress than did those without support. Pennebaker and O'Heeron (1984) contacted spouses of accidental death and suicide victims. Subjects who had talked about their spouse's death at length with close friends were less likely to report an increase in illness rate from before to after the death of the spouse and were less likely to ruminate or think constantly about the spouse's death.

These studies provide evidence for a positive relationship between social support and psychological and physical outcomes. There are, however, two important weaknesses in these and numerous similar studies: 1) measurements of social support are diverse, are based on self-reports, which may be biased, and generally do not allow for specification of actual behaviors that benefit recipients of social support; 2) correlational studies do not usually provide information about cause and effect. Available measures of social support classify social support in different ways:

...the number of support persons; the interrelatedness of the support group; whether the support is provided by family members, friends, or others; whether a close or confidant relationship is associated with the support; the functions the support fulfills and how they are matched with the person's needs; the adequacy of the support; the person's satisfaction with the support; and whether the support is actually provided or perceived to be available if needed. (Sarason, Shearin, Pierce, & Sarason, 1987, p. 814)

This variety makes it impossible to specify which variables actually account for the social support and coping relationship.

However, after comparing and contrasting several frequently used measures of social support, Sarason et al. (1987) concluded that 'each of the instruments assesses the extent to which an individual is accepted, loved, and involved in relationships in which communication is open' (p. 830). This view of social support emphasizes that, though supportive behaviors such as an exchange of information, money, or emotional expressiveness may be valuable, they contribute to social support only insofar as individuals perceive that one or more others care for them or are willing to do whatever they can for them. This implies that *perceived* social support may be more beneficial than the actual supportive behaviors in a social exchange between partners who are attempting to cope with a stressful event

Though research underscores the importance of perceived social support, it is difficult to disentangle from individuals' self-reports the relative benefits of perceived versus actual support (Gottlieb, 1984). The perceived availability of social support may or may not correspond with the actual support. Antonucci and Israel (1986) indicate that agreement between an individual and his or her network member in their reports of whether support was provided varied with relationship closeness. Agreement was highest between spouses (89%), next highest between family members (81%), and lowest between friends (55%). Antonucci and Israel (1986) concluded that instances of support in noncrisis, day-to-day situations may not be well defined and, therefore, imprecisely reported, and that perceptions of support may be influenced by perceptions of need.

Furthermore, personality differences may bias perceptions of social support. For instance, Procidano and Heller (1983) report that the perceived support from friends correlated positively with subscale scores for 'Good Impression,' 'Sociability' and 'Social Presence' on the California Psychological Inventory (Gough, 1956) and was associated with self-confidence, social competence, and social desirability. Procidano and Heller (1983) also found that subjects who read and thought about negative self-statements gave significantly lower ratings of perceived social support from friends than did subjects with no negative mood induction. Thus, current mood as well as personality characteristics may influence measures of social support.

Even if agreement among members of a social support network were perfect and self reports were unbiased the *behaviors* that convey social support would still be unidentified. Measures of social support have focused on subjects' perceptions that others are supportive rather than investigating actual (or even remembered) behaviors that led to the perceptions of support.

The emphasis in previous research on self reports of life experiences (e.g., social support and stress) also creates problems in determining cause and effect. As Wortman and Conway (1985, p. 282) note, 'most of the early studies demonstrating a relationship between support and health have employed cross-sectional, retrospective, or case-control designs.' It is difficult to specify a cause and effect relationship between social support and coping with stress using correlational data (Dooley, 1985; Heller, 1979; House, 1981; Thoits, 1982; Wortman & Conway, 1985). For example, though individuals who report having friends may be better able to cope with stressful events, the causal sequence may actually operate in a reverse direction such that well-adjusted persons who handle crises easily may have more friends or find it easier to confide in others.

Problems in the interpretation of survey-type studies could be reduced by conducting prospective longitudinal research. The goal would be to study how social support predicts health outcomes in the future while controlling for or examining the direct or interactional influence of other variables that have an effect on health outcomes, such as current psychological or physical health as well as other personality variables. However, failure to control for or examine crucial variables may also occur even in prospective longitudinal studies (cf. Dooley, 1985; Wortman & Conway, 1985). Another approach to improving correlational research is causal modelling. When data analyses are guided by a strong theory that generates the necessary *a priori* predictions, causal modelling is appropriate. Unfortunately, few precise models of the effects of social support exist (See, however, Hobfoll's (1988) recent model of conservation of resources which predicts how social support influences coping with stress).

Finally, as previously noted, current measures of social support do not provide information about specific supportive behaviors that subjects actually experienced. Hence, even prospective research using these measures will not reveal which social-support behaviors contribute to the benefits derived from social support. The diversity of measures of social support and their emphasis on perceived support have neglected the search for the particulars of social support, e.g., incidents, behaviors, or words that create the belief that one is supported. Also, the preference for real-life stressors has contributed to an abundance of survey studies without the controls that permit clear conclusions concerning the causal impact of social support.

EXPERIMENTAL RESEARCH ON SOCIAL SUPPORT

Having established a positive relationship between social support and stress reduction in many situations, social-support researchers are calling for experimental research to complement the survey studies (e.g., Sarason, 1987; Thoits, 1987). A major goal of our research program has been to conduct experiments on the effects of social support provided by same-sex friends in a stressful situation. We agree with Dooley's (1985) analysis of the use of the experimental approach to avoid the inferential difficulties associated with most survey methodologies:

> One way to avoid the spuriousness and reverse-causation rival hypotheses is to conduct controlled experiments. Experimental manipulation of the independent variable of social support assures that support is not caused by the dependent variable (i.e., reverse causation). Maximum control is provided by the random assignment of subjects to manipulated high-and-low support conditions. This type of assignment eliminates the association of irrelevant third variables with support (i.e., spuriousness). (Dooley, 1985, p. 111)

While experimental designs are relatively infrequent in the field of social support research (for exceptions, see Heller & Lakey, 1985; McGuire & Gottlieb, 1979; Sarason, I. G., 1981; Sarason, I. G. & Sarason, B. R., 1986; Whitcher & Fisher, 1979) and by definition not a 'natural' situation (Dooley, 1985), experimental interventions provide a straightforward way, based on internal validity considerations, to determine the types of relationships and social interactions that provide social support.

STUDY 1: SAME-SEX FRIENDSHIP AND COPING WITH STRESS

Study 1 (Winstead & Derlega, 1985) was designed to investigate whether an existing, positive social relationship, such as that between same-sex friends, helps individuals to cope more effectively with a stressful event. A major advantage of Study 1 in comparison to prior survey research is that it employed an experimental design, which allowed us to assess whether friends are more helpful than strangers in assisting individuals to cope with a stressful event.

Having friends is considered a desirable feature of American life. The State Department of Mental Health in California (see Fischer, 1983) adopted an advertising campaign featuring the message that 'Friends can be good medicine.' This message appeared on bumper stickers, shopping bags, and television and was publicized at public meetings. Measures of social support usually include friends as possible providers of social support and many of the positive findings in the social support literature rely on correlations between reports of having confidants or someone to talk to (i.e., friends) and reports of psychological and/or physical well-being (e.g., Fleming et al., 1982; Lowenthal & Haven, 1968). While the benefits of friendship may seem indisputable, some researchers have found that interactions with friends interfere with successful coping with stress (cf. Fischer, 1983; Hobfoll & London, 1986; Lehman, Ellard, & Wortman, 1986; Rook, 1984). Individuals may sometimes find it easier to discuss difficulties with someone whom they don't know. In the stranger *passant* phenomenon (Derlega & Chaikin, 1975; Simmel, 1950; Thibaut & Kelley, 1959) individuals are more open with strangers about a problem than with friends, especially when further encounters are unlikely, such as on an airplane, a train or bus, in a hotel far away from home, or perhaps in a psychology experiment.

Study 1 was designed to test the hypothesis that two same-sex friends are more successful than two same-sex strangers in helping one another cope with a stressful event. Subjects were recruited as pairs of same-sex friends. In the study, they were randomly paired with either a friend or stranger, told that they would be asked to handle a large, nonpoisonous snake, and then left to interact with one another before the stressful event occurred. In this way the effect of friendship on emotional responses to a fear-evoking situation was not confounded with the relative psychological health of the subjects. The study's design ensures that if subjects interacting with friends cope more effectively than subjects interacting with strangers in the stressful situation, then it is the 'friend' that has created this effect and not some other factor such as the subjects' level of psychological health.

Design and Subjects

The major independent variables in the first study were relationship (friends versus strangers) and subject sex (female versus male). The major dependent variables were paper-and-pencil measures of subjects' affect: fear of snakes, anxiety, depression, and hostility. The research participants were 62 female and 62 male undergraduate students randomly paired with either a same-sex friend or a same-sex stranger for the experimental session.

Procedure

Research participants were asked to sign up with a 'same-sex friend' for a study on 'participant modeling.' Two pairs of same-sex friends reported for the experimental session. Upon arriving, subjects were assigned as a partner either to their friend or to a same-sex stranger from the other pair of friends. One pair of partners was immediately taken to a room where the study began. The other pair waited in separate cubicles (to keep them from conversing with one another) for their turn in the study.

A female experimenter arrived shortly and described the study in which the subjects would be participating. The subjects were told that the study involved participant modeling, and they would be asked to handle a nonpoisonous snake after watching a model handle it. A detailed description of what the model would do with the snake was given, and subjects were told that they would be asked to do as many of these things as they felt comfortable doing. They were also told that they could handle the snake alone or with their partner.

After the explanation of the study, both subjects filled out a modified version of the Multiple Affect Adjective Checklist (MAACL) Today Form (Zuckerman & Lubin, 1965) which asked how they felt 'right now' and a single-item, eleven-point fear-of-snakes scale which asked how afraid of snakes they were.

Next, subjects were left alone for a four-minute period to give them an opportunity to interact with one another. During this time the experimenter was presumably checking to see if the equipment for the snake handling was ready. After the four minutes, the experimenter returned and took the subjects to separate rooms and asked them again to fill out the MAACL and the fear scale to provide a current measure of affect.

Results

A 2 (friend vs. stranger) x 2 (female vs. male) x 2 (time 1 vs. time 2) mixed design analysis of variance with time as the within-subjects factor was performed on the affect measures - the MAACL ratings of anxiety, depression, and hostility as well as the fear-of-snakes rating. There were significant friendship x time interactions on depression, $F(1,120) = 5.29$, $p < .05$, and hostility, $F(1,120) = 4.94$, $p < .05$. Tests of simple main effects were performed on the effects of time 1 versus time 2 for friends and strangers, respectively, on the depression and hostility measures. Depression scores were significantly lower at time 2 ($M = 15.59$) versus time 1 ($M = 16.77$) for friends, $F(1,128) = 7.63$, $p < .01$, one-tailed, whereas the depression scores were not significantly different at time 2 ($M = 15.79$) and time 1 ($M = 15.09$) for strangers, $F(1,122) < 1$. For friends, hostility scores were significantly lower at time 2 ($M = 9.22$) versus time 1 ($M = 9.70$), $F(1,128) = 3.73$, $p < .05$, one-tailed, whereas for strangers these scores were not significantly different at time 2 ($M = 9.31$) versus time 1 ($M = 9.01$), $F(1,122) < 1$. Friends had somewhat higher depression and hostility

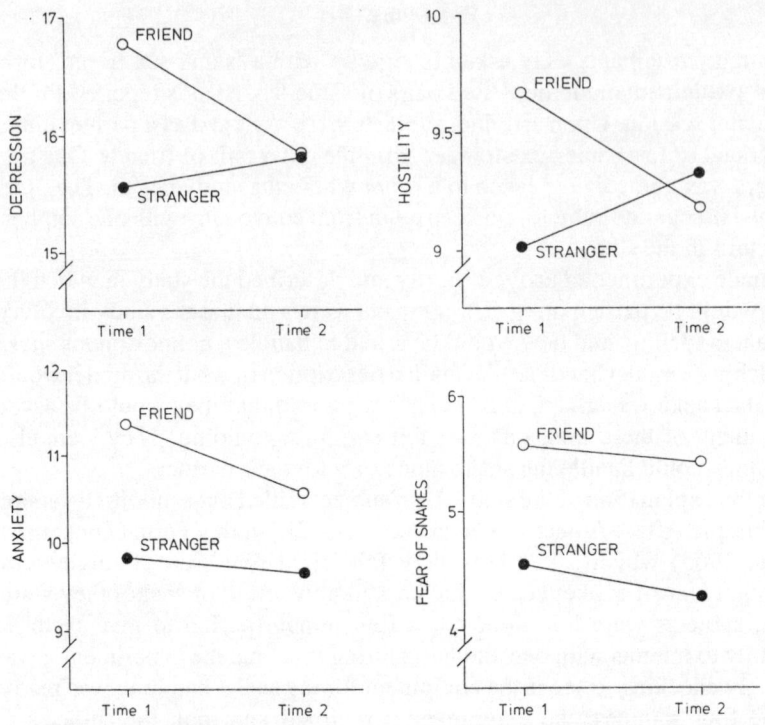

Figure 1. Means for the affect measures in Study 1 as a function of relationship and time.

scores than strangers at time 1; however, analyses of simple effects indicated that these mean differences were nonsignificant. There were no significant friendship x time interactions on either the anxiety or fear-of-snakes ratings. (See Figure 1 for a graphic summary of these results.)

The results provided experimental support documenting that friends can operate as social supports. These effects occurred, however, not for the emotions specifically aroused by the situation (i.e., fear[1] and anxiety) but for indirect signs of subjective distress (depression and hostility). For depression and hostility, being with a friend significantly reduced affect, whereas being with a stranger had no significant effect.

RESEARCH ISSUES RAISED BY STUDY 1

Friendship versus the Relative Psychological Health of Subjects

We have suggested that a major advantage of Study 1 is that it is an experimental and not a correlational study. Thus, the effects of friendship on emotional responses to a fear-evoking situation are not confounded with other variables, such as the relative psychological health of the subjects. Since all subjects were recruited in the same manner, that is, they were asked to come to the study with a friend, the effect of interacting with a friend or stranger cannot be attributed to differences in psychological health in the two groups. We did not measure psychological health, however. Thus, it is not possible to know if or how this variable affects the consequences of waiting with a friend or stranger.

The literature on social support has not usually focused on personality factors, but researchers have noted how it would be useful to consider how personality (e.g., psychological health) and relationship variables operate together to influence coping with stress (cf. Hobfoll, 1985; Hobfoll & London, 1986; Hobfoll, Nadler, & Leiberman, 1986; Jones, 1985). For instance, Hobfoll and Leiberman (1987) suggest that a close relationship (in which one feels accepted, loved and valued) and personality resources (such as self-esteem or a sense of one's own worth as a person) may serve as substitutable resources in coping with a stressful situation. When a given resource (e.g., a friend) is absent, a second resource (e.g., high self-esteem) can substitute for it. This idea is termed the *substitution hypothesis* by Hobfoll and Leiberman (1987). Based on the substitution hypothesis, it might be expected that persons in a stressful situation will be better able to cope if they possess either one or both types of resources (e.g., a friend's presence or high self-esteem), while those with neither resource will be less effective in their coping than those who have either one or both. Hobfoll and Leiberman (1987) found support for the substitution hypothesis in a study of women who had difficulties during their pregnancies (e.g., delivery by caesarean section, premature delivery of a baby under 2-kg weight, or spontaneous abortion before the third trimester). They found that the women who had either a supportive spouse, high self-esteem, or both resources, were less depressed than women who possessed neither resource at the occurrence of the stressful event. Using an experimental approach to investigate the substitution hypothesis, one could create levels of coping potential, ranging from low self-esteem, no partner to high self-esteem, with a partner, and then test responses of subjects at each level to a stressful situation.

Gender Differences in Friendships

Subjects were paired in Study 1 with either a male or a female same-sex friend or stranger. Studies on same-sex friendships indicate that females have emotionally close same-sex friendships in which the disclosure of personal feelings is valued and practiced. Males, on the other hand, have same-sex friendships based on shared activities and interests in which there is an emphasis on doing things together rather than on the sharing of feelings (see Winstead, 1986, for a literature review). It might have been expected that gender composition of relationships influences how effective friends, or strangers, are in helping one another cope with a stressful event. Females reported more anxiety ($F(1,120) = 10.09$, $p < .01$) and fear-of-snakes ($F(1,120) = 13.30$, $p < .01$) compared to the males, but there were no significant interactions with gender on the affect measures. Male friends were as successful as female friends in helping one another feel better. Reis, Senchak, and Solomon (1985) found that when asked to disclose intimately to a same-sex friend males and females did not differ in the level of intimacy of their disclosures. They concluded that although males may prefer to avoid intimate self-disclosure, they are capable of it. Similarly, males may be as capable as females of providing social support when it is called for.

Nevertheless, it seems worthwhile to examine in future studies the possible effects of gender composition of relationships on coping with stress. Parenthetically, there is limited research on cross-sex friendships (defined here as platonic, nonromantic relationships). Research indicates that males are more willing to self-disclose to female than to male partners (e.g., Derlega, Winstead, Wong, & Hunter, 1985) and males might be more open and perhaps experience more support with a female, platonic friend than with a male friend. Experimental studies in which subjects are paired with same-sex and cross-sex friends and strangers could provide useful information about the effects of gender composition of relationships on when and how friends or strangers help one another to cope with a stressful event.

STUDY 2: POSITIVE AND NEGATIVE FORMS OF SOCIAL SUPPORT AMONG SAME-SEX FRIENDS

Given that social support as provided by a friend does facilitate coping with stress, how does it perform this function? Talking about the stressful event may enable individuals to ventilate their feelings as well as encourage them to face a problem that they need to confront. Also, Festinger's (1954) and others' (Schachter, 1959; Wrightsman, 1960) work on social comparison processes suggests that comparing our thoughts and feelings with those of others gives us the opportunity to gain feedback and determine the appropriateness and 'normality' of our reactions. On the other hand, talking with a friend about a stressful event could make the person feel worse instead of better (see Coates & Winston, 1983/1987; Hobfoll, 1985). Verbally supportive behavior may be accompanied by unsupportive nonverbal behaviors; those trying to reassure the distressed person may convey the message that the person is overreacting or responding in an inappropriate or abnormal way. Worse, individuals who share their reactions with others who are in the same situation may be discouraged by discovering that their distress and anxiety are typical and common thus confirming their belief that the situation is desperate (Coates & Winston, 1983/1987).

A major goal of future laboratory-based research should be to develop a taxonomy of behavior exchanged by persons as they interact together before facing a stressful event. Though social support researchers have written about the kinds of social support provided by friends, this information is usually collected retrospectively (cf. Cobb & Jones-Cobb, 1984; Coates & Winston, 1983/1987; Lehman et al., 1986). For an important exception, see the work done on keeping diaries to measure the impact of social participation on physical and psychological health (Reis, Wheeler, Kernis, Spiegel, & Nezlek, 1985). By identifying the behaviors that are correlated with stress reduction in an actual situation, which would be possible with video- and audiotape equipment in the laboratory-type research we are conducting, future experimental research can be designed to assess the magnitude of effects of different types of interactions on coping with stress (cf. Winstead, Derlega, Sanchez-Hucles, & Lewis, 1986). In the absence of such research, however, we sought to investigate the effects of different types of conversation content between friends on coping with stress, based on a theoretical analysis of the functions of self-disclosure (Derlega & Grzelak, 1979; Derlega, Margulis, & Winstead, 1987) and past research concerning stress-coping strategies (e.g., Langer, Janis & Wolfer, 1975; Lazarus & Folkman, 1984; Thoits, 1986).

Talking with a friend will not inevitably lead to coping successfully with stress. Though many studies indicate that talking with friends can facilitate coping with stress (see Fleming & Baum, 1986, for a literature review), social support provided by talking with friends and neighbors can be associated with greater psychological distress. For instance, Hobfoll and London (1986) found that Israeli women whose male relatives or husbands had been mobilized into the Israeli military during the 1982 Israel-Lebanon conflict experienced greater psychological distress (state anxiety and state depression) if they had friends or neighbors with whom to talk. Intimacy with friends (e.g., 'I have friends with whom I can speak freely about what is important to me') was positively correlated with anxiety. Also amount of social support received during the crisis period (e.g., sharing of feelings, tangible assistance or advice received during the crisis period) was positively correlated to depression. Hobfoll and London (1986) suggest that interacting frequently with friends and neighbors who are also undergoing the same difficulty (for instance, having a male relative in combat) may have produced a 'pressure-cooker' effect. Talking to other members of one's social support group may have helped spread rumors and led to exaggerated accounts of what was actually happening in the war which, in turn, increased psychological distress.

We focused on three major conversation categories that may affect how well friends cope with a forthcoming crisis or stressor:

1. *Disclosure of feelings.* Talking about one's feelings, fears and anxieties concerning an anticipated stressor with a friend is one way of coping. The communication of one's feelings may have a cathartic value by dissipating the undesirable emotions that result from a stressful situation (cf. Derlega, Margulis, & Winstead, 1987; Freud, 1904/1954; Pennebaker & Beall, 1986). However, expressing one's feelings may aggravate one's negative mood state by calling attention to negative feelings that are now brought into sharper focus (Archer, Hormuth, & Berg, 1982). Thus, a strategy that involves talking about the negative feelings associated with the impending event may make the situation appear more threatening than it originally appeared.
2. *Problem-solving talk.* Engaging in a problem-solving conversation is a second way of dealing with a stressful event with a friend. Friends may provide social support by asking and answering questions such as 'What can be done about the situation?' Talking about how to solve the problem can provide a sense of control and confidence in overcoming an obstacle (Langer et al., 1975). Hence, talking that involves instrumental or problem-solving discussion could reduce negative affect if it suggests a way to deal with the stressor.
3. *Unrelated talk.* Talking about content unrelated to the stressful event represents another way of coping. Friends who talk about events unrelated to the stressor may experience reduced negative affect because they are distracted from thinking about the stressor (Averill & Rosenn, 1972; Houston & Holmes, 1974; Langer et al., 1975).

We predicted that talking with a friend about either problem-solving or unrelated content would produce less negative affect and less avoidance behavior than talking about one's feelings concerning the stressful event. This study represents among the first attempts to test experimentally how different modes of social support provided by friends, represented by the different conversational topics, can affect coping with stress.

In the second study that we conducted (Costanza, Derlega, & Winstead, 1988) the stressful event involved the anticipation of guiding a tarantula through a maze. Self-report data of negative mood state were collected before and after subjects talked with their friends in anticipation of handling the spider. Also, a behavioral fear measure was obtained based on how close to them subjects permitted the spider to be placed.

Method

Individuals had been asked to sign up with a 'same-sex friend' for a study on participant modeling. Subjects did not know at the time they signed up for the study that it involved possible contact with a tarantula. (See Figure 2 for a

Figure 2a. Subjects see the spider as the experiment is explained to them.

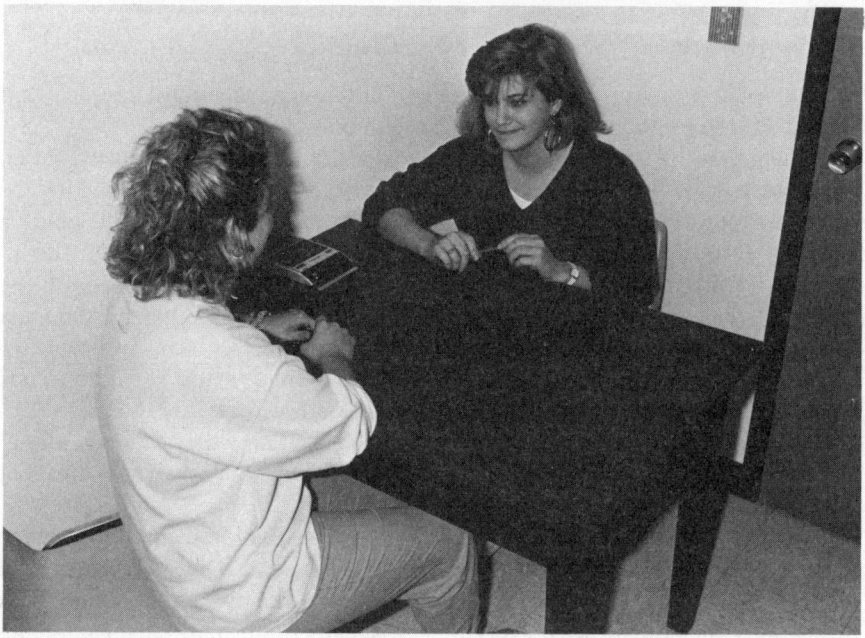

Figure 2b. A pair of friends talk together in one of the three conversation topic conditions.

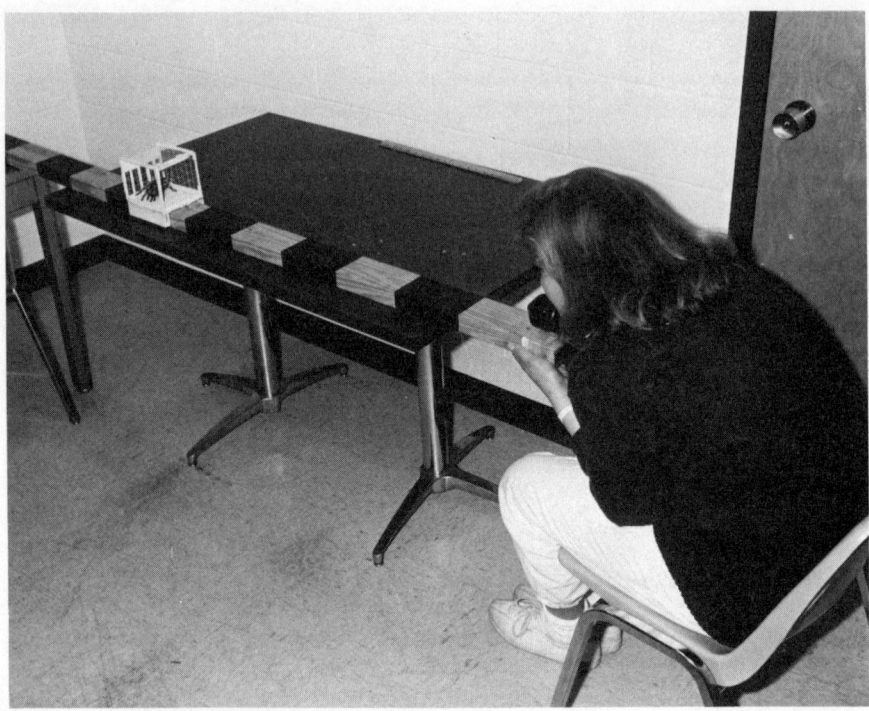

Figure 2c. Subject pulls the tarantula towards herself on the behavioral fear task.

photographic depiction of the various steps in this experiment for a typical pair of friends who might be assigned to talk with one another.)

When a pair of friends (either same-sex males or females) reported for an experimental session, the male experimenter described the study in which the subjects would ostensibly be participating. They would be asked to guide a tarantula through a maze after watching a model, the experimenter, do it. Subjects at this point were asked whether they agreed to continue with the research and they all agreed to participate. During this introduction, the tarantula was in a 10 gallon tank and could be seen by the subjects.

After the explanation of the study, subjects were taken to separate rooms where they filled out the modified version of the MAACL Today Form (Zuckerman & Lubin, 1965) used in Study 1 which asked how they felt 'right now' and a nine-point, single item fear-of-the-spider scale which asked how afraid of the tarantula they were.

Next, the subjects, in each of the three conversation topic conditions, were placed together in a room without the spider present. They were given an opportunity to talk together for three minutes while the experimenter was presumably checking to see if everything was ready for the participant modeling phase of the study. There were four major treatment conditions that represented the manipulation of the topic-of-conversation independent variable. Subjects waited with a friend talking about either their feelings, problem-solving, or unrelated topics, or they waited alone. Subjects' conversations were audiotaped both to provide data for a manipulation check and to encourage subjects to comply with instructions.

In the disclosure-of-feelings condition, the subjects were instructed to talk only about their feelings concerning the task with the tarantula (which they expected to involve participant modeling). Given a hypothetical example of going to a physician's office for an injection, discussing one's feelings about the situation might deal with how subjects felt about getting the injection. In the problem-solving condition, the friends were instructed to talk on problem solving about the participant-modeling task involving the tarantula. Subjects were given examples about what was meant by a problem-solving conversation. For instance, if subjects had gone to a physician's office for an injection, problem solving about that situation might involve talking about whether or not to look at the needle, how to act with the physician, or how to deal with the injection itself. In the unrelated content condition, the subjects were instructed to limit discussion to topics unrelated to the task with the tarantula. Given the example about going to a physician's office for an injection, unrelated talk might be about politics, about what they did last weekend, and so forth. In the fourth condition, each subject waited alone for a three-minute period for the next phase of the study to begin.

After the three minutes, the experimenter returned and took subjects to separate rooms and asked them again to fill out the MAACL and the fear scale to provide a current measure of affect.

After completing the mood measure for the second time, one subject was randomly selected to complete the behavioral fear measure. After the first person completed the task, he or she returned to their room and then the other subject completed the behavioral fear measure. Subjects did not know that either they or their partner had gone first on the behavioral task.

The fear stimulus was represented by a live orange-kneed tarantula (*brachypelma smithi*) that was approximately 3½ inches (8.89cm) in diameter. The tarantula was in a plywood-based cart with sides made out of a clear, nylon fishing line netting. The enclosure had ¾ inch (1.95 cm) openings in the top and on all four sides through which the spider could potentially extend its legs but could not escape.

Based on a behavioral fear task designed by Levis (1969), subjects had to pull the spider cart towards them with a fishing reel down a six-foot (182.74 cm) long runway. Subjects were asked to move the spider as close to themselves as they comfortably could. It was possible with this apparatus for subjects to reel the spider as close as 9.05 inches (23 cm) in a horizontal plane with their faces.

After each subject's data had been obtained on the behavioral fear measure, the two friends were reunited and a debriefing was conducted. During the debriefing, the experimenter talked to the subjects about what they had experienced during the session. This procedure was designed to eliminate any remaining fears that subjects may have felt about their participation as well as to inform subjects about the actual purpose of the research. During the debriefing the experimenter handled the spider himself and gave factual information about the tarantula's undeserved reputation for being dangerous.

Results

Audiotape recordings were made of the subjects' conversations and subsequently content analyzed by two judges. The frequency of statements made by each pair of friends was recorded for each of the following categories: disclosure of feelings, problem solving, and unrelated talk. The overall reliability between the two judges' ratings was $r = .92$ across the categories of social interaction.

The two judges' ratings were averaged and analyzed via 3 x 2 (communication mode X gender) ANOVAs on each conversation category to verify that subjects had followed instructions about what to talk about. Significant main effects were found for the conversation topic manipulation on the observed frequency of statements in the conversation categories: disclosure of feelings, $F(2,38) = 35.58$, $p < .001$; problem solving, $F(2,38) = 57.93$, $p < .001$; and unrelated content, $F(2,38) = 116.76$. Subjects generally talked about what they were instructed to discuss and avoided topics they were asked to ignore. The means associated with these effects are presented in Table 1.

Table 1: Mean frequency of statements in the conversation categories as a function of the conversation topic

Topic of conversation independent variable	Mean frequency of statements per dyad in each category		
	Disclosure of feelings	Problem solving	Unrelated talk
Disclosure of feelings	5.86 (3.75)	1.54 (0.77)	0.00 (0.00)
Problem solving	0.69 (0.27)	7.84 (2.54)	0.24 (0.04)
Unrelated talk	0.26 (0.12)	0.53 (0.21)	8.88 (2.15)

Note: The numbers in parentheses are the standard deviations. Results are not reported for the 'Alone' condition because no one had an opportunity to talk there.

A planned comparison of the adjusted mood ratings was conducted to test the hypothesis that negative mood state would be higher in the disclosure-of-feelings condition than in the problem-solving and unrelated-talk conditions. Anxiety scores were significantly higher in the disclosure-of-feelings condition than in the problem-solving and irrelevant-talk conditions, $F(1,103) = 9.81$, $p < .005$. Depression scores were also significantly higher in the disclosure-of-feelings condition than in the problem-solving and unrelated-talk conditions, $F(1,103) = 4.04$, $p < .05$. However, these same comparisons for the hostility and fear-of-the-spider[2] ratings as well as the behavioral fear measure were not significant (See Table 2).

Table 2: Means and standard deviations on the negative mood measures

Topic of conversation independent variable	Negative mood measures				
	Anxiety	Depression	Hostility	Fear-of-the-spider	Behavioral fear
Disclosure of feelings	12.7 (5.6)	16.3 (6.0)	9.5 (4.6)	5.8 (2.7)	51.0 (35.0)
Problem solving	9.9 (3.5)	14.1 (4.7)	8.8 (2.3)	5.5 (2.5)	39.4 (22.4)
Unrelated talk	9.7 (4.7)	14.4 (7.6)	9.0 (5.1)	5.5 (2.5)	35.4 (23.7)
Alone	11.4 (4.7)	14.6 (5.5)	8.8 (3.0)	5.9 (2.0)	58.9 (39.4)

Note: The numbers in the parentheses are the standard deviations. There are 28 subjects in each major treatment condition collapsed across subject gender. The means for the anxiety, depression, hostility and fear-of-the-spider measures are adjusted for pretest scores on the same measures. The behavioral fear means are not adjusted for any pretest measures: also, the behavioral fear scores are measured in centimeters.

Study 2 also provided an opportunity to test the relative advantage of talking with a friend about any of the conversation topics versus waiting alone for the start of the stressful event. Schachter (1959) found that subjects who anticipated receiving a severe electric shock preferred overwhelmingly to wait with others who would undergo the same experience rather than to wait alone, which may have been due partly to the opportunity to reduce one's fears by waiting with other persons. We did not find that interacting with a friend in the three conversation conditions produced lower negative mood states on any of the paper-and-pencil measures compared to waiting alone for the stressful event to begin. However, subjects in the alone condition kept a significantly greater distance from the spider than did subjects in the conversation topic conditions, $F(1,105) = 5.28$, $p < .025$. This was the only variable for which being with a friend, regardless of the content of the interaction, was more beneficial than being alone. However, despite this statistically significant result and the failure of the disclosure-of-feelings condition to differ from the other talk conditions for this measure, mean scores for behavioral fear indicate that talking about feelings is more similar to being alone that it is to the other talk conditions.

RESEARCH ISSUES RAISED BY STUDY 2

How Social Interaction Influences Coping with Stress

Interaction with friends may help or hinder how well one copes with stress depending on the type of contact that occurs. Our research indicates that talking about one's feelings with a friend in anticipation of a stressful event is less beneficial than problem-solving with a friend or talking with a friend about things unrelated to the stressor. Talking about one's feelings was associated with a higher level of negative affect (as measured by the MAACL anxiety and depression scores).

Future research could focus on how problem-solving and talking about unrelated content assist people in coping with stressful situations. Problem-solving may allow individuals to think about direct actions, aimed at the environment or themselves, that alter the threatening nature of the situation. Talking about an irrelevant topic may reduce stress by taking the individual's mind off a potentially unpleasant situation. The irrelevant-talk condition may be effective in a short, stressful situation, such as in the present experiment. However, if the stressful event were to persist for a longer time, the advantage of the irrelevant-talk condition (which directs subjects' attention away from the threatening situation) may not endure. For a stressful situation that poses continuing threats, the irrelevant talk might be usefully combined with strategies that focus also on the more favorable features of a situation as well as on the individual's inner resources for coping with stress.

Individual Differences in Coping Styles

The research documents the benefits of problem-solving and unrelated talk compared to the disclosure of feelings. However, individual differences in how people deal with threatening events may make a particular coping strategy better for some individuals than for others. For instance, the Folkman and Lazarus (1980) Ways of Coping Inventory provides a 68-item checklist identifying different ways of coping with problems. The inventory provides information about problem-solving and emotion-focused coping. Problem-solving coping gives an estimate of the extent individuals try to confront a problem directly (e.g., 'I make plans of action and follow them'). Emotion-focused coping deals with how concerned individuals are with the regulation of emotional responses when faced with a threat (e.g., 'I talk to people about how I am feeling'). It might be predicted that problem-focused individuals would benefit more from a situation where they talked with friends about how to solve a problem, but less where they were asked to talk about feelings or unrelated content. On the other hand, emotion-oriented individuals would benefit more from a situation where they talked about their feelings compared to situations where they talked about problem-solving or unrelated talk. Thus, the relative success of the different conversation modes may depend on the different coping styles favored by individuals as they talk about a threatening event.

Timing of Social Interaction and Its Impact on Coping with Stress

Study 2 focused on how conversational topics influenced negative affect *in anticipation* of handling a stressful situation. Talking about one's feelings was the least successful strategy in alleviating negative affect (compared to the other conversational topics). But data collected recently by Pennebaker and Beall (1986) indicates that writing about the emotions associated with a traumatic event (several years after the trauma has occurred) may have positive health benefits. Compared to control subjects who wrote about trivial topics, undergraduates who wrote about personally traumatic events and addressed either the facts and the associated emotions or the emotions only, for 15 minutes each day for four consecutive days, initially experienced increased blood pressure and negative moods, but in the long term had fewer health center visits for illness and fewer reported days of restricted activities due to illness. Another condition that involved writing only about the facts of traumatic events was similar in its effects to writing about trivial topics.

Though the procedures in Pennebaker and Beall's versus our own study differ considerably, the effects of talking about one's feelings may depend on its timing - whether it occurs before or after the stressful event is experienced. Subjects who talk with their friend about their feelings before the stressful event may magnify their negative feelings and perceived lack of control whereas those who talk about their feelings after the stressful event may undergo a cathartic experience comprised of ventilating and dissipating their negative feelings (cf. Derlega, Margulis & Winstead, 1987; Freud, 1904/1954; Pennebaker & Beall, 1986). The impact of timing as a mediator of social support has not been considered in past studies; however, it may help explain why some studies find that social support (at least when it involves talking about feelings) is beneficial after (e.g., Fleming et al., 1982) but not before (e.g., Hobfoll & London, 1986) confronting the stressful event.

Social vs. Nonsocial Expression of Thoughts and Feelings

We have studied *social* support, that is, help provided by an interaction with another person. Subjects in the Pennebaker and Beall study (1986), however, experienced positive health benefits by writing in a diary. No social interaction *per se* was involved. Derlega and Grzelak (1979) argue that one function of self-disclosure is self-clarification. Self-clarification occurs when thoughts and feelings are put into words in a manner that increases awareness and understanding. The presence of a listener or reader is not required. Social interaction nearly always involves some degree of self-expression and, thus, an opportunity for self-clarification. Does the presence of another person matter? Furthermore, distressed subjects have sometimes reported that the mere presence of a friend or family member provided support (Lehman, Ellard, & Wortman, 1986). The benefits of self-expression with and without various levels of social exchange and the benefits of social interaction with and without various levels of self-expression need further investigation.

Affected vs. Unaffected Social Supporters

In the stressful situation created in Study 2 both friends expected to experience the fearful event (that is, the participant modeling task involving the tarantula). While this situation is similar to real-life events where stressed persons also serve as sources of social support for one another, it is unlike many life crises where there are those directly affected and others in the social-support network who are relatively unaffected. The psychological state of those providing social support surely influences their effectiveness as sources of social support.

In Study 2 we found that disclosing one's feelings about a stressful event generated more negative affect than did problem solving or unrelated talk. The degree of distress experienced by the supportive other may have an especially important effect on outcome when emotions are being shared. For example, in the Hobfoll and London (1986) study, where Israeli women with male relatives or husbands mobilized during the 1982 Israeli-Lebanon conflict who had confidants were more anxious than women without confidants, it is likely that the confidants were also anxious (that is, the subjects were probably talking to women also worried about someone who had been mobilized). Interacting with a friend who shares the same concerns may accentuate both persons' feelings. In other situations, such as when a spouse or child is ill, some individuals (family members) are threatened with a more severe, personal loss than others (friends). Disclosure of feelings to friends experiencing much less threat may be effective in reducing negative affect because they can serve as concerned listeners without feeling pressure to ventilate their own feelings. The relative benefits of disclosing one's feelings about a stressful event or engaging in other forms of social support may depend on whether one's source of social support is or is not experiencing stress.

Perceived vs. Enacted Social Support

As stated in the introduction to this chapter, an implication of survey research on social support is that the subjective perception that others care and want to help may be the 'active ingredient' in social support rather than any specific behaviors that others actually emit. Study 2, however, examined what people do and found that some 'social-support' behaviors are more beneficial than others. We did not measure perceived social support and, therefore, cannot say whether it was affected by the different experimental conditions. Perceptions of social support may be important mediators of the effects of 'supportive' behaviors. For example, it could be that in the disclosure-of-feelings condition, especially since both friends were probably feeling anxious, subjects may have felt their friend was in need of support as much as or more than being a provider of it.

In the future we intend to measure perceptions of support as well as affective and behavioral outcomes. An advantage of the experimental approach advocated here is that it makes it possible to examine the impact of enacted support, as well as personality variables of the stressed individual and aspects of the stressful situation, on both perceptions of social support and affective and behavioral outcomes. Thus, the role of perceptions of support in the chain of events leading to successful coping can be determined.

Conclusions

In the past decade research on social support has burgeoned. The positive effects of social support and the possibility of negative consequences have been documented. We are now ready to ask questions such as what constitutes positive social support; when does social support fail to help or even harm and why; what are the situational and personal factors that influence the impact of social support? While survey studies will continue to be important in mapping the effects of social support in real-life situations, an experimental approach to the study of social support can provide more precise answers to these questions.

There are of course many problems with an experimental approach, including the 'unnaturalness' of the situational stressors that were employed, the reliance on undergraduate students as subjects, and the short time span of the experimental intervention. However, we have verified in a laboratory-based experiment that pairs of friends are more successful than pairs of strangers in helping one another reduce negative affect and that, in anticipation of stress, friends talking about problem-solving or unrelated topics feel better than friends who focus on their feelings or persons waiting alone. In a laboratory the ingredients of social support can be separated and tested. These studies suggest that it is possible to create experimental manipulations that can clarify how situational variables, such as the timing and type of stress, and personality variables, such as gender and coping style, influence the impact of social support on coping. Clearly, the laboratory-based experiment provides an excellent opportunity to assess how social support operates, thereby complementing the survey-type approaches that have dominated empirical enquiry into this topic over the last two decades.

AUTHORS' NOTE

We gratefully acknowledge the comments of Warren Jones, Robin Lewis, and Stephen T. Margulis on an earlier draft of this chapter. Preparation of this chapter was supported by NIMH Grant 1 RO3 NH42002-01A2.

FOOTNOTES

1. Failure to find an effect for the fear-of-snakes measure may have resulted from the relative insensitivity of this measure. It is a one-item scale and subjects could easily remember how they rated their fear from time 1 to time 2. The desire to be consistent may have interfered with subjects reporting of any actual change in affect.
2. As noted in footnote 1 the one-item fear measure was probably insensitive to change in affect.

REFERENCES

Antonucci, T. C., & Israel, B. A. (1986). Veridicality of social support: A comparison of principal and network members' responses. *Journal of Consulting and Clinical Psychology*, 54, 432-437.

Archer, R. L., Hormuth, S. E., & Berg, J. H. (1982). Avoidance of self-disclosure: An experiment under conditions of self-awareness. *Personality and Social Psychology Bulletin*, 8, 122-128.

Averill, J. R., & Rosenn, M. (1972). Vigilant and nonvigilant coping stress and psychophysiological stress reactions during the anticipation of electric shock. *Journal of Personality and Social Psychology*, 23, 128-141.

Brownell, A., & Shumaker, S. A. (Eds.) (1984). Social support: New perspectives in theory, research and intervention. Part I. Theory and research. *Journal of Social Issues*, 40 (4).

Coates, D., & Winston, T. (1983). Counteracting the deviance of depression: Peer support groups for victims. *Journal of Social Issues*, 39 (2), 169-194.

Coates, D., & Winston, T. (1987). The dilemma of distress disclosure. In V. J. Derlega & J. H. Berg (Eds.), *Self-disclosure: Theory, research, and therapy* (pp. 229-255). New York: Plenum.

Cobb, S., & Jones-Cobb, J. M. (1984). Social support, support groups and marital relationships. In S. Duck (Ed.), *Personal relationships: 5: Repairing personal relationships* (pp. 47-66). London: Academic Press.

Cohen, S., & Syme, S. L. (Eds.) (1985). *Social support and health*. Orlando: Academic Press.

Cohen, S., & Wills, T. A. (1985). Stress, social support, and the buffering hypothesis. *Psychological Bulletin*, 98, 310-357.

Costanza, R. S., Derlega, V. J., & Winstead, B. A. (1988). Positive and negative forms of social support: Effects of conversational topics on coping with stress among same-sex friends. *Journal of Experimental Social Psychology*, 24, 182-193.

Derlega, V. J., & Chaikin, A. L. (1975). *Sharing intimacy: What we reveal to others and why*. Englewood Cliffs, N. J.: Prentice-Hall.

Derlega, V. J., & Grzelak, J. (1979). Appropriateness of self-disclosure. In G. J. Chelune (Ed.), *Self-disclosure: Origins, patterns, and implications of openness in interpersonal relationships* (pp. 151-176). San Francisco: Jossey-Bass.

Derlega, V. J., Margulis, S. T., & Winstead, B. A. (1987). A social-psychological analysis of self-disclosure in psychotherapy. *Journal of Social and Clinical Psychology*, 5, 205-215.

Derlega, V.J., Winstead, B.A., Wong, P.T., & Hunter, S. (1985). Gender differences in an initial encounter: A case where men exceed women in disclosure. *Journal of Social and Personal Relationships*, 2, 25-44.

Dooley, D. (1985). Causal inference in the study of social support. In S. Cohen & S. L. Syme (Eds.), *Social support and health* (pp. 109-125). Orlando: Academic Press.

Festinger, L. (1954). *A theory of social comparison processes.* Human Relations, 5, 117-140.

Fischer, C. (1983, January). The friendship cure-all. *Psychology Today*, pp. 74-84.

Fleming, R., & Baum, A. (1986). Social support and stress: The buffering effects of friendship. In V. J. Derlega & B. A. Winstead (Eds.), *Friendship and social interaction* (pp. 207-226). New York: Springer-Verlag.

Fleming, R., Baum, A., Gisriel, M. M., & Gatchel, R. J. (1982). Mediating influences of social support at Three Mile Island. *Journal of Human Stress*, 8 (3), 14-22.

Folkman, S., & Lazarus, R. S. (1980). An analysis of coping in a middle-aged community sample. *Journal of Health and Social Behavior*, 21, 219-239.

Freud, S. (1904/1954). *The origins of psychoanalysis.* New York: Basic Books.

Gottlieb, B. H. (1984). *Social support and the study of personal relationships.* Paper presented at the Second International Conference on Personal Relationships, Madison, Wisconsin.

Gough, H. G. (1956). *California Psychological Inventory.* Palo Alto, California: Consulting Psychologists Press.

Heller, K. (1979). The effects of social support: Prevention and treatment implications. In A. P. Goldstein & F. H. Kanfer (Eds.), *Maximizing treatment gains: Transfer-enhancement in psychotherapy.* (pp. 353-382). New York: Academic Press.

Heller, K. (Ed.) (1986). Disaggregating the process of social support. *Journal of Consulting and Clinical Psychology*, 54, 415-470.

Heller, K., & Lakey, B. (1985). Perceived support and social interaction among friends and confidants. In I. G. Sarason & B. R. Sarason (Eds.), *Social support: Theory, research and applications* (pp. 287-300). Dordrecht, the Netherlands: Martinus Nijhoff.

Hobfoll, S. E. (1985). Limitations of social support in the stress process. In I. G. Sarason & B. R. Sarason (Eds.), *Social support: Theory, research and applications* (pp. 391-414). Dordrecht, the Netherlands: Martinus Nijhoff.

Hobfoll, S. E. (1988). *The ecology of stress resistance.* Washington DC: Hemisphere.

Hobfoll, S. E., & Leiberman, J. R. (1987). Personality and social resources in immediate and continued stress resistance among women. *Journal of Personality and Social Psychology*, 52, 18-26.

Hobfoll, S. E., & London, P. (1986). The relationship of self-concept and social support to emotional distress among women during war. *Journal of Social and Clinical Psychology*, 4, 189-203.

Hobfoll, S. E., Nadler, A., & Leiberman (1986). Satisfaction with social support during crisis: Intimacy and self-esteem as critical determinants. *Journal of Personality and Social Psychology*, 51, 296-304.

House, J. S. (1981). *Work, stress and social support.* Reading, Massachusetts: Addison-Wesley.

Houston, B. K., & Holmes, D. S. (1974). Effect of avoidant thinking and reappraisal for coping with threat involving temporal uncertainty. *Journal of Personality and Social Psychology*, 30, 382-388.

Jones, W. H. (1985). The psychology of loneliness: Some personality issues in the study of social support. In I. G. Sarason & B. R. Sarason (Eds.), *Social support: Theory, research and applications* (pp. 225-241). Dordrecht, the Netherlands: Martinus Nijhoff.

Langer, E. J., Janis, I. L., & Wolfer, J. A. (1975). Reduction of psychological stress in surgical patients. *Journal of Experimental Social Psychology*, 11, 155-165.

Lazarus, R. S., & Folkman, S. (1984). *Stress, appraisal, and coping*. New York: Springer.

Lehman, D. R., Ellard, J. H., & Wortman, C. B. (1986). Social support for the bereaved: Recipients' and providers' perspectives on what is helpful. *Journal of Consulting and Clinical Psychology*, 54, 438-446.

Levis, D. J. (1969). The phobic test apparatus: An objective measure of human avoidance behavior of small objects. *Behavior Research and Therapy*, 7, 309-315.

Lowenthal, M. F., & Haven, C. (1968). Interaction and adaptation: Intimacy as a critical variable. *American Sociological Review*, 33, 20-30.

McGuire, J. C., & Gottlieb, B. H. (1979). Social support groups among new parents: An experimental study in primary prevention. *Journal of Clinical Child Psychology*, 8, 111-116.

Pennebaker, J. W., & Beall, S. (1986). Cognitive, emotional, and physiological components of confiding: Behavioral inhibition and disease. *Journal of Abnormal Psychology*, 95, 274-281.

Pennebaker, J. W., & O'Heeron, R. C. (1984). Confiding in others and illness rates among spouses of suicide and accidental death victims. *Journal of Abnormal Psychology*, 93, 473-476.

Procidano, M. E., & Heller, K. (1983). Measures of perceived social support from friends and from family: Three validation studies. *American Journal of Community Psychology*, 11, 1-24.

Reis, H. T., Senchak, M., & Solomon, B. (1985). Sex differences in the intimacy of social interaction: Further examination of potential explanations. *Journal of Personality and Social Psychology*, 48, 1204-1217.

Reis, H. T., Wheeler, L., Kernis, M. H., Spiegel, N. & Nezlek, J. (1985). On specificity in the impact of social participation on physical and psychological health. *Journal of Personality and Social Psychology*, 48, 456-471.

Rook, K. S. (1984). The negative side of social interaction: Impact on psychological well-being. *Journal of Personality and Social Psychology*, 46, 1097-1108.

Sarason, I. G. (1981). Test anxiety, stress, and social support. *Journal of Personality*, 49, 101-114.

Sarason, I. G. (1987). *An interactional view of social support*. Paper presented at the Iowa Conference on Personal Relationships. Iowa City, Iowa.

Sarason, I. G., & Sarason, B. R. (Eds.) (1985). *Social support: Theory, research and applications*. Dordrecht, The Netherlands: Martinus, Nijhoff.

Sarason, I. G., & Sarason, B. R. (1986). Experimentally provided social support. *Journal of Personality and Social Psychology*, 50, 1222-1225.

Sarason, B. R., Shearin, E. N., Pierce, G. R. & Sarason, I. G. (1987). Interrelations of social support measures: Theoretical and practical implications. *Journal of Personality and Social Psychology*, 52, 813-832.

Schachter, S. (1959). *The psychology of affiliation*. Stanford: Stanford University Press.

Shumaker, S. A., & Brownell, A. (Eds.) (1985). Social support: New perspectives in theory, research and intervention. Part II. Interventions and policy. *Journal of Social Issues*, 41(1).

Simmel, G. (1950). The stranger. In K. H. Wolff (Ed.), *The sociology of Georg Simmel*. Glencoe, Illinois: Free Press.

Thibaut, J. W., & Kelley, H. H. (1959). *The social psychology of groups*. New York: John Wiley.

Thoits, P. A. (1982). Conceptual, methodological, and theoretical problems in studying social support as a buffer against life stress. *Journal of Health and Social Behavior*, 23, 145-159.

Thoits, P. A. (1986). Social support as coping assistance. *Journal of Consulting and Clinical Psychology*, 54, 416-423.

Thoits, P. A. (1987). *Prying open the black box: New directions for research on social support*. Paper presented at the Iowa Conference on Personal Relationships. Iowa City, Iowa.

Whitcher, S. J., & Fisher, J. A. (1979). Multi-dimensional reaction to therapeutic touch in a hospital setting. *Journal of Personality and Social Psychology*, 37, 87-96.

Winstead, B. A. (1986). Sex differences in same-sex friendships. In V. J. Derlega & B. A. Winstead (Eds.), *Friendship and social interaction* (pp. 81-99). New York: Springer-Verlag.

Winstead, B. A., & Derlega, V. J. (1985). Benefits of same-sex friendships in a stressful situation. *Journal of Social and Clinical Psychology*, 3, 378-384.

Winstead, B. A., Derlega, V. J. Sanchez-Hucles, J. & Lewis, R. (1986). *Friendships and coping with stress*. Unpublished grant proposal submitted to NIMH.

Wortman, C. B., & Conway, T. L. (1985). The role of social support in adaptation and recovery from physical illness. In S.Cohen & S. L. Syme (Eds.), *Social support and health* (pp. 281-302). Orlando: Academic Press.

Wrightsman, L. S. (1960). Effects of waiting with others on changes in level of felt anxiety. *Journal of Abnormal and Social Psychology*, 61, 216-222.

Zuckerman, M., & Lubin, B. (1965). *Manual for the Multiple Affect Adjective Checklist*. San Diego: Educational and Industrial Testing Service.

SOCIAL SKILLS AND INTERPERSONAL RELATIONSHIPS: INFLUENCES ON SOCIAL SUPPORT AND SUPPORT SEEKING

Ronald E. Riggio and Judy Zimmerman

Recent work in social support and personal relationships has been concerned with the health promoting properties of social relationships. Two lines of investigation seem to characterize this body of literature. One focus has been on supportive social relationships in the context of the stress and coping process, finding that social support (broadly defined) affords protection against the potentially harmful consequences of stress (see Cohen & Wills, 1985; Turner, 1983, for reviews). A second related area of inquiry has examined the impact of relationships on well being, irrespective of stress, finding that the presence of social support or companionship directly enhances well-being (Aneshensel & Frerichs, 1982; Rook, 1987; Turner, 1983; Williams, Ware, & Donald, 1981;

see also Cohen & Wills, 1985). Now that several studies have suggested that social support has both main and interactive effects on health and well-being, research has begun to shift its emphasis from documenting the mere existence of such effects to explicating the process underlying such findings.

One point that has been raised in recent refinements of the social support construct is the possibility that social skills or other personality factors may account for the noted relationship between social support and health (Cohen & Syme, 1985; Gottlieb, 1983, 1985; Heller, 1979; Heller & Swindle, 1983). Indeed, social skills and social support are empirically related, such that social skills are associated with higher levels of perceived support (Cohen, Sherrod, & Clark, 1986; Sarason, Sarason, Hacker, & Basham, 1985). Some recent findings have helped to clarify the nature of the relationship between social skills and social support, providing some evidence that social skills and social support are indeed distinguishable constructs (Cohen et al., 1986). In this latter study, stress-buffering effects were still found for social support, even after controlling for the effects of social skills. These findings are initially encouraging. Individual differences in social skills seems to be a key to the development of good interpersonal and supportive relationships, but further progress in understanding the influence of social skills on interpersonal relationships and social support is hampered by the apparent lack of consensus as to just what social skills are.

Given this current state of affairs, the intent of this chapter is to present a conceptual framework for the definition and assessment of social skills. In particular, we are concerned with the impact of global social skills, and specific social skill components, on the social support process. In examining this relationship between social skills and social support we will maintain the position that an understanding of the construction, development, and maintenance of relationships is necessary.

With this as a background, we will examine the mechanisms by which social skills, via the association with satisfying interpersonal relationships, influences facets of the social support construct. Specifically, we will be concerned with the characteristics of socially skilled persons and their close relationships as they affect subjective support perceptions, and the supportive functions that such close relationships may offer. We will also discuss the impact that social skills and support perceptions have on actual support seeking behaviors. Finally, we will attempt to show that the nature of emotionally supportive interactions, and the benefits to be derived from them, are strongly colored by the respective social skills of both participants. A necessary starting point in this overall discussion is the definition of social skills.

A FRAMEWORK FOR DEFINING AND ASSESSING SOCIAL SKILLS

Traditional Approaches to Measuring Social Skills

Social skills have been conceptualized in a variety of ways. Some of these approaches consist of short and rather diffuse measures that tend to lack clear construct definition, and are thus limited in their ability to tell us about the specific nature of social skills (e.g., Levenson & Gottman, 1978; Sarason et al., 1985). A number of other measurement approaches seem to be assessing social skill-related constructs, without specifically referring to these individual difference dimensions as social skills. Most notable of these are the standardized measures of empathy (e.g., Hogan, 1969; Mehrabian & Epstein, 1972), depth of self-disclosure (see, e.g., Cohen et al., 1986, using Jourard's 1971 scale), and assertiveness (Rathus, 1973). More recent approaches have taken the perspective that nonverbal skills, such as emotional sending ability (e.g., Friedman, Prince, Riggio, & DiMatteo, 1980), emotional decoding ability (e.g., Rosenthal, Hall, Rogers, DiMatteo, & Archer, 1979), or self-monitoring of nonverbal behavior (see Snyder, 1974), represent key elements of social skill.

Most of the aforementioned approaches claim to assess a single skill, or skill-related construct. However, global social skill is likely to be a complex, multi-faceted construct. Indeed, many of these skill-related constructs are, themselves, multidimensional (for example: self-monitoring, see Briggs, Cheek, & Buss, 1980; Riggio & Friedman, 1982; empathy, see Davis, 1983; assertiveness, see Galassi, Galassi, & Vedder, 1981).

Thus, investigating the role that social skills play in the development of relationships and in the social support process is a difficult task. There is no agreed upon method for assessing social skills, and even measures purporting to assess only a specific dimension of social skill may have measurement problems (see Riggio, 1986; Riggio, Widaman, & Friedman, 1985). Moreover, studies to date that have used social skill related constructs have largely failed to offer a rationale for the inclusion of the particular skill type (Cohen et al., 1986; Procidano & Heller, 1983; Heller & Swindle, 1983).

An Alternative View of Social Skills

Many current views of social skills are really personality traits in disguise, focusing on what people are , rather than on what they do. Friedman (1979) views social skills as the behavioral manifestations of underlying personality traits. For example, individuals may score high on the Extraversion scale of the Eysenck Personality Inventory (or on the Extraversion subscale of the Self-Monitoring Scale), however this does little to pinpoint the specific behaviors that a person might display that would lead others to perceive the individual as extraverted. Focusing on the observable cues resulting from possession of some social skill(s) may be a more reliable and valid measure of personality dimensions (see Friedman, 1979). Additionally, this perspective would also facilitate an examination of what occurs between persons in social interactions, by moving the focus of analysis from the person to the dynamics of the interaction.

Riggio (1986) has noted consistencies in many measures of social skills/personality, and offers a conceptual framework to integrate them. This framework draws on work in a number of areas: communication, clinical work in social skills training, and attempts by personality and social psychologists to measure factors related to interpersonal effectiveness. This conceptual framework springs most directly from work on individual differences in nonverbal communication skills.

In this orientation, social skills are of three basic types: skill in communication expressivity, sensitivity, and control. These three skills operate in two realms: the nonverbal, and the verbal (or social) domain. Skill in verbal and nonverbal communication are hypothesized to be prerequisites for effective communication and are likely related to success in interpersonal interactions (see Riggio, 1986, 1989).

The resulting six basic dimensions of social skill are measured by the self-report, Social Skills Inventory (SSI). In order to lay a foundation for subsequent discussion, each of the basic skill dimensions is described briefly below.

- *Emotional Expressivity* refers to general skill in nonverbal sending, and reflects the individual's ability to express, both spontaneously and accurately, felt emotional states, attitudes, and cues of interpersonal orientation.
- *Emotional Sensitivity* is general skill in receiving and decoding the nonverbal displays of others. High scores indicate a concern for observing the nonverbal displays of others, and an ability to decode emotions rapidly and with great accuracy. Emotionally sensitive individuals may be more easily aroused by others, thereby sympathetically experiencing others' emotional states.
- *Emotional Control* is the general ability to regulate nonverbal communication. High scorers on this dimension tend to moderate the expression of strong emotions, thus suppressing or altering the display of felt emotional states. High scores indicate facility in posing emotions on cue, and may also point to decreased emotional spontaneity.
- *Social Expressivity* deals with general speaking ability and skill in engaging others in social interaction. Persons high in social expressivity appear to be outgoing and extraverted. High scorers tend to be loquacious, smooth flowing talkers, who do so without apparent conscious effort.
- *Social Sensitivity* refers to an ability to decode and comprehend verbal communication, and also is a general knowledge of social norms and

conventions. High scorers are attentive listeners. In extremes, skill in social sensitivity may lead to an over concern with the appropriateness of one's own and others' social behavior.
- *Social Control* is a general skill in social self-presentation, acting, and role-playing. High scorers on this dimension are socially adept and confident, and can easily adjust behavior to be situationally appropriate.

Table 1 presents sample items from each of the subscales of the revised, 90 item Social Skills Inventory (This revised version of the SSI eliminates a seventh scale that was termed 'social manipulation.'). These six scales, when summed, provide an index of global social skill. Global social skill, as represented by a summed score of the SSI scales, is in many ways synonymous with what previous researchers have labeled 'social intelligence' (Thorndike, 1920), 'behavioral intelligence' (Guilford, 1967), or 'social competence' (Wine & Smye, 1981).

In regards to the psychometric properties of the SSI, factor analysis of the SSI lends support for the multidimensional structure of social skill (Riggio, 1986). Concerning the interrelations among the basic social skill dimensions, most of the subscales of the SSI are slightly to moderately positively correlated with one another. However, there are some notable exceptions. For example, possession of the skill of spontaneous emotional expressivity is, in the general population, slightly negatively correlated with the skill of emotional control. Yet, the truly socially skilled individual should possess some of both of these basic skills. Indeed, recent research indicates that both skills - emotional expressivity and emotional control - are linked to emotional sending ability, with emotional expressivity more strongly related to spontaneous emotional sending, and both emotional expressivity and emotional control implicated in the successful encoding of posed emotional expressions (Tucker & Riggio, 1988). There is no doubt that the interrelations among the basic components of social skill are complex, for global social skill is a complex construct. Moreover, the relation between any single social skill dimension and social effectiveness, may not always be linear. Possession of all of the basic components that make up global social skill is important, but the various skill components should also be 'in balance' with one another. For example, possessing high levels of one basic component of social skill, in relation to other key components, could be dysfunctional. In other words, too much emotional (or verbal) expressiveness, without possessing the regulatory skills of emotional and social control may lead an individual to appear shallow, overly long-winded, and excitable. Similarly, while social sensitivity is a key skill in being able to 'read' social cues and understand norms governing appropriate social behavior, possession of social sensitivity without having expressive skills can lead to social anxiety and withdrawal from social interaction.

The development of the SSI provides a tool for examining the links between social skills and social support, and for investigating the relationships among

Table 1: Basic Social Skill Dimensions and Sample Items from the Social Skills Inventory

Emotional Expressivity

When I get depressed, I tend to bring down those around me.
I have been told that I have "expressive" eyes.
Quite often I tend to be the "life of the party."

Emotional Sensitivity

It is nearly impossible for people to hide their true feelings from me.
At parties I can instantly tell when someone is interested in me.
People often tell me that I am a sensitive and understanding person.

Emotional Control

I am able to conceal my true feelings from just about anyone.
I am very good at maintaining a calm exterior, even when upset.
When I am really not enjoying myself at some social function, I can still make myself look as if I am having a good time.

Social Expressivity

At parties, I enjoy speaking to a great number of different people.
When in discussions, I find myself doing a large share of the talking.
I usually take the initiative and introduce myself to strangers.

Social Sensitivity

Sometimes I think that I take things that other people say to me too personally.
I often worry that people will misinterpret something that I have said to them.
While growing up, my parents were always stressing the importance of good manners.

Social Control

I find it very easy to play different roles at different times.
When in a group of friends, I am often spokesperson for the group.
I can fit in with all types of people, young and old, rich and poor.

---

social skills, social support and the development and maintenance of social relationships.

Since the heart of many supportive interventions relies on putting people in touch with potentially supportive networks or persons, it would seem that we need to know how relationships are initially formed, developed, and maintained if persons are to benefit from such interventions (see Gottlieb, 1985). Social support does not 'just happen' when people meet, nor does it easily spring forth among those experiencing similar life circumstances. Social support systems take time to develop and to be nurtured, in the same way that close relationships take time to form. Turning attention to the ways in which basic social skill influences the quality of social bonds, in addition to their initial acquisition, will help establish the basis for a deeper understanding of support processes, and promote more effective intervention design. For if people lack basic social skills, providing contact with potentially supportive others could prove futile, because barriers will exist that prevent the development of the close relationships out of which support systems arise.

SOCIAL SKILLS IN RELATIONSHIP DEVELOPMENT AND MAINTENANCE

Social Skills and Relationship Formation

Persons with greater social skills would be expected to have more frequent interactions with others than would persons deficient in important social skills. In an ongoing series of studies using the SSI, global social skills, as well as specific social skill dimensions, have predicted success in initial social interactions with strangers in laboratory settings (Riggio, 1986; Riggio & Throckmorton, 1988; Throckmorton, 1985). In these studies, socially skilled persons were rated by naive observers as being more likable and more successful interactants than individuals lacking these social skill dimensions. Socially skilled persons also have increased opportunities for social interaction, as they have a greater number of daily acquaintances, more social group memberships, and larger social networks, than do less skilled persons (Riggio, 1986; Zimmerman & Riggio, 1985).

Specific social skill dimensions are theoretically and empirically linked to success in the initial stages of a social interaction. Most notably, expressive skills are particularly important since one's behavior must be initially attention-getting or eye-catching in order to even begin making an impression on an observer. Emotional expressiveness, in particular, has been shown to be important in these initial stages of an interaction (Friedman et al., 1980; Friedman, Riggio, & Casella, 1988). Once a conversation begins, skill in social (i.e., verbal) expressivity is critical to keeping the conversation flowing and in providing the momentum for the interaction to develop further.

As the interaction moves beyond the initial opening stage, and the acquaintance process begins, social skills in controlling and regulating behavior become important. First and foremost, the skilled interactant must regulate both verbal and nonverbal expression. The basic social skills of emotional and social control allow the interactant to keep expressive behavior at an appropriate level, given the circumstances in which the interaction occurs.

Skill in social control also involves role-playing ability. Individuals possessing high levels of social control are good social role-players - able to perform well in just about any social situation. Persons high in social control thus develop a kind of social self-confidence. Through experience they learn that they are able to adapt to a variety of social situations. Indeed, our research has shown that possession of global social skills, and of social control in particular, is related to standardized, self-report measures of social self-confidence (such as the Lawson, Marshall, & McGrath, 1979 scale; see Dalton, 1985), and to observers' ratings of subjects' confidence (Riggio, 1987; see also Riggio & Friedman, 1986). Taken together, these data indicate that the socially skilled person is evaluated positively, is actively involved in forms of social participation, and has increased opportunities for constructing beginning relationships.

Social Skills and Relationship Development

While expressivity is important in initiating social interaction and forming acquaintanceships, when it comes to the development of deeper relationships, expressivity, is merely the tip of the iceberg. The other basic skill dimensions, namely sensitivity and control, are also crucial for adequate relationship development. Interestingly, because expressive skills are so easily observed, many social skill training programs emphasize the importance of expressive skills- sometimes to the exclusion of other skill components (see Curran & Monti, 1982; Trower, 1984 for reviews). These skill training programs might be successful in getting participants to establish initial contacts with others, but may do little towards helping establish deeper relationships.

Sensitivity skills and skill in emotional and social control are of prime importance to the development of relationship bonds, for it is sensitivity that is behind the ability to be a good listener and for being emotionally 'in-tune' with another person. Further, it is skill in regulating communication that is behind the 'give-and-take' processes of strong relationships. Relationships that progress to deep levels of involvement are critical, when we consider that social support is most likely to arise out of relationships that are characterized by feelings of closeness and intimacy. We will argue that it is precisely the skills of sensitivity and control that are central to adequate relationship development and maintenance.

While we have been focusing on the roles that each of the various social skill dimensions play in relationship formation and progression, it is also true that possessing a *balance* of the basic skills is important in facilitating relationship development. Making friends requires skilled performance in a variety of domains. For example, a person may score high on the social skill dimensions of expressivity and control, but lack sensitivity. Such a person would likely have little difficulty making initial contact with individuals and might fit in well in a group setting, but the person would probably come across as self-centered due to the lack of sensitivity to what others are saying or feeling. This individual may have many casual acquaintances, but few close or long term friendships.

Similarly, possessing extremes of any specific skill component (in relationship to the possession of the other basic skills) would be an indicator of potential dysfunctionality. For example, extreme social sensitivity could manifest itself in shyness, which has been shown to have adverse effects on relationship formation and development (see Jones, Cheek, & Briggs, 1986). This should serve as a caution against focusing on any one type of social skill and its relationship to interpersonal outcomes.

Social skills may be implicated in relationship formation and development in a number of ways. Social exchange theory holds that the ability to provide rewards influences relationship progression (Burgess & Huston, 1979; Hays, 1985; Levinger & Huesman, 1980). Relational rewards are those whose origin stems from the mere existence of the relationship itself. Because social skills are associated with receiving more positive evaluations from others, persons in relationships with socially skilled individuals may profit as attributions of positive characteristics carry over onto them.

Conversely, those in relationships with persons deficient in social skills may reap fewer rewards. People may be reluctant to enter into relationships with those of lower social skills because they are less able to furnish relational rewards.

Moreover, interactions with socially skilled individuals may be rewarding in and of themselves. Interactions with socially skilled persons should be 'high quality' interactions. Skills in expressivity contribute to lively, engaging conversations. Sensitivity skills allow the socially skilled individual to be responsive to interactants. Skills in control and social sensitivity mean that conversations will follow social conventions and rules of propriety. Rewarding interactions can facilitate the development of a budding relationship.

According to a social penetration theory framework, self-disclosure operates as a prime determinant of relationship progression, with interaction progressing from relatively superficial levels to more intimate levels (Altman & Taylor, 1973; Hays, 1984, 1985). More likely, however, it is not absolute increases in the breadth and depth of self-disclosure that matters in relationship development, but *appropriate* self-disclosure that counts. Two components of social skill seem relevant here. A knowledge of social convention is required. An interactant must know how much to disclose, given the stage of the relationship and the social circumstances. The skill of social sensitivity deals with knowledge of such social rules. However, this skill alone is not sufficient. Skill in social control - role playing ability - assists the individual in executing behavior consistent with the social norms.

Unfortunately, too much social control may be an inhibitor of relationship growth. Possession of extreme amounts of social control may result in the appearance of being distant or aloof, which may be interpreted as disinterest in the relationship. Additionally, excessive social control may lead to a decreased amount of self-disclosure. Conversely, too little social control may lead to too much self-disclosure - making the other dyad member uncomfortable, particularly if the nature of such disclosures is not consonant with the circumstances surrounding the newly forming relationship. Reciprocity norms could also be invoked, with the other dyad member unwilling to disclose at a similar level. These factors could contribute to lack of progression in the relationship. Again, we see that a balanced possession of the basic social skill components is required for satisfying relationship development.

Increased breadth of interaction also distinguishes progressing from non-progressing relationships (Altman & Taylor, 1973; Hays, 1985). Conversation and social activities in diverse areas are indicators of breadth. With respect to conversation, ease in speaking and facility in engaging a partner's attention and participation are necessary. Those with greater expressive skills will have an advantage. Social control is also helpful in that it is associated with comfort in wide-ranging social situations. Socially skilled persons are unlikely to feel inhibited in strange social situations, or in situations where the conversation moves to uncomfortable, unfamiliar, or overly personal territory.

In sum, social skills appear to have multiple influences on relationship formation and development. As we shall discuss, these same basic skills are likely to be used differently in dealing with the maintenance of ongoing relationships.

Relationship Maintenance and Social Skills

Persons with greater social skill report having more close friends than do nonskilled persons (Riggio, 1986). Why would this be so? Hansson, Jones, and Carpenter (1984) argue that social skills influence the attention that is devoted to relationships and the effectiveness of those efforts. Thus, socially skilled individuals are adept at maintaining relationships. What specific types of social skills might be related to these maintenance efforts?

Skillful communication of attitudes and feelings, such as expressions of affection, should come more easily and frequently from the socially skilled person. The socially skilled individual is also responsive to the needs and feelings of the other person. Empathy seems to be clearly implicated here.

Research on empathy has distinguished two general forms (see Davis, 1983). One type of empathy involves ability to take another's perspective (e.g., Hogan, 1969). The other form of empathy involves emotional responsiveness-the vicarious experience of another's emotion (e.g., Mehrabian & Epstein, 1972). The basic social skills framework allows a closer examination of the underlying components of these two types of empathy. Perspective-taking empathy is composed of skills in the verbal/social domain-social sensitivity, social expressivity and social control. Emotional responsiveness empathy is made up of the skills of emotional sensitivity and emotional expressivity (i.e., 'reading' another's emotional state and reflecting that emotion back to the other person). Empathy, which we hypothesize to be a combination of specific social skills, is critical to the maintenance and enhancement of ongoing relationships (see, e.g., Guerney, 1977).

According to social exchange formulations, relationships need to provide a variety of benefits to remain satisfying and healthy. In fact, benefits are more strongly correlated with long term maintenance of friendships than are costs (Hays, 1985). It is reasonable to suggest that social skills are related to the provision of benefits in long term relationships. Persons high in social skills have a richer and broader knowledge of social norms. They pay a great deal of attention to the reward/cost ratios in relationships, and take extra efforts to provide positive interpersonal experiences (a form of behavioral reward), and pay back resources in a socially appropriate time interval.

An ongoing state of indebtedness might likely be a source of strain in a relationship. As a result of increased attention to the relationship and the benefits present therein, socially skilled persons would be less likely to incur a state of indebtedness than would nonskilled individuals. Additionally, socially skilled persons are keenly aware of, and responsive to, aid reciprocity norms. They judiciously seek assistance from others, and pay back assistance in kind. The issue of indebtedness has important implications for social support perceptions and support seeking.

SOCIAL SUPPORT, APPRAISAL PROCESSES AND COPING WITH EVERYDAY STRESS

Perceptions of Social Support

We would like to maintain that social support perceptions are made considering the larger context of interpersonal relationships. These assessments are the product of the status of current relationships, be they satisfying and successful, or dissatisfying and problematic. Thus, factors that influence the quality of interpersonal relationships should also be expected to impact support appraisals because they form the basis for the psychological sense of feeling supported.

Common to many discussions of social support is the blurring of two related, though distinct, concepts: the *perception* of support and *actual support seeking*. While the former primarily refers to a phenomenological state or judgment, the latter is a coping strategy that may in many cases have little to do with subjective perceptions of support. An individual may have a large network of persons who are viewed as being supportive. The persons in the network may have provided adequate support in the past, and these relationships may be currently satisfying, yet the individual would not actually seek out or attempt to mobilize otherwise available support for a variety of reasons (e.g., embarrassment, a willingness to manifest independence, etc.). With the distinction between support perceptions and actual support seeking in mind, we will first turn attention to social skills and subjective evaluations of support.

Social skills should impact support appraisals in several ways. As we mentioned, socially skilled persons are more successful at maintaining intimate, high quality relationships. Moreover, they have larger social networks which means that they have more persons on which to base support assessments. These two factors work to increase perceptions of support quality and availability. Socially skilled persons have realistic ideas of what relationships can offer, and do not harbor idealized expectations about relationships. Skilled persons are quite capable of achieving desired types and quantities of interaction, which leads to less biased and more realistic support appraisals. Similarly, socially skilled persons should have little or no discrepancy between desired support and support that is actually available, in contrast to persons of inadequate skills (see Hansson et al., 1984).

Socially skilled persons should experience less distress from relationships due to the presence of interpersonal problem solving skills. When conflict arises, the socially skilled individual is well equipped to deal with it. The socially skilled person is also cognizant of the fact that conflict and disagreements are a normal part of social relations. Thus, support appraisals may be resistant to decreases that stem from negativity in relationships.

In contrast to nonskilled persons, socially skilled individuals are less likely to incur a state of indebtedness. Indebtedness leads one to believe that help cannot be sought, or would not be offered, by persons in the social network. As a result, perceptions of available support would be lowered. However, due to the more vigilant monitoring of cost/benefit balances in ongoing relationships, socially skilled persons will have made efforts to either provide support to others or to reciprocate in some other way, thereby avoiding an incurrence of interpersonal debt. Persons of lower skill would be less aware of, or concerned with, the implications that help seeking would have on relationships and might ask for help more often, make larger requests, or fail to reciprocate appropriately. These behaviors might discourage support seeking and thus perceptions of available support may decrease. Additionally, indebtedness may serve to increase the discrepancy between desired support and received support, as those who have not received their 'due' might be less willing to freely offer support or comply with a support request.

Embarrassment, defined as the situationally evoked fear of negative evaluation (Shapiro, 1983), is another social skill related construct that influences support perceptions. The skill component of social sensitivity, and its accompanying concern for the appropriateness of social behavior, are most closely linked to embarrassment.

The relationship of embarrassment to support appraisal is another instance where appraisal of support is dependent on desired or potentially anticipated support seeking and giving. If the nature of the problem that initiates the appraisal process is one that induces embarrassment, an individual may (erroneously) believe that others would be unwilling to offer help, if the need were known, or that others would refuse a request for aid. As a result, perception of available support would be diminished. Similarly, embarrassment would make persons reluctant to actually seek help, and thus, support perceptions would also decrease. However, since embarrassment is situationally determined, it is unlikely that support perceptions would suffer long-term decrements. Because socially skilled persons are confident and self-assured in a wide variety of social circumstances, it seems much less likely that embarrassment would operate to decrease social support perceptions for these persons.

The reactions of others to past requests for aid also influence support perceptions. Persons of lower social skills are likely to have received more support refusals in the past than persons of greater skills, and nonskilled persons may also have received fewer unsolicited offers of help. The probability of a refusal would seem to be based upon the current status of the relationship. If the relationship is being poorly maintained, a refusal is much more likely, and the chances for donor-initiated support giving are lessened. Second, persons of lower social skills would be less likely to have large social networks to turn to for help. Moreover, persons from the limited support network may be overburdened by requests and fail to provide support.

The character of past supportive interchanges also provides input into support perceptions. If these interactions have been of good quality, and adequate benefits have been derived from them, perceived support would be deemed satisfactory. However, those individuals of lower social skills would reap less benefit from interactions where support was sought or given, and as a result, past support satisfaction will be lower, with perceptions of current support suffering as a result.

Social Skills, Appraisal of Stress, and Support Seeking

According to the stress and coping paradigm of Lazarus and his colleagues (see Lazarus & Folkman, 1984, for a review), secondary appraisal of stress involves the evaluation of coping resources and options. Recall that social skill implies a sense of mastery and social efficacy. The socially skilled person is adept at handling a variety of social situations, is confident, and knows that control can be exercised over the social sphere of living. This mastery can result in the perception that coping resources within are adequate. This is one way in which social skills can impact secondary appraisal. What would have been appraised as threatening or harmful may instead be appraised as a challenge, or non-stressful, due to the interrelationship of primary and secondary appraisal processes.

Perceived social support is another type of coping resource that influences secondary appraisal. Since global social skill and the specific dimensions of emotional expressivity, emotional sensitivity, and social expressivity are all positively related to perceived support and social network size (Zimmerman & Riggio, 1985), social skills are related to secondary appraisals in a second way - by virtue of a relationship with subjective support assessments. In sum, social skills can have both a direct and mediated effect on secondary appraisal.

In many cases, support seeking may represent an adaptive coping response to a difficult situation. A graduate student may turn to a fellow student for help in preparing for qualifying examinations. A person suffering from a difficult personal problem may choose to share it with a friend. As yet, however, our knowledge of the antecedents of support seeking is just beginning (see DePaulo, Nadler, & Fisher, 1983, for a review). We know even less about the possible relationships between perceived support and actually seeking such support.

Pushing these entanglements aside for the moment, one somewhat obvious prediction that could be made is that perceived support and sought support are positively related. If one believes that a supportive network or confidante(s) exist, this may preclude the use of other coping strategies, and seeking support would then become the coping method of choice. Similarly, socially skilled persons may indeed prefer to use support seeking over other strategies that are less interpersonal in orientation, such as wishful thinking, rationalizing, or other palliative measures. These persons are adept at maintaining intimate and high quality relationships, so it seems likely that high levels of perceived support would make actual support seeking a more viable option.

There are many reasons why persons would choose not to draw upon otherwise available support. Seeking support often carries with it the unpleasant connotation that one is incapable of solving the problem independently-it is an admission of weakness. A desire to manifest independence may thus inhibit support seeking. On the other hand, persons with a large reservoir of perceived support may choose not to use it, as the psychological sense that others would rally to your aid may provide the impetus to cope independently. This would seem especially likely for socially skilled persons. Additionally, social skill carries with it a sense of competence and mastery, and when this is combined with a strong subjective sense of support, it may actually reduce the need to utilize support.

This brings us to our central thesis on the role of social skills in support seeking. We would like to argue that socially skilled persons are very wise and prudent users of social support. Despite the fact that these persons are rich in social resources, they may choose to limit their use. Socially skilled persons are keenly aware of the costs associated with helping. They would realize the strain that frequent or large support requests could place on relationships. If support were indeed sought, socially skilled persons would likely make attempts to minimize the impact that the request(s) have on the relationships. One way that this might occur is by timely and appropriate 'repayment' of support. Socially skilled persons find it easier to anticipate and be attentive to the donor's needs, and skilled persons are certainly able to offer a variety of forms of behavioral rewards, such as unsolicited expressions of affection.

Furthermore, if seeking support is deemed absolutely necessary, socially skilled persons may prefer to use indirect, rather than direct, requests for aid. These covert methods may be disguised as what Glidewell et al. (1983) call 'experience swapping,' whereby ideas or personal experiences are exchanged. This disguised informational support seeking minimizes costs to the recipient. Since no direct request is made, incurrence of debt, and possible resulting relational strain, are avoided. The success of this support seeking strategy relies heavily on one's ability to control cues of deception, as the support seeker must camouflage the real reason behind the request. (Recently, social skills have been implicated in ability to successfully deceive; see Riggio & Friedman, 1983; Riggio, Tucker, & Throckmorton, 1987). Successful experience swapping also has the dual function of maintaining the seeker's self image, or sense of mastery.

Socially skilled persons may also be more adept at sending out nonverbal cues or 'hints' that help is needed. This is another way in which the negative correlates of a direct request are circumvented. Finally, those of imbalanced possession of social skills, such as individuals with high amounts of social sensitivity in relation to other skill dimensions, may prefer indirect requests for support in order to reduce feelings of inadequacy or embarrassment.

Social Skills, Social Support, and Coping Strategies: A Preliminary Investigation

In an effort to provide some empirical support for the hypothesized relationships between social skills and social support and the strategies used in dealing with everyday stress, one hundred twenty-seven college freshmen (aged 18-20 years) were recruited from introductory psychology courses. Subjects completed the SSI and the Dimensions of Social Support Scale developed by Cohen (Cohen, 1977; Schaefer, Coyne, & Lazarus, 1981). The Dimensions of Social Support Scale measures both social network size and perceived social support from each social network member (using a 5-point rating scale) on informational support ('How much does this person give you information, suggestions, and guidance that you find helpful?') and emotional support ('How much does this person boost your spirits when you feel low?' and 'How much does this person make you feel he/she cares about you?').

Structured interviews were used to assess students' strategies of coping with everyday stress derived from five sources-Stress related to: (1) schoolwork/school performance, (2) family relationships, (3) dating and social life, (4) part-time or full-time jobs (if applicable), and (5) time management. Responses to the interview questions probing for coping strategies were categorized using a scheme developed by Cohen and Lazarus (1979) which groups coping strategies into five categories: *direct action, information seeking, intrapsychic mechanisms, inhibition of action,* and *turning to others.* Of prime importance for the present study were the categories of information seeking and turning to others - use of both strategies theoretically tied to possession of basic social skills.

Two independent coders made ratings of frequency of use of each of the coping strategies across the five stress source areas using a 5-point scale with '1' being 'uses the strategy infrequently or not at all' to '5' 'uses the strategy constantly.' Agreement between the judges was high (r = .85).

Table 2. Correlations Between the SSI and Measures of Social Support and Use of Coping Strategies

	Perceived emotional support	Perceived informational support	Social network size	Uses of information-seeking coping	Use of turning to others coping
SSI-Total	.25**	.23**	.22*	.20*	.33***
Em. Expressivity	.26**	.16	.11	.11	.28**
Em. Sensitivity	.31***	.27**	.15	.18*	.24**
Em. Control	.14	-.11	.01	.05	-.25**
Soc. Expressivity	.20*	.24**	.19*	.26**	.33***
Soc. Sensitivity	.03	.15	.16	.01	.39***
Soc. Control	.17	.09	.01	.16	.14

All n's = 127.
* p < .05; ** p < .01; *** p < .001

Table 2 presents the correlations between the SSI scales, SSI total score, and the measures of social network size, perceived informational support, perceived emotional support, use of information seeking coping strategies, and use of turning to others coping strategies. Total score on the SSI was significantly and positively correlated with all five measures. The relationships between the SSI subscales and social support and choice of coping strategies also followed predictable patterns. Specifically, scores on the expressivity scales and the emotional sensitivity scale were positively related to perceived emotional support and the use of social support (turning to others) coping strategies. Conversely, scores on the SSI were not significantly related to use of intrapsychic coping mechanisms or inhibition of action strategies. Although preliminary, these results tend to support previous research on the relationships between social skills and social support/coping, and provide some support for some of the contentions outlined in this chapter.

SOCIAL SKILLS AND EMOTIONALLY-SUPPORTIVE INTERCHANGES

Since talking about problems often involves revealing negative aspects of oneself, persons would tend to seek out someone with whom they have had a longstanding relationship (Wills, 1985). Socially skilled individuals are adept at maintaining relationships and should have at least one trusted confidante in their support networks. Persons with imbalanced social skills (particularly individuals who are high on the control dimensions, or individuals who are overly socially sensitive) may have self-presentational concerns when discussing sensitive personal problems. These concerns would be exemplified by failing to adequately disclose the nature of the problem, or by masking, suppressing, or otherwise altering, the expression of affective states. These behaviors work to the detriment of good support provision by restricting the amount and accuracy of information that is available to the support donor. Thus, supportive interactions may provide less benefit for persons with social skill deficiencies.

A common aspect of many conceptualizations of emotional support is feeling accepted, valued, and cared for by another (Cobb, 1976; Cohen & Wills, 1985; House, 1981). Emotional support therefore requires behaviors such as attentive listening, accurate reflection and feedback, empathy and communication of reassurance, advice-giving, and perhaps even intimate self-disclosure on the part of the support donor. This, in itself, calls for socially skilled behavior on the donor's part. How might the various social skill dimensions play a part in skills in providing support?

Effective listening skills are linked to skills in emotional and social sensitivity. The skilled donor must also know when to avoid eye contact and when to maintain it in order to avoid increasing the other's discomfort during a sensitive interaction, while concurrently communicating interest. Facility in decoding nonverbal behavior is important here, particularly skill in picking up cues of potential discomfort.

Expressive skills underlie the communication of sympathy, concern, and reassurance. Verbal and nonverbal messages must be consonant and both must be sent skillfully in order to appear genuine. In addition to the expression of reassurance and sympathy, support donors should feel comfortable with touching another and displaying other cues (e.g., suitable proximity, body posture, facial expressions, etc.) of interpersonal orientation that exemplify concern.

Although sympathy, reassurance, and concern, would, in most cases, imply the presence of caring for another, they can occur without the *empathic* understanding of another's plight. While the former rely on expressive skills, true empathy demands both expressive and sensitivity skills. Recall that one aspect of empathy involves the vicarious experience of another's emotion, plus the expression of that vicarious state. Thus, empathy is a more complex combination of basic social skills, one that seems likely to be a key in determining satisfaction with received support.

The skills of social and emotional control are important donor skills because they assist with the monitoring of both verbal and nonverbal communication. Skills in control contribute to the ability to refrain from excessive advice giving and criticizing. Emotional control allows a support giver to modulate potential expression of disgust, shock, or disfavor, which, if displayed, could prove harmful to the recipient and exacerbate the problem.

Although we have been discussing the role that specific social skill dimensions play in support giving, we must note, once again, that adequate provision of emotional and social support relies upon global and balanced possession of the various social skill components. In light of this, socially skilled persons are superior support givers. The ability to give adequate support to others is beneficial when they themselves are in need of support.

What can the socially skilled person expect from a support provider who is not socially skilled? Individuals of greater social skill are able to compensate for this potential problem. Recall that social skill involves facility in both verbal and nonverbal expression, and sensitivity to both types of information. It would seem that many persons have difficulty accurately expressing feelings, and that this would be especially true when sensitive topics are discussed. The person high in emotional expressivity is a good sender of affective information. The emotional communications of the expressive individual are thus easier to decode. As a result, much of the ambiguity surrounding the communication would be eliminated for the support provider - he or she can easily 'read' the emotional state of the skilled support seeker.

A prerequisite for sensitivity skills, particularly sensitivity to nonverbal and emotional communications, is an awareness of one's own internal emotional state. Research has indicated a positive correlation between the skill of emotional sensitivity and private self-consciousness (see Riggio, 1986). The socially skilled individual's awareness of his or her own emotional states, and an ability to label inner experience, may also serve to facilitate support requests, making the job of even a nonskilled support donor easier.

Supportive interchanges also involve the exchange of mutual feedback. The socially skilled person is well-equipped to be attentive to the information communicated by the support provider. Perceptions of such information would likely be more accurate. The socially skilled recipient is able to tell if the donor is accurately perceiving the nature of the problem, and the emotions being experienced. The socially skilled person, in a sense, serves as his or her own accuracy monitor, checking the perceptions of the support provider.

Although the preceding discussion has dealt primarily with the provision of emotional support, the same line of reasoning can be used in specifying the social skill components and behaviors necessary for high quality interaction. As Reis (1984) maintains, we need to identify the interactional antecedents of support if we are to know how social interaction becomes social support.

CONCLUDING COMMENTS

The question of how social skills affect the many facets of social support is quite complex and warrants continued research attention. The present chapter has sought to contribute to answering this question by offering a conceptual framework for understanding basic social skills.

As we have attempted to show, an examination of the role of social skills in the support process sets the stage for a clearer understanding of the interactional dynamics that allow socially skilled persons to construct relationships that remain socially supportive. This focus on the role of social skills in the development and maintenance of supportive relationships has important implications for future interventions designed to foster healthy and supportive relationships. Clearly there exist a variety of programs that attempt to provide participants with skills to help them in establishing social contacts (e.g., social skill training, shyness clinics), in the hope that these acquaintanceships will grow into socially supportive relationships. In addition, there are a variety of existing programs designed to provide participants with supportive others - volunteers or paraprofessionals - who can render social support (e.g., self-help groups). We are proposing that there may be an alternative, more general approach. This involves programs that take steps to cultivate individuals' basic social-communication skills. Enhancing social skills will lead to improvements in the quality of relationships and will assist individuals in eliciting needed support from existing social networks.

Future research would also profit by considering this multidimensional view of social skills. Global social skill, or social competence, is clearly a complex construct - one that has often been approached somewhat simplistically. The social skills framework outlined in this chapter, although preliminary, begins to capture some of the multidimensionality of the social skill construct, providing a starting point for future investigations of the role that social skill plays in the establishment, nurturance, and maintenance of support relationships.

REFERENCES

Altman, I., & Taylor, D. A. (1973). *Social penetration: The development of interpersonal relationships*. New York: Holt, Rinehart, & Winston.

Aneshensel, C. S., & Frerichs, R. R. (1982). Stress, support, and depression: A longitudinal causal model. *Journal of Community Psychology*, 10, 363-376.

Burgess, R. C., & Huston, T. L. (1979). *Social exchange in developing relationships*. New York: New York: Academic Press.

Briggs, S. R., Cheek, J. M., & Buss, A. H. (1980). An analysis of the Self-Monitoring Scale. *Journal of Personality and Social Psychology*, 41, 330-339.

Cobb, S. (1976). Social support as a moderator of life stress. *Psychosomatic Medicine*, 38, 300-314.

Cohen, F. (1977). *The Dimensions of Social Support Scale*. Unpublished manuscript. University of California, Berkeley.

Cohen, F., & Lazarus, R. S. (1979). Coping with the stresses of illness. In G. Stone, F. Cohen, N. Adler (Eds.), *Health Psychology*, (pp. 215-254). San Francisco: Jossey-Bass.

Cohen, S., Sherrod, D., & Clark, M. (1986). Social skills and the stress protective role of social support. *Journal of Personality and Social Psychology*, 50, 963-973.

Cohen, S., & Syme, S. L. (1985). Issues in the study and application of social support. In S. Cohen and S. L. Syme (Eds.), *Social support and health* (pp. 3-32). New York: Academic Press.

Cohen, S., & Wills, T. A. (1985). Stress, social support, and the buffering hypothesis. *Psychological Bulletin*, 98, 310-357.

Curran, J. P., & Monti, P. M. (Eds.). (1982). *Social skills training*. New York: Guilford Press.

Dalton, D. (1985). *Individual differences in single mothers' stress and coping processes*. Unpublished Masters thesis, California State University, Fullerton.

Davis, M. H. (1983). Measuring individual differences in empathy: Evidence for a multidimensional approach. *Journal of Personality and Social Psychology*, 44, 113-126.

DePaulo, B. M., Nadler, A., & Fisher, J. D. (1983). *New directions in helping (Vol. 2): Help-seeking*. New York: Academic Press.

Friedman, H. S. (1979). The concept of skill in nonverbal communication: Implications for understanding social interaction. In R. Rosenthal (Ed.), *Skill in nonverbal communication* (pp. 2-27). Cambridge, MA: Oelgeschlager, Gunn, & Hain.

Friedman, H. S., Prince, L. M., Riggio, R. E., & DiMatteo, M. R. (1980). Understanding and assessing nonverbal expressiveness: The Affective Communication Test. *Journal of Personality and Social Psychology*, 39, 333-351.

Friedman, H. S., Riggio, R. E., & Casella, D. F. (1988). Nonverbal skill, personal charisma, and initial attraction. *Personality and Social Psychology Bulletin*, 14, 203-211.

Galassi, J. P., Galassi, M. D., & Vedder, M. J. (1981). Perspectives on assertion as a social skills model. In J. D. Wine & M. D. Smye (Eds.), *Social competence* (pp. 287-345). New York: Guilford Press.

Glidewell, J. C., Tucker, S., Todt, M., & Cox, S. (1983). Professional support systems: The teaching profession. In A. Nadler, J. Fisher, & B. M. DePaulo (Eds.), *New directions in helping (Vol. 3): Applied perspectives on help-seeking and receiving* (pp. 189-212). New York: Academic Press.

Gottlieb, B. H. (1983). Social support as a focus for integrative research in psychology. *American Psychologist*, 38, 278-287.

Gottlieb, B. H. (1985). Social support and the study of personal relationships. *Journal of Social and Personal Relationships*, 2, 351-375.

Guerney, B. G. (1977). *Relationships enhancement: Skill-training programs for therapy, problem-prevention, and enrichment*. San Francisco, CA: Jossey-Bass.

Guilford, J. P. (1967). *The nature of human intelligence*. New York: McGraw-Hill.

Hansson, R. O., Jones, W. H., & Carpenter, B. N. (1984). Relational competence and social support. In P. Shaver (Ed.), *Review of personality and social psychology*, Vol. 5 (pp. 265-284). Beverly Hills, CA: Sage Press.

Hays, R. B. (1984). The development and maintenance of friendships. *Journal of Social and Personal Relationships*, 1, 75-98.

Hays, R. B. (1985). A longitudinal study of friendship development. *Journal of Personality and Social Psychology*, 48, 909-924.

Heller, K. (1979). The effects of social support: Prevention and treatment implications. In A. P. Goldstein & F. H. Kanfer (Eds.), *Maximizing treatment gains: Transfer enhancement in psychotherapy* (pp. 353-382). New York: Academic Press.

Heller, K., & Lakey, B. (1985). Perceived support and social interaction among friends and confidants. In I. G. Sarason & B. R. Sarason (Eds.), *Social support: Theory, research, and applications* (pp. 287-300). Dordecht, The Netherlands: Martinus Nijhoff.

Heller, K., & Swindle, R. (1983). Social networks, perceived social support, and coping with stress. In R. D. Felner, L. A. Jason, J. Moritsugu, & S. S. Farber (Eds.), *Preventive psychology, research, and practice in community intervention* (pp. 87-103). New York: Pergamon Press.

Hogan, R. (1969). Development of an empathy scale. *Journal of Consulting and Clinical Psychology*, 33, 307-316.

House, R. J. (1981). *Work stress and social support*. Reading, MA: Addison-Wesley.

Jones, W. H., Cheek, J. M., & Briggs, S. R. (Eds.) (1986). *Shyness: Perspectives on research and treatment*. New York: Plenum Press.

Jourard, S. M. (1971). *Self-disclosure: An experimental analysis of the transparent self*. New York: Wiley.

Lawson, J. S., Marshall, W. C., & McGrath, P. (1979). The social self-esteem scale. *Educational and Psychological Measurement*, 39, 803-811.

Lazarus, R. S., & Folkman, S. (1984). *Stress, appraisal, and coping*. New York: Springer.

Levenson, R. W., & Gottman, J. M. (1978). Toward the assessment of social competence. *Journal of Consulting and Clinical Psychology*, 46, 453-462.

Levinger, G. O., & Huesman, L. R. (1980). An incremental exchange perspective on the pair relationship: Interpersonal reward and level of involvement. In K. J. Gergen, M. S. Greenberg, & R. H. Willis (Eds.), *Social exchange: Advances in theory and research* (pp. 165-188). New York: Plenum Press.

Mehrabian, A., & Epstein, N. A. (1972). A measure of emotional empathy. *Journal of Personality*, 40, 525-543.

Procidano, M. E., & Heller, K. (1983). Measures of perceived social support from friends and family: Three validation studies. *American Journal of Community Psychology*, 11, 1-24.

Rathus, S. A. (1973). A 30 item schedule for assessing assertive behavior. *Behavior Therapy*, 4, 398-406.

Reis, H. T. (1984). Social interaction and well-being. In S. Duck (Ed.), *Personal relationships (Vol 5): Repairing personal relationships* (pp. 21-45). London: Academic Press.

Riggio, R. E. (1989). *Manual for the social skills inventory*. Palo Alto, CA: Consulting Psychologists Press.

Riggio, R. E. (1986). Assessment of basic social skills. *Journal of Personality and Social Psychology*, 51, 649-660.

Riggio, R. E. (1987). *The charisma quotient*. New York: Dodd, Mead.

Riggio, R. E., & Friedman, H. S. (1982). The interrelationships of self-monitoring, personality traits, and nonverbal social skills. *Journal of Nonverbal Behavior*, 7, 33-45.

Riggio, R. E., & Friedman, H. S. (1983). Individual differences and cues to deception. *Journal of Personality and Social Psychology*, 45, 899-915.

Riggio, R. E., & Friedman, H. S. (1986). Impression formation: The role of expressive behavior. *Journal of Personality and Social Psychology*, 50, 421-427.

Riggio, R. E., & Throckmorton, B. (1988). The relative effects of verbal and nonverbal behavior, appearance, and social skills on evaluations made in hiring interviews. *Journal of Applied Social Psychology*, 18, 331-348.

Riggio, R. E., Tucker, J., & Throckmorton, B. (1987). Social skills and deception ability. *Personality and Social Psychology Bulletin*, 13, 568-577.

Riggio, R. E., Widaman, K. F., & Friedman, H. S. (1985). Actual and perceived emotional sending and personality correlates. *Journal of Nonverbal Behavior*, 9, 69-83.

Rook, K. (1987). Social support versus companionship: Effects on life stress, loneliness, and evaluations by others. *Journal of Personality and Social Psychology*, 52, 1132-1147.

Rosenthal, R., Hall, J. A., DiMatteo, M. R., Rogers, P. L., & Archer, D. (1979). *Sensitivity to nonverbal communication: The PONS test*. Baltimore, MD: Johns Hopkins University Press.

Sarason, I. G., & Sarason, B. R. (1985). *Social support: Theory, research, and applications*. Dordrecht, The Netherlands: Martinus Nijhoff.

Sarason, B. R., Sarason, I. G., Hacker, T. A., & Basham, R. (1985). Concomitants of social support: Social skills, physical attractiveness, and gender. *Journal of Personality and Social Psychology*, 49, 469-480.

Schaefer, C., Coyne, J., & Lazarus, R. (1981). The health related functions of social support. *Journal of Behavioral Medicine*, 4, 381-406.

Shapiro, E. G. (1983). Embarrassment and help seeking. In B. M. DePaulo, A. Nadler, & J. D. Fisher (Eds.), *New directions in helping (Vol. 2): Help-seeking* (pp. 143-163). New York: Academic Press.

Snyder, M. (1974). The self-monitoring of expressive behavior. *Journal of Personality and Social Psychology*, 30, 526-537.

Throckmorton, B. (1985). *Interrelationships of communication skills and interviewing success*. Unpublished Masters thesis, California State University, Fullerton.

Thorndike, E. L. (1920). Intelligence and its uses. *Harper's Magazine*, 140, 227-235.

Trower, P. (1984). *Radical approaches to social skill training*. New York: Methuen.

Tucker, J. S., & Riggio, R. E. (1988). The role of social skills in encoding posed and spontaneous facial expressions. *Journal of Nonverbal Behavior*, 12, 87-97.

Turner, R. J. (1983). Direct, indirect, and moderating effects of social support upon psychological distress and associated conditions. In H. B. Kaplan (Ed.), *Psychological stress: Trends in theory and research*. New York: Academic Press.

Williams, A. W., Ware, J. E., & Donald, C. A. (1981). A model of human mental health, life events, and social support applicable to general populations. *Journal of Health and Social Behavior*, 22, 324-336.

Wills, T. A. (1985). Supportive functions of interpersonal relationships. In S. Cohen & L. S. Syme (Eds.), *Social support and health* (pp. 61-82). New York: Academic Press.

Wine, J. D., & Smye, M. D. (1981). *Social competence*. New York: Guilford.

Zimmerman, J. A., & Riggio, R. E. (1985). *Social skills and social support*. Paper presented at meeting of the Western Psychological Association, San Jose, CA.

PART III

ATTRIBUTIONAL AND STRATEGIC ASPECTS OF RELATIONSHIPS

COGNITION IN MARRIAGE:
A PROGRAM OF RESEARCH ON ATTRIBUTIONS

Frank D. Fincham and Thomas N. Bradbury

Although the scientific study of marriage can be traced to Pearson's early work on the anthropometric characteristics of spouses (Tharp, 1963), research psychologists have paid relatively little attention to marital relationships. Clinicians, in contrast, have emphasized the importance of the marital relationship. This is perhaps not surprising because marital problems are the primary reason people seek professional help in the United States (Veroff, Kulka & Douvan, 1981). However, it was not until the rise of behavior therapy in the late 1960s and early 1970s that the study of marriage began to receive much attention from psychologists. Since then studies comparing distressed and nondistressed couples across a variety of variables have appeared frequently in psychology journals.

Most recently, psychologists have begun to emphasize cognitive factors in intimate relationships and in marital therapy (e.g., Arias & Beach, 1987; Doherty, 1981a, 1981b; Epstein, 1982; Fincham, 1983; Newman & Langer,

1988; Weiss, 1984). The primary focus of these writings has been on the explanations or attributions that spouses give for events in their marriage, and a number of studies have been conducted on this topic (for reviews see Bradbury & Fincham, 1990a; Thompson & Snyder, 1986). To illustrate this emerging interest among marital researchers and to demonstrate its potential for understanding marital dysfunction, the present chapter reviews a program of research on attributions in distressed and nondistressed couples. In presenting this research we hope to achieve three specific goals: (a) to identify what we consider to be a new phase in marital research; (b) to examine the shortcomings of the research program in order to illustrate problems encountered in the study of cognition in marriage; and, (c) to discuss issues that remain unaddressed in the study of marital attributions and thereby provide guidance for further research.

In view of the above goals the chapter is organized into four sections. First, we outline the historical context within which our research arose. We then present and evaluate our program of research. In the third section, we consider marital attributions within the context of broader conceptual frameworks that we have outlined in an effort to integrate the investigation of attributions, satisfaction, and behavior in marriage. Finally, we summarize the contribution of our work to understanding marital dysfunction and for clinical practice.

RESEARCH PROGRAM

Introduction

There are two reasons for considering the historical forces that have influenced our research program. First, it leads to deeper understanding of the research itself. Second, it reveals that the research reflects broader trends in psychology and the study of marriage, some of which have yet to be acknowledged explicitly. In this section, we outline the historical setting within which the research arose and then identify the more immediate influences that shaped its implementation.

Historical Context

The critical self-scrutiny in psychology during the 1970s was felt most strongly in social psychology. Indeed, it was not uncommon to hear of the 'crisis' of social psychology and of the need for a 'new paradigm' (e.g., Elms, 1975; Silverman, 1977; Smith, 1972). In this context numerous boundary areas of research emerged between subspecialties in psychology, several of which involved social psychology. For present purposes, the most significant of these is the social-clinical interface, a development that was realized concretely with the appearance of the *Journal of Social and Clinical Psychology* in 1983 and several related books (e.g., Leary & Miller, 1986; Weary & Mirels, 1982). Although not new, this interface has reemerged as a closer approximation to the integration of the two subdisciplines than in the past (Leary & Maddux, 1987). The research reported in this chapter is a product of these developments and, indeed, our initial study on marital attributions was published in the first issue of the new journal.

A second significant development is the recent emphasis on close, intimate, or personal relationships as an area of inquiry in social psychology. One senses that this change also reflects the *zeitgeist* outlined above and the desire to keep social psychological theories 'from becoming Mandarin exercises' (McGuire, 1969, p. 45). The precedent for investigating close relationships in social psychology, however, has been present from the inception of the subdiscipline as evidenced in Lewin's (1948) own work on marriage. Although some research appeared subsequently on the psychology of relationships, most of it involved persons who were 'personally irrelevant' to each other (Huston & Levinger, 1978). The recent interest in intimate relationships is thus overdue. Moreover, it is clear from the appearance of the *Journal of Social and Personal Relationships* in 1984 and numerous volumes and series that the field now has a firm foundation. Although contemporary social psychologists have not paid much attention to marriage, this renewed interest in close relationships clearly created a favorable climate for the establishment of our research program.

A third historical factor, specific to the study of marriage, is central to the nature of our research. This factor concerns the evolution of research on the most frequently studied topic in the marital literature, namely, marital quality (Spanier & Lewis, 1980). The study of marital quality has three major foci: (a) development of various indices to measure marital quality; (b) attempts to account for variance in measures of this construct; and, (c) reviews and critical analyses of work pertaining to marital quality (Spanier, 1976). Our concern is with the evolution of research in the second of these areas. Although there is no definitive historical account of this research area, historical perspectives on the field of family studies (H. Christensen, 1964) and the area of family interaction and psychopathology (Jacob, 1987) provide useful supplements to original sources.

Two well-established research traditions have evolved since Burgess and Cottrell (1939) first stimulated interest in the study of marital satisfaction. The *sociological tradition* is characterized by large-scale surveys designed to uncover correlates of marital satisfaction and marital stability. A variety of potential correlates have been investigated, ranging from demographics (e.g., income, age, religion, race) to individual psychological variables (e.g., personality traits, childhood socialization). Despite its dominance for over a generation and the large quantity of data it generated, research within the sociological tradition has yielded a disappointing number of replicable findings (for reviews see Burgess, Locke & Thomes, 1971; Hicks & Platt, 1970). Moreover, the correlates discovered have been accompanied by 'little or no explanation of why the correlations exist' (Raush, Barry, Hertel & Swain, 1974, p. 4). In their review of this research, Hicks and Platt (1970) concluded that the collection of further data to discover the situational and dispositional correlates of marital quality was ill advised; they called instead for a major shift in research emphases that would require 'breaking away from the reliance on self-report' (p. 569). This call reflected growing discontent with the sociological tradition and coincided with the beginning of a second major phase in marital research.

The evolution of the *behavioral tradition* in research on marital quality reflects several developments, the most important of which was the emergence of a behavioral approach to marital therapy (e.g., Liberman, 1970; Stuart, 1969). The behavioral tradition began with the application of operant principles to marriage, a beginning that is noteworthy because of the strong emphasis it placed on overt behavior. This was consistent not only with the dissatisfaction expressed about the limitations of self-report data and with the view that marriage could only be understood fully by observing spouse behavior (e.g., Raush et al., 1974), but also with two related developments that began in the 1950s, namely, the appearance of programmatic research on human interaction and the application of general systems theory to the study of families (see Jacob, 1987).

Two research strategies have dominated the behavioral tradition. The first examines behavior coded from laboratory interactions and shows that the interactions of distressed spouses, compared to those of nondistressed spouses, are characterized by higher rates of negative behavior (and in some studies lower rates of positive behavior), more reciprocity of negative behavior, and a greater degree of predictability between spouses' behaviors (for reviews see Baucom & Adams, 1987; Schaap, 1984). The second research strategy related spouses' daily satisfaction to their reports of pleasing and displeasing partner behaviors. Both types of reported behavior, and in particular displeasing partner behavior, accounted for a significant portion of variance in daily satisfaction (see Bradbury & Fincham, 1987b). Research conducted in the behavioral tradition thus documents an association between behavior and marital satisfaction.

Notwithstanding the importance accorded to overt behavior, the behavioral tradition never fully relinquished reliance on self-report as the criterion variable to which behavior was related, marital quality, was assessed via this modality. It is therefore not surprising that social learning theory, with its emphasis on mediational constructs as explanatory variables, was soon introduced into behavioral marital therapy (e.g., Jacobson & Margolin, 1979; Stuart, 1980). In fact, dissatisfaction with research in the sociological tradition did not reflect a complete rejection of the importance of subjective experience. For example, the seminal study of Raush et al. (1974) was conceptualized in terms of object relations schemata or 'organized structures of images of the self and other' (p. 43). In a similar vein, Glick and Gross' (1975) early evaluation of marital interaction research strategies stressed the importance of spouse appraisals in marital interaction, and these authors recommended as optimal, research that contains a 'union of 'subjective' and 'objective' measures' (p. 511). Sociologists such as Campbell, Converse and Rogers (1976) also noted that 'it is only when we consider the subjective experience of married people that we begin to account for significant amounts of variations in their satisfaction with their marriages' (p. 331).

Given the circumstances that fostered the evolution of the behavioral tradition, the emphasis on overt behavior and lack of research attention given to subjective experience is perhaps understandable. However, the limitations of a purely behavioral account of marriage have become more apparent in the 1980s. For example, the discrepancy between coders' and spouses' views of interactional behaviors led Floyd and Markman (1983) to call for research on cognition in marriage, and the finding that spouses are unreliable observers of partner behavior has resulted in similar observations (e.g., A. Christensen, Sullaway & King, 1983; Jacobson & Moore, 1981). Not surprisingly, a shift in the focus of research on marital satisfaction can be seen.

Although not yet explicitly acknowledged, we argue that sufficient data have accumulated to propose that a third phase of research has begun. In the *mediational tradition*, greater emphasis is being placed on the study of affective and cognitive processes in marriage, factors that might (a) account for variance in marital satisfaction beyond that attributed to behavior and (b) clarify the association between behavior and marital quality (see Bradbury & Fincham, 1987a/1989). Thus, unlike the behavioral tradition, which arose out of dissatisfaction with research in the sociological tradition, the current phase of research represents an acceptance and expansion of the behavioral approach. Our research program reflects this new phase of marital research. In fact, the immediate influences on our research are representative of those that have shaped the emergence of the mediational tradition.

Starting Point

Our research was stimulated by a clinical experience. In conducting intakes for a marital clinic, the first author was struck by the sweeping generalizations spouses tended to make about their partners' faults and the sense of helplessness they expressed about changes in their partners' behavior. This apparently was not a unique experience as it was subsequently discovered that the clinical literature abounds with observations of the negative appraisals made by distressed spouses about their partner and their marriage. For example, Jacobson and Margolin (1979, p. 108) note that spouses 'typically view therapy as a way to demonstrate to the partner and to themselves that they are blameless, and that the other is at fault.'

Given such observations, and the often implicit inference made by clinicians that the spouse's position reflects his or her explanation of partner behavior, it was not surprising to find that 'Theories of ... causal attribution also figure prominently in the derivation of treatment strategies' (Jacobson & Margolin, 1979, p. 31). What was surprising, however, was the total absence of data on explanations or causal attributions in marriage (cf. Wright & Fichten, 1976). This lacuna was highlighted further by the fact that attribution research in social psychology had, with few exceptions, investigated explanations for the behavior of strangers or hypothetical others. Thus, our research was designed to provide an empirical basis for clinical practice and for the increasing number of claims concerning the importance of cognition, particularly attributions, in marriage (e.g., Berley & Jacobson, 1984; Fincham, 1985a).

The prominence given to attributions in cognitive accounts of marital dysfunction is no doubt due to the dominance of attribution theory and research in social psychology at the beginning of the 1980s. However, research in the marital area has not been influenced directly by the classic models of attribution (e.g., Heider, 1958; Kelley, 1967; Jones & Davis, 1965) and such papers are still rarely cited. Marital researchers (e.g., Baucom 1981, Fincham & O'Leary, 1983) were guided instead by Abramson, Seligman and Teasdale's (1978) attributional reformulation of learned helplessness. The emphasis in this model on the degree to which causes were viewed as internal vs. external, stable vs. unstable, and global vs. specific was particularly influential because it determined both the nature of attributions investigated (dimensions of *causal* attribution, rather than other sorts of attribution) and the manner by which attributions were measured.

The focus on attributions can be traced also to the two widespread and fundamental assumptions that attributions (a) initiate and/or maintain marital distress and (b) influence the behavior a spouse exhibits towards his or her partner. Although these assumptions are largely implicit in theoretical writings, when made explicit they have the potential to further our understanding of satisfaction and behavior in marriage. Determining the relevance of attributions for marital satisfaction on the one hand, and for marital behavior on the other, have been ongoing themes in our research program. Hence, they are used below to organize its presentation. It will become apparent that the research is still evolving and that our changing understanding of the relation of attributions to marital satisfaction and marital behavior has influenced the manner in which they have been investigated. An increasing awareness of related questions has also contributed to changes in our research. In turning to present our research program, we shall endeavour to clarify the reasons for the changes that have occurred during its brief existence.

The Association Between Attributions and Marital Satisfaction

Establishing That an Association Exists

The widespread notion that attributions may maintain or even initiate marital dissatisfaction presupposes an association between these two constructs. Studies 1, 2a, 2b, and 3 document such an association. Additional data relating to this association were obtained in seven subsequent studies. The findings of these studies, the sample characteristics, and the nature of the stimuli used in each study are summarized in Table 1.

Study 1. The first study investigated attribution differences between spouses seeking marital therapy and happily married spouses in the community, on several dimensions of perceived causality (Fincham & O'Leary, 1983). The significance of locating causes of relationship events in the partner is intuitively obvious yet it seems unlikely that this dimension alone can capture fully the psychological meaning of explanations for marital events. For example, attributing the partner's lateness to a factor that may affect many areas of the relationship and that may be difficult to change (e.g., 'because he is selfish') carries more damaging implications for the marriage than one that is unlikely to affect other areas of the relationship and that has no particular implications for the future (e.g., he misread the bus timetable); the locus of the cause is the same in both cases, but the causes vary considerably on the global-specific and stable-unstable dimensions. Thus, spouses were asked to indicate the extent to which they perceived the causes of hypothetical positive and negative partner behaviors to be (a) *located* in their partner versus in themselves, other people, or outside circumstances; (b) *stable* and therefore likely to be manifest on future occasions when the behavior occurs, versus unstable; and, (c) *global* and thus affecting other areas of the marriage, versus specific. Answers to each of the three questions were summed across stimulus events for each type of behavior.

The results of Study 1 showed that clinic and community spouses did not view the locus and stability of causes differently. However, clinic spouses saw the causes of positive partner behavior as less global than community spouses. For negative partner behavior clinic spouses rated causes as more global than community spouses. The results of this study were also encouraging because they showed that responses on each attribution dimension were somewhat consistent. Specifically, though they were less than optimal, alpha coefficients were comparable to those found for attribution dimensions in depression research (see Peterson et al., 1982).

In attempting to account for the above findings, it was argued that spouses describe relationship problems in general, nonspecific terms and that the full extent of attribution differences between distressed and nondistressed spouses might be evident only when judgments are made about relationship problems rather than discrete behaviors. Similarly, the study examined *causal* inferences whereas clinical observations regarding attributions are often couched in terms

Table 1. Descriptive information on Studies 1 to 10 and results pertaining to the association between attributions and marital satisfaction

Study Sample	Mean Satisfaction Scores Males / Females	Stimuli	Causal Attribution Dimensions Locus	Stability Globality	Intent Motivation	Responsibility Attribution Dimensions Praise/blame
1 16 CL couples	76 65	hypothetical partner behaviors				
16 ND couples	125 127	6 positive	ns	ns .02		
		6 negative	ns	ns .001		
2a 18 CL couples	86 77	2 important				
19 CM couples	98 109	marital difficulties	.03[a]	.05[b] .001		ns
2b 11 CL couples	87 72	2 important				
11 D couples	85 77	marital difficulties	.05[c]	ns .05[d]		
18 ND couples	119 117					
3 40 CL spouses	73 72	hypothetical partner behaviors				
40 ND spouses	127 128	6 positive	ns	.001 .001	.001 .001	.001
		6 negative	ns	ns .001	.001 .001	.001
4 42 CL wives	65	3 negative hypothetical				
42 ND wives	116	partner behaviors			.01 .01	ns
		marital problems			.01 .01	ns
5 40 CM wives	105	hypothetical partner behaviors				
		3 positive			Comp. index .001	
		3 negative			Comp. index .001	
6 20 D and depressed wives	77[e]	hypothetical partner behaviors				
16 D wives	85[e]	3 positive			Comp. index .01	
24 ND wives	120[e]	3 negative			Comp. index .001	
7 22 CL couples	86[e] 84[e]	marital events				
22 ND couples	100[e] 105[e]	over past 24 hours				
		positive	ns[a]	ns .05		
		negative	ns[a]	ns .05		
8 36 CL spouses	78 76	hypothetical				
40 ND spouses	125 127	partner behaviors[f]				
		3 positive		.001	.001 .001	.001
		3 negative		.001	.001 .001	.001
9 43 CM couples[g]	101 94	2 important marital difficulties	Comp. index females = .01 males = .07			
10 Time 1		2 important	Comp. index		Comp. index	
39 CM couples[g]	104 98	marital difficulties	females = .05		females = .01	
Time 2		3 negative	males = .01		males = .01	
34 CM couples	102 96	hypothetical partner behaviors	females = .01 males = .01		females = .05 males = .05	

Note: Values entered in table refer to probabilities obtained for group comparisons. Except for CL spouses, all subjects were recruited via advertisements in local newspapers.
CL = Clinic, CM = Community, D = Distressed, ND = Nondistressed
a. Refers to partner as locus (low versus high rating).
b. Refers to comparison between distressed and nondistressed community spouses.
c. Pertains to comparison between clinic and community spouses only.
d. Pertains to comparison between distressed and nondistressed spouses only.
e. Scores on the Dyadic Adjustment Scale (Spanier, 1976). All other satisfaction scores are for the Marital Adjustment Test (Locke & Wallace, 1959).
f. Attributions for own behavior were also assessed but are not included in the table.
g. A small proportion of the couples were seeking therapy.

---

of *blame*. This is an important consideration in view of evidence that people respond differently to questions of cause and blame (e.g., Fincham & Jaspars, 1980). Finally, later conceptual analysis revealed that inferences of causal locus are far more complex in a dyadic context than had been assumed initially (see Fincham, 1985a), a factor that may have accounted for the null effects obtained on this dimension.

Study 2a. In view of the above observations, a second study was undertaken to examine attributions for marital problems, to assess the extent to which spouses blamed their partner for these problems, and to investigate the locus dimension in a more refined manner (Fincham, 1985b). In Study 1 the locus dimension was assessed on a single bipolar scale (spouse vs. you, other people, or circumstances) thereby assuming that (a) attributions are only important when contrasted with other potential causes (contextual assumption); (b) attributions to all nonspouse causes have the same psychological meaning (equivalence assumption); and, (c) spouse and nonspouse causes are inversely related (hydraulic assumption). To examine each of these assumptions and to provide a more viable assessment of causal locus, distinctions were drawn between causes residing in the attributor, his or her spouse, the relationship, and outside circumstances. Judgments regarding each of these locus dimensions were made separately, for the two most important difficulties in the marriage. Responses to corresponding questions were summed across the two stimuli to form more reliable attribution measures.

The results of Study 2a were similar to those of Study 1 on the global-specific dimension, as clinic spouses, compared to community spouses, tended to view causes for negative events as more global. However, no group differences were found for blame and, as in Study 1, no effect was obtained for the perceived stability of causes. In regard to causal locus, no support was found for any of the assumptions made in using a bipolar scale, a finding that might explain the lack of results in the first study. In contrast, the assessment of several causal loci in Study 2a showed that clinic spouses, compared to community spouses, were more likely to see causes of marital difficulties as residing in the partner and in the relationship.

The findings regarding causal locus are best understood in light of the distinction between attributions that focus on the partner in relation to the self (e.g., 'She or he does not trust me') and those that involve the relationship per se (e.g., 'there is a lack of trust between us'). The former is an interpersonal attribution whereas the latter is a relationship attribution (Newman, 1981a, 1981b). Because responses to the partner and relationship loci were positively related to each other and to partner blame, it seems likely that *interpersonal* attributions, rather than *relationship* attributions, were assessed. This possibility points once again to the difficulty of conceptualizing and assessing casual locus, a problem that also has not been resolved satisfactorily in the social psychological literature (Ross & Fletcher, 1985).

Although clinic and community spouses did not differ in their stability and blame judgments, further analyses of these judgments had the most immediate impact on our research. In regard to stability it is important to note that in Study 2a the community group consisted of volunteer spouses who had not been screened for marital satisfaction. As it turned out, 25 % of the spouses in this group were maritally distressed. Although their exclusion did not change the pattern of differences between clinic and community samples, an interesting finding emerged when the distressed spouses from the community were compared to the happily married community spouses. Specifically, distressed spouses in the community saw the causes of their marital problems as more stable than nondistressed spouses, suggesting that whether a distressed spouse is seeking therapy may be an important factor in the attributions she or he makes. Spouses seeking therapy may believe that with some help the cause of the difficulty can be removed, a belief that is consistent with help-seeking. In contrast, distressed spouses who do not seek therapy may be resigned to their marital difficulties. Attributions may be important therefore not only because they lead to declines in marital satisfaction (see Study 10) but also because they may discourage spouses from seeking marital therapy.

To our knowledge, no attention has been paid to potential differences between distressed spouses seeking marital therapy and those who do not seek therapy. Instead, research in the behavioral tradition assumes that contrasting either group with happily married spouses will yield comparable results. Because this assumption underlies most research on marital satisfaction, we conducted a study to compare the attributions of distressed spouses seeking marital therapy, distressed spouses who were not seeking therapy, and happily married spouses.

Study 2b. The procedures used in Study 2a were again followed (Fincham & Bradbury, 1988a). The two distressed groups did not differ in their attributions. Thus, the suggestive finding obtained previously for perceived stability was not replicated. In contrast, we replicated the findings that distressed spouses were more likely than nondistressed spouses to view the causes of marital difficulties as global, as located in the partner and in the relationship. These differences, however, were not found consistently when each of the distressed groups was compared to the happily married group. The therapy-seeking group differed on the two locus questions, whereas spouses who were not seeking help differed on the global and relationship dimensions. These findings indicate that the type of distressed spouses investigated may affect statistical significance in some group comparisons. However, the lack of differences found between the two groups of distressed spouses, combined with the fact that both groups differed from happily married spouses in the same manner (though not always to the same degree), suggests that drawing a distinction between them may not be critical in marital research.

The second ancillary finding that gained our attention in Study 2a concerned blame judgments. Although no group differences emerged for blame in Study 2a, blame judgments were positively related to the casual dimensions that differentiated clinic and community spouses. This suggests that an evaluative judgment, albeit a subtle one, may account for the causal attribution differences found in the first two studies. Our third major study examined this possibility.

Study 3. The possibility that a subtle evaluative judgment might account for the association between causal dimensions and satisfaction was encouraging because it was consistent with the focus of our third study (Fincham, Beach & Nelson, 1987). A growing realization that the learned helplessness formulation may be incomplete for the study of marital attributions had already stimulated a study in which we attempted to examine in greater detail the hypothesis that *responsibility* attribution may be more powerful than causal attribution in discriminating distressed and nondistressed spouses.

The decision to investigate responsibility attributions was based also on two further considerations. First, responsibility is a core concept in social life. We do not act simply on the knowledge of what caused a social event but on whether the person who caused the event is liable or responsible for what happened. Second, in marriage there is typically little doubt concerning causation because marital behaviors usually consist of intentional actions. More commonly at issue is whether the spouse intended his or her action to have the effect that it did and whether he or she could have acted differently. Such issues concern the question of responsibility rather than causation because an act intended to bring about the consequences that in fact occur is the most obvious exemplar of an act for which one can be held responsible (Fincham & Jaspars, 1980).

Unlike causal attributions, which concern the factors that produce an event or behavior, attribution of responsibility is inherently interpersonal because it involves a judgment about a person's accountability to another for the event or behavior. Thus, a judgment concerning the acceptability of partner behavior according to a set of standards, duties, or expectations is central to attribution of responsibility. The two classes of attribution are distinct because responsibility rests on a number of criteria (e.g., the application of standards) and processes (e.g., determining a mismatch between actual and expected behavior) that do not characterize causal attribution. Nonetheless, causal and responsibility attributions are likely to correlate highly because responsibility judgments usually entail judgments of causation - people are typically held responsible only for outcomes that they cause (see Bradbury & Fincham, 1990a; Shaver, 1985 and Shaver & Drown, 1986 for further discussion of this distinction).

In Study 3 responsibility was assessed by asking spouses to assign blame versus praise for hypothetical negative and positive partner behaviors and to make judgments about the partner's motivation and intent. The latter judgments were used because they are important determinants of inferred responsibility for intentional behavior (Fincham & Jaspars, 1980). Causal attribution dimensions were measured in the same manner as in Study 1, thus permitting direct replication of its findings and allowing evaluation of the relative efficacy of causal and responsibility attributions in distinguishing distressed and nondistressed spouses. Participants in the study were happily married spouses from the community and spouses seeking marital therapy.

As before, limited results were obtained for causal attributions. Only the global dimension distinguished distressed and nondistressed spouses replicating the findings of Studies 1, 2a, and 2b. Distressed spouses in this study saw the causes of positive partner behavior as less global and the causes of negative partner behavior as more global than nondistressed spouses. However, for positive events the dimension of causal stability also distinguished the groups: nondistressed spouses saw positive partner behaviors as more stable than distressed spouses. This finding may reflect the positive relationship between perceived stability and praise for such events. In contrast, the groups differed in the expected manner on all three measures of responsibility, for both positive and negative events. For positive partner behaviors, nondistressed spouses assigned more praise, more unselfish motivation, and more positive intent. For negative behaviors, however, distressed spouses assigned more blame, more selfish motivation, and more negative intent. These impressive results led us to examine responsibility attributions in subsequent studies.

Although the data from Studies 1, 2a, 2b, and 3 suggest that causal attributions are associated with marital satisfaction, the results were not as consistent as anticipated. One factor that could account for these inconsistencies concerns our measurement of attributions, an issue that is discussed later in more detail. Although comparable to other attempts to assess attributions, our measures were not optimal from a psychometric perspective. Before turning to the task of developing a psychometrically sound instrument to assess attributions, we examined alternative explanations for the association between attributions and marital satisfaction. It will become apparent that attempts to test competing explanations for our findings, to understand why attributions and marital satisfaction might be related, and to determine the impact of attributions on satisfaction, provide further data to document a consistent and meaningful association between these two constructs (see Table 1).

Alternative Explanations for the Association Between Attributions and Marital Satisfaction

The association between causal and responsibility attributions and marital satisfaction would be of limited interest if it resulted from an irrelevant third variable or from one whose relevance to marital satisfaction was already established. Consequently, we examined whether our findings might be an artifact of either the hypothetical spouse behaviors used to assess attributions or of the fact that distressed spouses also tend to be depressed.

Study 4. Although attributions for actual marital events had been investigated in earlier studies (e.g., Study 2a), most of our findings were based on attributions for hypothetical spouse behaviors. As the two classes of stimuli had not been compared directly, the question of whether they would yield comparable results remained unanswered and was therefore addressed in Study 4 (Fincham & Beach, 1988). If results pertaining to the above two classes of stimuli diverge substantially, existing data would be of limited generalizability. However, if attributions made for actual, problem-related behaviors converge with those for hypothetical behaviors, greater confidence could be placed in our findings. Such convergence would also hold open the possibility that standardized, clinically useful measures of attributions may be developed using hypothetical events. Study 4 is therefore an important first step towards greater psychometric sophistication in the study of marital attributions. The attempt to investigate this issue was influenced by two further observations. First, sex differences were not found in our initial investigations and hence only wives were used in this study. Second, responsibility attributions were investigated because they had yielded the strongest results. Consequently, happily married wives and wives seeking marital therapy indicated the extent to which partner behaviors contributing to marital problems and negative hypothetical partner behaviors were motivated by selfish concerns, were intentional, and were worthy of blame.

A significant main effect was found for type of behavior, as hypothetical behaviors were perceived to be more selfishly motivated and more intentional than problem-related behaviors. More important, however, were the findings that (a) consistent with our earlier studies, distressed wives saw partner behavior that contributed to marital difficulties as more intentional and selfishly motivated than nondistressed wives; (b) the type of stimulus behavior did not influence differentially the attributions made in the marital groups; and (c) attributions for the two types of events predicted marital satisfaction equally well.

These results show that although the magnitude of responses is affected by the type of event for which attributions are made, the pattern of attributions shown by distressed and nondistressed spouses was not influenced by the nature of the stimulus events. Because the latter is the focus of research on attributions in marriage, greater confidence can be placed in the pattern of results obtained in our earlier studies. However, sole reliance on the use of wives and responsibility attributions restricts the conclusions that can be drawn from Study 4. It is therefore important to note that the findings are consistent with those of two further studies. In Study 7 participants rated the dimensions of causes of actual spouse behaviors that had occurred in the last 24 hours in their marriage. Distressed spouses once again differed from nondistressed spouses on the global causal dimension for both positive and negative events. In Study 10 responses to hypothetical behaviors and problem-related behaviors were combined to form composite attribution indices. These indices were highly reliable regardless of attribution type (causal or responsibility) or spouse gender. We can therefore be more confident that the association between marital satisfaction and attributions is not an artifact of the stimulus events investigated.

Studies 5 and 6. In view of the documented association between depression and marital satisfaction (e.g., Beach & O'Leary, 1986; Epstein, 1985) and between depression and attributions (e.g., Peterson & Seligman, 1984; Peterson, Villanova & Raps, 1985), two studies were undertaken to determine whether depressive mood might account for the results obtained in our research (Fincham, Beach & Bradbury, 1989). These studies thus speak to the issue of whether we are investigating a marital phenomenon per se. In turning to them it is worth noting that in Study 1 reliable relations were not found between causal attribution dimensions and depressed mood as measured by the Beck Depression Inventory (BDI; Beck & Beamesderfer, 1974).

In Study 5, wives who responded to an advertisement in the local newspaper made responsibility attributions for positive and negative hypothetical partner behaviors and completed measures of depressed mood (BDI) and marital satisfaction. Single composite attribution indices were computed separately for positive and negative behaviors by summing responses across the three responsibility judgments and across the stimulus behaviors. This was prompted by (a) the need to reduce the ratio of variables to subjects in order to conduct the appropriate statistical analyses and (b) the observation that it is the pattern of attributions across causal and responsibility dimensions that is emphasized in theoretical statements (e.g., the extent to which spouses see partner behavior as selfishly motivated, intentional, *and* blameworthy). Moreover, Study 3 showed that the responsibility judgments were highly intercorrelated for both positive and negative events and yielded highly reliable composite measures (alphas > .85).

As expected, depressed mood and marital satisfaction were inversely related, indicating that maritally distressed spouses tended to be more depressed. However, depression was not a significant predictor of satisfaction when entered into a regression equation with the two attribution indices. In contrast, the attribution indices together accounted for 44% of the variance in marital satisfaction even after depressed mood had been statistically controlled. These findings indicate that the attribution-satisfaction link is not simply a function of depression.

Because these findings rest on the validity of the BDI as a measure of depression and could reflect limited variation in BDI scores, Study 6 compared attributions of clinically depressed and maritally distressed wives (group 1), nondepressed and maritally distressed wives (group 2), and nondepressed, happily married wives (group 3). Depressed wives were diagnosed by structured diagnostic interviews and met the criteria for a major depression (DSM-III; American Psychiatric Association, 1980). Attributions were assessed in the same manner as in Study 5. If attributions simply reflect depression then groups 1 and 2, but not groups 2 and 3, should differ.

The pattern of results outlined above was not found. Instead, for both attribution indices, no differences were found between groups 1 and 2 while groups 2 and 3 differed significantly. That is, attributions varied as a function of marital distress and not as a function of depression. When BDI scores were used as a measure of depression and the data were analysed in the same manner as Study 5, similar results were obtained for the attribution indices: they accounted for a significant portion of the variance in marital satisfaction (20%) after depression had been taken into account. Finally, it is noteworthy that in both studies the attribution indices and BDI scores accounted for over half of the variance in marital satisfaction.

In view of the above findings we concluded that attributions in marriage are important in their own right and are not simply a function of the stimuli with which they have been assessed or of spousal depression. The existence of an apparently valid attribution-satisfaction relation raises the question of why this association exists, and it is to this question that we now turn.

Understanding the Association Between Attributions and Marital Satisfaction

To date we have examined two issues, namely, self-attributions and self-disclosure, that might help us better understand the relation between attributions and satisfaction.

Studies 7 and 8. In Study 2a, supplementary analyses were conducted on responses to the causal loci questions in order to understand the earlier results yielded by use of a bipolar locus scale. One analysis showed that group differences emerged when self-attributions were subtracted from spouse ratings. Specifically, distressed spouses were more likely to see their partner, rather than themselves, as the cause of marital difficulties when compared to nondistressed spouses. This finding suggested that a complete understanding of attributions in marriage would require consideration of attributions for partner behavior *relative* to those for one's own behavior. That is, the significance of attributions for partner behavior may result from their discrepancy with self attributions. Do these differences reflect a positive bias (i.e., a tendency to make more benign partner than self attributions) on the part of nondistressed spouses, a negative bias (i.e., a tendency to make less benign attributions for partner behavior than own behavior) on the part of distressed spouses, or both? Two studies were conducted to investigate these possibilities (Fincham, Beach & Baucom, 1987).

Study 7 attempted to examine this issue in regard to causal attributions made for partner and own behaviors in the last 24 hours that were judged to be positive, negative, or neutral. Unfortunately, the data obtained for husbands were incomplete. Where attribution-target differences emerged for wives, they showed that distressed wives made attributions that were more self-enhancing (e.g., wives saw their own positive actions as more reflective of global causes). In contrast, nondistressed wives made partner-enhancing attributions (e.g., wives saw the causes of positive partner behavior as more global). These differences were strongest on the global dimension but occurred also on the locus dimension.

Because the findings of Study 7 may reflect differences in the behaviors reported for self and partner in the two groups, a second study was conducted in which greater control was exerted over the stimuli. In Study 8, spouses rated the dimensions of causes for hypothetical positive and negative behaviors and made responsibility attributions for those behaviors. They responded to the behaviors when portrayed as performed by their partners and by themselves.

To summarize a complex set of findings, evidence was obtained for a self-enhancing attribution bias in distressed spouses and a partner-enhancing bias in nondistressed spouses. As might be expected on the basis of Study 3, these biases were strongest for responsibility attributions. The existence of attribution biases in both distressed and nondistressed spouses has important practical implications for working with couples. It is therefore important to note that we have only been able to replicate the self-enhancing bias exhibited by distressed spouses (see Fincham & Beach, 1988).

Study 9. The second factor that we examined in attempting to understand the attribution-satisfaction association is self-disclosure (Fincham & Bradbury, 1989). The rationale for investigating this factor follows from the supposition that communication of attributions in marriage allows feedback from the partner that, in turn, provides the attributor with the opportunity to change his or her attribution. Indeed, the very act of formulating one's perceptions for communication may itself lead to their alteration, even in the absence of partner feedback. Alternatively, the attribution may be validated by the partner. In either case, self-disclosure is likely to affect marital satisfaction.

Spouses in this study completed a variety of individual difference measures, including a self-disclosure inventory, and made attributions for behaviors relating to marital difficulties. Only the data pertaining to self-disclosure are reported here. No evidence was obtained to suggest that self-disclosure mediated the relation between a spouse's attributions and his or her marital satisfaction. This finding is perhaps best understood by recalling that some attributions are mindful and are made consciously, whereas others are overlearned or mindless and thus occur automatically (Langer, 1978). Mindless attributions are unlikely to be subject to self-disclosure, yet they presumably affect the attribution-satisfaction relationship.

Our knowledge of the processes that underlie the attribution-satisfaction association is rudimentary. However, it appears that the contrast between attributions made for partner behaviors and for own behaviors may provide further insight into this issue. Clearly, the processes underlying the attribution-satisfaction association merit additional attention, a topic that is discussed in the penultimate section of the chapter. Before turning to a more detailed critique of our research, we present a final study that addresses the longitudinal association between attributions and satisfaction.

The Longitudinal Association Between Attributions and Marital Satisfaction

Interest in marital attributions stems in part from the belief that they at least maintain and perhaps initiate marital dissatisfaction. Without a test of this belief, however, 'nagging doubts about the actual impact of the attribution process' are likely to persist (Sillars, 1985, p. 287). Owing to the difficulty of using experimental approaches in this domain, Olson and Ross (1985, p. 300) noted that longitudinal studies hold the most promise in addressing the need for 'clearer causal data.'

Study 10. In Study 10, we asked spouses to complete a measure of marital satisfaction and to provide causal and responsibility attributions for marital difficulties and for negative partner behaviors, at two times approximately 12 months apart (Fincham & Bradbury, 1987a). A causal and a responsibility attribution index were formed by summing the questions pertaining to each type of attribution across the two classes of stimuli. As noted earlier, this yielded very reliable measures.

Both attribution indices were associated with satisfaction at the two assessment points. More importantly, wives' causal and responsibility attributions predicted their later marital satisfaction even after the effects of earlier satisfaction had been removed. Specifically, rating the causes of negative partner behavior and marital difficulties as located in the husband, and as global and stable, was related to declines in marital satisfaction a year later. In a similar vein, attributing blame to the husband and inferring his behavior to be intentional and reflective of selfish motivation predicted declines in satisfaction. For husbands, attributions at Time 1 were unrelated to marital satisfaction at Time 2. Importantly, marital satisfaction did not predict later attributions for husbands or wives. This finding is inconsistent with the alternative hypothesis that the longitudinal association between attributions and marital satisfaction exists because of the influence of marital satisfaction on attributions over time. These results appear to be specific to attributions because similar analyses involving a second cognitive factor, unrealistic relationship beliefs, yielded nonsignificant findings.

The data from Study 10 are consistent with a causal relationship in which, at least for wives, attributions influence marital satisfaction rather than vice versa. In view of the short time lag used and the duration of the marriages investigated (mean = 7.3 years), both of which are likely to have restricted the changes in the variables investigated, these findings are particularly noteworthy. Although these data cannot demonstrate the existence of a causal relation, they do provide further evidence to support the importance of attributions in marriage.

Critique

The attempt to conduct programmatic research on the association between attributions and marital satisfaction has yielded handsome dividends. It has, however, made us keenly aware of the limitations of our data. Some of these limitations were mentioned earlier. In this section we provide a more detailed critique of our research.

Accuracy of attributions. In view of renewed interest in the accuracy of social judgments (e.g., Funder, 1987), it seems reasonable to ask a simple question: could it be the case that distressed and nondistressed spouses are simply providing accurate attributions for the marital events they experience? The concern expressed in this question reflects two issues. First, attributions of distressed and nondistressed spouses may differ only because the attributions pertain to different events. Second, even if the events are the same, the attribution differences may accurately reflect the explanations for the events when they occur in distressed and nondistressed marriages.

It is interesting to note that research in the behavioral tradition is also subject to the first concern. That is, one can argue that the problem-solving interactions from which behaviors are frequently coded differ in intensity for distressed and nondistressed spouses and are not therefore comparable - behavioral differences may emerge in the discussion of marital problems simply because the problems differ. This applies similarly to marital difficulties used to elicit attributions. It seems equally plausible, however, to argue that this difference in intensity is inherent to the phenomenon studied and that criticisms based on such differences are not relevant. In regard to attribution research, this first concern is weakened further by the observation that attribution differences emerge even when standard stimuli are used to elicit attributions.

The second issue, regarding the accuracy of attributions, is more complex. Attribution accuracy implies the existence of a normative model against which subjects' attributions can be compared. As noted earlier, normative models of attribution have had no impact on marital attribution research. Nor is it clear that they are easy or even appropriate to apply. In their absence the issue of accuracy is difficult to address. However, two pragmatic standards have been offered as criteria for the accuracy of social judgments in real world contexts (Funder, 1987). The first, inter-observer agreement, is problematic when applied to marital attributions. For example, attribution agreement between a spouse and observers for a given partner behavior presupposes that there is nothing idiosyncratic to the spouse (e.g., level of marital satisfaction) that will affect his or her attribution. It is extremely unlikely, however, that partner behavior has the same hedonic relevance, implications for future interaction and so on for spouses as they do for observers. Because such factors are known to influence attributions (Jones & Davis, 1965; Knight & Vallacher, 1981), it may be inappropriate to use observers' attributions as a standard against which spouse attributions should be judged. That is, given the differing perspectives of spouses and observers, it would be entirely appropriate for their attributions to differ and thus misleading to label either the spouse's or the observer's attributions as 'biased.'

The second criterion used to determine accuracy of social judgments concerns their ability to predict behavior. To the extent that accuracy remains relevant in the present context, it is noteworthy that the relation between attribution and behavior forms a major theme in our research program. Although we do not wish to preempt its presentation, our data show that attributions do predict the attributor's behavior. Currently no data exist concerning the ability of spouse attributions to predict partner behavior.

In sum, attribution accuracy is a complex issue and we do not claim to have provided an exhaustive treatment of this topic. At first glance it appears to raise concerns about the interpretation of marital attributions. However, closer examination shows that the issue of attribution accuracy cannot be applied in a straightforward manner to marital attributions and may not be appropriate in this context. As a result, we suggest that the attribution-satisfaction link should not be seen as an artifact of attribution accuracy without more detailed analysis and justification of such an interpretation.

Reactivity of attribution measures. In addition to being subject to the accuracy question, our studies also reflect a shortcoming of most attribution research - all of our studies use reactive attribution measures that may prompt respondents to be more thoughtful than they otherwise might be. It is therefore reasonable to ask whether attributions occur in relationships when they are not prompted. Two sources of evidence speak to this issue. The first comes from studies that have asked subjects simply to write down their thoughts about spouse behavior (Holtzworth-Munroe & Jacobson, 1985) and to describe their relationship (Fletcher, Fincham, Cramer & Heron, 1987). Both studies showed that attributions obtained via this free response format were related to measures of relationship quality. An advantage of this measurement strategy is that it allows one to determine the kinds of events for which attributions might occur (see Bradbury & Fincham, 1990a).

The second source of evidence concerns attributions coded from conversations (e.g., Holtzworth-Munroe & Jacobson, 1988; Stratton et al., 1986). Although promising, the complex problems raised by this procedure preclude unambiguous interpretation of these studies (see Bradbury & Fincham, 1988a). Moreover, it is important to note that even though these studies show that attributions occur spontaneously in close relationships, they investigate a different level of attributions (i.e., attributions communicated to the partner) than those examined in our own studies (i.e., private attributions). Nonetheless, the reactivity of our attribution measures is a legitimate concern.

Levels of attribution. Our research addresses only one level of attribution, namely, the *private* attributions that a spouse is able to articulate to him or herself. Nothing is known about the factors that determine whether and how such attributions become *public* and therefore can be coded from conversations. A third level of attribution, *implicit* attributions, has not yet gained the attention of marital researchers. Implicit attributions result from relatively unreflective and less conscious processes that imbue events with meaning (Langer, 1978; Newman, 1981a, 1981b). A complete understanding of this level of attribution requires investigation of how spouses segment the stream of marital interaction into units and how the description of these units constrains attributions, two topics that have received little attention in attribution research (see Ebbesen, 1980; Newtson, 1973). In any event, investigation of attributions at these three different levels should not be confused even though each is likely to be important for understanding marital satisfaction. Similarly, different types or kinds of attributions should not be confused, a problem that is evident in our own research despite attempts to avoid it.

Types of attribution. The confusion of different types of attributions is endemic in the marital literature where terms such as 'causal attribution' and 'blame' are often used interchangeably. As a first step, we attempted to distinguish between causal and responsibility attributions. However, it also seems necessary to distinguish responsibility from blame as the nature of the two judgments differ. Unlike responsibility, blame is primarily an evaluative judgment that determines liability for punishment or censure. Thus, an attributor may hold someone responsible for abrogating a duty but not blame him or her for doing so. This may occur typically when the attributor hears the person's account for his or her action. In fact, Shaver (1985) argues that responsibility is a judgment made before an account occurs and that blame can only be determined veridically once the account is given. The readiness with which spouses assign blame in the absence of partner input suggests, however, that this may not be a relevant factor that differentiates responsibility from blame in marriage. Nonetheless, distinguishing between these two judgments has proved fruitful because it has also shown that we have investigated only a limited number of responsibility dimensions, a factor that may have lead us to underestimate the importance of responsibility attributions in marriage.

In retrospect, it is clear that we confounded responsibility and blame. The significant correlations between blame and the other two ratings used to measure responsibility (i.e., intent and motivation) do not mean that they should be treated as measures of the same construct because responsibility and blame are distinct conceptually. The distinction is subtle but its importance is emphasized by the consistent group differences obtained for ratings of motivation and intent as compared to the inconsistent results found for judgments of blame.

A problem in making the distinction between responsibility and blame is that the dimensions underlying the two judgments are similar. In fact, blame is usually assigned only when someone is found to be responsible for an event. Despite the high empirical associations between judgments of cause, responsibility, and blame, research in social psychology shows that the three types of attribution should be retained (e.g., Critchlow, 1985; Fincham & Roberts, 1985; Fincham & Shultz, 1981). The importance of the distinction between cause and responsibility is already evident in our work, but the extension of the responsibility-blame distinction to marital research also warrants serious consideration.

Psychometric issues. The clarification of the attribution constructs discussed above needs to be accompanied by greater attention to the measurement of attributions. Perhaps the single most important limitation of attribution research, and of our research in particular, concerns the psychometric sophistication of the attribution measures. The significance of this problem can be illustrated by two observations.

First, the reliabilities with which causal attribution dimensions have been assessed are generally lower than those pertaining to responsibility-related judgments.[1] Because the reliability of measures limits the magnitude of correlations with other measures, this difference could result in misleading findings concerning the significance of different types of attributions in marriage. Although the magnitude of the alpha coefficients obtained for causal and responsibility ratings do not differ substantially, the tendency for responses regarding causes to be less consistent needs to be addressed in future research.

Second, the interplay between conceptual and measurement issues is also evident in the composite attribution measures investigated. We began to study composite attribution indices partly because of the need for more reliable measures. Fortunately, this strategy was consistent with the emphases evident in theoretical writings (e.g., Baucom, 1987). However, the need for measures of greater reliability may have prompted us to abandon prematurely the examination of individual attribution dimensions, and this finer level of analysis should not be ruled out solely on pragmatic grounds.

In retrospect, it is clear that any prior attempt to develop a standard psychometric instrument would have been ill advised because (a) insufficient data existed to document the relevance of attributions in marriage; (b) the reliability of existing measurement attempts, while less than optimal, approximated minimal psychometric criteria; and, (c) insufficient attention had been paid to clarifying types of attributions (see above). Enough progress has been made, however, such that an undertaking of the psychometric task is now timely.

Consequently, we are developing a more adequate attribution inventory using hypothetical behaviors as stimuli.

Finally, consideration of measurement issues has alerted us to a problem concerning the measurement of marital quality that might account for the association between the global causal dimension and marital satisfaction. Standard inventories of marital satisfaction contain numerous questions asking spouses to indicate the extent to which they agree with their partner across various areas of the marriage. It can be argued that an overlap exists in the content used to assess marital satisfaction and the global causal dimension and thus results in a spurious association between them (Bradbury & Fincham, 1990a). In the present context it suffices to note that this problem can be avoided by limiting the measurement of marital quality to global judgments of the marriage (Fincham & Bradbury, 1987b). Consequently, we have begun to assess marital satisfaction using measures that are restricted to overall judgments of the marriage (e.g., Norton, 1983).

Attribution style. It is important to note that our research has yet to address the question of whether there exists an attribution style, or a tendency to explain marital events in a consistent manner across time and situations. In fact, it is quite possible that attribution style itself may be related to marital satisfaction, such that distressed couples may explain events in a relatively invariant manner whereas nondistressed spouses may base their attributions on information specific to a given situation. This possibility is consistent with the stereotypy observed in the interactions of distressed couples.

Two related issues also need to made explicit in regard to attribution style. First, it is possible that the attributions exhibited by spouses for marital events may reflect a more general attribution style that is evident also in attributions for nonmarital events. The fact that Studies 5 and 6 found no association between attributions for marital events and spouse depression suggests that this is unlikely in view of the documented association between depression and attribution style. Nonetheless, this issue needs to be addressed directly. Second, the pattern of attributions we have investigated is a relative one as our studies tend to compare distressed and nondistressed spouses rather than evaluate the nature of their attributions according to absolute criteria (e.g., stable versus unstable). Whether the attributions of distressed and nondistressed groups can be characterized in differing ways according to such absolute criteria remains to be determined.

Several further factors, including the use of volunteer subjects, small samples, and self-report, limit our research program. Most of these are not specific to the study of attributions in marriage or unique to our research. Consequently, they are not discussed in any detail. Instead, we turn to the second major theme of our research, the association between attributions and marital behavior.

The Association Between Attributions and Marital Behavior

Establishing that an Association Exists

As noted earlier, the need to investigate attributions in relation to marital behavior is emphasized by the potential of such research to further our understanding of behavior exchanges in distressed and nondistressed couples. The often implicit causal assumption, that attributions influence a spouse's behavior toward his or her partner, presupposes an association between attributions and behavior. Our initial studies began to address this issue and we therefore return to them.

Studies 1 and 3 revisited. In Studies 1 and 3, spouses were also asked to indicate what they would do in response to each of the hypothetical partner behaviors for which attributions were made. Behavioral intentions were assessed in terms of the extent to which the respondent reported that he or she would react to the partner behavior in a rewarding versus punishing manner.

In both studies little evidence was obtained to support an association between causal attribution dimensions and behavioral intentions. When responsibility attributions were assessed (Study 3), however, a strong association was found with intended behavior. That is, the more partner behavior was seen as negatively intended, selfishly motivated, and blameworthy, the more punishing was the intended response. In fact, a composite responsibility attribution index accounted for nearly a third of the variance in responses to positive behavior and almost half of the variance in responses to negative behavior.

The conclusions that can be drawn from the above results are limited because behavioral intentions were investigated. In addition, it is possible that the association between responsibility attributions and behavioral intentions reflects common method variance. Finally, our results may also reflects spouses' lay theories of the relation between attributions and behavior. Thus, in our next attempt to investigate the attribution-behavior association we decided to code overt behavior from marital interaction.

Study 11. Because the behaviors that differentiate distressed and nondistressed spouses have been documented most thoroughly in regard to problem-solving discussions, we examined in this context the behavior of 40 couples varying widely in level of satisfaction (Bradbury & Fincham, 1990b). Spouses made attributions for marital difficulties and then engaged in a discussion under instructions to work toward a resolution of a difficulty that they had both identified as important to their marriage. Each spouse's speaking turns were coded according to whether they represented one of three conflict tactics: (a) avoidance acts that minimize the explicit discussion of conflict; (b) negative acts that are verbally competitive and seek concessions from the partner; and (c) positive acts that are verbally supportive and do not seek concessions from the partner (see Sillars, 1982).

Negative acts were related to a causal attribution index (i.e., the extent to which causes were located in the spouse, and were seen as global and stable) and a responsibility attribution index (i.e., the extent to which the partner was blamed, seen to act intentionally, and considered to be motivated by selfish concerns) for both husbands and wives. For wives, significant associations between positive acts and both attribution indices were also found. To examine whether the associations found between attributions and conflict behavior strategies simply reflected variability in marital satisfaction, marital satisfaction was partialled out of the correlations. The same pattern of results was obtained.

Although this study provides some support for the idea that attributions and marital behavior are related, the data are limited in that they do not show that an attribution for a specific partner behavior is related to the spouse's subsequent behavior toward the partner. We address this issue in turning to examine the nature of the association between attributions and marital behavior.

The Impact of Attributions on Marital Behavior

The belief that attributions mediate behavior exchanges in marriage assumes that attributions for a partner behavior influence subsequent behavior towards the partner. We examine this causal assumption in our next study.

Study 12. In Study 12 we attempted to manipulate attributions for partner behavior in 16 happily married and 16 distressed spouses recruited from the community. This was done by altering the instructions that apparently resulted in a partner writing a negative description of his or her spouse; in fact, the partner served as an experimental confederate and wrote a standard description (see Fincham & Bradbury, 1988c). The instructions either asked specifically for a negative description, thus providing the subject spouse with an explanation for the nature of what was written, or simply asked for a description. After reading the description, and the instructions under which the partner purportedly wrote it, the subject spouse engaged in a five-minute interaction with his or her partner, who had been coached to play a neutral role that would facilitate the interaction. The interaction was coded to examine the effect of the attribution manipulation on the behavior of the naive spouse.

It was found that the behavior of distressed spouses was affected by the attribution manipulation. As expected, negative behavior towards the partner was more likely when no obvious external reason for the description was available. Surprisingly, however, an increase in positive behavior was also obtained in this condition. In contrast, the behaviors of nondistressed spouses did not vary significantly across experimental conditions.

One interpretation of these findings is that when the negative description was read in the absence of experimental instructions to be negative (a condition designed to induce an attribution for the event that was internal to the partner), the level of arousal experienced by distressed spouses increased because of the attributions they made (e.g. 'as usual, he is trying to put me down in front of other people'). The feelings experienced by nondistressed spouses in this condition would be less arousing because they make less damaging attributions for partner behavior (e.g., 'he is probably annoyed with me about something'). In contrast, when an external explanation of the behavior was available (e.g., 'It's because he was following instructions') both distressed and nondistressed spouses would be expected to make an attribution that was unlikely to increase arousal. This assumption of an attribution-affect linkage is consistent with a large body of research in social psychology (see Weiner, 1986) and our own prior research (Fincham & O'Leary, 1983; Fincham, Beach & Nelson, 1987).

The above differences in affective responses are important because arousal can often motivate behavioral responding (e.g., Strongman, 1987) and, in the present context, the valence of the behavior resulting from this arousal may have been influenced by the constraints of the laboratory situation (i.e., public behavior recorded on videotape). That is, distressed spouses' generally negative response in the condition where no explanation was provided for the description was most likely moderated by concerns regarding self presentation, thus leading them to present themselves in a balanced way to the experimenters. This explanation may account for the higher rate of positive behaviors exhibited by distressed spouses.

Unfortunately, the data collected in this study speak to only one part of this explanation. Although it was shown that the attribution manipulation affected the perceived locus of the cause equally for distressed and nondistressed spouses, no data were collected on other causal dimensions or on levels of arousal. Our interpretation therefore remains speculative. Nonetheless, this study provides the only data in the marital literature that speak to a possible causal relation between attributions and behavior.

Critique

The relative paucity of research on the relation between attributions and behavior in our research program parallels that in the marital literature (see Bradbury & Fincham, 1990a) and in social psychology (see Harvey & Weary, 1984; Ross & Fletcher, 1985). In fact, studies on the consequences of attributions are relatively rare despite the clear need for research on this topic (Kelley & Michela, 1980). The limitations of our studies emphasize the considerable challenge encountered in attempting to redress this imbalance.

Types of attributions and behaviors. The types of attributions and behaviors we investigated are likely to influence the relation found between these two variables. The earlier critique, in which we outlined different types of attributions and emphasized the importance of distinguishing between them, is therefore relevant here. Clearly we need to investigate the impact of perceived blame because this is the attribution that is most directly relevant to behavior.

In regard to behavior, our studies are limited by the investigation of behaviors that arise in negative contexts. Two considerations apply to the choice of behavior studied in future research. First, the belief that attributions mediate the relation between behavior and marital satisfaction suggests that behaviors reliably related to satisfaction be the subject of inquiry. Second, behaviors that have been found to instigate attributions (e.g., negative and unexpected behaviors) might be selected. The investigation of such behaviors has the advantage of simultaneously addressing questions regarding the external validity of findings. Nonetheless, there is a need to study different behaviors in different settings to understand fully the association between attributions and behavior.

Specificity of measures. Regardless of the types of attributions and behaviors investigated, both classes of variables can be measured at different levels of specificity. At the most general level, attributions can be assessed for global marital phenomena (e.g., relationship maintenance) and then related to broad classes of interactional behavior (e.g., problem solving strategies). Although Study 11 documents an association between attributions and behavior at a relatively global level, data concerning attributions for specific partner behaviors and specific spouse responses are likely to be more informative, especially for determining the influence of attributions on behavior. Study 12 approximates but does not attain this ideal because attributions for a specific event were examined in relation to a number of subsequent responses summed to represent broad classes of behavior. To the extent that the measure of attribution or behavior is molar rather than molecular, a greater degree of inference is required to sustain the argument that the attributions are likely determinants of the behavior.

Conceptual status of attributions. Even when attributions and behavior are investigated at the fine-grained level outlined above, it is important to note that attributions are unobserved internal events. Consequently, it is not possible to demonstrate that they actually influence behavior. It is thus reasonable to ask how conclusions regarding the influence of attributions on behavior can be best justified. In our judgment, two converging lines of evidence would allow this causal inference to be made with the greatest confidence.

First, the assumption that attributions mediate responses to partner behavior requires that attributions satisfy the criteria of a mediating variable (Baron & Kenny, 1986). That is, it must be shown that (a) variation in partner behavior accounts for a significant portion of the variance in spouse attributions; (b) variation in spouse attributions is reliably related to changes in spouse behavior; and, (c) when spouse attributions are held constant, a previously significant relation between partner behavior and spouse behavior is no longer significant. The mediational hypothesis could be investigated by requiring spouses to engage in a conversation that is structured so that only one person talks at a time and rates the perceived intent of the partner's message before responding to it. This variation of the commonly used 'talk table' paradigm (see Gottman, Notarius, Markman, Banks, Yoppi & Rubin, 1976) would allow a spouse response to be examined in relation to the preceding partner behavior *and* the spouse's attribution for the behavior.

Second, data from experiments would be useful. However, serious ethical and practical problems encountered in manipulating spouse attributions limit this source of data. To the extent that experimental investigations of the impact of attributions on behavior are feasible, they should meet two criteria. Because it is actually the experimental conditions, rather than attributions themselves, that are manipulated, it is necessary to show that the manipulation was effective in leading the spouse to attribute the event in the manner intended. A check on the manipulation is thus required that is obtained independently of the behavioral consequences investigated. In addition, it should be shown that attributions relate to the behaviors investigated within each cell of the experimental design.

Clearly our research does not yet meet the ideals outlined above. Nonetheless, the need for converging lines of evidence to support causal inferences regarding attributions and marital behavior is underscored because it would constitute an important contribution to the general attribution literature which, as noted earlier, focuses largely on the determinants of attributions rather than their consequences. In addition, testing the mediational hypothesis shifts the level of analysis from an entirely intrapersonal one (the association between a spouses's attributions and his or her own behavior) to a level that also takes into account interpersonal processes (the role of partner behavior in relation to a spouse's response). This has the desirable effect of avoiding the assumption that a spouse's behavior reflects only his or her individual characteristics, when behavior in fact reflects the larger interactive context in which it occurs (see Duncan, Kanki, Mokros, & Fiske, 1984).

Finally, it is noteworthy that even though data meeting all the criteria outlined above might suggest strongly that attributions affect marital behavior, such data would not show that this influence occurs in the natural environment. In sum, clarity regarding the conceptual status of attributions as unobservable hypothetical entities is important because it facilitates recognition of the type of data relevant to judging their status as a causal variable that mediates behavior exchanges in marriage.

Many of the issues mentioned in our earlier critique (e.g., levels of attribution) apply equally to our research on the relation between attributions and behavior. Rather than dwell on these issues in an attempt to provide an exhaustive critique of this topic, we consider next how a more comprehensive understanding of attributions in marriage might be achieved. Informed by the wisdom that comes with hindsight, our cartography for future research is guided by the limitations of existing data.

TOWARDS A MORE COMPREHENSIVE ACCOUNT OF ATTRIBUTIONS IN MARRIAGE

Relative to the accumulation of data, conceptual developments have been slow to emerge in the literature on marital attributions. However, the need for further conceptual analysis is evident from the critiques provided above and from the lack of any framework that integrates the study of attributions, behavior, and marital satisfaction. Because 'we shall not attain a conceptual framework by collecting more experimental results' (Heider, 1958, p .4), our recent efforts have been directed toward conceptual development. In this section we outline some of these developments and attempt to place the study of attributions in a broader context.

Conceptual Developments

The distinction noted earlier, between private and public attributions, has guided our conceptual analysis and has resulted in two foci for future research (Fincham & Bradbury, 1988b). Each is outlined in turn.

An Integrative Framework

Our studies investigate private attributions in relation to marital satisfaction and marital behavior, respectively. The need to integrate these two research themes lead to the development of a framework relating attributions, behavior, and satisfaction.

According to this framework, partner behavior leads a spouse to engage in primary processing. During primary processing a spouse attends to and extracts information from the behavior. Although the results of primary processing are available to the individual (e.g., an intense affect), primary processing itself takes place outside of conscious awareness. To the extent that primary processing results in the behavior being seen as negative, unexpected, and self-significant, secondary processing is initiated.

Unlike primary processing, both the product and the content of secondary processing are potentially available to the individual. The goal of secondary processing, to understand partner behavior in terms of existing knowledge, is achieved largely by making attributions for the behavior. Because it is assumed that spouses do not always make attributions for partner behavior, primary processing may not lead to secondary processing. Thus, given that secondary processing is initiated, a causal attribution is likely to occur that could be followed by attributions of responsibility and blame. The nature of the attribution experienced by the spouse will depend on the degree of mindfulness with which it is made. Thus, even though a spouse is initially aware only of blaming

Cognition in Marriage

his or her partner for a marital event (a mindful attribution), this does not imply the absence of implicit causal and responsibility judgments.[2]

Before describing the relations depicted among attributions, behavior, and marital satisfaction, a second aspect of the framework requiring elaboration is the distinction between short-term and long-term satisfaction. Short-term or momentary satisfaction is likely to reflect long-term satisfaction but is also likely to update long-term satisfaction over the course of time. Attributions for specific partner behaviors affect short-term satisfaction and thus do not necessarily carry implications for stable judgments of the marriage. To the extent that an attribution reflects a pervasive explanatory style it is likely to relate more strongly to long-term satisfaction. However, a specific attribution may affect long-term satisfaction directly when it pertains to an event that is highly significant to the spouse and his or her appraisal of the marriage (e.g., an extramarital affair).

In turning to the associations among attributions, behavior, and satisfaction (see Figure 1), it can be seen that our framework depicts the direct relation between attributions and marital satisfaction assumed in prior research (Path e). However, the integrative contribution of the framework stems from the incorporation of an indirect link between these two variables that is mediated by

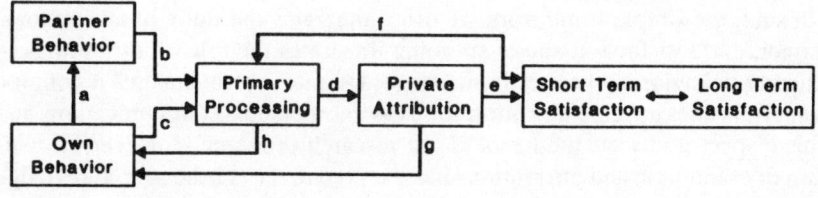

Figure 1. Framework for integrating the investigation of attributions, behavior, and satisfaction in marriage

behavior. That is, an attribution leads the spouse to act in a particular way (Path g) which, either alone or in combination with a partner response, mediates the relationship between the attribution and marital satisfaction (e.g., Path g, c, f or Path g, a, b, f). For example, a wife may attribute the grease she finds on a plate that her husband has washed to his laziness and respond by complaining to him (e.g., 'I am tired of always having to do your chores for you!'). She may appraise her behavior (e.g., 'It is not much fun complaining all the time') which may then influence her satisfaction (i.e., Path c, f) or go on to make an attribution for the behavior (e.g., 'He's causing me to become a real nag') that influences her satisfaction (i.e., Path c, d, e). Alternatively, she may appraise her husband's angry response (e.g., 'Get off my back!') and this appraisal could influence her satisfaction (i.e., Path a, b, f) or she might, in addition, make an attribution for his response (e.g., 'His shouting shows that he doesn't care about me') that influences her satisfaction (i.e., Path a, b, d, e).

This conceptual framework points to four issues of potential interest in future research. First, the indirect relations portrayed between attributions and satisfaction stress the significance of research on self-appraisals and self-attributions, a research direction that is also evident from the self-enhancing attributions found in Study 8. Second, because these indirect relations assume that attributions mediate behavior, they emphasize the critical need for research on this topic. Third, our analysis raises the question of whether current research underestimates the association between attributions and satisfaction because only the direct relation between these two variables has been studied. Finally, the proposed influence of satisfaction on primary processing suggests that greater attention be given to the possibility that a reciprocal causal relation exists between attributions and marital satisfaction.

In sum, the simple framework we offer integrates the study of attributions, behavior, and satisfaction and in so doing illustrates the role of attributions in mediating behavior exchanges in marriage. Despite the advantages it confers, this analysis does not consider attributions as interpersonal communications and in this respect it reflects the focus of our research program. However, investigation of communicated attributions has the potential to further our knowledge of marriage and we therefore turn to this topic.

Attributions as Communications

Although public attributions have recently gained the attention of marital researchers (e.g., Holtzworth-Munroe & Jacobson, 1988), they have not been conceptualized as dynamic, conversational behaviors (Bradbury & Fincham, 1988a). The implications of a dynamic conception of attributions are far reaching and relate the study of attributions to large, interdisciplinary bodies of literature (e.g., pertaining to symbolic interactionism, ethnomethodology, ordinary language analysis) that deal with social interaction as interpretation (see Semin & Manstead, 1983). Of particular relevance is the work pertaining to interpersonal communication, the significance of which is emphasized by the view that marital conversations allow spouses to order their lives and construct a reality that is experienced as objective (Berger & Kellner, 1970). We attempt to illustrate the utility of this work for marital researchers by outlining briefly the relevance of such notions as 'facework' and 'motive talk' that are found in these literatures.

Goffman (1955) uses the term 'facework' to refer to the coping behaviors that occur when an actor's identity is threatened in the course of social interaction. It suffices to note that some of these behaviors are employed to prevent the occurrence of actions that might disconfirm the actor's identity. In the present context, this suggests the intriguing possibility that spouses might offer attributions for their behavior in the absence of prompting by the partner. Whether such attributions result from perceived threats to identity is less important than the idea that attributions themselves can serve as stimuli in marital interaction. Is there anything unique about these stimuli, or can they be treated as equivalent to any other behavior in understanding their role in behavior exchanges? Under what conditions do attributions give rise to other attributions (e.g., 'He says he helped out because he loves me. I think he really said that because he wants a favor from me')? Do these meta-attributions show the same properties as attributions? Such questions suggest a fertile area of future inquiry.

A second class of facework behaviors is remedial. For our purposes the most important of these occur following an initial challenge in which the actor is held responsible or accountable for an event. His or her response is to engage in 'motive talk,' or talk designed to minimize negative interpretations of the incident. The most relevant type of motive talk in the present context consists of an account or explanation for one's behavior (see Lyman & Scott, 1970). Such accounts usually take the form of either an excuse, in which a spouse admits to behaving in an offensive manner but points to factors that mitigate his or her responsibility (e.g., lack of intent: 'I admit that I was late but I really didn't mean to spoil your evening'), or a justification, where it might be argued that the behavior was not offensive ('I was not being inconsiderate. I just had to call the director to let him know that I won't be at work tomorrow'). These accounts are important in marriage because they can lead to misunderstanding or to a negotiated understanding of events between spouses. Consequently, the study of accounts and the interaction that follows an account is likely to be critical to a complete understanding of marital dysfunction. For example, marital distress may result from the absence of corrective feedback that comes from communicating attributions because they tend to infer ('mindread') their partner's views. Alternatively, distress may reflect an unwillingness or inability to communicate attributions in a productive (e.g., nonthreatening) manner. As a third possibility, marital distress may be due to spouses' inability to successfully negotiate accounts with each other (e.g., due to high arousal, deficits in communication skills). Again a variety of potentially fruitful avenues of research is evident.

In the present context, it suffices to acknowledge the relation between the study of communicated attributions and a larger body of interdisciplinary work, and to note that this attempt complements the detailed description we have provided elsewhere of the accounting sequence and how it relates to types of attributions (see Fincham & Bradbury, 1988b). This topic is likely to prove important in future marital research, and an emerging interest in accounts that occur in the context of relationships augurs well for its realization (see Burnett, McGhie & Clarke, 1987).

Viewing Attributions in a Broader Context

The work described thus far has focused largely on attributions. However, a complete understanding of attributions in close relationships requires that they be examined in relation to other cognitions and viewed within a more comprehensive portrayal of the variables relevant to understanding close relationships. We therefore address each of these needs.

Cognition in Marriage

Building on the work of Doherty (1981a, 1981b), we recently outlined a cognitive model for conflict in close relationships (Fincham & Bradbury, 1987c). According to Doherty (1981a, 1981b), conflict instigates two cognitive processes relating to (a) the reason for the conflict (causal attribution) and (b) whether it can be resolved (efficacy expectations). Both of these processes are hypothesized to influence various dimensions of the conflict, including the extent to which conflict on a specific topic generalizes to other areas of the marriage, the foci of attempts to resolve the conflict, and whether such attempts occur. Because these relations are numerous and because the revised model that we propose is complex, we refer the reader to the original paper for a full account of the model and limit ourselves to making three observations.

First, data pertaining to marital conflicts provided greater support for the attribution component of the model than for the efficacy component (Fincham & Bradbury, 1987c, Study 2). This is consistent with the finding from Study 10 that attributions, but not the other cognitive variable investigated (relationship expectations), reliably predicted later satisfaction. Although the results for nonattribution variables have been disappointing, this in no way detracts from the need to investigate attributions in a broader cognitive framework.

Second, the cause-responsibility distinction used to revise Doherty's original model received strong empirical support in that responsibility judgments tended to mediate the relation between causal attribution dimensions and conflict dimensions. Moreover, consideration of this distinction made salient an aspect of responsibility that we had not previously applied to marriage, namely, the capacities that a person must possess before he or she can be held responsible or accountable for his or her behavior (see also Fincham & Emery, 1988; Shaver,

1985). Thus, for example, a husband's responsibility for marital conflict is mitigated to the extent that he lacks the ability to carry out conflict-avoidant behavior (e.g., he has a skill deficit). The clinical significance of further research on perceived capacities, responsibility, and marital dysfunction is emphasized by the fact that therapists often attempt to reattribute conflicts as being due to skill deficits in order to change the blaming attitudes exhibited by distressed couples.

Third, close examination shows that our data, like nearly all attribution research (see Smith & Miller, 1979, 1983 for exceptions), pertain only to cognitive content, or the outcome of attribution judgments. This is an important limitation because it tends to reinforce the view that attributions are static, rather than dynamic, entities. Moreover, such data do not explore directly the attribution *processes* that are postulated to occur in marriage. For example, even though the hypothesized linear causal relationship among different attribution constructs (i.e., cause → responsibility → blame) is consistent with the results of path analyses (Fincham & Bradbury, 1987c), a more direct test of this process model might be obtained by use of reaction time measures. As a possible index of cognitive processing (Pachella, 1974), reaction time should vary as a function of which attribution is measured according to this linear model. Because blame judgments imply the occurrence of causal and responsibility attributions, they should exhibit the longest reaction time, followed by responsibility attributions and then causal attributions. In a similar vein, the paradigm used by Smith and Miller (1983), in which subjects make one judgment about a stimulus event and then another, could be used to test the linear model. The pattern of reaction times obtained for the second attribution should vary systematically depending on the nature of the first attribution (e.g., a longer latency should be associated with a responsibility judgment that follows a causal judgment rather than one that follows a blame judgment). Pursuing this logic, competing models of the relations between cause, responsibility, and blame could be tested for a variety of stimuli.

Examination of the processes that underlie attributions and the factors that affect these processes has the potential to integrate the study of attributions within a broader conceptual framework. This makes salient the importance of information processing for attributions (see Wyer, 1981) and raises a whole new realm of questions for marital researchers interested in cognition. How do happily married and maritally distressed spouses organize and represent knowledge about their marriage? Do they seek out information that is consistent with their knowledge structures while avoiding information that is inconsistent with them? Does marital satisfaction make certain concepts and schemas chronically accessible and thereby influence the encoding of marriage-relevant information? Are nondistressed spouses more likely than distressed spouses to counterargue information regarding negative partner behavior so that the resulting cognitive representation is less influenced by this information? Do the opposite processes occur for processing of positive partner behavior? The value of addressing such questions is underscored not only by their potential to enrich our understanding of marriage but also by their ability to enhance the ecological validity of social cognition research, an area that has mushroomed since the social psychologists adopted the methods and perspectives of cognitive psychology. These considerations led us to consider a number of postulates derived from social cognition research in developing a more inclusive model of marriage in which cognition is one element.

A Contextual Model of Marriage

The contextual model of marriage (Bradbury & Fincham, 1987a, 1989) was prompted by three observations: (a) the need to gain some perspective on the role of attributions in marriage in order to balance the current emphasis placed on the study of this variable; (b) the absence of models in the mediational tradition that integrate behavior with the more recent study of cognition and affect; and, (c) the fact that existing theories of marriage 'either effectively explain a small segment of the marital interaction, but lack the scope and range of the many factors involved, or else have the range and broad perspective, but lack the detail and intricacy at the practical dyadic level of analysis' (Newcomb & Bentler, 1981, p. 92). In view of these observations, the contextual model takes as its starting point partner behavior and considers the spouse's cognitive and affective responses to the behavior as influenced by transient and stable contextual factors.

Briefly stated, a given partner behavior leads a spouse to engage in primary processing of the behavior in which (a) the behavior is attended to and interpreted and (b) a primary affective response occurs that is positive, neutral, or negative in tone. Following primary processing, the spouse may then engage in a behavior. However, to the extent that the behavior is appraised as negative, unexpected, and self-significant, and is accompanied by a negative primary affective response, secondary processing is likely to occur. In secondary processing the basic goal is to understand the partner behavior by engaging in a causal search and, if necessary, determining responsibility and blame; it is proposed that the attribution processes can be influenced by the primary affective response. As shown in Figure 2, spouse behavior can also occur after this secondary processing.

Although the processes described thus far incorporate the constructs studied in the behavioral and mediational traditions, the spouse is portrayed as functioning independently of prior events in the interaction and of the more stable psychological characteristics studied in the sociological tradition. Accordingly, the psychological *context* of the spouse needs to be considered. We propose that two broad classes of contextual variables influence the processing of behaviors in marriage. The thoughts and feelings experienced by the spouse immediately prior to processing a given partner behavior constitute the proximal context. In

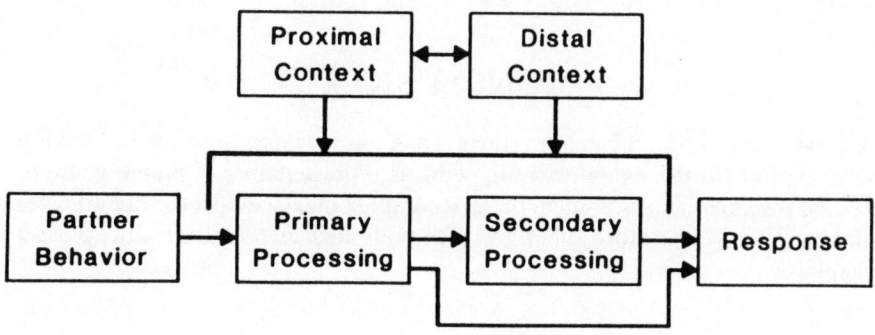

Figure 2. Intraindividual processes in the contextual model of marriage

contrast, the distal context comprises the more stable and continuing characteristics of the spouse and includes personality factors, attitudes, semantic and episodic memory, goals, chronic mood states, and learning history. The relationship between proximal and distal contexts is one of interdependence - the distal context influences the proximal context which in turn updates the distal context over the course of time (see Bradbury & Fincham, 1987a for further details).

The integration of variables studied in the sociological, behavioral, and mediational traditions within the common framework represented by the contextual model constitutes a distinct departure from most approaches to the study of close relationships.[3] The contextual model has proven useful in integrating disparate lines of marital research (Bradbury & Fincham, 1989) and in guiding our recent research (Bradbury & Fincham, 1988b). Although the model requires further refinement, some interesting questions are already apparent. For example, which proximal and distal factors account for variance in a spouse's interaction behavior? Do some variables evolve over the course of a relationship from being relatively proximal (e.g., an attribution for a specific relationship event) to being relatively distal (e.g., a generalized tendency to make certain sorts of attributions in the relationship)? What elements of the distal context exert the most influence over variables in the proximal context, and is this influence uniform over all variables in the proximal context? In sum, the contextual model illustrates the need to extend current cognitive accounts of marital dysfunction beyond a consideration of attributions and to integrate these accounts into a broader theoretical framework for the study of marriage.

CONCLUSION

A great deal of ground has been traversed in our research program over a very short period. To the extent that this work is representative of a new genre of marital research, an assessment of its accomplishments and its shortcomings is timely. We have therefore attempted to provide such an appraisal in the present chapter.

Contribution to Understanding Marital Dysfunction

Considerable progress has been made in examining the two major assumptions that have stimulated attribution research in marriage. First, a reliable association between attributions and marital satisfaction has been documented (Studies 1, 2a, 2b, and 3). Second, alternative explanations for this relation have been ruled out (Studies 4, 5, and 6), and data have been collected to suggest that attributions are causally related to marital satisfaction (Study 10). Third, our attempts to understand why there is an association between attributions and marital satisfaction showed that attributions for partner behavior may assume their significance because they are discrepant with those made for one's own behavior (Studies 7 and 8). Fourth, preliminary data support the existence of an association between attributions and marital behavior (Studies 1, 3, and 11) and show that attributions influence behavior (Study 12).

These data are quite modest, however, relative to the numerous claims made regarding the importance of attributions in marriage and in marital therapy. Nonetheless, their importance is emphasized by the fact that they are among the first on marital attributions. In fact, our research appears to provide the only data regarding (a) a causal relation between attributions and marital satisfaction, (b) the factors that might give rise to the attribution-satisfaction relation, (c) an association between marital attributions and marital behavior, and (d) the possible causal nature of this association. Moreover, we are not aware of any other attempts to offer conceptual frameworks for integrating research on marital attributions or for understanding data relating to other pertinent phenomena in marriage. Perhaps more importantly, the observation that 'the study of cognition in intimate relationships' suffers from a 'lack of focus and direction' (Baucom, Epstein, Sayers & Sher, 1989, p. 31), suggests that the programmatic nature of our research speaks to a critical lacuna in this area.

Contribution to Clinical Practice

Our research also makes an important contribution at the level of clinical application. The most significant implications result from our attempt to illustrate conceptually the central role of responsibility attributions in marriage. Conceptualizing spouses' attributions as responsibility judgments provides a framework for integrating several disparate interventions in marital therapy (see Fincham, 1985a). For example, 'relabeling' typically involves ascribing a negative spouse behavior to a skill deficit and thereby mitigating the spouse's responsibility for the behavior. Similarly, 'reframing' can be conceived of having an impact because of its effect on responsibility - negative behaviors or symptoms are usually presented as having positive motivations.

Awareness of the issue of responsibility in therapy also alerts the clinician to the fact that seemingly innocent attribution inquiries communicated to the partner raise the issue of accountability and might be experienced as accusations. Examining more effective ways for the couple to handle such inquiries leads naturally to communication training, another commonly used intervention in marital therapy. As a final example, attending to the issue of responsibility in therapy necessarily entails consideration of the expectations spouses hold about marriage and partner behavior because responsibility only arises in relation to expectations or duties. This is significant because the exploration of expectations comprises 'much of what occurs in good marital therapy' (O'Leary & Turkewitz, 1978).

Final Comment

Notwithstanding the achievements noted above, the foregoing critiques point to several limitations of our work and to a number of basic issues that remain to be investigated. Perhaps the most important task for future research is to investigate directly the role of cognitive and affective variables as mediators of the relation between marital behavior and marital satisfaction. The prevailing lack of mediational research is understandable, however, in the light of several observations.

First, it can be argued that the case for studying potential mediating variables required demonstration of their relevance to marriage. With the relevance of attributions now firmly established, researchers can turn to the more difficult task of investigating their mediational role. Second, the absence of integrative theory to guide research on attributions may account for the lack of research on this topic. As a consequence, we have devoted our attention recently to conceptual analyses that integrate various factors studied in marital research (see above). Third, the emergence of a mediational research tradition has not been recognized explicitly. We hope that our earlier analysis of the historical factors influencing our research will make the emergence and goals of a mediational research tradition explicit and thereby facilitate mediational research. Investigating attributions as a mediating variable poses a considerable challenge that may be best realized by attending to another limitation of existing studies.

Although research on attributions in marriage was prompted by clinical observations, its closeness to the clinical context has diminished over time. Thus, there has been no attempt to investigate directly the application of its findings to the clinical situation or to provide data that are guided by clinical needs.[4] Yet recognition of the cross fertilization between social and clinical issues that gave rise to this field of inquiry may be the key to advancing research on attributions in marriage and to realizing the potential of the social-clinical interface.

One way to advance mediational research and to address clinical concerns more directly is by means of analogue intervention studies. By comparing the impact of an attribution and a behavioral intervention relative to each other and to a wait list control group, it is possible to determine whether changes in behavior and marital satisfaction occur independently of changes in attributions. Similarly, changes in attributions may lead to changes in satisfaction that are independent of changes in behavior, thereby suggesting that attributions may be important in their own right and not simply as a variable that mediates the relation between behavior and satisfaction. Thus, an important theoretical issue can be examined in the context of addressing an applied concern.

Clearly, a great deal of work remains and our research program reveals only some of the issues that need to be addressed in advancing our understanding of attributions in marriage. As with any new and developing research area, the precise nature of future research is difficult to predict because it will be shaped by issues that emerge as the field evolves. In our view, the collective effort of social and clinical psychologists is likely to be essential in meeting the challenges that lie ahead, for it is apparent that the next steps in this area are going to be more demanding than those taken to date.

ACKNOWLEDGEMENTS

The authors thank Steve Beach and Glenn Reeder for their helpful comments on an earlier draft of the manuscript. This chapter was written while the first author was supported by a Faculty Scholar Award from the W.T. Grant Foundation and by Grant # 44078-01 from the National Institute of Mental Health.

FOOTNOTES

1. This could result, in part, from the format used to assess casual dimensions. Spouses sometimes have difficulty specifying the major cause of an event and then restricting their responses to

consideration of the cause alone and not the event that it explains. Consequently, we have begun to use a simpler format for assessing causal dimensions in our recent research.
2. When spouses blame their partner for an event, they also tend to report that their partner is the cause of the event and is responsible for its occurrence (Fincham & Bradbury, 1987c). However, this may reflect their lay theory of the relations among cause, responsibility, and blame. Although knowledge of spouses' lay theories is significant in its own right, the possibility that data regarding their relation may reflect such theories emphasizes the absence of research on the *processes* underlying attribution, a topic dealt with later in greater detail.
3. Although the model appears similar to those offered by Kelley et al. (1983) and Levinger and Rands (1985), closer examination shows that it differs from these models on several dimensions, including the level at which psychological processes are specified, the phenomena addressed, the relative emphases given to features common to the models, and the extent to which the models are data-based (see Bradbury & Fincham, 1988b).
4. The application of attribution principles to marital therapy thus still lacks an empirical basis. The three studies that have examined the effect of cognitively oriented interventions in marital therapy fail to investigate specifically the effect of reattribution because they used multifaceted cognitive interventions and failed to assess whether the intervention had actually altered attributions (Baucom & Lester, 1986; Epstein, Pretzer & Fleming, 1982; Margolin & Weiss, 1978). Moreover, none utilise findings from marital attribution research to design interventions.

REFERENCES

Abramson, L. Y., Seligman, M. E. P., & Teasdale, J. (1978). Learned helplessness in humans: Critique and reformulation. *Journal of Abnormal Psychology*, 87, 49-74.

American Psychiatric Association (1980). *Diagnostic and statistical manual of mental disorders* (3rd ed.). Washington, DC: American Psychiatric Association.

Arias, I., & Beach, S. R. H. (1987). The assessment of social cognition in the context of marriage. In K. D. O'Leary (Ed.), *Assessment of marital discord* (pp. 109-137). Hillsdale, NJ: Erlbaum.

Baron, R. M., & Kenny, D. A. (1986). The mediator-moderator variable distinction in social psychological research: Conceptual, strategic, and statistical considerations. *Journal of Personality and Social Psychology*, 51, 1173-1182.

Baucom, D. H. (1981, November). *Cognitive behavioral strategies in the treatment of marital discord*. Paper presented at the meeting of the Association for Advancement of Behavior Therapy, Toronto.

Baucom, D. H. (1987). Attributions in distressed relations: How can we explain them? In S. Duck & D. Perlman (Eds.), *Intimate relationships: Development, dynamics, and deterioration* (pp. 177-206). London: Sage.

Baucom, D. H., & Adams, A. N. (1987). Assessing communication in marital interaction. In K. D. O'Leary (Ed.), *Assessment of marital discord* (pp. 139-181). Hillsdale, NJ: Erlbaum.

Baucom, D. H., Epstein, N., Sayers, S., & Sher, T. G. (1989). The role of cognition in marital relationships: Definitional, methodological, and conceptual issues. *Journal of Consulting and Clinical Psychology*, 57, 31-38.

Baucom, D. H., & Lester, G. W. (1986). The usefulness of cognitive restructuring as an adjunct to behavioral marital therapy. *Behavior Therapy*, 17, 385-403.

Beach, S. R., & O'Leary, K. D. (1986). The treatment of depression occurring in the context of marital discord. *Behavior Therapy*, 17, 43-49.

Beck, A. T., & Beamesderfer, A. (1974). Assessment of depression: The Beck Depression Inventory. In P. Pichot (Ed.), *Psychological measurement in psychopharmacology* (Vol. 7, pp. 151-169). Paris: Karger.

Berger, P., & Kellner, H. (1970). Marriage and the construction of reality: An exercise in the microsociology of knowledge. In H. P. Dreisel (Ed.), *Recent sociology No. 2: Patterns of communicative behavior* (pp. 50-73). New York: Macmillan.

Berley, R. A., & Jacobson, N. S. (1984). Causal attributions in intimate relationships: Toward a model of cognitive-behavioral marital therapy. In P. Kendall (Ed.), *Advances in cognitive - behavioral research and therapy* (Vol. 3, pp. 1-60). New York: Academic.

Bradbury, T. N., & Fincham, F. D. (1987a). Affect and cognition in close relationships: Towards an integrative model. *Cognition and Emotion*, 1, 59-87.

Bradbury, T. N., & Fincham, F. D. (1987b). Assessment of affect in marriage. In K. D. O'Leary (Ed.), *Assessment of marital discord* (pp. 59-108). Hillsdale, NJ: Erlbaum.

Bradbury, T. N., & Fincham, F. D. (1988). Assessing spontaneous attributions in marital interaction: Methodological and conceptual considerations. *Journal of Social and Clinical Psychology*, 7, 122-130.

Bradbury, T. N., & Fincham, F. D. (1988). Individual difference variables in close relationships: A contextual model of marriage as an integrative framework. *Journal of Personality and Social Psychology*, 54, 713-721.

Bradbury, T. N., & Fincham, F. D. (1989). Behavior and satisfaction in marriage: Prospective mediating processes. *Review of personality and social psychology: Vol 10. Close relationships* (pp. 119-143). Newbury Park, CA.: Sage.

Bradbury, T. N., & Fincham, F. D. (1990a). Attributions in marriage: Review and critique. *Psychological Bulletin*, 107, 3-33.

Bradbury, T. N., & Fincham, F. D. (1990b). *The impact of attributions in marriage: A behavioral analysis*. Manuscript submitted for publication.

Burgess, E. W., & Cottrell, L. S. (1939). *Predicting success or failure in marriage*. New York: Prentice.

Burgess, E. W., Locke, H. J., & Thomes, M. M. (1939). *The family: From institution to companionship*. New York: American Book Company.

Burnett, R., McGhie, P., & Clark, D. (Eds.) (1987). *Accounting for relationships: Explanation, representation and knowledge*. London: Methuen.

Campbell, A., Converse, P. E., & Rogers, W. L. (1976). *The quality of American life*. New York: Sage Foundation.

Christensen, A., Sullaway, M., & King, C. E. (1983). Systematic error in behavioral reports of dyadic interaction: Egocentric bias and content effects. *Behavioral Assessment*, 5, 129-140.

Christensen, H. T. (1964). Development of the family field of study. In H. T. Christensen (Ed.), *Handbook of marriage and the family* (pp. 1-22). Chicago: Rand McNally.

Critchlow, B. (1985). The blame in the bottle: Attributions about drunken behavior. *Personality and Social Psychology Bulletin*, 11, 258-274.

Doherty, W. J. (1981a). Cognitive processes in intimate conflict: I. Extending attribution theory. *American Journal of Family Therapy*, 9, 3-13.

Doherty, W. J. (1981b). Cognitive processes in intimate conflict: II. Efficacy and learned helplessness. *American Journal of Family Therapy, 9,* 35-44.

Duncan, S., Kanki, B. G., Mokros, H., & Fiske, D. W. (1984). Pseudounilaterality, simple-rate variables, and other ills to which interaction research is heir. *Journal of Personality and Social Psychology, 46,* 1335-1348.

Ebbesen, E. B. (1980). Cognitive processes in understanding ongoing behavior. In R. Hastie, T. M. Ostrom, E. B. Ebbesen, R. S. Wyer, D. L. Hamilton, & D. Carlston (Eds.), *Person memory: The cognitive basis of social perception* (pp. 179-225). Hillsdale, NJ: Erlbaum.

Elms, A. C. (1975). The crisis of confidence in social psychology. *American Psychologist, 30,* 967-976.

Epstein, N. (1982). Cognitive therapy with couples. *American Journal of Family Therapy, 10,* 5-16.

Epstein, N. (1985). Depression and marital dysfunction: Cognitive and behavioral linkages. *International Journal of Mental Health, 13,* 86-104.

Epstein, N., Pretzer, J. L., & Fleming, B. (1982, November). *Cognitive therapy and communication training: Comparison of effects with distressed couples.* Paper presented at the meeting of the Association for Advancement of Behavior Therapy, Los Angeles.

Fincham, F. D. (1983). Clinical applications of attribution theory: Problems and prospects. In M. Hewstone (Ed.), *Attribution theory: Social and functional extensions* (pp. 187-203). Oxford: Blackwell.

Fincham, F. D. (1985a). Attributions in close relationships. In J. H. Harvey & G. Weary (Eds.), *Attribution: Basic issues and applications* (pp. 203- 234). New York: Academic.

Fincham, F. D. (1985b). Attribution processes in distressed and nondistressed couples: 2. Responsibility for marital problems. *Journal of Abnormal Psychology, 94,* 183-190.

Fincham, F. D., & Beach, S. R. (1988). Attribution processes in distressed and nondistressed couples: 5. Real versus hypothetical events. *Cognitive Therapy and Research, 12,* 505-514.

Fincham, F. D., Beach, S. R., & Baucom, D. H. (1987). Attribution processes in distressed and nondistressed couples: 4. Self-partner attribution differences. *Journal of Personality and Social Psychology, 52,* 739-748.

Fincham, F. D., Beach, S. R., & Bradbury, T. N. (1989). Marital distress, depression, and attributions: Is the distress-attribution association an artifact of depression? *Journal of Consulting and Clinical Psychology, 57,* 768-771.

Fincham, F. D., Beach, S. R., & Nelson, G. (1987). Attribution processes in distressed and nondistressed couples: 3. Causal and responsibility attributions for spouse behavior. *Cognitive Therapy and Research, 11,* 71-86.

Fincham, F. D., & Bradbury, T. N. (1987a). The impact of attributions in marriage: A longitudinal analysis. *Journal of Personality and Social Psychology, 53,* 510-517.

Fincham, F. D., & Bradbury, T. N. (1987b). The assessment of marital quality: A re-evaluation. *Journal of Marriage and the Family, 49,* 797-809.

Fincham, F. D., & Bradbury, T. N. (1987c). Cognitive processes and conflict in close relationships: An attribution-efficacy model. *Journal of Personality and Social Psychology, 53,* 1106-1118.

Fincham, F. D., & Bradbury, T. N. (1988a). *Attributions in distressed couples seeking therapy, distressed couples not seeking therapy, and happily married couples.* Unpublished manuscript.

Fincham, F. D., & Bradbury, T. N. (1988b). The impact of attributions in marriage: Empirical and conceptual foundations. *British Journal of Clinical Psychology, 27,* 77-90.

Fincham, F. D., & Bradbury, T. N. (1988c). The impact of attributions in marriage: An experimental analysis. *Journal of Social and Clinical Psychology*, 7, 122-130.

Fincham, F. D., & Bradbury, T. N. (1989). The impact of attributions in marriage: An individual differences analysis. *Journal of Social and Personal Relationships*, 6, 69-85.

Fincham, F. D., & Emery, R. E. (1988). Limited mental capacities and perceived control in the attribution of responsibility. *British Journal of Social Psychology*, 27, 193-207.

Fincham, F. D., & Jaspars, J. M. (1980). Attribution of responsibility: From man the scientist to man as lawyer. In L. Berkowitz (Ed.), *Advances in experimental social psychology*, (Vol. 13, pp. 81-138). New York: Academic.

Fincham, F. D., & O'Leary, K. D. (1983). Causal inferences for spouse behavior in maritally distressed and nondistressed couples. *Journal of Social and Clinical Psychology*, 1, 42-57.

Fincham, F. D., & Roberts, C. (1985). Intervening causation and the mitigation of responsibility for harm doing: II. The role of limited mental capacities. *Journal of Experimental Social Psychology*, 21, 178-194.

Fincham, F. D., & Shultz, T. R. (1981). Intervening causation and the mitigation of responsibility for harm doing. *British Journal of Social Psychology*, 20, 115-120.

Fletcher, G. J. O., Fincham, F. D., Cramer, L., & Heron, N. (1987). The role of attributions in the development of dating relationships. *Journal of Personality and Social Psychology*, 53, 481-489.

Floyd, F. J., & Markman, H. J. (1983). Observational biases in spouse observation: Toward a cognitive/behavioral model of marriage. *Journal of Consulting and Clinical Psychology*, 51, 450-457.

Funder, D. C. (1987). Errors and mistakes: Evaluating the accuracy of social judgment. *Psychological Bulletin*, 101, 75-90.

Glick, B. R., & Gross, S. J. (1975). Marital interaction and marital conflict: A critical evaluation of current research strategies. *Journal of Marriage and the Family*, 37, 505-512.

Goffman, E. (1955). On face-work: An analysis of ritual elements in social interaction. *Psychiatry: Journal for the Study of Interpersonal Processes*, 18, 213-231.

Gottman, J. M., Notarius, C., Markman, H., Banks, S., Yoppi, B., & Rubin, M. E. (1976). Behavior exchange theory and marital decision making. *Journal of Personality and Social Psychology*, 34, 14-23.

Harvey, J. H., & Weary, G. (1984). Current issues in attribution theory and research. *Annual Review of Psychology*, 35, 427-459.

Heider, F. (1958). *The psychology of interpersonal relations*. New York: Wiley.

Hicks, M. W., & Platt, M. (1970). Marital happiness and stability: A review of research in the sixties. *Journal of Marriage and the Family*, 32, 553-574.

Holtzworth-Munroe, A., & Jacobson, N. S. (1985). Causal attributions of married couples: When do they search for causes? What do they conclude when they do? *Journal of Personality and Social Psychology*, 48, 1398-1412.

Holtzworth-Munroe, A., & Jacobson, N. S. (1988). Toward a methodology for coding spontaneous causal attributions: Preliminary results with married couples. *Journal of Social and Clinical Psychology*, 7, 101-112.

Huston, T. L., & Levinger, G. (1978). Interpersonal attraction and relationships. *Annual Review of Psychology*, 29, 115-156.

Jacob, T. (1987). Family interaction and psychopathology: Historical overview. In T. Jacob (Ed.), *Family interaction and psychopathology: Theories methods and findings* (pp. 3-24). New York: Plenum.

Jacobson, N. S., & Margolin, G. (1979). *Marital therapy: Strategies based on social learning and behavior exchange principles.* New York: Brunner/Mazel.

Jacobson, N. S., & Moore, D. (1981). Spouses as observers of the events in their relationship. *Journal of Consulting and Clinical Psychology, 49,* 269-277.

Jones, E. E., & Davis, K. E. (1965). From acts to dispositions: The attribution process in person perception. In L. Berkowitz (Ed.), *Advances in experimental social psychology* (Vol. 2, pp. 219-266). New York: Academic.

Kelley, H. H. (1967). Attribution theory in social psychology. In D. Levine (Ed.), *Nebraska symposium on motivation* (Vol. 15). Lincoln, NE: University of Nebraska Press.

Kelley, H. H., Berscheid, E., Christensen, A., Harvey, J. H., Huston, T. L., Levinger, G., McClintock, E., Peplau, L. A., & Peterson, D. (1983). *Close relationships.* San Francisco: Freeman.

Kelley, H. H., & Michela, J. L. (1980). Attribution theory and research. *Annual Review of Psychology, 31,* 457-501.

Knight, J. A., & Vallacher, R. R. (1981). Interpersonal engagement in social perception: The consequences of getting into the action. *Journal of Personality and Social Psychology, 40,* 990-999.

Langer, E. J. (1978). Rethinking the role of thought in social interaction. In J. H. Harvey, W. Ickes, & R. F. Kidd (Eds.), *New directions in attribution research* (Vol. 2, pp. 35-58). Hillsdale, NJ: Erlbaum.

Leary, M. R., & Maddux, J. E. (1987). Progress towards a viable interface between social and clinical-counseling psychology. *American Psychologist, 42,* 904-911.

Leary, M. R., & Miller, R. S. (1986). *Social psychology and dysfunctional behavior.* New York: Springer-Verlag.

Levinger, G., & Rands, M. (1985). Compatibility in marriage and other close relationships. In W. Ickes (Ed.), *Compatible and incompatible relationships* (pp. 309-331). New York: Springer-Verlag.

Lewin, K. (1948). The background of conflict in marriage. *Resolving social conflicts: Selected papers on group dynamics* (pp. 84-102). New York: Harper & Row.

Liberman, R. P. (1970). Behavioral approaches to family and couple therapy. *American Journal of Orthopsychiatry, 40,* 106-118.

Locke, H. J., & Wallace, K. M. (1959). Short marital adjustment and prediction tests: Their reliability and validity. *Marriage and Family Living, 21,* 251-255.

Lyman, S. M., & Scott, M. B. (1970). *A sociology of the absurd.* New York: Apple-Century-Crofts.

Margolin, G., & Weiss, R. L. (1978). Comparative evaluation of therapeutic components associated with behavioral marital treatments. *Journal of Consulting and Clinical Psychology, 46,* 1476-1486.

McGuire, J. W. (1969). Theory-oriented research in natural settings: The best of both worlds for social psychology. In M. Sherif & C. Sherif (Eds.), *Interdisciplinary relationships in the social sciences* (pp. 21-51). Chicago: Aldine.

Newcomb, M. D., & Bentler, P. M. (1981). Marital breakdown. In S. Duck & R. Gilmour (Eds.), *Personal relationships: 3. Personal relationships in disorder* (pp. 57-94). New York: Academic.

Newman, H. M. (1981a). Interpretation and explanation: Influences on communicative exchanges within intimate relationships. *Communication Quarterly*, 29, 123-131.

Newman, H. M. (1981b). Communication within ongoing intimate relationships: An attributional perspective. *Personality and Social Psychology Bulletin*, 7, 59-70.

Newman, H. M., & Langer, E. J. (1988). Investigating the development and courses of intimate relationships: A cognitive model. In L. Y. Abramson (Ed.), *Social cognition and clinical psychology*. New York: Guilford.

Newtson, D. A. (1973). Attribution and the unit of perception of ongoing behavior. *Journal of Personality and Social Psychology*, 28, 28-38.

Norton, R. (1983). Measuring marital quality: A critical look at the dependent variable. *Journal of Marriage and the Family*, 45, 141-151.

O'Leary, K. D., & Turkewitz, H. L. (1978). Marital therapy from a behavioral perspective. In T. J. Paolino & B. S. McCrady (Eds.), *Marriage and marital therapy* (pp. 240-297). New York: Brunner/Mazel.

Olson, J. M., & Ross, M. (1985). Attribution: Past, present and future. In J. H. Harvey & G. Weary (Eds.), *Attribution: Basic issues and applications* (pp. 282-311). New York: Academic.

Pachella, R. G. (1974). The interpretation of reaction time in information- processing research. In B. H. Kantowitz (Ed.), *Human information processing: Tutorials in performance and cognition*. Hillsdale, N. J.: Erlbaum.

Peterson, C., & Seligman, M. E. P. (1984). Causal explanations as a risk factor for depression: Theory and evidence. *Psychological Review*, 91, 347-374.

Peterson, C., Semmel A., von Baeyer, C., Abramson, L. Y., Metalsky, G. I., & Seligman, M. E. P. (1982). The Attributional Style Questionnaire. *Cognitive Therapy and Research*, 6, 287-299.

Peterson, C., Villanova, P., & Raps, C. S. (1985). Depression and attributions: Factors responsible for inconsistent results in the published literature. *Journal of Abnormal Psychology*, 94, 165-168.

Raush, H. L., Barry, W. A., Hertel, R. K., & Swain, M. A. (1974). *Communication, conflict, and marriage*. San Francisco: Jossey-Bass.

Ross, M., & Fletcher, G. J. O. (1985). Attribution and social perception. In G. Lindzey & E. Aronson (Eds.), *Handbook of social psychology: Vol. 2. Special fields and applications* (3rd ed., pp. 73-122). New York: Random House.

Schaap, C. (1984). A comparison of the interaction of distressed and nondistressed married couples in a laboratory situation: Literature survey, methodological issues, and an empirical investigation. In K. Hahlweg & N. S. Jacobson (Eds.), *Marital interaction: Analysis and modification* (pp. 133-158). New York: Guilford.

Semin, G. R., & Manstead, A. S. R. (1983). *The accountability of conduct: A social psychological analysis*. London: Academic.

Shaver, K. G. (1985). *The attribution of blame: Causality, responsibility, and blameworthiness*. New York: Springer-Verlag.

Shaver, K. G. & Drown, D. (1986). On causality, responsibility, and self-blame: A theoretical note. *Journal of Personality and Social Psychology*, 50, 697-702.

Sillars, A. L. (1982). *Verbal tactics coding scheme*. Unpublished coding manual. Ohio State University.

Sillars, A. L. (1985). Interpersonal perception in relationships. In W. Ickes (Ed.), *Compatible and incompatible relationships* (277-305). New York: Springer-Verlag.

Silverman, I. (1977). Why social psychology fails. *Canadian Psychological Review*, 18, 353-358.

Smith, M. B. (1972). Is experimental social psychology advancing? *Journal of Experimental Social Psychology*, 8, 86-96.

Smith, E. R., & Miller, F. D. (1979). Salience and the cognitive mediation of attribution. *Journal of Personality and Social Psychology*, 37, 2240-2252.

Smith, E. R., & Miller, F. D. (1983). Mediation among attribution inferences and comprehension processes: Initial findings and a general method. *Journal of Personality and Social Psychology*, 50, 697-702

Spanier, G. B. (1976). Measuring dyadic adjustment: New scales for assessing the quality of marriage and similar dyads. *Journal of Marriage and the Family*, 38, 15-28.

Spanier, G. B., & Lewis, R. A. (1980). Marital quality: A review of the seventies. *Journal of Marriage and the Family*, 42, 825-839.

Stratton, P., Heard, D., Hanks, H. G. I., Munton, A. G., Brewin, C. R., & Davidson, C. (1986). Coding causal beliefs in natural discourse. *British Journal of Social Psychology*, 25, 299-313.

Strongman, K. T. (1987). *The psychology of emotion* (3rd ed). New York: Wiley.

Stuart, R. B. (1969). Operant interpersonal treatment for marital discord. *Journal of Consulting and Clinical Psychology*, 33, 675-682.

Stuart, R. B. (1980). *Helping couples change.* New York: Guilford.

Tharp, R. G. (1963). Psychological patterning in marriage. *Psychological Bulletin*, 60, 97-117.

Thompson, J. S., & Snyder, D. K. (1986). Attribution theory in intimate relationships: A methodological review. *American Journal of Family Therapy*, 14, 123-138.

Veroff, J., Kulka, R. A., & Douvan, E. (1981). *Mental health in America: Patterns of help seeking from 1957-1976.* New York: Basic Books.

Weary, G., & Mirels, H. L. (Eds.). (1982). *Integrations of clinical and social psychology.* Englewood-Cliffs, NJ: Prentice-Hall.

Weiner, B. (1986). *An attributional theory of motivation and emotion.* New York: Springer-Verlag.

Weiss, R. L. (1984). Cognitive and behavioral measures of marital interaction. In K. Hahlweg & N. S. Jacobson (Eds.), *Marital interaction: Analysis and modification* (pp. 232-252). New York: Guilford.

Wright, J., & Fichten, C. (1976). Denial of responsibility, videotape feedback and attribution theory: Relevance for behavioral marital therapy. *Canadian Psychological Review*, 17, 219-230.

Wyer, R. S. (1981). An information-processing perspective on social attribution. In J. H. Harvey, W. Ickes, & R. F. Kidd (Eds.), *New directions in attribution research* (Vol. 3, pp. 359-404). Hillsdale, NJ: Erlbaum.

PLANNING AND PERFORMING INTERPERSONAL INTERACTION: A COGNITIVE-MOTIVATIONAL APPROACH

Daniel Bar-Tal, Yoram Bar-Tal, Nehemia Geva, and Kerry Yarkin-Levin

One of the central concerns of social psychology is the study of interpersonal interaction. Interpersonal interaction, which is by definition a social behavior, takes place frequently and continuously in human life. It is, therefore, important to understand how individuals carry on their interpersonal interactions. The purpose of the present chapter is to describe cognitive motivational processes involved in planning and performing interpersonal interaction. This description is based on recent developments in the literature on cognitive social psychology (i.e., information processing, social cognition, and lay epistemology).

We hope that the proposed model can serve as an integrative framework for work which has been published on this topic. The need for such a framework stems from our feeling that the present studies of interpersonal interaction are mostly specific rather than general. The specific analyses cannot be generalized to every interpersonal interaction. Therefore, in order to explain many of the interpersonal interactions, the analysis should strive towards universalism rather than particularism, and it should focus on a process rather than on contents. But, in order to accomplish this task, it is first necessary to define the meaning of the term process and to distinguish it from content. This distinction will allow us to demarcate a line between what is particularistic and what can be generalized over people, time and situations (see also, Bar-Tal & Bar-Tal, 1988).

PROCESS AND CONTENT

The universal generalization involves generalization over individuals, places, situations, and time. Particular generalization, on the other hand, is limited to certain individuals, situations, time or places. The latter generalization is limited to individuals who are known to maintain a similar repertoire of beliefs and therefore may behave similarly in some situations, or to certain situations which may affect similarly different individuals. The universal versus particular generalization differentiation is sometimes referred to in social psychology as the process versus content distinction (e.g., Kruglanski, 1980; Newell & Simon, 1972).

Process refers to a sequence of operations performed by individuals which describe principles of overt and covert behaviors. Contents refer to the cognitions that individuals use to characterize people, behaviors, topics, events, objects, places or situations (see Bar-Tal, D. & Bar-Tal, Y., 1988). Both contents and processes can be found on different levels of universality. It is possible to find a content which may be held by an individual in a certain situation and time and it is possible, as well, to identify content which may be held by a large portion of the human population or even by all human beings. In the same way, it is possible to describe a particular process of specific behaviors that pertains to certain individuals, times, or situations and it is possible to describe a general underlying process of behavior category that pertains to all human beings (see also Bar-Tal, Y. & Bar-Tal, D., in press). We assume that it is easier to formulate a description of generalizable processes than contents. Processes can be described by the analyst of human behavior in general and abstract terms, independently of contents. In contrast, nobody can assure which specific contents in a person's conceptual repertoire are available and accessible in the individual's mind. Moreover, processes, which describe the sequence of operations, focus on the explanation of behavior, in addition to its description, while contents do not necessarily fulfill an explanatory function.

The present chapter argues that the process of interpersonal interaction is greatly affected by the knowledge available to the participants during the interaction. Therefore, of special importance for the model of the interpersonal interaction process is the process model of knowledge acquisition and change (lay epistemology theory) proposed by Kruglanski (Kruglanski, 1980/1989; Kruglanski & Ajzen, 1983). The principles of this model will serve as an underlying basis in the stages of our process.

EPISTEMIC PROCESS

The epistemic process of knowledge acquisition consists of two phases. First, there is the *cognitive generation phase*, which addresses the issue of the generation of the contents of our knowledge. Second, there is the *cognition validation phase* in which a degree of confidence is attributed to the generated contents. The first phase of cognitive generation focuses on what was metaphorically described by Karl Popper's (1973) 'search light' - analogy of human consciousness. Since human mental capacity is limited, at any given time individuals can only generate a restricted number of contents on the basis of incoming information and/or their own insights. The second phase of cognitive validation is performed via a deductive principle. The individual deduces from the generated cognitions implications and tests them against the evidence he/she possesses. If the evidence is logically consistent with the implications, then the individual's confidence in the validity of this cognition is strengthened. But, if the evidence is inconsistent, then individuals' confidence in the cognition may be undermined. A central postulate of the theory is that the described process does not have a natural point of termination. In principle, at least, it is always possible to come up with a number of alternative hypotheses (contents) which may be inconsistent with the same body of evidence. In reality, however, individuals end the epistemic process with regard to certain cognitions by bestowing on them a certain degree of confidence without considering further various alternatives. This cognitive phenomenon is conceived as epistemic freezing. In contrast, a phenomenon of entertaining alternative contents, validating them, and eventually substituting them instead of previously held beliefs represents epistemic unfreezing.

Generation of alternative cognitions to the frozen ones depends on three types of factors: the availability of information, cognitive determinants, and motivation. *Availability of information* refers to the existence of information in the environment that individuals can collect and test against their own knowledge. *Cognitive determinants* affecting hypotheses generation reflect the knower's stable and momentary capacity to come up with ideas. This has to do with the availability of ideas in a person's cognitive repertoire (cf. Bruner, 1957) and with their accessibility at a given point in time (cf. Higgins & King, 1981). Three identified motivations affect both the cognition generation phase and the cognition validation phase (Kruglanski & Ajzen, 1983): a) *Motivation for cognitive structure*, defined as a desire to have firm knowledge on a given topic; b) *motivation for validity* (also described as fear of invalidity), defined as a desire to avoid mistaken judgments and to have 'true' knowledge; and c) *motivation for specific content*, defined as a desire to maintain a particular belief as a truth.

The first motivation disposes the person to generate a pertinent content and to validate it as a belief. Under this motivation individuals freeze. They commit themselves to a belief and refrain from critical challenge of it. They prefer structure as opposed to ambiguity, confusion, and uncertainty. The second motivation disposes a person to generate alternative hypotheses and to search for relevant information. This motivation implies unfreezing, since under this motivation, individuals are opened to collect new information, to think about new ideas and to entertain them as alternative beliefs, even when they contradict the old ones. The third motivation disposes the individuals to avoid any relevant information inconsistent with the specific content that he/she wants to uphold and to collect information which is consistent with the desired content. This motivation is a result of needs which underlie the specific desired belief. The specific content of knowledge serves the needs and therefore individuals have a desire to maintain that content. On the basis of the epistemic model of knowledge acquisition, we will outline in the coming pages a general cognitive motivational process model of planning and performing interpersonal interaction. Although a number of specific cognitive-motivational models which deal with particular contents have been presented, the present chapter proposes a process model formulated in abstract terms which can be used for an analysis of any intentional interpersonal interaction. Most of the earlier models describe specific interpersonal interactions involving such contents as ingratiation (Jones, 1964), negotiation (Pruitt & Smith, 1981), or self-presentation (Schlenker, 1980). By contrast, the present model describes a general process of interpersonal interaction independent of specific contents. It provides an integrative framework for various proposed content-oriented models which are underlied by the same processes described herein. The model we will present focuses specifically on dyadic interaction, although we believe that the implications of the model can be also generalized to interactions involving more than two people.

A PROCESS MODEL OF INTERPERSONAL INTERACTION

We propose a model of planning and performing interpersonal interaction which consists of four stages. These stages portray the sequential nature of the processes within the individual (intraprocesses) activated during the interaction.

The first stage in the model involves setting a goal that an individual desires to achieve in an interpersonal interaction. The second stage focuses on generation of a plan or plans to achieve the set goal. Then, comes the stage of evaluation and validation of the plan. Finally, the fourth stage consists of the execution of the plan. In all four stages the epistemic process of knowledge acquisition plays an essential function. Setting a goal, generation of interaction plans, evaluation and selection of the plan and execution of the plan involve the epistemic processes of content generation and content validation. Also, each of these four operations is influenced by the three factors described before; the availability of information, the cognitive abilities of the individual and his/her epistemic motivations.

As an example to illustrate the described sequence, imagine the case of John who is anticipating a job interview. First, he generates and validates a goal for his interaction. Let us assume that John's goal during the interview is to make a positive impression by exhibiting characteristics he presumes to be highly valued by his potential interviewer (e.g., motivation, competence). Next, he plans his interaction. In order for John to successfully prepare a plan for his behavior during the interview, he first collects information about the publicized job and the interview to find out, for example: (1) what skills are essential for the job; (2) what the interviewer is like; (3) what questions the interviewer is likely to ask; and (4) where and in what situation the interview will take place. In order to collect this information, John talks with individuals who were interviewed in the past by the company, and he talks with individuals who know the interviewer and the company, and he talks with individuals who performed the same job he applied for in other companies and in the company for whom he wants to work. While collecting the information, John is involved in the epistemic process of considering whether or not he has enough information to generate plans. When he feels that he has enough available information, he generates plans for his interaction. In the next stage, he selects the best plan among the generated alternatives. Ultimately, John decides to come to the interview in a three-piece suit and during the conversation with the interviewer to emphasize his self-confidence and motivation. At the interview, as he forms his own impression of the interviewer and his intentions, John slightly modifies his plan in order to present himself as compatible with the newly perceived demands of the job. Thus, during the interaction, new information is added and the interviewer's behavior serves as feedback concerning the success of the plan. On the basis of this new information John generates new ideas and modifies his old plan. This part, in which John acts and reacts at the same time, continues until the end of the interaction.

Prior to describing the delineated stages in details, four points should be noted.

(a) Because the proposed model is cognitive-motivational, it focuses on the intrapersonal processes. Therefore, the analysis deals with one member in the interaction. However, this does not prevent the reader from understanding interpersonal dynamics, since the same process is activated by all the interacting individuals. Further, as the interaction commences, both individuals are undoubtedly influencing one another, so that the behavior or reaction of one person provides informational cues for the other person. This information provides the interactors with the opportunity to evaluate their performance and to modify their behavioral plan and/or goals.

(b) Individuals define their goals on different level of generality. Since we are concerned with the analysis of specific interpersonal interactions, we focus on specific, tactical goals which pertain to a particular situation, time, and place.

(c) The present model focuses on intentional interactions, where the interacting individuals have goals in mind prior to initiating the interaction. In line with Langer's (1978) analysis, though we do recognize the possibility of interactions that may be carried out accidentally without intentional objectives. It is recognized that not all interpersonal interactions involve all the operations described above. Individuals do not always actively collect information or spend time evaluating their knowledge. On occasion, individuals set a goal and select a stored plan of behavior from their memory in order to achieve their goal. It is argued that this type of modified process will occur in situations that have been previously experienced by the individual (Abelson, 1976), and the individual is not under motivation for validity. For example, a person who is helped by his neighbors decides to please the helper (a situation he experienced in the past). He, then, expresses his thanks, gratitude, and compliments to the neighbor. Another example is a woman who wants to convince her husband to go to a movie in the evening. On the basis of their past experiences, she selects the plan of behavior that has worked successfully in the past. The factors affecting these modifications will be described while analyzing the main steps of the model.

(d) It should be noted that though we discuss intentional interactions, it is unlikely that individuals can always report the goal which they set or the plan which they selected. Often individuals have limited access to cognitive processes and as a result they base their verbal reports on implicit, a priori theories about the causal relationships between causes and effects (Nisbett & Wilson, 1977). On the same basis, it should be also pointed out that individuals may not be aware and thus unable to describe the stages of the interpersonal interaction that they go through.

Setting a Goal

The idea that individuals are often goal-oriented in their behavior has a long history in psychology (e.g., Lewin, 1935; McClelland, 1951; Miller, Galanter, & Pribram, 1960; Murray, 1938). Individuals set goals to satisfy their needs or motivations and perform behaviors to achieve these goals. Interpersonal interactions are often the means by which individuals can achieve their goal, as they are ends by themselves. Different goals may be set in a variety of interpersonal contents. For example, individuals may want to influence another person's behavior, perception, emotion, or attitude in order to get something, to make a good impression, to hurt a person, or to convince a person. They also may want to satisfy another person's needs by, for instance, assuring them of love or recognizing the other's authority and power. Jones and Thibaut (1958) have identified the three following categories of goals which may characterize interpersonal interactions: (a) goals which aim to gratify personal needs; (b) goals which aim to determine the causes of the other person's behavior; and (c) goals which aim to establish whether the other person behaves appropriately in accordance to norms. Obviously, the list of goals people might entertain is endless and they can be classified in various ways. Individuals' repertoires of goals depend upon their dispositions, past experiences, culture, and the environment in which they live. The onset of an interactional goal corresponds to the analysis of cognition generation and validation by the lay epistemology model. First, the person generates a goal or goals and then validates one of them. Later, as long as the freezing continues, the validated goal guides the interpersonal interaction. A goal may be triggered as a consequence of internal stimulation (flow of associations), or as a result of cues evolving from a situation. Thus, the specific content of a goal which sets on the whole interaction process is a function of the availability and accessibility of various ideas in the cognitive repertoire and the availability and saliency of cues in the environment (see Wyer & Srull, 1980). For example, a woman remembering her own birthday may decide to please her friend as a reciprocity for previously received help, or a man may watch a TV program about good manners and decide to apologize to his friend for his own inappropriate behavior at a recent cocktail party. A goal does not have to be newly generated, but may be retrieved from a stored repertoire. Various goals are stored in the form of schemata and retrieved on the basis of appropriate cues. The retrieval of a goal indicates its accessibility.

One of the factors contributing to the accessibility of a goal is its centrality (i.e., importance) for the self. Obviously, some goals are more important to self than are other goals. A number of psychologists have suggested that personal goals vary with regard to their centrality to self and are hierarchically arranged along this dimension (Harvey & Schroeder, 1963; Reykowski, 1982; Staub, 1980). Thus, the more central the goal is, the more accessible it will be in the person's repertoire (Bar-Tal, 1986). However, it should be pointed out that the repertoire of an individual's goals and their relative importance to the self is likely to change over time or circumstances.

The stage of setting a goal is also influenced by the specific epistemic motivation that the person has. The predominance of an epistemic motivation for structure may result in the emergence of the most accessible goal for a specific person, because that person strives for a quick and firm selection. For example, a person under pressure to decide quickly how to react to an insult from his neighbor may be primed by a conversation with a friend about a movie describing conciliation between two foes. Under these circumstances, the person might immediately select a goal of rapprochement. In contrast, motivation for validity may increase the chances for the emergence of more than one goal for a given social interaction, depending on personal capacity to come up with ideas and the availability of environmental cues. Such a motivation may increase the hesitation over which goal to use as a guideline for further processing. In addition, one can incorporate assumptions detailed in the cognition validation phase of the lay epistemology theory, and hypothesize that this motivation may drive the person to additional explorations with regard to the suitability of an emerging goal for the given situation or its compatibility with other goals. For example, a student may wonder if his or her desire to compliment a professor is appropriate in a particular situation, or whether it is compatible with another goal of presenting oneself as sincere.

A different behavior will be exhibited by a person with motivation for a specific content. In this case, a person selects goals which are functional to his or her own needs. For example, we can visualize a person with a strong power motive for whom the likelihood of an interaction with others instinctively raises the goal of domineering. A study by Kruglanski and Freund (1983) serves as an example of how epistemic motivations affect the formation of new knowledge structures. Specifically, it demonstrated that under motivation for structure individuals tend to use their preexisting knowledge, while under motivation for validity they are more inclined to use situational information.

While we suggested the possibility of having, at any given moment, more than one goal for the interaction, the following steps of the model will assume that a particular goal is predominant (chosen because of its relative centrality to the self in a given situation) and thus, the individual is about to realize this goal, provided he or she knows how to achieve it. Naturally, two or more goals may be more or less equally central and also conflicting. This case of contradictory cognitions will be discussed later, while analyzing the generation and evaluation of plans for interaction.

Generation of a Plan

The idea that individuals behave according to a plan is not a new one and has been presented in the past (e.g., Goffman, 1967; Hayes-Roth & Hayes Roth, 1979; Miller, Galenter, & Pribram, 1960; Newell & Simon, 1972; Schank & Abelson, 1977). In their influential book about *Plans and the structure of behavior*, Miller et al. (1960) analyzed how individuals generate their various plans of behavior. They defined a plan as '...any hierarchical process in the organism that can control the order in which a sequence of operations is to be performed' (p. 16). A hierarchical process refers to a set of instructions which guide behavior. Generation of a plan involves planning a sequence of actions and reactions that a person anticipates using in his/her interpersonal interactions. A plan may involve verbal and/or nonverbal behavior. As Schneider (1981) suggested, a plan of behavior for presenting oneself in a certain way can be accomplished through verbal behavior, expressive behaviors such as smiles, eye contact, artifactual displays such as clothing or ornaments, and nonverbal behavior consisting of motoric acts. Goffman (1959) described the principles of planning interpersonal interaction in theatrical terms. He compared an individual's behavior in interpersonal interaction to a theatrical performance in which an individual may 'act in a thoroughly calculating manner, expressing himself in a given way solely in order to give the kind of impression to others that is likely to evoke from them a specific response he is concerned to obtain' (p. 6). An illustrative study by Shure and Spivack (1972) demonstrates how the generation of plans for behavior can be examined empirically. In this study, children ages 10 to 12 were presented with a description of an interpersonal situation that began with a certain event and concluded with another event. For example, first, the children were told that one child said something nasty to another child and, then, were told that the latter child got even. The children were then asked to describe what happened between the two events. The investigators were interested in studying means-end thinking - or in our terminology, planning. The results showed that children differed with regard to their ability to plan behavior. That is, children's ability to verbalize details of a plan, their awareness of potential obstacles, and their recognition of the time necessary to reach the stated goal differed significantly.

Over the years, social psychological research has devoted attention to the study of behavioral plans, and several investigators have addressed the problem of planning interpersonal behavior. These writings have focused mostly on elucidation and description of specific plans (i.e., contents). Thus, for example, Jones (1964), in his widely acclaimed book, analyzed a general plan of ingratiation. This plan is used to increase the attractiveness of the person in order to acquire something from another person at a minimum cost, to prevent a potential attack from another person, or to increase one's own respectability in the eyes of another person. According to Jones, ingratiation can be carried out in three different ways: (1) by flattering the other person; (2) by conforming to the other person; or (3) by presenting one's own positive characteristics. Later, Jones and Pittman (1982) proposed five classes of self-presentational strategies (i.e., plans) that individuals may use in situations in which they want to influence another person's perception of themselves. In addition to ingratiation, they discussed intimidation, self-promotion, exemplification, and supplication. The plan of intimidation involves presenting one's self as a dangerous person who has the resources to harm. In using a self-promotion plan, a person presents himself/herself as a competent person either with respect to his/her general ability or his/her specific skills. A person using a plan of exemplification presents himself/herself as having integrity and moral worthiness. Finally, the plan of supplication involves advertising one's dependence and weakness.

Pruitt and Smith (1981) discussed behavioral plans that a bargainer may wish to use in interpersonal negotiations. For example, individuals who decide to use a plan of firmness may start with high demands and concede slowly, may use verbal decoupling formulas after making concessions, and/or may commit themselves to particular demands. Another example of a plan is shyness. Leary and Schlenker (1981) suggested that this plan can be used in situations in which individuals 'are motivated to make a favorable impression on others but doubt their ability to project images of themselves that will produce satisfactory reactions from the others' (p. 343). Specific behaviors that reflect shyness involve doing little in the interaction, being quiet, or showing friendly interest. Collectively, these contributions indicate that individuals may generate different plans to achieve the same goal. Conversely, often the same plans of behavior may be used to achieve different goals. Of course, the list of plans that an individual might generate is unlimited. Rather than documenting various specific plans, the present chapter concentrates on delineating the processes that take place during the planning of interpersonal interactions. As stated earlier, our knowledge includes a repertoire of stored plans, i.e., what to do in case we want to accomplish certain goals. Similarly to other parts of our knowledge, the existing plans may be general or specific, holistic or with certain conditional constraints, well rehearsed or rarely applied. As part of our knowledge, the stored plan is a cognitive unit acquired by various learning techniques. Thus, once a goal is pending performance, the first question concerns whether a person has a plan of behavior to achieve that goal. According to the present formulation, the search for a plan, like the emergence of a goal, is performed according to the principles previously mentioned in our discussion of the cognitive generation phase of the epistemic process. That is, a person raises a plan or several plans to consciousness.

Retrieval of a stored plan. As implied by the functional principle of human performance (i.e., the principle of 'least effort'), the generation of a plan is first directed at the search for stored plans. The accessibility of such plans is determined by their saliency (Tversky & Kahneman, 1974). The saliency of a plan may be affected by the strength of the link between the specific goal and the specific plan. One factor that influences the strength of the link is the frequency of past successful accomplishment of a given goal in a certain way. In addition, a plan may acquire 'functional autonomy'. By the last term we want to imply that certain plans (those which were very successful in various situations) become so accessible that they may emerge in different situations almost regardless of the particular goal. For example, a person who achieves several different goals by acting very violently may eventually use this tactic for trying to reach almost any interpersonal interactional goal. Also, individuals constantly repeat types of interaction as a result of role prescription. For example, a salesman typically uses similar sales pitches across a variety of contexts to sell his merchandise. Similarly, a physician who wants to know the history of an illness within a patient's family may repeatedly use the same techniques to elicit this information from a wide range of patients. Importantly, individuals also often engage in similar interactions with the same person. For example, a father may consistently try to scold his son who is performing poorly in school. Or, a husband may repeatedly try to convince his wife to dress properly for social engagements. Finally, it is also likely that certain situations have an implicit set of learned rules which guide behavior (see Argyle & Henderson, 1984). For example, a person who is unexpectedly helped by a stranger may decide to please the helper and, therefore, express gratitude and thanks. Another example may be a person who witnesses the aggressive behavior of a customer and decides to intervene and reprimand the aggressor. In all the described interpersonal interactions, individuals may use plans of behavior developed in the past. The plans are stored in the memory and the appropriate goal or situation may evoke the plan automatically. In these cases, as Jones and Thibaut (1958) have pointed out, 'The perceiver in any social interaction will act in such a way as to reduce the need for information to sustain the interaction process. This blanket statement, which deserves at least a celexis paribus, implies a general tendency to adopt simplifying strategies which are in the service of cognitive and emotional economy' (p. 152).

In fact, Miller et al. (1960) suggested that plans of behavior are stored in memory after their execution. Later, these plans are used again more or less automatically whenever the situation is similar to the one experienced in the past. Abelson (1976) advanced a similar idea, suggesting that individuals often behave according to stored scripts. According to Abelson, a script is 'a coherent sequence of events expected by the individual involving him either as a participant or as an observer' (p. 33). The 'basic ingredient' of a script is a vignette which is 'an encoding of an event of short duration, in general including both an image (often visual) of the perceived event and a conceptual representation of the event' (p. 34). Vignettes are the basic units stored in memory. Scripts, which consist of sequences of vignettes, are learned on the basis of past experiences and modified throughout one's life. Individuals often use stored scripts as plans of behavior, especially for previously experienced interactions (Abelson, 1981; Schank & Abelson, 1977). Abelson (1981) suggested three necessary conditions for the scripted behavior to occur. First, the individual must have a stable cognitive representation of the particular script. Second, the individual must encounter a cue which evokes the script. Third, the individual must activate the script and start to behave on the basis of action rules. As Langer (1978) pointed out: 'Much of the interaction that people mundanely enact in the every day world would seem to rely on the scripted structure of typical activities rather than on the active processing of incoming information' (p. 50). This economic process of using a script in interpersonal interaction supposedly is considered functional for individuals. Importantly, it enables individuals to react in a quick way with minimal investment. Besides the factors associated with the cognitive property of a plan (i.e., availability, saliency), the search for and hence the generation of an existing plan can be influenced by the epistemic motivations underlying the process. Motivation for structure implies a restricted search, and a superficial inspection of the details of the retrieved plan. Under this motivation, a person is disposed to select a plan as quickly as possible to avoid delay, ambiguity, or hesitation. He/she, therefore, tends to freeze with the first plan that becomes accessible.

Motivation for validity, on the other hand, calls for an extensive search and careful examination of the sequence of actions advocated by the plan, in order to prevent errors and failures in the execution. Such a motivation, promoting the meticulous inspection of various retrieved plans for their feasibility and capacity to achieve the goal, may result in a failure of finding a satisfactory stored plan. Finally, the motivation for specific content may direct the person to a specific desired plan, which is functional to person's needs, without searching for alternative possibilities.

The failure to retrieve an applicable plan from the existing repertoire requires a construction of a new plan. However, it is also plausible to assume that in a case of a less central goal, a person may abandon efforts to find a plan for achieving the goal. Yet, in other cases, the individual may embark on the trail of planning.

Construction of a new plan. Formation of a new plan (including plan modification) involves collection and processing of information. In this vein, Lanzetta (1963) suggested that 'when faced with uncertainty the organism may first search in memory for information which can provide a basis for choice and attempt to evaluate and integrate such data to assess its implication for the problem at hand. Only when these processes are completed and only if they fail to produce data or relevance will the organism seek to acquire further information' (p. 263). The search of relevant information in the memory is described at length by cognitive psychologists (Anderson & Bower, 1973; Simon, 1979). However, memory is only one source of information. The active search for information in order to form a plan may entail, in addition to the individual's own memory, a diversified list: Individuals may ask other people, read available material, etc. The topic of information selection and processing is discussed at length elsewhere (e.g., Carver, 1979; Kruglanski, 1980; Nisbett & Ross, 1980; Schroder, Driver, & Streufert, 1967; Wyer, 1974).

The present chapter, in line with its epistemological approach, suggests at least the following three categories of variables which are assumed to influence the collection of information: (1) conditions of the information collection, (2) personal ability and (3) the motivational state of the person.

(1) Conditions of the information collection - naturally, the collection of information is limited by the circumstances of the situation. The availability of the information and the constraints underlying the collection of information represent the variables which may characterize the conditions of the information collection. It is possible that some desired information is simply unavailable, because nobody knows it. Also, sometimes a person who plans his/her inter-

personal interaction is limited by a set of constraints. For example, he/she may have only a limited amount of time to collect the information or he/she may be restricted to specific geographic locations. The individual's perception of the conditions of the information collection may direct his/her effort towards memory search only, reliance on external sources or the use of both of these sources.

(2) Personal ability - personal ability also affects the process of information collection. First, individuals' ability to collect information is determined by their perceptual ability, as reflected in their span of attention, and visual and auditory capability. Second, individuals differ with respect to their creativity in collecting information (Simon, 1979). Finally, individuals differ with regard to their ability to think about the implications of the available information. These differences may exist due to the individuals' momentary cognitive set, past experience, or more stable cognitive capacities.

(3) Motivational state - the three epistemic motivations which served to analyze the previous steps are also relevant in this substage. The motivation for structure restricts the search or collection of information. Under this motivation individuals strive to have firm knowledge as quickly as they can. They collect the first information available and refrain from critically challenging it. The motivation for specific content biases the person to a search for certain type of information. Individuals' needs dispose them to search for information consistent with the plan that they want to construct and to avoid information which is inconsistent with this plan. Under these two motivations it is possible to subsume all the biases and errors that cognitive social psychologists have observed (see Kruglanski & Ajzen, 1983 for details). Finally, the motivation for validity extends the scope and amount of search. Under this motivation, a person makes special effort to collect all the available information even if it may be contradictory to a set goal or an entertained plan. Of special relevancy to the analysis of this factor is the study by Peri, Kruglanski and Zakai (1986) which investigated the effects of epistemic motivation on information search. They found that epistemic motivations, together with the subjects' level of initial confidence in their existing knowledge, affected information search, as described in the analysis.

Naturally, the reader may raise a question with regard to the criteria for information selection. The present model postulates that the main criterion for information selection is the perceived relevancy (or deducibility) of an item to a potential plan, which in turn is perceived to be relevant for the focal goal. An example of this criterion occurs when an interviewee is collecting information about his/her interviewer. The interviewee would be more sensitive to knowledge about 'what the interviewer likes in one's personal appearance' which implies what to do, than 'what the interviewer eats for breakfast', since this knowledge probably implies nothing of relevance for the future interview. The collection of information proceeds until the person feels that the integrated knowledge is culminated in what he or she feels is a plan for action. The next stage involves the evaluation and validation of the plan. But, it should be noted that the onset of the information search which was triggered by a lack of a plan does not by any means guarantee generation of a plan as an end product. The fear of invalidity about the information encountered during the search may lead the frustrated planner to abandon (even temporarily) the goal. For example, consider the man who wants to get married but cannot come up with a plan for interacting with potential candidates, thus remaining a bachelor for years.

Evaluation and Validation of a Plan

The previous stage of plan generation may end with one of the following options: (a) the person cannot form a plan to accomplish his or her goal, or (b) as the consequence of plan retrieval, or planning, the person may come up with a plan, or a number of plausible plans, for achieving the goal. Whether one or more than one plan is under consideration, an evaluation and validation stage is requisite prior to implementing the plan into action. This stage corresponds to the cognition validation phase of the epistemic process, because it involves evaluation of the plan or plans against one's knowledge and attributing high confidence to the selected plan. The validated plan must be consistent with existing knowledge (e.g., other goals, plans).

The evaluation and validation of a plan includes at least three examinations. First, the generated plan has to be consistent with the goal a person wants to achieve in the interpersonal interaction. Since, in the most general way, all the plan's search or construction was oriented by this principle, the availability or generation of a plan usually fulfills this criterion. Yet the degree of consistency may be a function of the detailed processing at the previous stage which in turn could have been affected by the prevalence of a certain epistemic motivation, and saliency of various cognitive elements during the search or construction of plans. Since it is plausible to assume changes in motivation during the process, it is possible to imagine a case in which a plan was generated with the general view that it is consistent with the goal, but just before its enactment a more detailed inspection may identify several of its flaws - or inconsistencies with the goal. When more than one plan emerges, the epistemic question rather than being: 'Is the plan consistent with the goal?' turns to be 'Which of the plans is most consistent with the goal?' An inconsistent plan is modified and, in order to increase its consistency, a person sometimes has to again collect information. In rare cases, a person may also change a goal and either use the generated plan or construct another one.

The second factor in the evaluation of a plan (or plans) relates to the person's belief that the plan is adequate. Adequacy of the plan indicates that this is the best behavioral plan for an individual under the given circumstance. That is, the plan has a high likelihood of success, at a minimum of cost. Under this criterion, questions relating the correspondence of the plan with one's own ability may become salient. For example, a person may think that helping a friend to move to a new apartment is consistent with his/her goal to reciprocate previously received favors. Yet, this help may be inconsistent with the person's time schedule, physical ability, etc. Lack of adequacy turns the person back to the first or second stage.

Finally, the individual examines whether the generated plan conflicts with other goals that he/she may have. Individuals may have several other goals in mind, not necessarily even related to interpersonal interactions, and the plan may conflict with one of them. Once more, the determinants of such a potential 'clash' between a plan and other goals are the epistemic motivations underlying the processing at this particular step and the cognitive properties affecting the saliency of the other goals. Whether the conflicting plan is changed or not depends on the relative standing of the conflicting goals in the hierarchy of centrality. Goals which are more central to self predominate over goals which are less central to self. Thus, plans of behavior pertaining to a more central goal are executed, if they conflict with less central goals. A plan or a goal may be changed, if the two goals are more or less equally central to self or the set goal is less central than the conflicting one. However, in all the cases, a person may try to select a plan which will be the least conflicting (least costly) with respect to the other goals. (For further elaboration of inconsistency resolution relevant to all the conflicting cognitions see Kruglanski and Klar, 1987). One point should be noted. A feeling of an inconsistency between a generated plan and other central goals which becomes salient sends the person back either to the plan generation stage for the required changes, or to the first stage of setting a new goal. In some cases, when the goal cannot be achieved, the process may be terminated.

Although we did not find research which explicitly investigated the process of plan selection, several studies reflect on the use of the selected plan in social situations. For example, a study by Jellison and Gentry (1978) showed that individuals selected a plan on the basis of the available information which had the highest likelihood of achieving the desired goal. In this study, half of the subjects were told that the job interviewer tends to hire a person whom he likes and the other half were told that he tends to hire a person whom he dislikes. It was found that subjects behaved in accordance to the information they had received. That is, the former subjects expressed opinions that increased the likelihood that the interviewer would like them, whereas the latter subjects expressed opinions which increased the likelihood that the interviewer would dislike them.

A study by Baumeister and Jones (1978) also demonstrated how already collected information influences the selection of a plan of behavior. This study investigated how the information a person has about the knowledge of another person influences the behavior exhibited toward that person. Subjects were led to believe that the other person received either positive or negative information about them. It was found that a person who realized that another person had unfavorable information about him/her did not challenge this impression directly, but compensated for it by presenting himself/herself in areas in which the other lacked information. By contrast, a person who realized that another person had favorable information about him/her tended to depreciate his/her qualities in an attempt to appear modest.

Studies by Quattrone and Jones (1978) and by Schneider (1969) demonstrated how individuals selected a plan of behavior in accordance with the circumstances. For example, in the former study, subjects were asked to imagine themselves trying out for a dramatic role in a play. Some subjects were led to assume that they had impressed the director with a highly relevant performance audition. Other subjects were led to assume that no such audition took place. The results showed that the subjects in the no audition condition disclosed facts about themselves to the director that were evaluated positively and corresponded to the specific dramatic role requirement (e.g. that they had acted the same part previously). By contrast, subjects who assumed they had performed successfully on the audition chose to tell facts that augmented the impression, by referring to the limitations of performing one role (e.g. that they had acted very well in a role different than the one they were asked to play). The reviewed studies illustrate plans for interpersonal interaction which were evaluated, selected and executed. They demonstrate that individuals construct their plans on the basis of available information and situational constraints. The collection of information enables them to select an adequate plan under given circumstances.

The reader should not assume that the proposed analysis of interpersonal interaction implies that observers are always able to recognize a correspondence between a goal and subsequent performance of behavior by an actor. The selected behavior is always consistent with the set goal from the perspective of the performer, but may look 'irrational' to an observer. That is, the performed behavior may look to the observer as being unsuitable for the goal. Several examples may illustrate this phenomenon: (1) an adolescent may initiate aggressive behavior in order to receive parental love and attention; (2) a person who needs approval may engage in a confrontation while interacting with his friend; or (3) a husband who wants to express love to his wife may also make clumsy remarks about the cleanliness of the house. It is suggested that in all these examples the behavior is consistent with individual's goal. The apparent inconsistent pattern can be explained in at least two ways. The first explanation focuses on goals. As was stated previously, the performed behavior must not only be consistent with the goal for which the person initiates the interaction, but also with other goals which are higher or equal to that goal on the hierarchy of centrality to self. Therefore, the selection of behavior may be limited and may look as though it does not correspond to the goal. This may be the case of a husband whose goal is keeping his wife in line with her 'traditional' role, but also wants to express his love for her. The second explanation focuses on the behavior. It suggests that as a consequence of environmental constraints, past experiences and/or personal limitations, individuals may learn to perform behaviors to achieve their goals which may look inconsistent with the goal. For example, an adolescent who is ignored by his parents learns that through aggressive and hostile remarks he can obtain their attention. Similarly, a person who confronts his friend learned to do so in order to get approval.

This line of reasoning is consistent with Kruglanski and Yaffe's (1988) theorizing that cognitive processes of neurotic patients are not different than that of normal individuals. However, what is dysfunctional, according to Kruglanski and Yaffe, is the specific contents of the patient's inferences. Consistent with our present argument, this would represent the goals that individuals set, or plans of behavior that individuals ultimately execute.

Interaction

Once the individual knows what he or she wants to achieve in the course of the interpersonal interaction (i.e., has a goal) and knows how to achieve it (i.e., has a plan), the goal directed behavior begins. During the interaction, the person attempts to carry out his/her plan. But, since the person usually can only plan his or her own behavior and predict the behavior of the other, often the behavior of the other does not correspond entirely to the plan. In these cases, the person has to modify and adjust his/her plan according to the development of the interaction. This proposition is based on an assumption that interpersonal interactions are constructed of series of behavioral units. Each unit consists of two acts, one by each person in the interaction. Each act serves as an informative stimulus and a reaction. That is, it provides new information to the other person, on the one hand, and it functions as a reaction and feedback to other's previous behavior, on the other hand.

Specifically, during the interaction new information constantly is added. A person can collect the new information from the content of the verbal conversation, from the nonverbal behavior cues, or from the artifacts in the situation (e.g., clothing, furniture, etc.). Jones and Thibaut (1958) noted that information collection depends on the type of goals for which a person is striving in the interaction situation. That is, the goals that a person sets determine, to a large extent, the cues to which he/she will attend and the meaning he/she is most likely to assign them. On the basis of this information, the person may modify his/her plan or even change his/her goal during the interaction. Naturally, the other person is the most important source of information. During the interaction, the person may form impressions about the other person's personality, intentions, or attitudes and respond in accordance with these impressions. Social psychologists have devoted much attention to this area (e.g., Asch, 1946; Hastie et al., 1980; Schneider, Hastorf, & Ellsworth, 1979) and it is beyond the scope of this chapter to discuss its principles or outcomes. But, one note should be made. An article by Swann (1984) is of special relevancy to the proposed model. He shifts the focus of person perception to the interpersonal context suggesting that during an interaction the two people negotiate the identities that both try to assume. Therefore, person perception should be viewed as part of interpersonal process.

Also, the behavior of the other person serves as feedback. On the basis of verbal and nonverbal reactions, individuals can determine whether they have successfully performed their plans to achieve their goals. Symbolic interaction theorists argue that individuals use other people's reactions to them as a measure of what they are really like and how they succeed in the performance of their behavior (Mead, 1934). The reactions of others provide a person with feedback of how he/she appears to them, and the actor can then discover whether or not this is in accordance with the way in which he/she planned to perform.

In addition to the described interpersonal 'ping pong', we would like to illuminate the intrapersonal processes which take place during the interaction itself. In each unit of the sequence, the epistemic processes of generation and validation of cognitions are involved. On the basis of the incoming information, individuals generate ideas about their success with the plan, and validate them. Then, on the basis of these ideas, they generate a decision on how to continue their interaction, and validate it. This process is greatly affected by (a) the cognitive abilities of the person to collect and understand incoming information, as well as to generate modifications to the plan and b) the three epistemic motivations. With regard to cognitive abilities, Athay and Darley (1981) recognized the effect of human competencies on performing interpersonal interaction. They defined interaction competencies as 'abilities or capacities to construct innovative patterns of performance by reconstructing familiar practiced paradigms to meet the instrumental demands of constantly varying interaction situations' (p. 299). For example, cognitive abilities such as social sensitivity, flexibility or empathy may facilitate interpersonal interaction.

The second factor consists of the three epistemic motivations which also have a differential effect in the performance of interpersonal interactions. The motivation for validity tends to increase the sensitivity of the actor to the incoming information and the willingness to consider alternatives to the plan. The need for structure lowers the dependence of the person on external cues and the readiness to change his/her plan. Under this motivation, the person freezes with the plan and avoids making any changes, since he/she is disposed to have a structure, any structure. The held plan fulfills this wish. Indeed a study performed by Langer, Blank, and Chanowitz (1978) demonstrated that individuals sometimes enact social behavior in interpersonal interactions without much conscious attention to relevant semantics. This was particularly the case in situations where effortful responding was not required, or which had been experienced before. Finally, motivation for specific content may bias the person to search for information supporting the given plan during the interaction, on the one hand, and to avoid information indicating that the plan does not work, in the other hand. This motivation can explain the behavior of interacting individuals who form expectations and become sensitive to information confirming them, as reported by Darley and Fazio (1980). Goffman (1959, 1967, 1969) has provided an extensive description of the dynamics of interpersonal interactions. In his description, he especially emphasized the interdependence of the interacting individuals, the reciprocal influence on the flow of the interaction, the information which each of the interacting individuals can collect, the acting that they enact, and the rules that guide the interpersonal interaction. Kelley (1979) in his analysis of interpersonal relationships suggested three key properties of interpersonal interaction: (a) the effects that interacting persons have on each other, (b) mutual responsiveness to one another's outcomes, and (c) attribution of behavior to stable dispositions by the two interacting persons.

For our purpose, two empirical studies can serve as demonstrations of how individuals adapt their behavior in the course of an interaction. Schneider and Eustis (1972) showed an adjustment of individuals' behavior in accordance to the behavior of the other person. In this study, individuals who had a goal of making a good impression matched the other person in their behavior. That is, they presented themselves more positively to bragging partners rather than to modest partners and were more revealing to a revealing partner. Similarly, a study by Gergen (1965) demonstrates how individuals modify their plan of behavior as a consequence of another person's reactions. In this study, subjects who were instructed to create the most favorable impression possible in interpersonal interaction were reinforced in the process of enacting their plan of behavior. The results showed that subjects were more responsive to reinforcement by raising the favorability of their self-presentation than were subjects who were not reinforced.

Taken together, these studies indicate that the performance of planned behavior may be dependent on the information collected during the interpersonal interaction and on the behavior of the other person. Individuals may not perform the planned behavior mechanistically, but rather actively collect information during the interaction and react to the stimulation provided in the situation. A change of the plan due to its incompatibility with the information collected during the interaction, or a change of the goal as information analysis implies, or even smooth activation of the sequence of the plan, are general consequences of the cognitive-motivational process described previously. Hence, despite the intra-personal focus and the concentration on micro processes, the present formulation suggests a dynamic model of the interpersonal interaction.

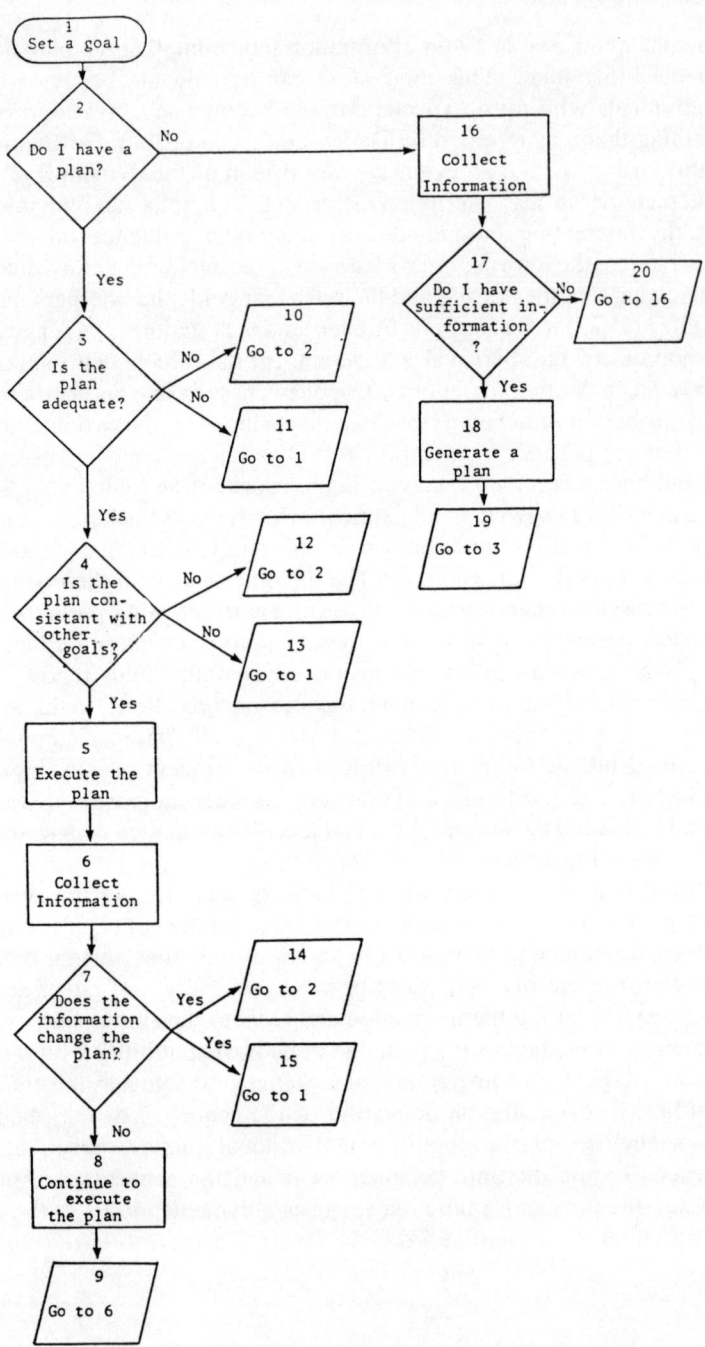

Figure 1. The process of planning and performing interpersonal interaction

Summary

The analyzed process is depicted graphically in a flow chart (see Figure 1). The flow chart starts with the setting of the goal that a person desires to achieve in interpersonal interaction. The first question which preoccupies the person is whether he/she has a plan of behavior to achieve the set goal. If the person has a plan, then the decision to use this plan is preceded by two examinations: (a) whether the plan is adequate and (b) whether it is consistent with other goals. If the plan is adequate and the planned behavior is consistent with the other goals, the person begins to execute the plan in the interpersonal interaction. Later, he/she may change the plan to a more adequate one, as new information is collected during the interaction. Also, during the interaction he/she may even change the goal, because of newly collected information. In the case in which the person does not have an available plan of behavior, the actor evaluates his or her own knowledge concerning whether it is possible to generate a plan. If he/she has sufficient knowledge, he/she tries to come up with a plan of behavior. But, if he/she does not have sufficient information, he/she begins to collect information until coming up with the best plan of behavior under the circumstances. Finally, he/she executes the plan of the interaction.

IMPLICATIONS

The last part of the chapter will address two major implications of this model. The first deals with the nature of the interpersonal interaction and the second discusses its utility.

The Nature of Interpersonal Interaction

The presented model describes the dynamics of interpersonal interaction. This description implies that the interaction is mediated by cognitive and motivational factors which mold the information coming from the environment, and together with it determine the direction of the social behavior. The model conceptualizes interpersonal interaction as consisting of four stages of which the behavior is only one of them. The sequence of interaction begins with the goal that the individual sets to achieve via the interpersonal encounter. Then, the model pays special attention to the part of planning. The next stage pertains to the cognitive processes of evaluation and validation of the selected plan. Finally, the sequence culminates with behavior which comes in the last stage, in the performance of the interaction. In all these stages, the epistemic process of cognition generation and validation as well as the influence of the three epistemic motivations play an essential role.

On the basis of this description it is possible to claim that the model makes an attempt to relate the structure of thought (in this case, goals and plans) to the dynamics of cognitive functioning, motivations, and actions. These relationships are of special importance because of two reasons. First, the model implies continuities between goals, plans, and actions. This line of reasoning corresponds to recent suggestions that cognitive functioning and overt behavior are part of the same sequence. That is, actions are simply plans that are 'filled out' with motor values (e.g., Rumelhart & Ortony, 1977). Second, the model emphasizes the effect of motivations on cognitive functioning. It recognizes that the outcomes of cognitive processes are dependent on epistemic motivations (Kruglanski & Ajzen, 1983). This complex approach is important in view of the tendency to see in the study of social cognition 'parsimony of a single process, unencumbered by motives and emotions or dynamic factors intrinsic to the internal structure of the cognitive content...' (Markus & Zajonc, 1985, p. 214).

The interaction itself is viewed as consisting of a series of behavioral units. The behavioral unit includes two acts - one by each of the interacting persons. An act functions at the same time as a feedback and reaction to the previous act of the other person and as a stimulus and information for the next act. It is therefore not surprising that each act is preceded by cognitive and motivational processes of cognition generation and validation in which the act is planned. This picture presents interpersonal interaction as reciprocal. The two individuals in interaction mutually influence each other.

The proposed conceptualization presents an active model of a man during the interaction. Individuals participating in interpersonal interaction utilize their own knowledge and potentials, and actively search for information in the environment. Then, they collect this information, process it and later act in accordance to it. But, a rational way of carrying the interaction should not necessarily be inferred. Motivation for validity does not dominate over the other two epistemic motivations. Motivation for structure and motivation for specific content cause biases in individuals' functioning. These two motivations account for the specific biases and errors described in the recent cognitive literature and utilized in works concerned with self presentation and impression management.

Also, the present model sets forth the shortened process, often called automatic, which may bias the interaction. People do not necessarily act on the basis of either an information search or an evaluation and validation of knowledge. They may use a goal and/or a plan automatically from their stored repertoire. This way is often functional in the face of the circumstances and individual needs, but it is also often biased because of its sole dependence on the actor's own knowledge.

The described process of planning and performing interpersonal interaction implies its subjective nature. The process is determined by the individual's cognitive repertoire, cognitive abilities, and motivation. Individuals differ with regard to these characteristics and in spite of frequent commonalities, the list of goals and plans, which is of unlimited scope, varies from individual to individual. Individuals may use various plans to achieve the same goal and use the same plan to achieve different goals. Their choices represent subjectively-based preferences for a given conclusion over possible alternatives, since in principle, human inferences do not have objective basis for their conclusions (see Popper, 1959, 1972). It is, therefore, not surprising that observers frequently cannot correctly identify either the actor's goals or his/her plans.

Finally, the present model reflects an underlying assumption that interpersonal interaction is often a goal directed behavior. Goals, which determine the direction of behavior, can be of different kinds. The list of possible goals guiding interpersonal interaction is unlimited. This view extends the traditional emphasis on self-presentation and impression management (e.g., Baumeister, 1982; Schlenker, 1980; Tedeschi, 1981), which narrows the possible range of goals.

Utility of the Model

The model describes the general process which underlies specific interpersonal interactions. It presents (a) the sequence of stages through which people go in their planning and performing interpersonal interaction, and (b) general variables which affect the outcomes of each stage. It is assumed that various interpersonal interactions can be analyzed on the basis of the presented model. Thus, the cognitive-motivational model does not intend to list various goals that individuals may set, or plans that they may use. Instead, the model is designed to serve as an interpretive framework for descriptions of specific types of interpersonal interactions which use particular goals and plans. It describes the organization of behavior and the interconnection between cognition and behavior as influenced by epistemic motivations and cognitive abilities, regardless of the specific contents of goals and plans.

The model not only describes the sequence of operations involved in the interaction process, but also explains the basis for progression from one stage to another, as well as regression to previous stage(s). Thus, it allows an understanding and even a prediction as to when the process should run smoothly and when it should be detained or even stopped. Situations of information search, having conflicting goals, having an inadequate plan, or having inconsistent plans with goals imply a delay which should be overcome. Moreover, the model enables construction of specific hypotheses. It suggests how different epistemic motivations affect the stages of the process; when conflict situations may arouse in the individual's head; when individuals may discontinue the process and change the goal or the plan; and when individuals may act automatically. Finally, the model generates a series of variables that can be used specifically in the investigation of interpersonal interaction. Variables such as salience of goals, adequacy of a plan, epistemic motivations, familiarity with the plan, may shed light on how individuals plan and perform their specific interaction.

It is suggested that the proposed process can be utilized in an analysis of any specific contents involved in interpersonal interactions not addressed previously. That is, the underlying process can serve as a basis for a description of a specific type of interpersonal interaction which may be characteristic of certain individuals, at a certain time and place. Thus, for example, the described process can be used for the analysis of interpersonal interactions between husband-wife, lawyer-client, therapist-patient, and worker-supervisor. In each of these examples the interacting individuals may have different goals, collect different information, and utilize different plans of behavior. But, in each case, the *underlying process* is the same.

It should be noted that a study of contents is an essential task for social psychologists. The study of contents is an important objective for the understanding of individuals' behavior in specific social context. Importantly, only the contents provide the specific meaning to social contexts (see for example, Bar-Tal, 1990). In specific social contexts, individuals have particular goals, collect certain information, and generate certain plans of behavior, while planning and performing interpersonal interactions. In order to study specific contents, the process must be known. Through the description of the process, it is possible to understand the dynamics of interpersonal interaction and to identify the particular variables which are needed for studying specific interpersonal interactions. We believe that the present model provides an important step in that direction.

ACKNOWLEDGEMENTS

The authors would like to thank Harold Kelley for providing valuable comments on the earlier draft of this chapter.

REFERENCES

Abelson, R. P. (1976). Script processing in attitude formation and decision making. In J. S. Carroll & J. W. Payne (Eds.), *Cognition and social behavior* (pp. 33-45). Hillsdale, NJ: Erlbaum.

Abelson, R. P. (1981). Psychological status of the script. *American Psychologist*, 36, 715-729.

Anderson, J. R., & Bower, J. G. (1973). *Human associative memory*. Washington: Winston.

Argyle, M., & Henderson, M. (1984). The rules of friendship. *Journal of Social and Personal Relationships*, 1, 211-237.

Asch, S. E. (1946). Forming impressions of personality. *Journal of Abnormal and Social Psychology*, 41, 258-290.

Athay, M., & Darley, J. H. (1981). Toward an interaction-centered theory of personality. In N. Cantor & J. F. Kihlstrom (Eds.), *Personality, cognition, and social interaction* (pp. 281-308). Hillsdale, NJ: Lawrence Erlbaum.

Bar-Tal, D. (1986). The Masada Syndrome: A case of central belief. In N. Milgram (Ed.), *Stress and coping in time of war* (pp. 32-51). New York: Brunner/Mazel.

Bar-Tal, D. (1990). *Group beliefs*. New York: Springer Verlag.

Bar-Tal, D., & Bar-Tal, Y. (1988). New perspective for social psychology. In D. Bar-Tal & A.W. Kruglanski (Eds.), *Social psychology of knowledge.* (pp. 83-108) Cambridge: Cambridge University Press.

Bar-Tal, Y., & Bar-Tal, D. (1985). Decision making models pf helping behavior: Contents and process. In W. M. Kurtines and J. L. Gewirtz (Eds.), *Handbook of moral behavior and development* (volume 2). Hillsdale, NJ: Lawrence Erlbaum.

Baumeister, R. F. (1982). A self-presentational view of social phenomena. *Psychological Bulletin*, 91, 3-26.

Baumeister, R. F., & Jones, E. E. (1978). When self-presentation is constrained by the target's knowledge: Consistency and compensation. *Journal of Personality and Social Psychology*, 36, 608-618.

Bruner, J. (1957). On perceptual readiness. *Psychological Review*, 64, 123-152.

Carver, C. S. (1979). A cybernetic model of self-attention processes. *Journal of Personality and Social Psychology*, 37, 1251-1281.

Darley, J. N., & Fazio, R. H. (1980). Expectancy confirmation: Processes arising in the social interaction sequence. *American Psychologist*, 35, 867-881.

Gergen, K. J. (1965). The effects of interaction goals and personalistic feedback on the presentation of self. *Journal of Personality and Social Psychology*, 1, 413-425.

Goffman, E. (1959). *The presentation of self in everyday life*. Garden City, NY: Doubleday Anchor.

Goffman, E. (1967). *Interaction ritual*. Chicago: Aldine Publishing Co.

Goffman, E. (1969). *Strategic interaction*. Philadelphia: University of Pennsylvania Press.

Harvey, O. J., & Schroder, H. M. (1963). Cognitive aspects of self and motivation. In O. J. Harvey (Ed.), *Motivation and social interaction* (pp. 95-133). New York: Ronald Press.

Hastie, R., Ostrom, T. M. Ebbesen, E. B., Wyer, R. S., Hamilton, D. L., & Carlston, D. E. (Eds.) (1980). *Person memory: The cognitive basis of social perception*. Hillsdale, NJ: Erlbaum.

Hayes-Roth, B., & Hayes-Roth, F. (1979). A cognitive model of planning. *Cognitive Science*, 2, 275-310.

Heider, F. (1958). *The psychology of interpersonal relations*. New York: John Wiley.

Higgins, E. T., & King, G. (1981). Accessibility of social constructs: Information-processing consequences of individual and contextual variability. In N. Cantor & J. F. Kihlstrom (Eds.), *Personality, cognition, and social interaction* (pp. 69-121). Hillsdale, NJ: Lawrence Erlbaum.

Jellison, J. M., & Gentry, K.W. (1978). A self-presentation interpretation of the seeking of social approval. *Personality and Social Psychology Bulletin*, 4, 227-230.

Jones, E. E. (1964). *Ingratiation*. New York: Appleton-Century-Crofts.

Jones, E. E., & Davis, K. E. (1965). From acts to dispositions: The attribution process in person perception. In L. Berkowitz (Ed.), *Advances in experimental social psychology* (Vol. 2, pp. 219-266). New York: Academic Press.

Jones, E. E., & Gerard, H. B. (1967). *Foundations of social psychology*. New York: Wiley.

Jones, E. E., & Pittman, T. S. (1982). Toward a general theory of strategic self-presentation. In J. Suls (Ed.), *Psychological perspectives on the self* (pp. 231-262). Hillsdale, NJ: Erlbaum.

Jones, E. E., & Thibaut, J. W. (1958). Interaction goals as bases of inference in interpersonal perception. In R. Tagiuri & L. Petrullo (Eds.), *Person perception and interpersonal behavior* (pp. 151-178). Stanford, CA: Stanford University Press.

Kelley, H. H. (1979). *Personal relationships: Their structures and processes.* Hillsdale, NJ: Lawrence Erlbaum.

Kruglanski, A. W. (1980). Lay epistemologic-process and contents: Another look at attribution theory. *Psychological Review,* 87, 70-87.

Kruglanski, A. W. (1989). *Lay epistemics and human knowledge: Cognitive and motivational bases.* New York: Plenum.

Kruglanski, A. W., & Ajzen, I. (1983). Bias and error in human judgment. *European Journal of Social Psychology,* 13, 1-44.

Kruglanski, A. W., & Freund, T. (1983). The freezing and unfreezing of lay-inferences: Effects on impressional primacy, ethnic stereotyping, and numerical anchoring. *Journal of Experimental Social Psychology,* 19, 448-468.

Kruglanski, A. W., & Jaffe, Y. (1988). Curing by knowing: A lay epistemic approach to cognitive therapy. In L.Y. Abramson (Ed.), *Social cognition and clinical psychology: A synthesis* (pp. 254-291). New York: Guilford Press.

Kruglanski, A. W., & Klar, Y. (1987). A view from a bridge: Synthesizing the consistency and attribution paradigms from a lay epistemic perspective. *European Journal of Social Psychology,* 17, 211-241.

Langer, E. J. (1978). Rethinking the role of thought in social interaction. In J. H. Harvey, W. Ickes, & R. F. Kidd (Eds.), *New directions in attribution research* (Vol. 2, pp. 35-58). Hillsdale, NJ: Erlbaum.

Langer, D. J., Blank, A., & Chanowitz, B. (1978). The mindlessness of ostensibly thoughtful action: The role of 'placebic' information in interpersonal interaction. *Journal of Personality and Social Psychology,* 36, 635-642.

Lanzetta, J. T. (1963). Information acquisition in decision making. In O. J. Harvey (Ed.), *Motivation and social interaction* (pp. 239-265). New York: Ronald Press.

Leary, M. R., & Schlenker, B. R. (1981). The social psychology of shyness: A self-presentation model. In J. T. Tedeschi (Ed.), *Impression management theory and social psychology* (pp. 335-358). New York: Academic Press.

Lewin, K. (1935). *A dynamic theory of personality: Selected papers.* New York: McGraw.

Markus, H., & Zajonc, R. B. (1985). The cognitive perspective in social psychology. In G. Lindzey & E. Aronson (Eds.), *Handbook of social psychology* (3rd ed., Vol. 1, pp. 137-230). New York: Random House.

McClelland, D. C. (1951). *Personality.* New York: Holt, Rinehart, & Winston.

Mead, G. H. (1934). *Mind, self and society.* Chicago: University of Chicago Press.

Miller, G. A., Galanter, E., & Pribram, K. H. (1960). *Plans and the structure of behavior.* New York: Holt, Rinehart & Winston.

Murray, H. A. (1938). *Explorations in personality.* New York: Oxford University Press.

Newell, A., & Simon, H. A. (1972). *Human problem solving.* Englewood Cliffs, NJ: Prentice Hall.

Nisbett, R. E., & Ross, L. (1980). *Human inference: Strategies and shortcomings of social judgment.* Englewood Cliffs, NJ: Prentice-Hall.

Nisbett, R. E., & Wilson, T. D. (1977). Telling more than we can know: Verbal reports on mental processes. *Psychological Review*, 24, 231-259.

Peri, N., Kruglanski, A.W., & Zakai, D. (1986). *Interactive effects of initial confidence and epistemic motivations on the extent of informational search*. Unpublished manuscript. Tel-Aviv University.

Popper, K. R. (1959). *The logic of scientific discovery*. New York: Harper.

Popper, K. R. (1973). *Objective knowledge: An evolutionary approach*. Oxford: Clarendon.

Pruitt, D. G., & Smith, D. L. (1981). Impression management in bargaining: Images of firmness and trustworthiness. In J. T. Tedeschi (Ed.), *Impression management theory and social psychological research* (pp. 247-267). New York: Academic Press.

Quattrone, G. A., & Jones, E. E. (1978). Selective self-disclosure with and without correspondent performance. *Journal of Experimental Social Psychology*, 14, 511-526.

Reykowski, J. (1982). Social motivation. *Annual Review of Psychology*, 33, 123-154.

Rumelhart, D. E., & Ortony, A. (1977). The representation of knowledge in memory. In R. C. Anderson, R. J. Spiro, & W. E. Montague (Eds.), *Schooling and the acquisition of knowledge* (pp. 99-135). Hillsdale, NJ: Lawrence Erlbaum Associates.

Schank, R. C., & Abelson, R. (1977). *Scripts, plans, goals, and understanding*. Hillsdale, NJ: Erlbaum.

Schlenker, B. R. (1980). *Impression management: The self-concept, social identity, and interpersonal relations*. Monterey, CA: Brooks/Cole.

Schneider, D. J. (1969). Tactical self-presentation after success and failure. *Journal of Personality and Social Psychology*, 13, 262-268.

Schneider, D. J. (1981). Tactical self-presentations: Toward a broader conception. In J. T. Tedeschi (Ed.), *Impression management theory and social psychological research* (pp. 23-40). New York: Academic Press.

Schneider, D. J., & Eustis, A. C. (1972). Effects of ingratiation motivation, target, positiveness, and revealingness on self-presentation. *Journal of Personality and Social Psychology*, 22, 149-155.

Schneider, D. J., Hastorf, A. H., & Ellsworth, P. C. (1979). *Person perception* (2nd Ed.). Reading, Mass: Addison-Wesley.

Schroder, H. M., Driver, M. J., & Steufert, S. (1967). *Human information processing*. New York: Holt, Rinehart, & Winston.

Shure, M. B., & Spivack, G. (1972). Means-end thinking, adjustment, and social class among elementary-school-aged children. *Journal of Consulting and Clinical Psychology*, 38, 348-353.

Simon, H. A. (1957). *Models of man*. New York: Wiley.

Simon, H. A. (1979). *Models of thought*. New York: Yale University Press.

Staub, E. (1980). Social and prosocial behavior: Personal and situational influences and their interactions. In E. Staub (Ed.), *Personality: Basic aspects and current research* (pp. 237-294). Englewood Cliffs, NJ: Prentice Hall.

Swann, W. B. (1984). Quest for accuracy in person perception: A matter of pragmatics. *Psychological Review*, 91, 457-477.

Tedeschi, J. T. (Ed.) (1981). *Impression management theory and social psychological research*. New York: Academic Press.

Tversky, A., & Kahneman, D. (1974). Judgment under uncertainty: Heuristic and biases. *Science*, 185, 1124-1131.

Wyer, R. S. (1974). *Cognitive organization and change: An information processing approach*. Potomac, MD: Erlbaum.

Wyer, R. S., & Srull, T. K. (1980). The processing of social stimulus information: A conceptual integration. In R. Hastie, T. M. Ostrum, E. B. Ebbessen, R. S. Wyer, D. L. Hamilton, & D. E. Carlston (Eds.), *Person memory: The cognitive basis of social perception* (pp. 227-300). Hillsdale, NJ: Lawrence Erlbaum Associates.

INTER-PERSONALISM: UNDERSTANDING PERSONS IN RELATIONSHIPS

Lynn Carol Miller and Stephen John Read

PREDICTING AND UNDERSTANDING BEHAVIOR IN RELATIONSHIPS

'Well?' said Molly, now very critical.

Anna, in the face of this unspoken but clear determination not to discuss it, said: 'I've been thinking about it all during the last few months...no I'd like to talk about it with you. After all, we both went through it, and with the same person...'

'Well?'

Anna persisted: 'I remember that afternoon, knowing I'd never go back. It was all that damned art all over the place.'

Molly drew in her breath, sharp. She said, quickly: 'I don't know what you mean.' As Anna did not reply, she said accusing, 'And have you written anything since I've been away?'

The Golden Notebook, Doris Lessing, pages 5-6.

Consider these two characters - Molly and Anna. It seems apparent in the above that Anna wants to discuss a topic that Molly does not. How can we understand such exchanges and predict the interpersonal behavior of Molly and Anna in their relationship with one another? One traditional approach is to ask what individual differences predict willingness to disclose in relationships (Jourard, 1959). For example, are some individuals, perhaps like Anna, more willing to discuss intimate topics than individuals like Molly? Unfortunately, individual difference measures of disclosure have not consistently predicted behavioral disclosure (for reviews see Cozby, 1973; Miller, 1982). Partly in reaction to such inconsistencies, other researchers have focused on relationship effects such as disclosure reciprocity (Cozby, 1973) or disclosure-liking effects (Cozby, 1973; Goodstein & Reinecker, 1974). That is, if individuals like Anna disclose, do their partners generally disclose in return? And do social norms dictate that they reciprocate disclosure even if they don't want to? During these exchanges what is the relationship between disclosure and liking?

Although these are interesting questions, they don't seem to get at the heart of the interaction. The exchange between Molly and Anna seems based on a long history of interactions and experience. We would need to understand their unique relationship to better understand this conversation between them. How do we separate what Anna and Molly will typically be like from what is unique to their special relationship? Past researchers have not typically pulled apart variance in disclosure at the individual level (extent to which individuals generally disclose to others or receive disclosure) from variance in disclosure due to the *unique relationships* that individuals form. Yet, recent work (Miller & Kenny, 1986) suggests that in close relationships, most of the variance is explained at the dyadic or relationship level. But, while our methods allow us to partition and assess the amount of variance due to individual differences and unique relationships (Kenny & LaVoie, 1984), our theoretical approaches to predicting and understanding the *unique* and complex *relationships* that *persons* form have lagged behind.

The primary concern of this chapter is to introduce a theory of Interpersonalism that provides a more detailed, richer framework for understanding persons and how persons create unique relationships. Central to the theory is an attempt to develop a detailed model of persons. In this model, individual differences and traits are viewed as goal-based structures composed of chronic configurations of the individual's goals, plans, resources, and beliefs. Situations, also, can be conceptualized as goal-based structures consisting of the goals that can be satisfied within them and the behaviors and resources associated with them. By viewing persons and situations in terms of a common language of goal-based structures, it is argued that we have more useful 'units' for understanding the complex meshings and frictions that occur as unique individuals create unique relationships.

Although the model is intended for general application to the study of interpersonal relations, to provide greater focus, we will begin by examining previous assumptions concerning individual differences in self-disclosure. We have chosen self-disclosure, or communication of the more personal and private aspects of self, as our 'behavior of interest' for several reasons. First, self-disclosure has been considered of central importance in the development and maintenance of relationships (Altman & Taylor, 1973; Levinger, 1974) and intimacy of disclosure has been related to such variables as liking and marital satisfaction (Burke, Weir, & Harrison, 1976; Hendrick, 1981; Jourard & Landsman, 1960). Second, 'self-disclosure' is an appropriate and salient interpersonal phenomena with which to illustrate a model of 'Inter-personalism'. Third, 'self-disclosure' is a well-researched area, but one in which basic assumptions and questions regarding individual differences and relationship effects seem to demand further clarification. Before exploring this model, we will briefly examine some of the assumptions of previous approaches to self-disclosure and suggest that it might be fruitful for researchers in self-disclosure to begin to ask a new set of questions.

Questioning Assumptions

The meaning of disclosures. Although self-disclosure researchers have begun to differentiate a number of different types of disclosing behaviors (cf. Morton, 1978 on the distinction between 'discriptive' and 'evaluative' intimacy) in ongoing interactions, we have typically assumed that we could code the meaning of a particular disclosure outside of the context of the particular ongoing conversation and relationship. Such a view is too simple. Instead, we must consider what the explicit and implied meaning of that disclosure is for the person who reveals it and the person who receives it in a particular interaction and a particular relationship. For example, if I say, 'I'm feeling well...OK', what does such a disclosure mean? On the surface, it's relatively low in intimacy. But, it might - depending upon the context and the relationship - mean, do you care enough about me to ask me 'what's really going on?' Or, I may tell you about a particular 'favorite' self-story. For strangers, such 'stories' may suggest that the speaker has a variety of goals (e.g. attention, self-presentation, self-verification, intimacy) while for a spouse the same 'self-stories' may become codes that indicate that a partner has a particular concern, need, or problem (e.g. 'OK, this is the story about overcoming difficult obstacles, she/he must be dealing with one now.').

The meaning of a particular disclosure is probably going to depend upon the goals or perceived goals of the discloser. Thus, an important goal for self-disclosure researchers may well be to expand existing theoretical distinctions regarding the functions and meanings of disclosures (e.g. Derlega & Grzelak, 1979; Stiles, 1987). However, as suggested earlier, the meaning of a disclosure is apt to depend upon where it is embedded in an ongoing interaction and relationship. It is important, then, to have a more detailed understanding of conversations and how listeners infer meanings from the sequence of behaviors. Related work on language and understanding of conversations is especially exciting in this regard (for a review see McLaughlin, 1984)

Is self-disclosure usefully viewed as a trait? Historically self-disclosure has been viewed as a relatively stable personality characteristic. Unfortunately, the relationships between self-report disclosure measures and other variables (including behavioral disclosure) have been inconsistent and weak (cf. Cozby, 1973; Miller & Read, 1987). Perhaps, then, it would be useful to take a step back and ask, what do we mean by a 'trait' and how might different trait conceptions aid us in understanding disclosure in relationships.

As Magnusson and Endler (1977) point out there are a number of ways to view the concept of 'trait'. According to a trait personality theory (cf. Magnusson, & Endler, 1977), traits are viewed as latent dispositions to respond in a certain way: individuals differ in the extent to which, by their reactions, they manifest a rank order on this dimension. Such an approach assumes that although individuals may differ in their absolute level of behavior across situations, individual rank ordering will be maintained. It is clear that the research in self-disclosure does not support a consistent view of self-disclosure as a trait, defined in this way. For example, the work by Miller, Berg, and Archer (1983) indicates that the characteristics of the recipient of disclosure (Opener level) significantly interact with subject's chronic willingness to disclose (disclosure level) in predicting disclosing behavior.

Alternatively, traits have been viewed (see for example Cattell, 1965) as a 'summary of consistent reactions (with respect to a variable) across a number of situations' in which 'no inferences are made about latent dispositions' (Magnusson & Endler, 1977, p. 17). However, in the work by Miller and Kenny (1986; 1987) differences in the extent to which individuals perceive themselves to generally disclose across a number of others and the extent to which others perceive them to generally self-disclose did not predict important relationship phenomena. For example, among women who knew one another in a sorority (Miller & Kenny, 1986; 1987) individuals who tended to disclose consistently to others across the members of the group did not tend to be liked better or to be disclosed to more in return. Thus, while we can measure willingness to reveal personal and private information across a broad range of individuals, it is not altogether clear where such a strategy takes us.

A third way of viewing a trait is as:

a certain aspect of the mediating system's way of selecting, interpreting, and treating information as a basis for coherent behavior across situations. The basis for identification of a trait would be the coherent patterns of behavior across situations of different kinds that characterize individuals and groups of individuals, according to the interactional model of behavior (Magnusson & Endler, 1977, page 17).

Unfortunately, little research and theory in self-disclosure has been explicitly concerned with individual differences at the 'mediating level' (Magnusson & Endler, 1977). Such an interactional approach to 'traits' in the area of self-disclosure seems, on the surface to make a great deal of intuitive sense given the extent to which self-disclosure is an interpersonal behavior. How might we develop a more systematic model of some of the mediating variables in the area of disclosure?

A Search for Mediating Structures

One approach is to consider concrete examples of disclosure patterns of individuals and to abstract possible mediators from those examples. Thus, one low disclosing individual might have goals that involve avoiding intimacy (e.g. avoid getting too close to others, avoid commitments) or the individual may have conflicting goals (e.g. to develop a close relationship, to avoid rejection) that might restrict their disclosing behaviors, lead to less 'risky' compromise behaviors, or lead them to use sub-plans to increase the chances that the other will be accepting. Another may hold beliefs about disclosing and relationships that may restrict disclosure patterns. He may believe that other people aren't interested in his problems, that disclosing is a sign of weakness, or that there is no point in disclosing because it's not going to change anything. Other low disclosers may lack important resources or effective plans for bringing up self-related information.

Alternatively, one can imagine an individual who feels that disclosing positive things about himself will impress others and increase his chances of being successful but who withholds negative information to reduce interference with self-presentational goals. Or, he may disclose positively about himself in one context (at work) and disclose more negative facets of self in close, established relationships where self-presentational concerns are reduced, or other goals are more salient (e.g. desire for intimacy and emotional closeness). All of the above are examples of individuals whose disclosing behaviors would be restricted or dependent upon their interaction partner, the circumstances, or the nature of the relationship.

The above examples suggest some interesting possibilities. Let us consider the following potential mediators and the relationships among them:

(1) Individuals' goals and the relations among them. It is important to consider the relation among goals and how such relations can restrict, change and compromise strategies individuals enact. Different goals may be related to very

different types of disclosing behaviors and part of very different sets of interpersonal strategies. Recent work indicates that as interaction goals shift in salience, differences in both the type and amount of disclosure result (Berg & Archer, 1982). How do individuals combine their goals and how are these configurations of goals for the individual as well as for the couple, related to the meaning attached to a particular disclosure within a particular conversation?

(2) Plans and strategies for enacting these goals. We need to understand how these are associated with configurations of goals regarding disclosure and also how the different disclosing behaviors fit in with other interpersonal sets of strategies (e.g. positive disclosures may be part of a class of self-presentational strategies). We need to better understand individuals' hierarchies of plans and strategies, how they are developed and how individuals choose among them.

(3) Resources and constraints on resources for acting out these plans. We need to better understand what resources are needed for individuals to enact specific plans associated with interpersonal goals and how chronic differences in resources affect individuals' salient interpersonal goals, plans and beliefs.

(4) Beliefs that are consistent or inconsistent with these goals, plans, and the use of various resources. We need to have a better understanding of individuals' belief systems that (a) facilitate or inhibit their goals in social interaction, (b) affect their choice of plans and strategies, and (c) affect how they construe, interpret and respond to their interactions with others.

Essentially, we are arguing (Miller & Read, 1987) that it may be useful to view disclosures as acts in sets of strategies (e.g., disclosing positive information about self, negative information, intimate information, etc.) and procedures (e.g., steer the conversation to this topic so I can bring up this positive thing about myself) that enable one to reach various goals (e.g., conveying a particular image of self). Such procedures are activated in interpersonal relationships and exchanges in which the potential discloser is evaluating and making inferences about whether her partner will facilitate or interfere with her goals and whether her partner or the changing context will make additional goals salient. Often, as in the example of the conversation between Molly and Anna, complex inferences about the meaning of the sequence of actions need to be made. Understanding a sequence of disclosures and actions between individuals such as Molly and Anna may require a fairly detailed understanding of them and how they perceive themselves, each other, the situation and their relationship. Let us proceed to take a closer look.

INTER-PERSONALISM: PERSONS IN RELATIONSHIPS

> When the two women went out together, Anna deliberately effaced herself and played to the dramatic Molly. When they were alone, she tended to take the lead. But this had by no means been true at the beginning of their friendship. Molly, abrupt, straightforward, tactless, had frankly dominated Anna. Slowly, and the offices of Mother Sugar had had a good deal to do with it, Anna learned to stand up for herself. Even now there were moments when she should challenge Molly when she did not. She admitted to herself she was a coward; she would always give in rather than have fights or scenes. A quarrel would lay Anna low for days whereas Molly thrived on them. She would burst into exuberant tears, say unforgivable things, and have forgotten all about it half a day later. Meanwhile Anna would be limply recovering in her flat.
>
> *The Golden Notebook*, Doris Lessing, pages 9-10

Although the above description is fiction, such relationships are probably not atypical of naturally occurring relationships. In any event, the reader must try to make sense out of a complex web of perceptions, understandings, and exchanges to understand these characters and the nature of their relationship with one another. What are Anna's goals? How does she go about accomplishing them? What are her beliefs? Why is it, for example, that Anna 'deliberately effaces herself' in public? Why does she play 'to the dramatic Molly'? Why does Anna see Molly as she does? Is that the way Molly sees herself? Why are there differences in their relationship in private and public contexts? How does Anna, as an individual, perceive that she has changed over time and how has that changed their relationship? How does their relationship affect them as individuals? How have their relationships with others (Mother Sugar) affected how they view themselves and their relationships with others? What are the conflicts that Anna faces and why does she resolve them as she does? How might the self-concepts and goals of these women differ and how might they differ in their interpretations of and reactions to relationship outcomes?

Inter-personalism, a goal-based theory of persons in relationships, is one attempt to address some of these issues. In this chapter we suggest that goal based structures provide a common language for a theory incorporating not only a model of persons and situations, but also a model of how we perceive our partner and understand our relationships in varying contexts and over time.

A Goal-based Theory

A number of theorists (e.g., Miller, Galanter, & Pribram, 1960; Murray, 1938; Schank & Abelson, 1977; and Wilensky, 1983) have argued that social interaction can be analyzed in terms of people's goals, and the plans and strategies necessary to achieve those goals. Implicit in these analyses are two additional considerations: an individual's beliefs as they relate to these goals and strategies, and the resources necessary to carry out the plans and attain these goals. Because differences in these four components are an important source of differences between individuals in their social behavior, let us consider each in greater detail.

Goals. For our present purposes a goal is, quite simply, something which the individual desires or wants to attain because it is rewarding in its own right. Among the wide range of possible goals are basic biological needs such as food, sleep, and sex, social needs such as companionship, respect, love, and success, and more abstract needs or goals such as truth, and justice. Examples of goals particularly relevant to disclosure may include impressing another, understanding oneself and others, making friends, having an intimate relationship, and avoiding rejection and ridicule. Most of the time, we may not be 'consciously' aware of these goals, or the execution of these goals. But, individuals may be more or less consciously *aware* of various beliefs, standards, and goals depending upon the situation (Duval & Wicklund, 1972), and their ability to reach their goals. Furthermore, individuals clearly differ in the extent to which they may be chronically aware of their thoughts, feelings, and motives (Carver & Scheier, 1981).

Plans and Strategies. In addition, there are the plans and strategies which an individual uses to attain those goals. Plans are organized sequences of behavior aimed at the attainment of some end goal or set of goals. Oftentimes, a given plan is composed of several subsequences or subplans linked together into an overall plan in order to attain the goals in a particular situation. In terms of disclosure such plans would include what to disclose (and not disclose) about oneself, the way one would go about disclosing it, when and where it would be disclosed and how it is likely to be construed as the interaction unfolds. Often an individual may have a hierarchy of possible plans and strategies. The use of a particular strategy probably depends upon a variety of factors including one's perception of the context, the rapidity with which such a choice must be made, expectations (based on experience or simulations) of probable success associated with a strategy, and the probable impact of the strategy. In addition, as Mandler (1975) points out, higher order plans involve organized sequences of behaviors which can be fairly 'automatic' or relatively 'unconscious'. Berscheid (1983) gives the following excellent example.

> For many people the early-morning rising and breakfast routine is a highly organized action sequence. Triggered by the alarm clock, for example, Joan gets up, puts on her robe, yells at Johnny to get up, stumbles downstairs, makes the coffee, yells at Johnny to get up again, waits to hear his feet land on the floor, unloads the dishwasher, puts plates on the table, and so forth. The sequence has been performed so many times in the past, in just that invariant order and with each response in the intrachain sequence of activities serving as the stimulus for the next, that she can do it in her sleep-and often does....Many organized action sequences are part of higher - order plans that are in the process of execution...Joan's highly organized morning routine, for example, may be part of several of her higher-order plans, including seeing to it that Johnny gets an

education and arrives at school on time, as well as preserving her marriage to a man who believes a good wife and mother always provides a hardy breakfast for her family. Higher order plans, then, are response sequences initiated and in some state of completion. (pp. 150-151)

Beliefs. An individual's beliefs and knowledge about the world are apt to be instrumental to the choice and successful completion of a plan. Among these may be such things as knowledge about the locations of objects (such as an airport) necessary to a plan, evaluations of the morality and effectiveness of various plans, and knowledge about the likely behavior of physical and social objects. Among these beliefs are beliefs about people ('people are basically worthwhile and trustworthy') and also oneself ('if I tell her this, she'll continue talking to me') which may influence one's behavior and set one apart from others. There are beliefs (ends-beliefs) that may relate more to goals *per se*, such as 'having people like me is rewarding', while other beliefs, such as 'disclosing about myself is a good way to get others to like and pay attention to me', are beliefs about the strategies or plans an individual would adopt to reach his goals (these will be referred to as means-beliefs). Some beliefs individuals may have such as, 'I must be loved and adored by my spouse and it would be horrible if such love was not forthcoming', have been described as illogical (Ellis & Harper, 1977). Individuals may often be unaware of the extent to which their beliefs may influence their responses (Ellis & Harper, 1977).

Resources. Most plans carry with them numerous conditions which must be satisfied for the plan's successful completion. Some of these conditions simply depend on the particular state of the world and are beyond the control of the individual trying to enact the plan. However, most of the time, plans require certain resources to carry them out. Among resources commonly required in social interaction (Foa & Foa, 1976) are such things as money, access to information, speed and ways of processing information, time, attributes (e.g., attractiveness, strength), and various skills and abilities. Clearly, people differ considerably in these things.

Goal-based Configurations and Behavior

While people may have a large repertoire of goals, the salience of these goals in social interaction is apt to vary depending upon the context and the nature of their interpersonal relationship. Activating a goal or set of goals is apt to also activate a consideration of plans, strategies, beliefs associated with the goals and plans, and an assessment of resources needed to carry out the plans to attain the goals. For any given individual, at a given time, some goals and goal-configurations are apt to be more salient than others. It is expected that the hierarchies and relationships among this complex of activated goal configurations and the nature of the constraints on behavior imposed by the context and the interpretation of responses from ongoing interactions would affect the content, style and timing of plans, strategies, and behavioral sequences that are executed.

Intra-personal goal relations. Wilensky (1983) has argued that there are two types of goal relations at the level of the individual. 'Goal conflict' involves goals at the intra-personal level (within the individual) that are negatively related (e.g., in opposition to one another). Goals may be negatively related to one another because of a variety of reasons: (1) resource limitations such as not having enough time to carry out all of one's plans, restrictions on material resources, and limitations on abilities or skills needed to carry out one's plans, (2) state limitations (e.g., we can't physically be in two places at the same time), and (3) preservation goals and limitations (e.g., engaging in disclosing in order to be close to another endangers another goal, being viewed positively). Wilensky (1983) argues that when people are faced with negative goal relations, they typically try to circumvent them either by figuring out a new plan that will allow them to attain all their goals, or by determining which goals are most important and focusing on achieving those, abandoning the others.

In coming up with a new plan, people can do one of the following: (1) find a new plan without the problems of the first, or (2) remove the reason for the negative goal relation. Thus, for example if the first plan failed because of a resource limitation, find a plan that doesn't require the same resource. Another strategy, if the original plan failed for lack of a resource, such as money, is to first try to get more of the resource and then retry the old plan.

Fortunately, goals are not always negatively related. Some goals are unrelated to one another while for others there is what Wilensky (1983) describes as 'Goal overlap'. These are goals at the intra-personal level that are consistent with one another, for example, because they can be achieved by the same plan or because they can be achieved more easily together than apart.

This analysis of goal relations suggests that if we wish to predict which plan an individual is apt to execute, we first need to know that individual's goals and the relations among them. And, we will need to know what factors will facilitate or interfere with their likelihood of enacting a particular plan (e.g., knowledge of the plan, resources for enacting plans of action, beliefs about various plans).

Individual Differences

Idiographic configurations

Across situations, however, we would expect that for most individuals some higher order goals form a stable core. We have argued (Miller & Read, 1987) that most stable individual differences at the mediating level can be viewed as chronic configurations of (1) an individual's goals, (2) the plans and strategies for attaining those goals, (3) the resources required for successfully carrying out the plans, and (4) beliefs about the world which affect the execution of their plans. Similar arguments concerning the importance of one or more of these components have been made by Allston (1970, 1975) and Carbonnell (1979). Mischel (1973) has also argued for the importance of plans and goals in understanding individual differences. Obviously, the exact complex chronic configurations of goals, plans, resources and beliefs are apt to be unique and idiographic for different individuals.

Traits

We argue that while many of these chronic configurations are idiosyncratic, some configurations are shared as 'fuzzy sets' (Rosch, 1975; 1978) by a large number of people and as a result are apt to be recognized with a trait label. These configurations may differ in how prototypical (Rosch, 1975, 1978; Rosch & Mervis, 1975) they are of a particular trait, with configurations varying in their similarity to the central members or prototypes of the category. Thus, we are adopting a prototype notion of traits (Buss & Craik, 1983, 1984; Cantor & Mischel, 1977, 1979), in which these configurations may share a 'family resemblance' (Rosch & Mervis, 1975) to each other and so form a coherent set, even though they may differ in their similarity to the central members of the category. Our approach, however, differs from previous approaches that have examined the prototypicality of traits. First, we are concerned with traits as mediating systems unlike Buss & Craik (1983, 1984). Second, in contrast to previous approaches (Buss & Craik, 1983, 1984; Cantor & Mischel, 1977, 1979) we are concerned with the configuration and organization of components or 'units' (e.g., goals, plans, resources and beliefs) that make up structures prototypically viewed as traits.

For a concrete example of how such a configuration can be viewed as a trait, let's consider Alan. Alan very much wants and likes to be with people, engages in various plans and behaviors to interact with them, possesses the skills and resources to successfully interact with them, and has certain beliefs and knowledge which are instrumental to carrying out his plans. In terms of the present model, Alan has a chronic configuration of goals, plans, resources and beliefs that might best be described by the trait sociable. An example is given in Figure 1a.

To be called sociable Alan presumably has to have the goal of wanting to be with people. Further, a truly sociable individual should be able to successfully carry out various plans for social interaction. An individual who is not able to interact successfully (e.g., achieve his or her goal to be with others), would probably not be considered sociable but instead may be chronically lonely. Figure 1 contrasts sociability with chronic loneliness. As you can see, the sociable person and the lonely person may have very similar goals. However, because their beliefs, strategies and resources differ considerably, we would expect only one of these individuals to be construed as falling on the high end of the sociability dimension.

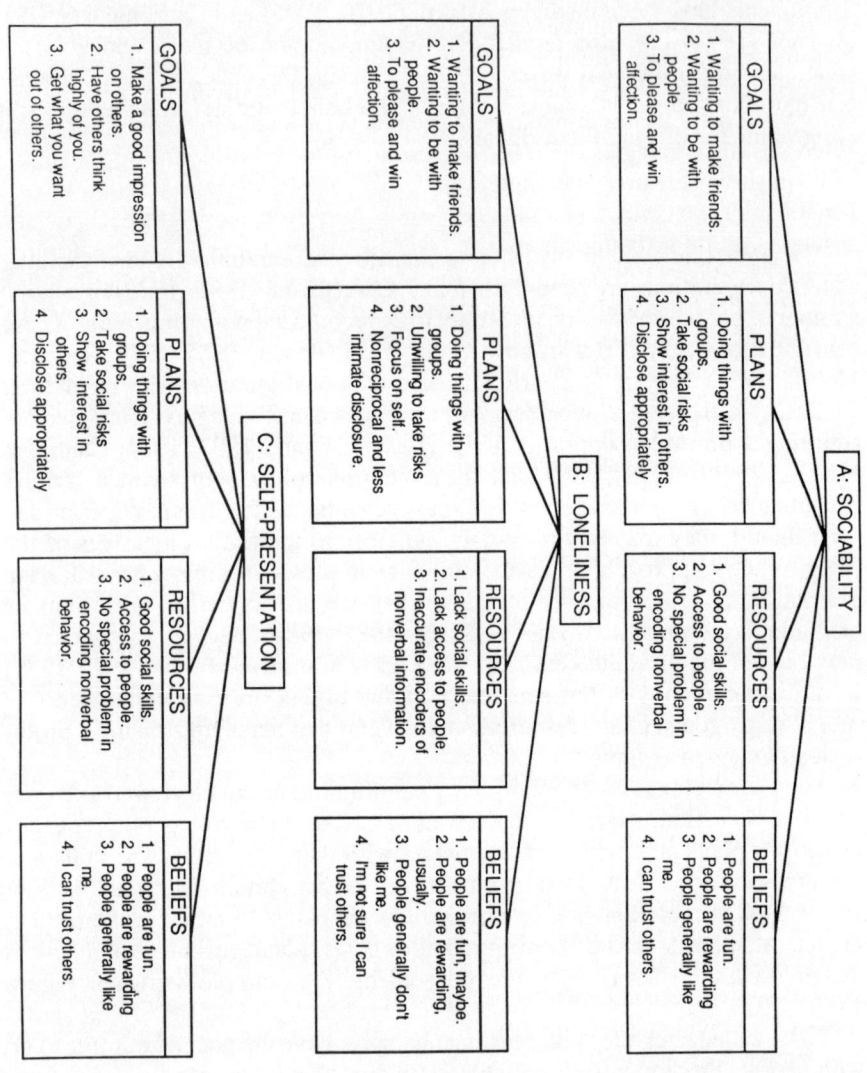

Miller, L. C., and Read, S. J., (1987). Why am I telling you this? Self-disclosure in a goal-based model of personality. In V. J. Derlega & J. Berg (Eds.). *Self-disclosure: Theory, research, and therapy*. Plenum. Reprinted with permission from the publisher

Figure 1. A Comparison of Sociability, Loneliness and Self-Presentation.

Likewise, individuals may have similar strategies but associate these strategies with the attainment of different goals. Thus, one individual, Ellen may be quite likely to self-disclose intimate information about herself when she is trying to impress others, while another person, Alan, may typically self-disclose only when he is trying to make new friends. Given a chronic configuration of Ellen's goals, strategies, beliefs, and resources, as indicated in Figure 1c, the trait 'positive self-presenter' might be a more useful way to describe Ellen's constellation of goals and strategies, while Alan's constellation of goals and strategies might be better summarized (see Figure 1a) as involving 'sociability' (Cheek & Buss, 1981), or 'need for affiliation' (Murray, 1938). In short, although both Ellen and Alan may have similar, overlapping strategies, because these strategies are associated with different chronic goals, Alan and Ellen could be said to possess different traits. (This suggests that individuals who are attempting to make inferences about others' traits on the basis of limited observations may often have difficulty. We discuss this problem further in the portion of this manuscript concerned with 'perceiving and understanding others').

Goal relations and traits. As suggested earlier, in considering the probability of a particular plan being executed, researchers should consider an individual's goals, plans for enactment, resources pertinent to enactment, and beliefs relevant to the goals and plans. By considering these goal structures as components of traits, researchers should be better able to understand why expected behaviors do not consistently occur (e.g., a resource was unavailable) and why and when we might expect behavioral change (e.g., a person develops new social skills or learns alternative strategies to more effectively enact a behavior critical to a plan). In addition, it is critical for researchers to consider how relations among goals may influence plan execution. In an earlier example, one individual wanted to be intimate to establish a close relationship while simultaneously avoiding rejection. He may want to disclose his fears but considers this too 'risky'. Instead, he engages in a more moderate, compromise behavior (listening) that satisfies these multiple goals to some extent but that may not be the most effective strategy for either goal by itself. By viewing traits in terms of goal structures, researchers may have a more useful language for understanding those factors which affect the nature, frequency, and perceived coherence and consistency of behaviors.

A Model of Situations

The preceding analysis of individual differences provides a major part of an explicit conceptual framework for a general goal based model of Inter-personalism. One missing piece, however, is a specification of the features of social situations. This missing piece is provided by Argyle, Furnham, and Graham's

(1981) recent analysis of situations. Several of the major aspects of situations which they identify have a parallel in our analysis of traits.

First, according to Argyle et al., the chief component of a situation is the goals whose satisfaction it affords. Second, situations have associated with them rules governing the appropriateness of behavior in that situation. Third, different situations have different roles that people can fill. Each role specifies particular behaviors that are appropriate for people filling those roles. The rules and roles associated with situations make certain kinds of plans more salient, while at the same time restricting other kinds of plans. Fourth, situations often provide or make available resources and objects that are important to carrying out different plans. Finally, associated with any given situation are elements and sequences of behavior that can be used to attain goals within that situation.

Thus, both personality and situation can be analyzed in a common language. As a result it becomes much easier to specify precisely what the interaction should be between any given situation and any given person. For instance, we have argued that central to most traits is a goal, and central to Argyle et al.'s conception of a situation is the goals whose satisfaction it affords. Thus, the behavior of individuals in any given situation should depend on the degree and type of match between the goals of the individuals and the goals whose satisfaction is afforded by the situation. While the goals afforded by the situation are important, the behavior of an individual should also depend on the degree and type of match between the plans and resources in the individual's repertoire, and the plans of action which are appropriate for attaining the goals of that situation. Individuals often possess a number of different ways for attaining a particular goal. The situation should affect which, if any, of these plans are chosen and how smoothly and effectively chosen plans are enacted.

Analyzing traits and situations in this way provides an explicit conceptual framework for the analysis of person-situation interactions. We can think of them in terms of the interplay between the goals, plans and resources of the individual, and the goals, plans, resources and roles associated with the situation.

This approach bears a strong similarity to Murray's (1938) attempt to characterize person and situation in a common language. Murray referred to characteristics of the individual that directed behavior as needs, while referring to aspects of the situation that activated those needs as press. Thus, if an individual had a need for achievement or a need for affiliation, the situation would be characterized in terms of its press for achievement or its press for affiliation. However, the present formulation goes beyond Murray in its emphasis on the additional components of plans, resources and beliefs and the way in which these additional characteristics of person and situation also interact.

This model also makes it quite easy to analyze person-person interactions in terms of how the goals, plans, resources and beliefs of each member of a dyad are affected by the perceived goals, plans, resources and beliefs of the other. Since the perception and understanding of the other is central to analyzing person-person interactions we need a model of how people understand others. In the following we outline a model of person perception and attribution that seems particularly appropriate for dyadic interactions.

Perceiving and Understanding Others

Understanding the Meaning of Actions

How do we make sense of our partner's behavior in our ongoing interactions with him or her? According to Read (1987) understanding such extended sequences of behavior is our fundamental attribution problem since only rarely do single behaviors have meanings outside of such sequences. This seems particularly true in trying to make sense of dyadic interactions, where people must deal with behaviors that extend over minutes, days or even years.

As several theorists have noted (e.g., Miller, Galanter, & Pribram, 1960; Schank & Abelson, 1977) behavioral episodes have a characteristic general form consisting of four components: (1) the goal of the sequence, (2) the factors that instigated the goal, (3) the behaviors that make up a plan aimed toward the achievement of that goal, and (4) the outcome of the sequence, whether the goal is achieved or not. Since episodes have this form, understanding a behavioral sequence requires people to determine how the individual actions form a plan, what the goals of that plan are, what factors instigated the goals and precisely how that plan would achieve that goal (Read, 1987). Essentially, people must try to figure out how the events fit together into a coherent, plausible scenario or story. In most behavioral sequences the information necessary to create this scenario is not explicit. We must make numerous inferences to tie the events together, relying on highly detailed knowledge about the social and physical worlds.

Before we consider how individuals may attempt to 'fit' events together we will outline a number of different sources of detailed social knowledge that individuals need. Then we will consider how perceivers may go through a series of steps in understanding particular interactions using metarules to form coherent understandings of interactions, other people, and relationships.

Sources of Detailed Knowledge

Below we outline some of the numerous forms of information used to interpret an interaction partner's behavior. Due to space considerations we have restricted our discussion to sources of social knowledge.

Social norms, rules, and maxims. First, there are structures that prescribe what one ought to do in a social interaction (norms and rules) and assumptions (maxims) that individuals in a given culture subscribe to (cf. McLaughlin, 1984 for a fascinating review). There are a variety of types of rules. These can be very detailed and used for a number of purposes including interpreting behavior. For example, in the conversation between Molly and Anna at the beginning of this chapter, Molly asks what appear to be a series of questions. Two types of rules appear relevant to Molly's question asking behavior (Collett, 1977; Pearce, 1976, as cited in McLaughlin, 1984). First there are *regulative rules* (e.g., answers should follow questions). But in order to follow these rules (Collett, 1977) one must first invoke *constitutive rules* (e.g., understandings of which behaviors count as 'questions' and what constitutes an 'answer'). For example, is Molly's statement to Anna, 'I don't know what you mean' really the question, 'What do you mean?' In addition to rules, Grice (1975) suggests that there are a number of maxims that if followed tend to result in a 'cooperative contribution' (McLaughlin, 1984). In Molly and Anna's conversation, a number of maxims appear to have been violated. For example, Molly's question at the end of the conversation, 'And have you written anything since I've been away', changes the topic and seems to violate Grice's (1975) 'Relevancy Maxim' (e.g., a contribution should be pertinent in the context). When violations occur, conversants are apt to engage in 'conversational implicature' (Grice, 1975) to consciously ascertain why maxims have been violated. Structures such as norms, rules and maxims, then provide members of a given culture with a background of what is 'normal' or 'expected' against which to predict and understand behavior and to make inferences about why violations occur.

For example, one could infer from Molly and Anna's conversation that this topic deeply disturbs Molly. That would explain why her tone is so negative, and why in the end she engages in procedures to 'cut off' or 'change' the topic. In so doing, Molly may violate one maxim (relevancy) to prevent violating either other maxims (e.g., politeness maxim) or social norms (e.g., If I let Anna disclose to me about this, I should reciprocate but I won't be able to). But, why didn't Molly just come out and tell Anna directly that she didn't want to talk about the topic? Such a statement would be reasonable among strangers or even acquaintances because an acquaintance would not have wanted to violate the 'morality maxim' (Bach & Harnish, 1979, p. 64 cited in McLaughlin, 1984) by asking Molly to tell her personal or privileged information. On the other hand, if Molly and Anna are supposed to have a close friendship, then Molly may not want to come out and say, 'I don't want to discuss this with you'. To say that might violate norms about close friendships (e.g., close friends talk to one another things that are troubling them and try and meet the needs of the other). Such violations might indicate that Anna and Molly really weren't all that close.

Scripts, plans, goals, and themes. Schank and Abelson (1977) outline a number of additional sources of social knowledge (see Read, 1987 for a summary). Scripts are representations of stereotyped or routinized action sequences (e.g., going to a restaurant) that provide information about a number of different characteristics of the action such as: (1) its typical goals (2) the actors and roles found in that context, (3) objects and instruments that play an important role in behavior in that script, (4) the context in which the script is typically enacted, (5) conditions that must be fulfilled to enact the script and (6) the sequence of actions that constitute the script. Such knowledge can make a major contribution to our understanding of a sequence. For instance, if we recognize that a particular sequence is the 'pick up in a bar script' it allows us to make inferences about the likely goals of the individuals in that script.

When knowledge of more concrete, stereotyped action sequences is unavailable, we can still understand people's actions using our knowledge of plans. These tend to be more abstract and general than scripts, but provide many of the same kinds of knowledge such as the goals of the sequence, typical objects and people that play a role in the plan, and the conditions necessary for successfully carrying out the plan.

Understanding others also depends on detailed knowledge of people's possible goals. Associated with different goals is information such as the conditions that initiate them and plans that can be used to achieve them.

Knowledge about an individual's goals often comes from knowing what roles they fill and the nature of their interpersonal relationships. These themes (Schank & Abelson, 1977) provide information about the expected characteristics of people in particular roles, such as the behaviors they enact, their goals, and the conditions that initiate these goals. Role themes also provide information about the likely behavior of people who interact with the role member.

Traits and social stereotypes. Earlier (see also Miller & Read, 1987) we argued that traits can be viewed as chronic configurations of goals, plans, resources and beliefs. People should make attributions from behavior about an individual's likely configuration of goals, plans, resources, and beliefs. This information should, in turn, be used to make trait attributions. Conversely, people should use information about traits to make inferences about goals, plans, resources, and beliefs.

In natural interactions, individuals are privileged to an array of information about individuals. Perceivers try to make coherent inferences from this array, even trying to 'fit together' information that, at least on the surface, seems incongruent. Part of this task is probably ascertaining which behaviors go with which plans and how plans might be organized to achieve different hierarchies and configurations of goals. Eliminating possibilities is probably an important part of the process. For example, recent research (Pines, Berg & Miller, 1987) suggests that the timing of a behavior may allow perceivers to eliminate probable primary goals (e.g., she wasn't just being polite because that behavior at this time was not prescribed by social norms and was not expected).

In fitting this information together, single behaviors are apt to vary in their role in overall trait attributions. A single behavior that is highly prototypical (Buss & Craik, 1983; 1984) of a trait should lead to quicker and more confident attributions of the trait than should a less prototypical behavior (Cantor & Mischel, 1979). In addition to the effects of prototypicality, Reeder and Brewer

(1979) have argued that some trait inferences tend to be asymmetric. For instance, people are more willing to infer that someone is intelligent from one intelligent behavior than they are to infer that someone is stupid from one stupid behavior.

How are behaviors that are prototypical or diagnostic of the same trait related to one another? Interestingly, Buss and Craik (1983, 1984) have noted that behaviors which are prototypical of a trait are frequently not topographically similar, suggesting that what makes these behaviors prototypical is not similarity among members of a category. Barsalou (1985) has recently argued that for some kinds of categories, among them what he calls goal-based categories, typicality judgments are based on the extent to which the category member fits an ideal. One kind of ideal is defined by the goal of the category and the extent to which members of the category fit that goal. Thus for traits, typicality of a category member or trait related behavior may be based, at least partially, on the degree to which the behavior achieves the goal of the trait.

This suggests that even diagnostic and prototypical *single behaviors* need to be understood in the context of the goals of the ongoing interaction and the relationships among individuals to form a coherent understanding of the interaction. Furthermore, while individuals may make confident initial trait inferences based on single prototypical or diagnostic behaviors, these may be vulnerable to change if they are not embedded in a rich, coherent, supporting array.

Social stereotypes triggered by such things as gender, race, physical appearance, clothing, and mannerisms are also an important source of information in social inference (Cantor & Mischel, 1979; Hamilton, 1981). Stereotypes carry with them beliefs about typical behaviors, goals, interests, traits, etc., of the individuals who fit these stereotypes. People should be particularly likely to rely on stereotypes in the early parts of a social interaction, when other kinds of information are scarce.

Self schemas, other schemas, and mental models. A number of authors have argued for the importance of self-schemata (c.f. Markus & Smith, 1981) and self-concepts (Swann, 1983) in person perception and interpersonal processes. While space limitations preclude an extensive discussion, it seems likely that what we believe or know to be our characteristics affects our interpretation of other's behavior toward us. For instance, a rich woman probably responds differently to people's overtures than someone who is middle-class. She is apt to have more alternative explanations (e.g., her money, her other qualities) for why others befriend her, that may be difficult to differentiate. This ties in with attribution principles such as 'non-common effects' (Jones & Davis, 1965) and the use of the 'discounting principle' (Kelley, 1971).

Other sources of knowledge are what might be called mental models of what people in general are like and what relationships are like (Bowlby, 1973; Collins & Read, 1987; Hazan & Shaver, 1987). These mental models are presumably based on our interactions with other people, in particular our parents (cf. Waring, 1987). Thus, if we think people are trustworthy we will tend to make different inferences about someone's goals than if we tend to think that people can't be trusted. Or, if we think that marriage is typically a relationship in which each partner tries to exploit the other then we will be biased toward interpreting actions by our spouse as an attempt to take advantage of us.

Understanding and Developing Unique Relationships

Mental models of unique relationships. The types of knowledge discussed so far are fairly general. Yet, during the course of an interaction and indeed during the course of a relationship people develop mental models (Park, 1986; see also Gentner & Stevens, 1983; Johnson-Laird, 1983) of both their interaction partner and the relationship itself. These models are dynamic representations that are continually updated in response to new information (Park, 1986). They can be used to guide our interactions with the individual, and to predict and explain behavior. Among other things we can use our model of a person to simulate how they might respond to some action of ours.

As individuals enter relationships they are apt to make inferences about the likely goals, beliefs, plans and resources of the other. As they do, they gradually start developing a model of their partner and a model of their unique relationship with one another by combining their own goals, plans, resources, and beliefs with their perception of their partner's. As they learn more about their partner, more concrete and individualized information can be filled in. This is changed and elaborated as the relationship progresses and there are more connections among their own goal-based structures and those of their partner. Some of these inter-connections involve discovering goals, strategies, and beliefs that the other may not view positively or that may be incompatible with the other's goals, strategies and beliefs. Although there are probably a number of possible responses to such 'discoveries', among them will be attempting to either work out a unique understanding of these differences, or deactivating incompatible structures. For example, imagine that we discover in the course of a developing relationship that in order to get 'a word in edgewise' we need to violate a rule about interrupting another (which we may believe indicates rudeness). One approach is to deactivate this belief (which doesn't seem to be how our partner interprets the meaning of interruptions). Unfortunately, couples may often have difficulty 'working through' these incompatible structures. Learning to understand and articulate beliefs, feelings, and motives within one's relationships may therefore be critical to marital satisfaction (cf. Waring, 1987 for a discussion of cognitive restructuring of disclosure in marital therapy).

In developing a relationship, partners may also try out new strategies that they wouldn't have felt comfortable enacting previously. And, partners may discover how their unique relationships allow them to achieve goals that they previously could not have achieved. For example, as part of a relationship, individuals may possess resources they previously lacked that enable them to achieve personal as well as interpersonal goals. Or, individual's perceptions that their partner is 'accepting' may reduce the salience of some goals (e.g., avoid rejection) enabling the individual to more effectively enact plans to reach other, previously blocked goals (e.g., enhanced intimacy). In short, we would argue that individuals develop mental models of relationships that affect the activation, deactivation, and creation of goal-based structures guiding behavior in relationships. Because part of this model of one's partner and unique relationships depends upon understanding the connections among partner goals, we elaborate these below.

Inter-personal relations among goals-based structures. The relations among the goal-based configurations of both members of a dyad are central to understanding their relationship. Wilensky's (1983) analysis suggests that there are two kinds of inter-personal goal relations:

(1) Goal Competition - individuals' goals are negatively related to one another.
(2) Goal Concord - individuals' goals are positively related, say because they both possess the same goal, or each individual's goals facilitate the other's.

Wilensky (1983) outlines three classes of reasons why goals may be negatively related to one other. One is resource limitations (e.g., time, knowledge, materials, abilities). For example, consider a couple in which one member wishes the other to be more intimate and open up about his feelings. But, the husband has never really thought about his feelings and lacks the ability to 'get in touch' with what he is really experiencing.

Goals may also be negatively related because achieving them would require us to be in two mutually exclusive states. For instance, because of our laws it is illegal to be married to two different people at the same. Finally, goals may be negatively related because achieving one goal threatens a goal we have already achieved. Wilensky (1983) (see also Schank & Abelson, 1977) refer to this as the creation of a Preservation goal. For instance, we may think that it would be a good idea to date other people, even though we are married, until we realize that doing so would probably threaten the happiness of our marriage. One type of preservation goal that is quite important in social interaction is the preservation of self-esteem or face.

Earlier we discussed some of the ways in which individuals may deal with intra-personal goal conflict, including changing plans. In interpersonal relations, however, we cannot typically make a unilateral change in an ongoing plan. But we can try to get the other member of the relationship to change or abandon their goals. There are a number of ways we could do this, such as persuasion, negotiation or perhaps even the use of force. A variation on this would be to get our partner to postpone the achievement of their goals to a later time.

Fortunately, different individuals' goals and plans are not always negatively related. People often possess similar goals. Oftentimes, these goals may be achieved more quickly or with less effort than by either individual working alone. In other cases achievement of the goals may be possible only if they both work together. But, having similar goals does not always lead to positive goal relations. If both members of a couple wanted the last ice cream bar in the freezer, this would not lead to a positive goal relation. It is also possible to have cases where people may have quite different goals, but where the same plan, which requires action by both members, can be used to achieve both goals at the same time.

Further, Kelley (1979) has argued that as relationships develop, motives are often transformed from more individualistic ones to ones centered on the outcome of the dyad. For example, members of a dyad may shift from trying to maximize individual outcomes to trying to maximize the outcomes of the dyad.

Also, in close relationships, one member of a couple may have a higher order goal about the other such that achievement of a wide range of different goals by the partner will satisfy that goal. For instance, if one member has the goal of making the other happy, there are a number of different things the other person can do that would be consistent with that goal.

Other factors that contribute to positive goal-based relations are:

(1) similar beliefs about other people and the world. For example, even when two individuals share the same compatible goals, if one individual uses a strategy that the other individual views as morally unacceptable, there is apt to be conflict.

(2) use of similar strategies, both in terms of style and content. Generally, if our partner uses a strategy that we would use to accomplish the same goal, we are more apt to understand what our partner is trying to do and to more accurately predict their behavior. Whether the strategies are similar or not, if the behavioral enactments in our strategies easily 'mesh' with the behavioral enactments in our partner's strategies (Kelley et al., 1983), there is less apt to be an interruption in an ongoing sequence that might lead to negative affect (Berscheid, 1983). Furthermore, as couple's behavioral sequences become 'meshed' (Kelley et al., 1983), each member's behavior may play a major role in the other's plans, helping each to facilitate partner and relationship goals.

(3) similar and complementary resources. Complementary skills, abilities, and knowledge, may allow one individual to fill in a gap left by the other. Similar skills (e.g., cognitive abilities) are often needed to meet important needs of the partners (e.g., to have a mutually intellectually stimulating conversation).

In many respects the present analysis is similar to and compatible with the causal chain analysis presented by Kelley et al. (1983). While Kelley et al. (1983) acknowledge that dyadic relationships can be analyzed at many levels, including the level of goals and plans, their analysis focuses primarily on the level of causal relations among behaviors and does not examine, in detail, the level of goals and plans. The present analysis places its primary emphasis on the relationship of the goals and the plans of the members of the dyad and how these are related to their beliefs and resources. In addition, our theory emphasizes the importance of understanding persons in detail (and their goal-based configurations) in order to understand the unique relationships that emerge among unique persons over time. The theory therefore provides a language of relationships compatible with both a language of persons who make up these relationships (Miller & Read, 1987) and a language of situations (Argyle, Furnham, & Graham, 1981) in which these relationships occur.

Developing Models of the Interaction, Our Partner, Our Relationship

What we do in understanding a dyadic interaction is very similar to what happens when we read a short story or novel. As we progress we build a representation of the sequence of events. New information must be integrated with the pre-existing representation. We are continually building and adding to our model of the characters and the sequence of events (Read, 1987).

Initially, we may categorize people (e.g., gender, race or role) and situations, thus activating a set of knowledge structures. As the interaction proceeds, new information activates additional knowledge structures and subsequent actions are interpreted within the context of previous actions and connected to our current scenario. To connect new actions to the existing scenario we do the following: (a) We examine whether this action could be part of a plan or causal sequence suggested by our current scenario. If it is, then the action is connected to the scenario and it is at least partially explained. (b) If we fail to connect the action to our scenario, we then try general world knowledge to search for a plan it may be part of which might connect to the existing scenario and thereby be partially explained. This new plan or causal sequence may generate expectations and be used to interpret subsequent input. If the action is part of a plan, we try to identify its goal. Once identified, we examine whether it is merely part of a larger plan or whether it is an end in itself. If the latter, we try to identify its source, such as an interpersonal role, a personal relationship, or some occurrence that instigated the goal. We see if this information 'fits' with other information or if it is discrepant from our existing mental models and representations of this person, the roles they are apt to enact, and/or their relationships with others.

In proceeding through such steps, how might individuals go about 'fitting' information together to form a coherent understanding of the dyadic interaction, of the persons in the context of the interaction, and the unique relationships of those individuals. Several writers (see Wilensky, 1983) have identified a number of principles, or metarules, of story comprehension that Read (1987) argues should affect people's representations of social interactions. We would argue that they apply as well to people's representations and developing models of persons. For example, the *principle of exhaustion* says that people should pick the interpretation that accounts for the most data. Thus, the observer is taking information from the total array of sequences of actions (not just single behaviors) as well as observable attributes and stylistic facets of the person as the observer construes them (e.g., in light of their stereotypes, beliefs, goals, prior knowledge and model of this person, etc.) and trying to come up with a plausible representation of this person while trying to test out 'alternative explanations and models' concerning this person. Presumably some individuals (e.g., openers) may be able to extract more information from their partners, and the more individuals are willing to disclose about themselves within their unique relationships, the more likely they are to give their partners information to create more 'accurate' mental models.

Another metarule, the *principle of parsimony*, instructs people to produce an interpretation that maximizes the connections among inputs. For instance, if one interpretation of a sequence is of two unrelated plans and the second interpretation is of two plans that are part of a broader plan, people should choose the second interpretation. To elaborate this, let's consider the following behavioral sequence:

1. Mary congratulates Ellen, saying she's just heard from Bill the happy news that he's going to propose to Ellen. Ellen is delighted and goes off to plan the wedding.
2. An hour later, Mary tells Bill she's crazy about him and she'll agree to his proposal if they elope immediately. Bill embraces Mary.

On the basis of the first behavioral sequence alone, we might infer that Mary's plan is to be friendly and helpful. On the basis of the second sequence alone, we might infer that Mary's plan is to enhance commitment and intimacy in her relationship with Bill. However, on the basis of the entire behavioral sequence we might infer that Mary is trying to hurt Ellen.

There are several interesting things to note from this example. First, this interpretation would not have been probable if we had not tried to find a parsimonious explanation that maximized the connections among inputs. Second, it's hard to see how the individual behaviors by themselves could be viewed as prototypical of possible negative traits (e.g., hostile, manipulative, aggressive). Yet the whole sequence taken together strongly suggests such traits. Furthermore, this example suggests that when our interaction partners use indirect or deceptive strategies or strategies that involve 'hidden' goals, it may take longer to develop coherent interpretations of behavior and models of persons.

Explaining the Unexpected

While typically unaware of our goals and goal structures, we are more apt to be consciously aware of them when something unexpected happens, when there is plan failure, or when we are entering into a relatively novel situation and we need to actively plan out how to approach it. Because research on unexpected events is apt to provide insights into goal structures, we detail a number of these unexpected events below. An unexpected event may:

1) violate what is typical or acceptable behavior for a given situation,
2) violate our model of ourself,
3) violate our expectancies of what people are like in general,
4) violate expectations based on knowledge of social stereotypes or roles,
5) contradict some aspect of our model of our partner,
6) contradict some aspect of our model of our relationship with our partner,
7) be incompatible with a particular interpretation of a sequence of behaviors. Many an eager male has been jolted by a sisterly kiss on the cheek and a door quickly closing in his face at the end of an evening.

Successful interpersonal coordination is much easier if we understand what our partner is doing and why they are doing it. When they do something unexpected, we may consciously generate a set of hypotheses to explain it. While there are innumerable explanations specific to the concrete details of the situation, two major classes (Lalljee & Abelson, 1983) are the possibility that the partner has different goals than we thought, or they are having problems enacting plans. When something unexpected happens, people consider the following possibilities (among others):

(1) what the partner is doing is really quite consistent with what we know to be their goals, but their plan was misidentified. Once we realize what they are doing, we see that it actually fits quite nicely with our model of them.

(2) we were, in fact, mistaken about the other's goals. We may have attributed to them goals they don't actually possess or failed to realize that they also possess additional goals that override or affect the first set. To explain their behavior we must figure out what their actual goals are.

(3) the other does possess the goals that we attributed to them, but can't carry out the necessary plans. They may lack a necessary resource, not know how to carry out the plan, or environmental factors may block plan enactment. Here we must explain what could be keeping them from enacting the plan.

(4) one's partner may possess the hypothesized goal, but not share the beliefs you do about ways to achieve that goal. For example, the two authors of this paper differ considerably on the meaning associated with different kinds of gifts.

(5) our partner misidentified our goal. We have all been in the midst of an interaction that is going badly when our partner says something like, 'I thought you wanted X. I was just trying to help.' To which you reply, 'What made you think that?' Here our partner's goal has been to help us attain our goal, only to discover that they had misidentified the goal we wanted.

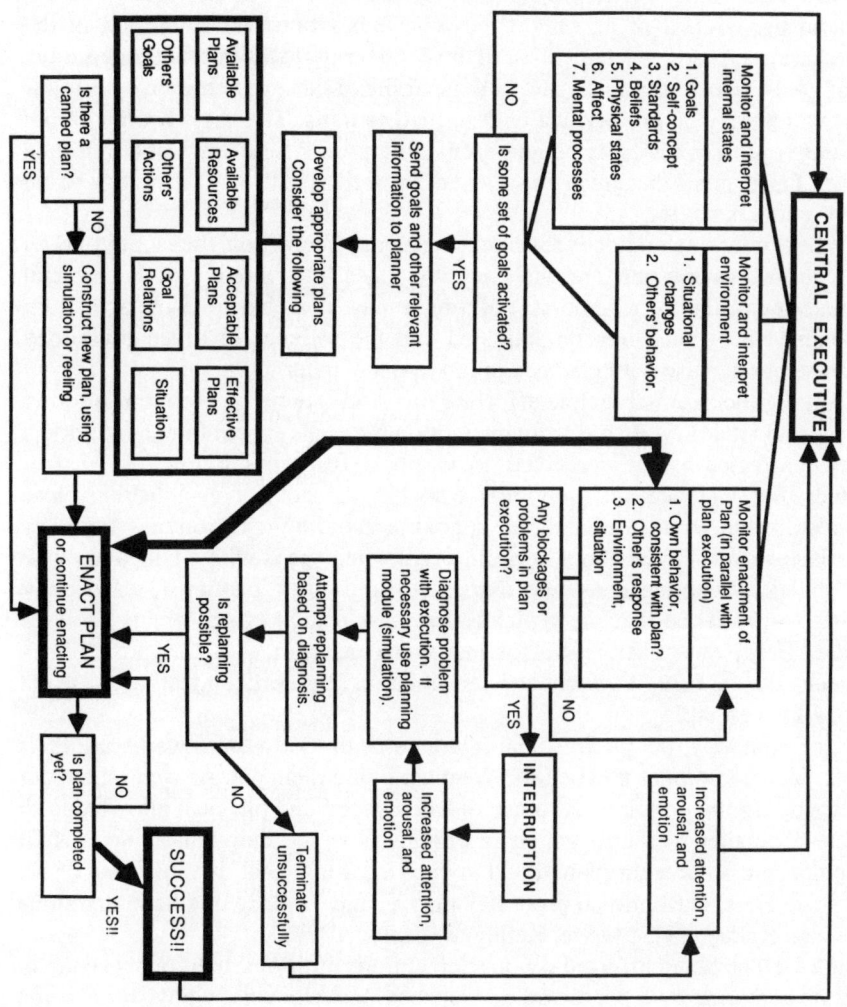

Miller, L. C., and Read, S. J., (1987). Why am I telling you this? Self-disclosure in a goal-based model of personality. In V. J. Derlega & J. Berg (Eds.). *Self-disclosure: Theory, research, and therapy*. Plenum. Reprinted with permission from the publisher

Figure 2. A flowchart representing the general process model.

Inter-personalism: In Process

Now that we have outlined some of the facets of the model, how would it work in the context of an ongoing dyadic interaction? As suggested in the flowchart in Figure 2, each member of the dyad brings to the interaction a unique set of goals, plans, resources, and beliefs. Some of these are chronic configurations which may be prototypically described as traits. The goals form a partial hierarchy, with some goals being chronically more salient and important than others. Those goals that are most salient or important will, all other things being equal, guide behavior.

When individuals enter or consider entering an interaction, they monitor both the external environment and their internal states. This monitoring has several results, one of the most important of which may be a change in the activation of goals. New goals may be activated and the salience of other goals may increase or decrease with changes in internal and external factors.

Among the external factors affecting our goals are our perceptions of other people and situations. In a dyadic interaction the goals salient to one individual may be affected by the perceived goals, plans, resources and beliefs of their partner. For instance, an individual who has the goal of establishing close friendships but who chronically has a goal of avoiding rejection may typically not disclose very much about herself except when she is with a colleague who is especially accepting and supportive. Here fear of rejection may be sufficiently reduced in salience that the typically low disclosing person 'opens up' (see Miller, Berg, & Archer, 1983 for research consistent with this possibility). Salience can be further affected by the situation (e.g., office meeting vs. tea at a cozy kitchen table).

Unfortunately, people in social interactions do not wear signs listing their goals, plans, resources and beliefs. We must figure them out. As we pointed out earlier doing this requires us to use detailed social and physical knowledge to create a detailed scenario which represents how the individual's actions fit together into a coherent plan aimed toward the attainment of some goal or set of goals. Thus, attributional processes play a central role in dyadic interactions (see also Kelley, 1979; Orvis, Kelley, & Butler, 1976).

As well as being affected by our perceptions of our partner, our goals may also be activated by a perceived discrepancy between what we wish to be the case and what is the case. For example, if a friend's behavior indicates that his view of us differs from our own, this may threaten our self-concept and motivate us to reassert our own self view (Swann, 1983; Swann & Read, 1981a, 1981b). Or noticing that we have failed to live up to our standards for behavior may motivate us to meet those standards (Duval & Wicklund, 1972).

The chronic importance of a goal may affect the likelihood of its activation, with more important goals more likely to be activated. For instance, people may selectively encode features that are relevant to chronic, important goals. Higgins and King (1981) (see also Bargh, 1984) argue that the interpretation of social stimuli is affected by both chronic and temporary differences in the accessibility of relevant constructs. Postman et al. (1948) (cited in Bargh & Pratto, 1986) showed that the importance of various abstract social values, such as discovery of truth or aesthetics, affected people's recognition threshold for words related to those values. When we really want to become closer to someone, we may be particularly vigilant for a behavior that we can respond to, a request that we can fulfill or a way in which we can better meet their needs.

Finally, greater internal focus or self-awareness (e.g., Duval & Wicklund, 1972; Carver & Scheier, 1981) should increase the chance that goals are activated by internal cues, while greater focus on the environment should increase the chance that goals are activated by external cues. This suggests that the goals of people who are dispositionally self-aware (privately self-conscious) should be less affected by characteristics of other people and the situation and should be more affected by the individual's internal states.

Thus, the importance of a goal in a given situation is a joint function of: (1) its chronic salience or importance to the individual, and (2) the extent to which it has been activated by aspects of the particular context, including other people. Characteristics of one's interaction partner and the situation then, may change the configuration and hierarchy of goals guiding behavior. This is a crucial point, for it argues that even if there are strong and consistent individual differences in these chronic configurations, an individual's behavior in any given interaction can be only partially predicted by knowledge of that individual's traits and idiosyncratic configurations of goals, plans, resources and beliefs. Greater predictability seems likely only when we simultaneously consider how one such unique individual interacts with another within a specific situation.

Once some goal or set of goals is activated, we must decide what to do. As can be seen from the model in Figure 2, knowledge of our own goals, and relevant additional information, such as our perception of the goals and characteristics of our interaction partner and knowledge about the situation, is used to develop an appropriate plan.

To develop a plan, we must consider numerous factors. First, we must assess the relations among our own goals and actions and their relation to the possible goals and actions of those with whom we are interacting. If we have multiple goals we must consider various relations among them, such as which are most important, which conflict with each other, which might compete with the goals of our partner, and which might possibly be achieved by the same plan. Thus, the plan we choose depends on whether we think the other person will facilitate or interfere with it. This suggests that the success of our plan partially depends on the accuracy with which we perceive the goals and plans of our partner. Second, we need to consider what we know about our situation. For instance, what goals does it easily afford (Argyle, Furnham, & Graham, 1981) and what resources are available? Third, we must look both at the plans we know, and whether they are available in this particular situation, with this particular partner.

Fourth, we then need to know whether these are likely to be effective in achieving our goals, and whether they are socially and morally acceptable. Finally, we need to assess whether we possess the resources necessary to carry out possible plans. And if we do possess the resources, but they are limited, we need to decide whether the benefits of attaining our goals are worth the expenditure of resources such as time, money, effort, etc.

People's expectancies about likely outcomes and the reactions of others play an important role in many parts of the planning process. For instance, an individual's expectancies influence which particular plan components are chosen, and even whether a developed plan will be enacted. Essentially, we consider the probability of success of various courses of action and the associated costs and benefits of each course. In this sense the present model is related to the class of expectancy - value models (See Feather, 1982, for a useful compendium of these approaches).

Earlier we argued that people build mental models of other people and use such models to simulate their behavior. People also build models of the current interaction and use that to predict the direction in which it is progressing. Thus in a dyadic interaction, our expectancies about the interaction are based on our mental model of ourselves, our partner, our relationship and our model of the interaction.

The planning process can be viewed in terms of an analysis of person-person and person-situation interactions. Essentially, the person is trying to integrate his or her goals, plans, resources and beliefs with those of the other member of the dyad and at the same time with the goals, plans, roles and rules associated with the particular social situation.

If we are fortunate, a canned plan or script (Schank & Abelson, 1977) may already exist and we won't need to spend very much time in the planning process. We can just take the script and act it out.

However, frequently we don't have such canned plans available and must spend time developing them. One way to develop plans is to mentally simulate the enactment of a possible plan or sequence of plans (Wilensky, 1983), mentally trying out different plans or parts of plans, seeing how they fit together, seeing what role one's partner will play in these plans, and simulating how both people and the environment will respond to those plans. Such simulations are often useful in identifying potential problems, such as undesirable interactions between components of a plan, or unfavorable reactions from other people.

The completeness of this simulation probably depends greatly on the extent to which an individual is internally focused. The greater the degree to which an individual chronically focuses internally on his/her own mental processes (e.g., private self-consciousness, Carver & Scheier, 1981) and thus focuses on this simulation and its development, the more complete and adequate the simulation should be.

Plans in social interaction vary greatly in detail. At one extreme we may enter an interaction with a very detailed, well worked out plan. At the other extreme we may have only the vaguest idea of what we want to achieve.

Once we develop a plan we can enact it. During enactment we continually monitor our performance, the responses of our interaction partner, and the nature of the situation. At the same time, we are continually updating our model of our partner's characteristics, goals, and the reasons for their actions. We are also updating our models of the situation and the interaction. The results of this can modify our current plans and the goals guiding our behavior. Consider the following example in which one such interaction evolves.

Ellen starts out liking her partner, Tom, and desires to become more intimate with him; she decides to disclose some personal feelings to him. However, he doesn't seem responsive to these initial disclosures and she perceives that he has become more distant. So, Ellen becomes more distant in turn, and Tom perceive that Ellen doesn't like him. Since his self-concept involves perceiving himself as likable (cf. Swann, 1983 for research addressing this issue) he becomes extremely friendly. Ellen responds positively but she is wary of becoming too intimate. Meanwhile Tom decides that Ellen is a friendly person and begins to feel that he can 'open up' to her. Since he does desire to become more intimate and close with someone, he decides to tell her something moderately intimate about himself. Because Ellen responds warmly to this, Tom feels more relaxed and less concerned about 'making a fool of himself'.

Most plans in social interaction require a coordinated response from our partner. Whether we are gossiping, going on a date, or negotiating a business deal, successfully carrying out our plan typically requires certain responses from our partner. Thus, we must monitor their behavior to see whether and how it fits into our plans. Does it fit or facilitate our plan, is it a slight variation which can be handled with minimal adjustment, or is it a more major deviation, perhaps something which will totally block our plan? The answers tell us what modifications, if any, must be made.

At the same time, our interaction partner has his or her own set of goals and corresponding plans, and will be trying to enact those plans. Thus, interactions are a continuing process of negotiation between both partners as each tries to let the other know what he wants and tries to constrain the other's behavior so it fits one's own plan (Carson, 1969; McClintock, 1983). Each individual says and does things to carry out his or her own plan and hopes that the other responds in line with the offered behavior. The other person, by their response, indicates whether they are willing to go along or not. Carson (1969) presents a particularly insightful analysis of such coordination and the negotiation which supports it. In a similar vein, Berscheid (1985) and Kelley et al. (1983) have argued that one can analyze the level of compatibility in relationships in terms of the extent to which the behavioral sequences of each member of the dyad facilitate or interfere with the behavioral sequences of the other member. There are a number of different reasons why coordination may be difficult or even fail. Among them are such things as competing goals, misunderstanding of what the other is trying to do and lack of the skills or resources necessary to carry out one's part.

Problems during the enactment of our plans produce an interruption (Mandler, 1975), which increases both our attention to what is happening and our arousal and emotional responses. The severity of the interruption is a function of the extent to which the ongoing goals or plans are blocked. Slight deviations from a plan create only minor interruptions and arousal, while major threats to a plan's success should create high levels of arousal and strong emotional responses. This is especially likely, when we have few good alternative plans, and the plans are critical to important goals. Berscheid (1983) has argued that such interruptions are an important source of emotion in close relationships.

An interruption, if serious enough, leads us to explain the problem, and throws us into a replanning mode where we use our explanation to come up with a new plan which can overcome the source of the interruption. In nonstereotyped social interaction, such replanning occurs continually as we attempt to adjust our behavior to our partner. In the example of Ellen and Tom, Ellen had to do some replanning when her initial disclosure to Tom was not met with as responsive a reply as Ellen expected. While, as in Ellen and Tom's case, the required replanning is usually relatively minor, sometimes major replanning is required.

Wilensky (1983, p. 76) argues that attempts to deal with problems in plans depend on the explanation for the problem. Earlier we discussed how people might deal with unexpected outcomes, some of the possible explanations, and how this process is affected by different kinds of knowledge. For example, the explanation will depend on individuals' belief systems. Consider a depressive or lonely person who receives the type of rebuff that Ellen initially may have received from Tom. Instead of changing gears as she did, she might have decided that Tom was really rejecting her because she wasn't a likable person and that was terrible. Some people's belief systems and attributional styles may prevent them from easily replanning and initiating a new plan that will enable them to reach their goals.

If replanning is possible, we should proceed to enact the new plan. However, if replanning is impossible or impractical, we will stop, having failed to attain our goals.

SUMMARY

We started this chapter questioning some of the assumptions that guided prior research on individual differences in self-disclosure. We have argued that self-disclosure might best be re-examined as a set of strategies that individuals use to achieve a variety of goals. And further, that individuals may differ in their goals, strategies, resources and beliefs related to disclosure. Essentially, we have argued for examining individual differences in terms of mediating cognitive structures that influence behavior. In predicting individual differences we should take into account individuals' unique configurations of goals, strategies, beliefs and resources (e.g., differences in mediating structures). At the individual level we need to consider how an individual's goals facilitate and inhibit other goals (e.g., desiring to avoid embarrassment may block the desire to be intimate), and how different disclosure strategies fit in with classes of other strategies that meet diverse goals. We should also assess how different chronic configurations of goals, strategies, resources and beliefs (some of which may be viewed as specific trait dimensions) are related to different types of disclosure behaviors as they are embedded in particular conversations and interactions (for a discussion of methodologies for uncovering such representations see Read, 1987).

At the interpersonal level, we need a language that allows us sufficient flexibility to understand the unique dynamics of persons and to discuss and analyze the ever changing mutual influences among complex individuals. The present theory of interpersonalism provides one such language with which to examine the stable and changing configurations of individuals' goals, plans, resources, and beliefs and how these influence and are influenced by mutual interactions among them. And, it suggests how individuals go about combining their own goal-based structures with their perception of their partner's structures to create unique models of relationships that guide behavior. As such, inter-personalism is a general model that stresses the importance and complexity of unique persons who create dynamic, unique relationships.

ACKNOWLEDGEMENTS

This project was supported in part by a grant from the National Institute of Mental Health (MH39510-03) to the first author and a grant from the National Science Foundation (BNS-8406262) to the second author.

REFERENCES

Allston, W. P. (1970). Toward a logical geography of personality: Traits and deeper lying personality characteristics. In H. D. Krefer & M. K. Munitz (Eds.), *Mind, science and history* (pp. 59-92). Albany, NY: SUNY Press.

Allston, W. P. (1975). Traits, consistency and conceptual alternatives for personality theory. *Journal for the Theory of Social Behaviour*, 5, 17-48.

Altman, I. & Taylor, D. A. (1973). *Social penetration: The development of interpersonal relationships*. San Francisco: Jossey-Bass.

Archer, R. L., & Earle, W. B. (1983). The interpersonal orientations of disclosure. In P. B. Paulus (Ed.), *Basic group processes* (pp. 289-314). New York: Springer-Verlag.

Argyle, M., Furnham, A. & Graham, J. A. (1981). *Social situations*. Cambridge, England: Cambridge University Press.

Bargh, J. A. (1984). Automatic and conscious processing of social information. In R. S. Wyer, Jr., & T. K. Srull (Eds.), *Handbook of social cognition* (Vol. 3, pp. 1-43). Hillsdale, NJ: Erlbaum.

Bargh, J. A., & Pratto, F. (1986). Individual construct accessibility and perceptual selection. *Journal of Experimental Social Psychology*, 22, 293-311.

Barsalou, L. W. (1985). Ideals, central tendency, and frequency of instantiation as determinants of graded structure in categories. *Journal of Experimental Psychology: Learning, Memory, and Cognition*, 11, 629-654.

Berg, J. H., & Archer, R. L. (1982). Responses to self-disclosure and interaction goals. *Journal of Experimental Social Psychology*, 18, 501-512.

Berscheid, E. (1983). Emotion. In H. H. Kelley et al. (Eds.), *Close Relationships* (pp. 110-168). New York: W. H. Freeman.

Berscheid, E. (1985). Compatibility, interdependence, and emotion. In W. Ickes (Ed.), *Compatible and Incompatible relationships* (pp. 143-161). New York: Springer-Verlag.

Bowlby, J. (1973). *Attachment and loss: Vol. 2. Separation: Anxiety and anger*. New York: Basic Books.

Burke, R. J., Weir, T. & Harrison, D. (1976). Disclosure of problems and tensions experienced by marital partners. *Psychological Reports*, 38, 531-542.

Buss, D. M., & Craik, K. H. (1983). The act frequency approach to personality. *Psychological Review*, 90, 105-126.

Buss, D. M., & Craik, K. H. (1984). Acts, dispositions, and personality. *Progress in Experimental Personality Research*, 13, 241-301.

Cantor, N., & Mischel, W. (1977). Traits as prototypes: Effects on recognition memory. *Journal of Personality and Social Psychology*, 35, 38-48.

Cantor, N., & Mischel, W. (1979). Prototypes in person perception. In L. Berkowitz (Ed.), *Advances in experimental social psychology* (Vol. 12, pp. 3-52). New York: Academic Press.

Carbonnell, J. G. (1979). Subjective understanding: Computer models of belief systems. *Computer science technical report* 150, Doctoral Dissertation, Yale University.

Carson, R. C. (1969). *Interaction concepts of personality*. Chicago: Aldine Publishing.

Carver, C. S., and Scheier, M. F. (1981). *Attention and self-regulation: A control-theory approach to human behavior*. New York: Springer-Verlag.

Cattell, R. B. (1965). *The scientific analysis of personality*. Chicago: Aldine Publishing.

Cheek, J. M., & Buss, A. H. (1981). Shyness and sociability. *Journal of Personality and Social Psychology*, 41, 330-337.

Collins, N. L., & Read, S. J. (1987). *Early attachment experience and adult romantic love: Continuities in social relationships from childhood to adulthood*. Unpublished manuscript, University of Southern California.

Cozby, P. C. (1973). Self-disclosure: A literature review. *Psychological Bulletin*, 79, 73-91.

Derlega, V. J., & Grzelak, J. (1979). Appropriateness of self-disclosure. In G. J. Chelune (Ed.), *Self-disclosure: Origins, patterns, and implications for openness in interpersonal relations* (pp. 151-176). San Francisco: Jossey-Bass.

Duval, S., & Wicklund, R. A. (1972). *A theory of objective self-awareness*. New York: Academic Press.

Ehrlich, J. H., & Graven, D. B. (1971). Reciprocal self-disclosure in a dyad. *Journal of Experimental Social Psychology, 7*, 389-400.

Ellis, A., & Harper, R. (1977). *A guide to successful marriage*. Los Angeles: Wilshire.

Feather, N. T. (Ed.). (1982). *Expectations and actions: Expectancy-value models in psychology*. Hillsdale, NJ: Erlbaum.

Foa, E. B., & Foa, U. G. (1974). *Societal structures of the mind*. Springfield, IL: Thomas.

Gentner, D., & Stevens, A. (1983). *Mental models*. Hillsdale, NJ: Erlbaum.

Goodstein, L. D., & Reinecker, V. M. (1974). Factors affecting self-disclosure: A review of the literature. In B. A. Maher (Ed.), *Progress in experimental personality research* (Vol. 7, pp. 49-77). New York: Academic Press.

Grice, H. P. (1975). Logic and conversation. In P. Cole & J. L. Morgan (Eds.), *Syntax and semantics, Vol. 3: Speech acts* (pp. 83-106). New York: Academic Press.

Hamilton, D. L. (1981). (Ed.). *Cognitive processes in stereotyping and intergroup behavior*. Hillsdale, NJ: Erlbaum.

Hazan, C., & Shaver, P. (1987). Romantic love conceptualized as an attachment process. *Journal of Personality and Social Psychology, 52*, 511-524

Hendrick, S. S. (1981). Self-disclosure and marital satisfaction. *Journal of Personality and Social Psychology, 40*, 1150-1159.

Higgins, E. T., & King, G. (1981). Accessibility of social constructs: Information-processing consequences of individual and contextual variability. In N. Cantor & J. F. Kihlstrom (Eds.), *Personality, cognition, and social interaction* (pp. 69-121). Hillsdale, NJ: Erlbaum.

Johnson-Laird, P. N. (1983). *Mental models*. Cambridge, MA.: Harvard University Press.

Jones, E. E., & Davis, K. E. (1965). From acts to dispositions: The attribution process in person perception. In L. Berkowitz (Ed.), *Advances in experimental social psychology* (Vol. 2, pp. 219-267). New York: Academic Press.

Jourard, S. M. (1959). Self-disclosure and other-cathexis. *Journal of Abnormal and Social Psychology, 59*, 428-431.

Jourard, S. M., & Landsman, (1960). Cognition, cathexis, and the 'dyadic effect.' *Merrill-Palmer Quarterly, 6*, 178-186.

Kelley, H. H. (1971). Attribution in social interaction. In E. E. Jones, D.E. Kanouse, H. H. Kelley, R. E. Nisbett, S. Valins, & B. Weiner (Eds.), *Attribution: Perceiving the causes of behavior* (pp. 1-26). Morristown, NJ: General Learning Press.

Kelley, H. H. (1979). *Personal relationships: Their structures and processes*. Hillsdale, NJ: Erlbaum.

Kelley, H. H., Berscheid, E., Christensen, A., Harvey, J. H., Huston, T. L., Levinger, G., McClintock, E., Peplau, L. A., & Peterson, D. R. (Eds.). (1983). *Close Relationships*. New York: W. H. Freeman.

Kelley, H. H., & Thibaut, J. W. (1978). *Interpersonal relations: A theory of interdependence*. New York: Wiley.

Lalljee, M., & Abelson, R. P. (1983). The organization of explanations. In M. Hewstone (Ed.), *Attribution theory: Social and functional extensions* (pp. 65-80). Oxford: Blackwell.

Levin, F. M., & Gergen, K. J. (1969). *Revealingness, ingratiation, and the disclosure of self*. Paper presented at the 77th convention of the American Psychological Association, Washington, DC.

Levinger, G. (1974). A three-level approach to attraction: Toward an understanding of pair relatedness. In T. L. Huston (Ed.), *Foundations of interpersonal attraction* (pp. 99-120). New York: Academic Press.

Levinger, G., & Senn, D. J. (1967). Disclosure of feelings in marriage. *Merrill Palmer Quarterly of Behavior and Development, 13*, 237-249.

McClintock, E. (1983). Interaction. In H. H. Kelley et al. (Eds.) *Close Relationships* (pp. 68-109). New York: W. H. Freeman.

McLaughlin, M. L. (1984). *Conversation: How talk is organized*. Beverly Hills, CA: Sage.

Magnusson, D., & Endler, N. S. (1977). Interactional psychology: Present status and future prospects. In D. Magnusson & N. S. Endler (Eds.) *Personality at the crossroads* (pp. 3-31). Hillsdale, NJ: Erlbaum.

Mandler, G. (1975). *Mind and emotion*. New York: Wiley, 1975.

Markus, H., & Smith, J. (1981). The influence of self-schemata on the perception of others. In N. Cantor & J. F. Kihlstrom (Eds.) *Personality, cognition, and social interaction* (pp. 233-262). Hillsdale, NJ: Erlbaum.

Miller, G. A., Galanter, E., & Pribram, K. H. (1960). *Plans and the structure of behavior*. New York: Holt, Rinehart, and Winston.

Miller, L. C. (1982). *Patterns of two individual differences relevant to recipient and revealer roles in dyadic interactions*. Unpublished doctoral dissertation, University of Texas at Austin.

Miller, L. C., Berg, J. H., & Archer, R. L. (1983). Openers: Individuals who elicit intimate self-disclosure. *Journal of Personality and Social Psychology, 44*, 1234-1244.

Miller, L. C., & Kenny, D. A. (1986). Reciprocity of self-disclosure at the individual and dyadic levels: A social relations analysis. *Journal of Personality and Social Psychology, 50*, 713-719.

Miller, L. C., & Kenny, D. A. (1987). *Disclosure-liking effects at the individual and dyadic level: A social relations analysis*. Unpublished manuscript, Scripps College, Claremont, CA.

Miller, L. C., & Read, S. J. (1987). Why am I telling you this? Self-disclosure in a goal-based model of personality. In V. J. Derlega & J. Berg (Eds.) *Self-disclosure: Theory, research, and therapy* (pp. 35-58). Plenum.

Mischel, W. (1973). Toward a cognitive social learning reconceptualization of personality. *Psychological Review, 80*, 252-283.

Mischel, W. (1977). On the future of personality measurement. *American Psychologist, 32*, 246-254.

Morton, T. L. (1978). Intimacy and reciprocity of exchange: A comparison of spouses and strangers. *Journal of Personality and Social Psychology, 36*, 72-81.

Murray, H. et al. (1938). *Explorations in personality*. New York: Oxford University Press.

Orvis, B. R., Kelley, H. H., & Butler, D. (1976). Attributional conflict in young couples. In J. H. Harvey, W. J. Ickes, & R. E. Kidd (Eds.), *New directions in attribution research* (Vol. 1, pp. 353-386). Hillsdale, NJ: Erlbaum.

Park, B. (1986). A method for studying the development of impressions of real people. *Journal of Personality and Social Psychology, 51*, 907-917.

Piner, K. E., Berg, J. H., & Miller, L. C. (1987). *Is your timing off? Role of timing in interpersonal communication*. Unpublished manuscript, University of Mississippi, University, Mississippi.

Postman, L., Bruner, J. S., & McGinnies, E. (1948). Personal values as selective factors in perception. *Journal of Abnormal and Social Psychology, 43*, 142-154.

Read, S. J. (1987). Constructing causal scenarios: A knowledge structure approach to causal reasoning. *Journal of Personality and Social Psychology, 52*, 288-302.

Reeder, G.D., & Brewer, M. B. (1979). A schematic model of dispositional attribution in interpersonal perception. *Psychological Review*, 86, 61-79.

Rosch, E. (1975). Cognitive reference points. *Cognitive Psychology*, 7, 532-547.

Rosch, E. (1978). Principles of categorization. In E. Rosch & B. B. Lloyd (Eds.), *Cognition and categorization* (pp.27-48). Hillsdale, NJ: Erlbaum.

Rosch, E., & Mervis, C. B. (1975). Family resemblances: Studies in the internal structure of categories. *Cognitive Psychology*, 7, 573-605.

Schank, R. C., & Abelson, R. P. (1977). *Scripts, plans, goals, and understanding*. Hillsdale, NJ: Erlbaum.

Stiles, W. B. (1987). 'I have to talk to somebody': A fever model of disclosure. In V. J. Derlega & J. H. Berg (Eds.), *Self-disclosure: Theory, research, and therapy* (pp. 257-301). New York: Plenum.

Swann, W. B. (1983). Self-verification: Bringing social reality into harmony with the self. In J. Suls & A. G. Greenwald (Eds.), *Psychological perspectives on the self* (Vol. 2, pp. 33-66). Hillsdale, NJ: Erlbaum.

Swann, W. B., & Read, S. J. (1981a). Self-verification processes: How we sustain our self-perceptions. *Journal of Experimental Social Psychology*, 17, 351-372.

Swann, W. B., & Read, S. J. (1981b). Acquiring self-knowledge: The search for feedback that fits. *Journal of Personality and Social Psychology*, 41, 1119-1128.

Waring, E. M. (1987). Self-disclosure in cognitive marital therapy. In V. J. Derlega & J. H. Berg (Eds.) *Self-disclosure: Theory, research, and therapy* (pp. 283-301). New York: Plenum.

Wilensky, R. (1983). *Planning and understanding: A computational approach to human reasoning*. Reading, MA.: Addison-Wesley.

AUTHOR INDEX

Abelson, R. P. 210, 212, 215, 239, 247, 248, 249, 252, 256, 260
Abramson, L. Y. 164
Ackerman, K. 24, 29
Adams, A. N. 162
Adelman, M. B. 2, 11, 12, 14, 15, 23, 24, 29
Ainsworth, M. D. S. 59
Ajzen, I. 207, 217, 226, 251
Allston, W. P. 243
Altman, I. 3, 5, 70, 241, 142, 235
American Psychiatric Association 173
Anderson, B. 14
Anderson, J. R. 216
Aneshensel, C. S. 133
Antonucci, T. C. 109
Archer, D. 135
Archer, R. L. 118, 236, 258
Argyle, M. 215, 246, 254, 259
Arias, I. 159
Asch, S. E. 221
Athay, M. 222
Averill, J. R. 118
Avery, A. W. 1, 2, 3, 9

Bach, K. 248
Back, K. W. 5
Baldwin, M. P. 74
Balling, S. S. 2
Banks, S. 184
Bar-Tal, D. xii, xiii, 206, 211, 228
Bar-Tal, Y. xii, 206
Bargh, J. A. 258, 259
Baron, R. M. 184
Barry, W. A. 162
Barsalou, L. W. 250
Basham, R. 134
Bates, A. 13
Baucom, D. H. 162, 164, 174, 179, 194, 197
Baum, A. 108, 117
Baumeister, R. F. 219, 227
Beach, S. R. 159, 169, 171, 172, 174, 183
Beall, S. 118, 125
Beamesderfer, A. 172
Beck, A. T. 172
Bentler, P. M. 192
Berg, J. H. 26, 64, 70, 71, 118, 236, 238, 244, 249, 257, 258
Berger, C. R. 5, 15
Berger, P. 76, 189
Bergler, E. 2
Berkowitz, S. 11
Berley, R. A. 164
Berscheid, E. 2, 3, 4, 5, 66, 82, 96, 240, 252, 261
Blank, A. 222

Blau, P. 11, 65, 73
Borden, V. M. H. 45, 69, 76
Bower, J. G. 216
Bowlby, J. 58, 59, 251
Bradac, J. J. 15
Bradbury, T. N. xi, 160, 162, 163, 168, 170, 172, 174, 175, 177, 178, 180, 181, 182, 185, 188, 190, 191, 192, 193
Braiker, H. G. 64, 75, 76, 81
Brehm, S. S. 65, 66, 71
Brewer, M. B. 96, 250
Brewin, C. R. 203
Brickman, P. 73, 79
Briggs, S. R. 141
Brownell, A. 108
Bruner, J. S. 207
Buber, M. 35
Buck, R. 61
Burgess, E. W. 14, 161
Burgess, R. C. 141
Burke, R. J. 235
Burnett, R. 190
Burr, W. 14
Buss, A. H. 245
Buss, D. M. 243, 249, 250
Butler, D. 258
Byrne, D. 3

Calabrese, R. J. 5, 15
Campbell, A. 163
Cantor, N. 243, 250
Caplow, T. 5
Carbonell, J. G. 243
Carlston, D. E. 229
Carpenter, B. N. 142
Carson, R. C. 261
Cartwright, D. 13
Carver, C. S. 216, 240, 259, 260
Casella, D. F. 139
Cate, R. M. 1, 71
Cattell, R. B. 236
Chaiken, S. 79, 93
Chaikin, A. L. 70, 112
Chanowitz, B. 222
Cheek, J. M. 141, 245
Chelune, G. J. 2
Christensen, A. 163
Christensen, H. T. 161
Clark, D. 190
Clark, M. S. 64, 70, 71, 72, 134
Clore, G. L. 3
Coates, D. 116, 117
Cobb, S. 117
Cohen, F. 147, 148
Cohen, S. 108, 133, 134, 135, 149
Collard, J. 23, 28
Collett, P. 248
Collins, N. L. 251
Converse, P. E. 163

Conway, T. L. 108, 110
Cooley, C. H. 35
Costanza, R. S. 118
Cottrell, L. S. 14, 161
Cox, S. 152
Coyne, J. 147
Cozby, P. C. 234, 236
Craik, K. H. 243, 249, 250
Cramer, L. 177
Cramer, R. E. 2
Critchlow, B. 179
Curran, J. P. 140

Dalton, D. 140
Darley, J. 222, 223
Davidson, C. 203
Davis, J. 11, 13
Davis, K. E. 14, 66, 75, 164, 177, 250
Davis, M. H. 135, 142
DePaulo, B. M. 146
Derlega, V. J. xii, 70, 111, 112, 116, 117, 118, 125, 236, 244, 257
Deutsch, M. 36, 62
DiMatteo, M. R. 135
Dion, K. K. 65, 67, 80
Dion, K. L. 65, 67, 80
Doherty, W. J. 61, 159, 190
Donald, C. A. 133
Dooley, D. 110, 111
Douvan, E. 159
Dreyer, A. 61
Driscoll, R. 14, 17, 18, 66, 75, 80
Driver, M. J. 216
Drown, D. 170
Duck, S. 2
Duncan, S. 185
Duval, S. 240, 258, 259

Ebbesen, E. B. 178
Eggert, L. L. xi, 1, 2, 9, 11, 15, 18, 19, 20, 21, 22
Eidelson, R. J. 22, 64, 75
Ellard, J. H. 112, 126
Ellis, A. 241
Ellsworth, P. C. 221
Elms, A. C. 160
Emery, R. E. 190
Endler, N. S. 236, 237
Epstein, N. 135, 143, 159, 172, 194, 197
Erikson, E. H. 58, 59, 63
Eustis, A. C. 223

Fazio, R. H. 74, 223
Feather, N. T. 260
Fehr, B. 3
Fei, J. 66
Festinger, L. 5, 116
Fichten, C. 164
Fincham, F. D. xiii, 159, 160, 162, 163, 164,

165, 167, 168, 169, 170, 171, 172, 174, 175, 177, 178, 179, 180, 181, 182, 183, 185, 188, 190, 191, 192, 193, 195
Fischer, C. 112
Fisher, J. A. 111
Fisher, J. D. 146
Fiske, D. W. 185
Fitzgerald, N. M. 1
Fleming, B. 197
Fleming, R. 108, 112, 117, 125
Fletcher, G. J. O. 168, 177
Floyd, F. J. 163
Foa, E. B. 241
Foa, U. G. 241
Folkman, S. 117, 124, 145
Forman, R. 5
French, J. P. 39
Frerichs, R. R. 133
Freud, S. 9, 118, 125
Freund, T. 212
Friedman, H. S. 135, 136, 139, 140, 147
Fujino, D. C. 71
Funder, D. C. 176
Furnham, A. 246, 254, 259

Galanter, E. 210, 212, 239, 247
Galassi, J. P. 135
Galassi, M. D. 135
Gatchel, R. J. 108
Gentner, D. 251
Gentry, K. W. 219
Gerard, H. B. 78
Gergen, K. J. 223
Gisriel, M. M. 108
Glick, P. 4
Glick, B. R. 162
Glidewell, J. C. 147
Goffman, E. 189, 212, 213, 223
Gold, M. 59
Goode, W. J. 10
Goodstein, L. D. 234
Gottlieb, B. H. 109, 111, 134, 139
Gottman, J. M. 67, 95, 135, 184
Gough, H. G. 110
Graham, J. A. 246, 254, 259
Graziano, W. 4, 5
Grice, H. P. 248
Gross, S. J. 162
Gruber-Baldini, A. L. 51
Grzelak, J. 117, 125, 236
Gschneidinger, E. 98
Guerney, B. G. 143
Guilford, J. P. 136

Hacker, T. A. 134
Hall, J. A. 135

Index

Hallinan, M. 11
Hamilton, D. L. 250
Hammer, M. 11
Hanks, H. G. I. 203
Hansson, R. O. 142, 144
Harary, F. 13
Harnisch, R. 248
Harper, R. 241
Harrison, D. 235
Harvey, J. H. 183
Harvey, O. J. 211
Hastie, R. 221
Hastorf, A. H. 221
Haven, C. 108, 112
Hayes-Roth, B. 212
Hayes-Roth, F. 212
Hays, R. B. 3, 141, 142, 143
Hazen, C. 59, 60, 67, 96
Heard, D. 203
Hecht, M. L. 19
Heider, F. 13, 164, 186
Heller, K. 108, 110, 111, 134, 135
Henderson, M. 215
Hendrick, C. 65, 67
Hendrick, S. S. 65, 67, 70, 235
Henton, J. 71
Heron, N. 177
Hertel, R. K. 162
Hicks, M. W. 161, 162
Higgins, E. T. 207, 258
Hill, C. T. 66
Hill, R. 14
Hobfoll, S. E. 112, 115, 116, 117, 125, 126
Hogan, R. 135, 142
Holland, P. 11
Holmes, D. S. 118
Holmes, J. G. xii, 61, 62, 63, 66, 67, 71, 72, 73, 74, 78, 79, 82, 85, 94, 97
Holtzworth-Munroe, A. 177, 188
Hormuth, S. E. 118
House, J. S. 110
House, R. J. 149
Houston, B. K. 118
Huesmann, L. R. 33, 41, 66
Hunter, S. 116
Huston, T. L. 1, 3, 9, 10, 13, 61, 65, 68, 70, 81, 96, 141, 161

Israel, B. A. 109

Jacob, T. 161, 162
Jacobson, G. F. 24, 28
Jacobson, N. S. 162, 163, 164, 177, 188
Jaffe, Y. 221
Jamieson, D. W. 72
Janis, I. L. 117
Jaspars, J. M. 167, 169, 170
Jellison, J. M. 219
Johnson, M. P. 10, 13, 14, 15, 16, 23, 28, 29
Johnson-George, C. 61, 68
Johnson-Laird, P. N. 251
Jones, E. E. 78, 164, 177, 208, 211, 213, 215, 219, 220, 221, 250
Jones, W. H. xiii, 115, 141, 142

Jones-Cobb, J. M. 117
Joreskog, K. 17
Jourard, S. M. 135, 234, 235

Kafka, J. S. 14
Kahneman, D. 214
Kanki, B. G. 185
Kelley, H. H. 3, 12, 29, 36, 38, 39, 41, 42, 43, 44, 45, 47, 52, 53, 63, 64, 66, 67, 68, 69, 71, 73, 75, 76, 78, 81, 112, 164, 223, 250, 252, 261
Kellner, H. 76, 189
Kelly, E. L. 45
Kelman, H. C. 39, 54
Kenny, D. A. 184, 234, 236
Kerckhoff, A. C. 6, 11, 13, 45
Kernis, M. H. 117
King, C. E. 163
King, G. 207, 258
Klar, Y. 219
Klinger, E. 65
Knight, J. A. 177
Krain, M. 10, 14, 17, 22, 28
Kruglanski, A. W. 206, 207, 212, 216, 217, 219, 221, 226
Kulka, R. A. 159

La Gaipa, J. J. 9
La Voie, L. 234
Lakey, B. 111
Lalljee, M. 256
Landsman, M. J. 235
Langer, D. J. 222
Langer, E. J. 117, 118, 159, 174, 178, 210, 215
Lanzetta, J. T. 216
Larzelere, R. E. 61, 65, 68, 70, 81, 96
Lawson, J. S. 140
Lazarus, R. S. 117, 124, 145, 147, 148
Leary, M. R. 161, 214
Lefcourt, H. M. 61
Lehman, D. R. 112, 117, 126
Leiberman, J. R. 115
Leinhardt, S. 11
Leslie, L. A. 10, 13, 14, 16, 18
Lester, G. W. 197
Levenson, R. W. 95, 135
Levinger, G. xii, 3, 5, 9, 15, 36, 41, 45, 49, 52, 64, 66, 69, 73, 76, 79, 94, 141, 161, 235
Levis, D. J. 121
Levitz-Jones, E. M. 60
Lewin, K. 2, 29, 161, 210
Lewis, R. 117
Lewis, R. A. 1, 3, 6, 9, 10, 11, 12, 13, 14, 16, 18, 22, 23, 25, 26, 28, 29
Liberman, R. P. 162
Lipetz, M. E. 14, 66, 75
Lloyd, S. 71
Locke, H. J. 14, 161, 167
London, P. 112, 115, 117, 125, 126
Lott, A. J. 3, 11

Lott, B. E. 3, 11
Lowenthal, M. F. 108, 112
Lubin, B. 113, 120
Lydon, J. E. 72
Lyman, S. M. 189

Maddux, J. E. 161
Magnusson, D. 236, 237
Mahler, M. S. 60
Mandler, G. 240, 262
Manstead, A. S. R. 188
Margolin, G. 162, 163, 164
Margulis, S. T. 117, 118, 125
Markman, H. J. 163, 184
Markus, H. 226, 250
Marshall, W. C. 140
McClelland, D. C. 210
McClintock, C. G. 43, 46
McClintock, E. 261
McFarland, C. 67
McGhie, P. 190
McGrath, P. 140
McGuire, J. C. 111
McGuire, J. W. 161
McLaughlin, M. L. 236, 247, 248
McQuinn, R. D. 26
Mead, G. H. 222
Mehrabian, A. 135, 143
Menne, J. M. C. 5
Mervis, C. B. 243
Metalsky, G. I. 202
Michela, J. L. 183
Miell, D. 2
Milardo, R. M. 1, 3, 6, 9, 10, 11, 12, 14, 15, 16, 22, 23, 24, 26, 28, 29
Miller, A. A. 24
Miller, D. T. 63, 74
Miller, F. D. 191
Miller, G. A. 210, 212, 215, 239, 247
Miller, G. R. 24
Miller, L. C. xiii, 234, 236, 238, 242, 244, 249, 254, 257, 258
Miller, P. C. 61, 76
Miller, R. S. 161
Mills, J. 71, 72
Mirels, H. L. 161
Mischel, W. 243, 250
Mitchell, A. K. 23
Mokros, H. 185
Monti, P. M. 140
Moore, D. 163
Morton, T. L. 235
Morton, T. U. 70
Munton, A. G. 203
Murray, H. A. 210, 239, 245, 246
Murstein, B. I. 6

Nadler, A. 115, 146
Nelson, G. 169, 183
Newcomb, M. D. 13
Newcomb, T. M. 192
Newell, A. 206, 212
Newman, H. M. 159, 168, 178
Newtson, D. A. 178
Nezlek, J. 117
Nisbett, R. E. 210, 216
Norton, R. 180
Notarius, C. 184

O'Heeron, R. C. 109
O'Leary, K. D. 164, 165, 172, 183, 195
Olson, D. H. 14
Olson, J. M. 175
Orlofsky, J. L. 59, 60
Ortony, A. 226
Orvis, B. R. 258
Osgood, C. E. 68
Ostrom, T. M. 229

Pachella, R. G. 191
Park, B. 251
Parks, M. R. xi, 1, 2, 3, 9, 10, 11, 13, 14, 15, 17, 18, 19, 20, 21, 22, 23, 24, 25, 29, 30
Pennebaker, J. W. 109, 118, 125
Peplau, L. A. 66
Peri, N. 217
Perlman, D. xiii, 23
Peterson, C. 165, 172
Peterson, D. R. 55, 201, 265
Pierce, G. R. 109
Pietromonaco, P. 49
Piner, K. E. 249
Pittman, T. S. 213
Platt, M. 161, 162
Popper, K. R. 207, 227
Postman, L. 259
Pratto, F. 259
Pretzer, J. L. 197
Pribram, K. H. 210, 212, 239, 247
Prince, L. M. 135
Procidano, M. E. 110, 135
Pruitt, D. G. 50, 62, 69, 208, 213

Quattrone, G. A. 120

Rands, M. 45
Raps, C. S. 172
Rathus, S. A. 135
Rauem, B. 39
Raush, H. L. 162, 243
Read, S. J. xiii, 236, 238, 242, 244, 247, 248, 249, 251, 254, 257, 258, 263
Reeder, G. D. 96, 250
Reinecker, V. M. 234
Reis, H. T. 116, 117, 151
Rempel, J. K. 67, 68, 73, 74, 78, 79, 85, 94, 95, 96, 97
Reykowski, J. 211
Ridley, C. A. 1, 2, 3, 9
Riggio, R. E. xii, 135, 136, 137, 139, 140, 142, 146, 147
Roberts, C. 179
Rogers, P. L. 135
Rogers, W. L. 163
Rook, K. S. 49, 112, 133
Rosch, E. 243
Rosenn, M. 118
Rosenthal, R. 135
Ross, L. 216
Ross, M. 67, 168, 175
Rotter, J. B. 61
Rubin, M. E. 16, 18, 184

INDEX

Rubin, Z. 66
Rumerhart, D. E. 226
Rusbult, C. E. 3, 64
Ryder, R. G. 14, 61

Sabatelli, R. M. 61, 62
Saleh, W. 61
Salzinger, L. L. 11, 12, 24, 29
Sanchez-Hucles, J. 117
Sarason, B. R. 108, 109, 111, 134, 135
Sarason, I. G. 108, 111, 134
Sayers, S. 194
Schaap, C. 162
Schachter, S. 5, 116, 123
Schaefer, C. 147
Schaffer, A. 11
Schaie, K. W. 51
Schank, R. C. 212, 215, 239, 247, 248, 249, 252, 260
Scheier, M. F. 240, 259, 260
Schlenker, B. R. 208, 214, 227
Schneider, D. J. 212, 220, 21, 223
Schroder, H. M. 211, 216
Schwartz, N. 98
Scott, M. B. 189
Seligman, C. 74
Seligman, M. E. P. 164, 172
Semin, G. R. 188
Semmel, A. 202
Senchak, M. 116
Shapiro, E. G. 145
Shaver, K. G. 170, 178, 191
Shaver, P. 59, 60, 67, 86, 251
Shearin, E. N. 109
Sher, T. G. 194
Sherrod, D. 134
Shultz, T. R. 179
Shumaker, S. A. 108
Shure, M. B. 213
Sillars, A. L. 175, 181
Silverman, I. 160
Simmel, G. 112
Simon, H. A. 206, 212, 216, 217
Sinnett, R. E. 5
Slater, P. 10
Smith, D. L. 208, 213
Smith, E. R. 160, 191
Smith, M. B. 160
Smye, M. D. 137
Snoek, J. D. 35, 36
Snyder, D. K. 4, 160
Snyder, M. 5
Solomon, B. 116
Solomon, L. 62
Sorbom, D. 17
Spanier, G. B. 161, 167
Spiegel, N. 117
Spivack, G. 213
Srull, T. K. 67, 79, 211
Stahelski, A. J. 63
Stan, C. M. 1
Staub, E. 211
Steigleder, M. K. 2
Stern, D. 59
Sternberg, R. J. 65
Stevens, A. 251
Stiles, W. B. 236
Stoufe, L. A. 58, 59, 60

Strack, F. 98
Stratton, P. 177
Streufert, S. 216
Strickland, L. H. 62
Strongman, K. T. 183
Stuart, R. B. 162
Sullaway, M. 163
Surra, C. A. 1, 10, 11, 12, 26
Sussman, M. 13
Swain, M. A. 162
Swann, W. B. 222, 250, 258, 261
Swap, W. 61, 68
Swindle, R. 134, 135
Swinth, R. L. 69
Syme, S. L. 108, 134

Taylor, D. A. 3, 5, 70, 141, 142, 235
Teasdale, J. 164
Tedeschi, J. T. 227
Terman, L. M. 2
Tharp, R. G. 159
Thibaut, J. W. 3, 12, 36, 39, 41, 43, 44, 52, 63, 66, 67, 68, 69, 112, 211, 215, 221
Thoits, P. A. 110, 111, 117
Thomes, M. M. 161
Thompson, J. S. 160
Thorndike, E. L. 137
Thornes, B. 28
Throckmorton, B. 139, 147
Titus, S. L. 14
Todt, M. 152
Traupmann, J. 66
Trower, P. 140
Tucker, J. S. 137, 147
Tucker, S. 152
Turkewitz, H. L. 195
Turner, R. J. 133
Tversky, A. 214

Vallacher, R. R. 177
Vedder, M. J. 135
Veroff, J. 159
Villanova, P. 172
von Baeyer, C. 202

Wallace, K. M. 167
Waller, W. 14
Wallin, P. 2
Walster, E. H. 2, 3, 66, 71
Walster, G. W. 66
Ware, E. E. 61
Ware, J. E. 133
Waring, E. M. 251
Weary, G. 161, 183
Webb, W. M. 62
Weiner, B. 183
Weir, T. 235
Weiss, R. F. 2
Weiss, R. L. 160
Wheeler, L. 117
Wheeless, L. 16, 18
Whitcher, S. J. 111
Wicklund, R. A. 240, 258, 259
Widaman, K. F. 135
Wilensky, R. 239, 242, 252, 254, 260, 262
Williams, A. W. 133
Wills, T. A. 108, 133, 134, 149
Wilson, M. 70

Wilson, T. D. 210
Wine, J. D. 137
Winstead, B. A. xiii, xiv, 116, 118, 125
Winston, T. 116, 117
Wolfer, J. A. 117
Wong, P. 116
Worchel, P. 62
Wortman, C. B. 108, 110, 112, 126
Wright, J. 164
Wrightsman, L. S. 61, 116
Wyer, R. S. 67, 79, 191, 211, 216

Yanof, D. S. 59
Yates, S. 79, 93
Yoppi, B. 184

Zajonc, R. B. 226
Zakai, D. 217
Zanna, M. P. 67, 73, 74, 78
Zelditch, M. 24, 29
Zimmerman, J. A. xii, 139, 146
Zuckerman, M. 113, 120

SUBJECT INDEX

Accessibility
  of goals 211
  of plans 214
Accommodation 36, 37, 38, 39, 46, 47, 49, 52, 53, 54
  and conflict style 76
  and convergence 49
Adaptation 38, 39, 45
Altruism 36
Ambivalence 60, 75, 78, 79, 80, 81, 95-97, 99
Appraisal processes 81-85
Assertiveness 135
Asymmetry 51
Attachment
  anxious-ambivalent 59, 60, 96
  avoidant 59, 60
Attraction *see* interpersonal attraction
Attributional dimensions *see* causal dimensions
Attributional style 180
Attribution of responsibility 166, 169-172, 174, 175, 178, 181, 182, 191, 195
  compared to causal attribution 178-179
  dimensions of 166
Attributions
  accuracy of 176
  and depression 172
  and efficacy 190
  and helping-seeking 168
  and marital behavior 181-185
  and marital satisfaction *see* marital satisfaction
  and marital therapy 195
  and self-disclosure 174
  as communications 188
  causal vs responsibility 178-179
  dimensions of 166
  for hypothetical and real behaviors 171-172
  interpersonal 168
  levels of 178
  measurement 179
  partner-enhancing bias 174
  reactivity of 177
  self-enhancing bias 174
  spontaneous 178
  types of 178

Beck Depression Inventory 172, 173
Behavioral intelligence 137
Beliefs 241

Blame 167, 168, 169, 170, 171, 172, 175, 178, 181, 182, 183, 186, 191, 192
Break up of relationships 24-26

Causal attributions
  compared to responsibility attributions 178
  dimensions of *see* causal dimensions
Causal conditions
  environment 47-48
  personality 48-49
  relationship system 49-51
Causal dimensions
  global vs specific 164-167, 169, 170, 172, 174, 175, 180, 182
  internal vs external (causal locus) 165, 166, 167, 168, 173
  stable vs unstable 165, 166, 167, 168, 170, 175
Cognition generation 207, 211, 225
Cognition validation 207, 211, 212, 218, 225
Cognitive abilities 222
Cognitive balance 13
Coherence 249, 250, 254, 255
Commitment 18, 20-22, 75
Communal relationships 71
Communication, amount 16-17, 25
Communication networks
  and relationship initiation 7-9
  and relationship development 9-23
  see also networks
Compliance 39, 54
Consistency 236
Contextual model of marriage 192-194
Control, *see* power
Convergence 36, 37, 44, 49, 50, 52
Coordination 52
Coping 145-146
Coping strategies 147-149
Coping with stress 110-112, 115-118, 124-125
Cross sex friendships 116
Dependability 68

Depression 172, 173, 180
Disclosure of feelings 118, 121, 122, 123
Disclosure reciprocity 70
Dispositional transformation 36, 45, 46, 47, 54
Distressed vs nondistressed couples 159, 160, 162, 165, 166, 168, 169, 170, 171, 172, 173, 174, 176, 180, 181, 182, 183, 191
Divergence 53
Dyadic withdrawal hypothesis 9-11

Effective matrix 41, 42
Emotional control 136, 137, 150
Emotional sending ability 135, 137
Emotional sensitivity 136, 138, 143, 146, 148, 150
Emotions, self-regulation of 66
Empathy 135, 142-143, 149-150
Episodes 247
Epistemic motivations
  for specific content 208, 212, 216, 217, 222, 226
  for structure 208, 211, 212, 216, 217, 226
  for validity 208, 212, 216, 217, 222, 226
Epistemic process 207-208
Equity in exchange 26, 71

Facework 189
Feedback *see* interaction

Gender differences 115
Given matrix 41, 42
Goal setting 210-212
Goal-based categories 250
Goals, relationship among 242, 252

Identification 39, 54
Idiographic 242
Information collection 216-217, 219, 221, 223
Information, availability of 219
Ingratiation 208, 213
Interaction
  and feedback 222
  intentional 210
  nature of 225
Internalization 39, 54

Interpersonal attraction 2, 3, 4, 13, 14, 15, 16, 17, 18, 19, 20, 21, 22, 28
Interpersonal disposition 40, 44, 69
Interpersonal transformation 45-47
Intimacy 18, 20-22, 57, 58, 59, 60, 65, 75, 76, 97, 98, 99

Jointly oriented 35

Knowledge structures 212

Lay epistemology theory 207, 212
Learned helplessness 164, 169
Liking 18
Locus of control 61, 62

Marital satisfaction 70, 161, 162, 163, 164, 165, 166, 168, 170, 171, 172, 173, 174, 175, 176, 178, 180, 182, 184, 186, 187, 188, 191, 194, 195, 196
  and attributions 164, 165, 166, 170, 171, 172, 173, 174, 175, 176, 178, 180, 186, 187, 188, 194, 196
  and depression 172
  behavioral perspective 162-163
  mediational perspective 163
  sociological perspective 161-162
Marital therapy 195, 251
Mental models 250-252
Metarules 247, 254, 255
Motivational transformation 36, 39, 41-43, 47, 253
Motives 253
Multiple Affect Adjective Checklist (MAACL) 113, 120, 121, 124

Needs 246
Networks
  and dyads 9-22
  and the break up of relationships 23-26
  see also communication networks
Nonverbal skills 135

INDEX

Outcome correspondence 39, 41
Outcome matrix 39, 40
Overaccommodation 49, 50
Overconvergence 49, 50

Parsimony, principle of 255
Perceived similarity 18, 19, 20, 21, 22
Perceived support 108-111, 134, 143-146
Person perception 250
Person-situation interaction 246
Plans 209, 210, 212-223
  and interaction 221-223
  evaluation and validation of 218-221
  generation of 216-218
  retrieval of 214
  selection of 219
  simulation of 260
Power 62, 212
Predictability 67, 68, 79
Preference complementarity 41
Preference similarity 41
Preservation goal 242, 252
Press 246
'Pressure cooker' effect 117
Primary processing 186, 192
Principles of
  exhaustion 254
  story comprehension 254-255
Problem-solving 61, 85, 118, 121, 122, 124, 127
Process vs content 206
Prototypicality 243, 250
Proximity 5

Reciprocity 70, 71, 72, 99
Relationship development 140-142
  Communication networks and 9-23
Relationship formation 139-140
Relationship initiation 4-9
Relationship maintenance 142-143
Resources 241
Responsibility, see attribution of responsibility
Risk aversiveness 96
Roles 246
Romeo and Juliet effect 17-18
Rules 247-249

Same sex friendships 20-22, 111-118, 118
Scenario 247, 254
Scripts 215, 248
Secondary processing 186, 192
Self-awareness 259
Self-concept 258
Self-consciousness 259
Self-disclosure 70, 174, 235-237

see also disclosure of feelings
Self-monitoring 4, 135
Self-orientation 35, 44
Self-presentation 208, 226, 227
Self-schema 250
Shyness 141, 151
Situations 245-247
Social competence 137, 151
Social control 137, 138, 140, 142, 143
Social efficacy 145
Social expressivity 136, 143, 146
Social networks 1, 139, 144-148
Social norms 247
Social penetration theory 141
Social sensitivity 137, 138, 141, 143, 145, 147, 149
Social skills 135-151
Social stereotypes 249-250
Social support 133, 134, 138-140, 143, 147, 148, 150, 151
  and anxiety 113, 117, 123
  and depression 113, 117, 123
  and hostility 113, 123
  correlational studies 108-111
  experimental research 111
  perceived vs enacted 126-127
Socio-emotional behavior 52
Spontaneous attributions 178
Stability 165, 166, 167, 168, 170, 175
Story comprehension, principles of 254-255
Stranger *passant* phenomenon 112
Strategies 238, 240, 241, 243, 245, 253, 255, 263
Stress 133, 145, 147, 148
Stress appraisal 145
Structural interdependence 12
Substitution hypothesis 115
Support seeking 145-147
Sympathy 149, 150

Tactical transformation 44, 45, 54
'Talk table' technique 184
Task behavior 52
Themes 248-249
Trust
  and affective responses 88-89
  and early development 58-59
  and evaluation of interactions 89-94
  and expectations 87
  and responsiveness 59
  and risk taking 62
  and the need for closure 78
  basic trust 58
  breakdown of 94
  general trust 58-64
Traits 236-237, 243, 245

Uncertainty reduction 14, 15, 67

Ways of coping inventory 124